£3.99

A JEWISH CHILDHOOD

Edited by Antony Kamm
and A. Norman Jeffares

First published in Great Britain in 1988
by Boxtree Limited

Copyright © in introduction and selection 1988 Kamm and Jeffares

Printed and bound in Great Britain by
Richard Clay plc, Bungay, Suffolk
for Boxtree Limited, 36 Tavistock Street,
London WC2E 7PB

British Library Cataloguing in Publication Data
A Jewish childhood
  1. Literature. Jewish writers. Special
  subjects. Childhood. Anthologies
  I. Kamm, Antony   II. Jeffares, A.
  Norman (Alexander Norman), *1920* -
  808.8'0354

ISBN 1-85283-216-9

Contents

Introduction vii
HEINRICH HEINE *A Child's Conception of God* 1
BENJAMIN DISRAELI *Out of This World* 1
FELIX MENDELSSOHN-BARTHOLDY *A Letter from Switzerland* 4
KARL MARX *School Report* 7
SARAH BERNHARDT *Understudy!* 8
BENJAMIN FARJEON *Waiting for Father* 12
SIGMUND FREUD *Case Study* 16
AHAD HA-AM *Parental Choice* 18
SHALOM ALEICHEM *The Night of Hakafoth* 20
ISRAEL ZANGWILL *Sugarman's Bar-Mitzvah* 23
MARCEL PROUST *The Actress* 26
WILLIAM ROTHENSTEIN *Collector of Curiosities* 31
HELENA RUBINSTEIN *Mama's Beauty Cream* 33
CHAIM WEIZMANN *Timber* 35
LEON TROTSKY *The Little Mud Hut* 40
GERTRUDE STEIN *A Nineteenth-Century Girl* 45
BERNARD BARUCH *Country Boy* 49
JACOB EPSTEIN *The Artist's Eye* 52
LEONARD WOOLF *The Pulling of the Queen's Doctor's Nose* 56
SHOLEM ASCH *My Father's Greatcoat* 59
STEFAN ZWEIG *The Seductive City* 64
ISAAK LÖWY *The Lure of the Theatre* 66
MARY ANTIN *Within the Pale* 69
ANZIA YEZIERSKA *The Promised Land* 74
SOPHIE TUCKER *The Price of Personality* 81
FRANZ KAFKA *A Filial View* 86
EMANUEL SHINWELL *No Tailor!* 89

GILBERT FRANKAU *Crack Shot* 91
HUMBERT WOLFE *The Fancy Dress Ball* 92
BETHEL SOLOMONS *Sabbath Rugby* 96
ANDRÉ MAUROIS *'Dissenters, Withdraw'* 98
JEAN STARR UNTERMEYER *A Man* 101
EDNA FERBER *Down the Mississippi* 102
SELY BRODETSKY *Whitechapel Ghetto* 106
MARC CHAGALL *Once Bitten* 109
ISAAK BABEL *Karl-Yankel* 112
SCHMUEL DAYAN *The Journey* 118
BORIS PASTERNAK *The Train* 122
SERGEI EISENSTEIN *Image of Cruelty* 123
GOLDA MEIR *The Cossacks and the Swamps* 125
VICTOR GOLLANCZ *Childhood Fears* 128
G.B. STERN *Potted History* 132
LOUIS GOLDING *Advenchers* 134
BUD FLANAGAN *The Runaway* 138
S.N. BEHRMAN *Blighted Passion* 143
GROUCHO MARX *Lucky Date* 147
DOROTHY PARKER *Fulfillment* 149
HARRIET COHEN *Overtures* 150
SOLLY ZUCKERMAN *The Laws of Gravity* 152
ISAAC BASHEVIS SINGER *The Young Philosopher* 155
ARTHUR KOESTLER *Overbaked Beans* 159
LILIAN HELLMAN *The Fig Tree* 160
RUTH MICHAELIS-JENA *Under the Weimar Republic* 164
MEYER LEVIN *Escape* 168
KENNETH HART *The Hall, Hampstead* 171
JOSEPHINE KAMM *Lunch at Grandfather's* 176
ROY WELENSKY *Watcher of the Dead* 179
LEO ROSTEN *A Book Was a Book* 181

IRENE MAYER SELZNICK *I Had a Little Lamb . . .* 184
DAVID DAICHES *The Two Worlds* 187
RALPH GLASSER *Soap Boy* 191
BUD SCHULBERG *Sammy's Stand* 193
HOWARD FAST *My Father* 194
LARRY ADLER *Expulsion* 199
HERMAN WOUK *The Purple Suit* 201
SAUL BELLOW *'Like My Own Boy'* 204
ARTHUR MILLER *Second Sight* 207
NORMAN MAILER *The Trains* 212
MICHAEL MEYER *Into the Arch* 215
MARTYN GOFF *A Mild Case of Scum* 219
DANNIE ABSE *The Clytemnestra Bust* 221
WOLF MANKOWITZ *The Hammer v The Python* 225
DAVID MARCUS *Only the Best* 232
SAMMY DAVIS *Show Business* 236
ALLEN GINSBERG *Gregory Corso's Story* 238
BERNARD MALAMUD *Black Writing* 238
MARGHANITA LASKI *The Orphan* 241
LIONEL BLUE *Pickles and Piety* 243
BERNARD LEVIN *The Taste of Food* 245
EVELYN COWAN *Betty the Hen* 251
JOHN D. RAYNER *Kristallnacht* 254
ANNE FRANK *Hiding* 257
ELIE WIESEL *The Violin Player* 259
BERNARD KOPS *Jewish Christmas* 261
JACK ROSENTHAL *Evacuees* 265
NORMAN PODHORETZ *Improperly Dressed* 268
CHAIM BERMANT *Bar-Mitzvah Boy* 273
T.G. ROSENTHAL *Not Kosher* 274
FREDERIC RAPHAEL *A Second Childhood* 278

LEONARD COHEN *For Wilf and His House* 283
MORDECAI RICHLER *Pre-Med?* 284
PHILIP ROTH *My Baseball Years* 286
YAËL DAYAN *A Case of Security* 289
JULIA PASCAL *Ballerina!* 292
JOSEPH HELLER *My Daughter Is Unhappy* 297
JULIA NEUBERGER *Belief and Practice* 303
GARY KASPAROV *Checkmate* 306
ACKNOWLEDGEMENTS 310
INDEX 312

INTRODUCTION

This is a collection of reminiscences, impressions, observations, and interpretations of childhood, written by men and women of Jewish birth or of Jewish origin. It includes authors both of whose parents were Jewish; those whose mothers only were Jewish (Sarah Bernhardt, for example, and Marcel Proust); also those whose fathers but not mothers were Jewish (as Dorothy Parker and Gary Kasparov); and those, like Karl Marx, whose fathers were forced to renounce Judaism.

The pieces are arranged roughly in chronological order, according to when the incident, or a main incident in them, occurred, though some illustrating similar, or contrasting, themes have been grouped together. Extracts from novels, notably by Marghanita Laski, Bernard Malamud, and Joseph Heller, have been placed approximately in the period about which the author is writing. These particular extracts have been selected because although the child so graphically depicted in each is not Jewish, they represent interpretations and observations of childhood by writers of Jewish birth and upbringing.

We have taken into account the quality of expression of an experience, as well as the experience itself, and have included a wide variety of geographical and social backgrounds.

In researching and drawing from an even richer field of writing about childhood than we had first believed existed, we have continually been struck by the manifestations of Jewish resilience in the face of uncertainty and deprivation, of the ability to adapt to disparate social conditions without loss of collective identity, and of the sense of humour which pervades so many of the factual as well as fictional accounts. Heinrich Heine opens the selection by reason of the year of his birth, but regarded by Jews as a renegade, by Christians as a Jew, and by the French, in whose country he finally settled, as a German, he brought upon himself contradictions, such as Jewish children have often had to meet. He was also the first writer of Jewish birth who seems to have felt free enough to indulge in humour, besides being a European poet of lasting stature.

The confused innocence of childhood is nowhere better illustrated than in the experiences of emigrants or the children of emigrants, as with mixed success they endeavour to embrace the 'two worlds' so splendidly evoked by David Daiches. Sometimes, as in the extract from Anzia Yezierska's story, the initial shock of the new world was as dehumanising as the hopelessness of the old. The pioneering spirit of the early twentieth-century settlers in Palestine, like Schmuel Dayan, was not shared by many of their compatriots who made the journey westwards to Britain or America. That children survived so philosophically and often with such apparent good humour upheavals, transplantings of roots, and changes of language and culture, is in large measure due to the position of the family in Jewish tradition.

The particular role of a family is that its essential qualities of caring and togetherness should be extended to the community, and beyond it to other citizens of the state and, ultimately, to the world. Too often in history, outside influences and attitudes have caused the togetherness to be confined within a Jewish community, whose members have become aliens in their own country, and objects of suspicion in the alien countries in which they have sought refuge and freedom from oppression. Hence the existence of the London 'ghetto', described by Israel Zangwill and Sely Brodetsky.

It is the nature of writers to be egotistical when describing their own lives; indeed everyone tends to be selective when, consciously or unconsciously, recalling the events of their childhood – a further anthology could have been compiled entirely of accounts of *bar mitzvah* celebrations! Yet few Jewish children have not encountered, and not been affected by, anti-Semitism in some form. This is a fact of Jewish childhood, which has not been ignored here.

To have omitted any reference to the Holocaust would have been an even greater distortion of human experience. To represent it adequately and readably, an extract from one of the autobiographical novels of Elie Wiesel has been included, as well as two letters to her imaginary correspondent from Anne Frank's diary, written shortly before she was taken away to her death; while Rabbi John D. Rayner has been persuaded to record aspects of his life in Berlin before, during, and immediately after *Kristallnacht*. His account is made all the more moving by the deliberate spareness of the telling.

Jewish literary talent, whether oral or written, has always deployed a wide variety of expression, and this richness is particularly effective in accounts and interpretations of childhood, which range from tragic to sentimental, from comic to heroic, from the attitudes of loners, to those deep in the close nexus of family life. The details are firmly etched, but the situations go beyond any temporary detail, because the authors are concentrating on those universal factors which blend with and shape the individual's own intensely felt experiences.

A.K. and A.N.J.
July 1988

Heinrich Heine

A Child's Conception of God

God was always the beginning and the end of all my thoughts. If now I ask: What is God? what His nature? even as a small child I already asked: What is God like? what does He look like? And at that time I could spend whole days looking up at the sky, and in the evening I was quite disconsolate, that I had never glimpsed the most holy countenance of God, but had only seen the silly grimaces of the grey clouds. I grew entirely confused by all the information learned from astronomy, which subject even the smallest child was not spared in that period of enlightenment. I could not get over the wonder of it, that all these thousands of millions of stars were great and beautiful globes, like our own, and that one simple God ruled over all these gleaming myriads of worlds. Once in a dream, I remember, I saw God, in the farthest distance of the high heavens. He was gazing contentedly out of a little window of heaven, a pious old face with a little Jewish beard; He was scattering handfuls of seeds, which as they fell from heaven opened out, as it were, in the immeasurable space, and grew to tremendous size, until they finally became bright, flourishing, inhabited worlds, each one as large as our own. I have never been able to forget this face; I often saw this cheerful old man in my dreams again, scattering the seeds of worlds out of His tiny window: I once even saw Him cluck with his lips, just as our maid used to do when she gave the hens their barley. I could only see the falling seeds, always expanding to vast shining globes: but the great hens, which were possibly lying in wait somewhere with wide-open beaks, to be fed with these world-spheres, those I could never see.

HEINRICH HEINE (1797–1856), German poet and philosopher, was born in Düsseldorf and studied law, before devoting his life to writing.

Benjamin Disraeli

Out of This World

When I was eight years of age a tutor was introduced into the house, and I was finally and formally emancipated from the police of the nursery and the government of women. My tutor was well qualified for his office, according to the existing ideas respecting education, which substitute for the noblest of sciences the vile art of teaching words. He was learned in his acquirements, and literary in his taste, with a calm mind, a bland manner, and a mild voice. The Baroness, who fancied herself a great judge of character, favoured him, before the commencement of his labours, with an epitome of mine. After a year's experience of his pupil, he ventured to express his opinion that I was by no means so slow as was supposed; that, although I had no great power of application, I was not averse to acquiring knowledge; and that if I were not endowed with any remarkable or shining qualities, my friends might be consoled for the absence of these high powers by my being equally destitute of those violent passions and that ungovernable volition usually attendant upon genius, and which too often rendered the most gifted miserable.

I was always a bad learner, and although I loved knowledge from my cradle I liked to acquire it my own way. I think that I was born with a detestation of grammars. Nature seemed to whisper me the folly of learning words instead of ideas, and my mind would have grown sterile for want of manure if I had not taken its culture into my own hands, and compensated by my own tillage for my tutor's bad husbandry. I therefore in a quiet way read every book that I could get hold of, and studied as little as possible in my instructor's museum of verbiage, whether his specimens appeared in the anatomy of a substantive, or the still more disgusting form of a dissected verb.

This period of my life, too, was memorable for a more interesting incident than the introduction of my tutor. For the first time I visited the theatre. Never shall I forget the impression. At length I perceived human beings conducting themselves as I wished. I was mad for the playhouse, and I had the means of gratifying my mania. I so seldom fixed my heart upon anything, I showed, in general, such little relish for what is called amusement, that my father accorded me his permission with pleasure and facility, and, as an attendant to this magical haunt, I now began to find my tutor of great use.

I had now a pursuit, for when I was not a spectator at the theatre, at home I was an actor. I required no audience; I was happier alone. My chivalric reveries had been long gradually leaving me: now they entirely vanished. As I learnt more of life and nature, I required for my private world something which, while it was beautiful and uncommon, was nevertheless natural and could live. Books more real than fairy tales and feudal romances had already made me muse over a more real creation. The theatre at once fully introduced me to this new existence, and there arose accordingly in my mind new characters. Heroes succeeded to knights, tyrants to ogres, and boundless empire to enchanted castles. My character also changed with my companions. Before, all was beautiful and bright, but still and mystical. The forms that surrounded me were splendid, the scenes through which I passed glittering, but the changes took place without my agency, or if I acted, I fulfilled only the system of another, for the foundation was the supernatural. Now, if everything were less beautiful, everything was more earnest. I mingled with the warlike and the wise, the crafty, the suffering, the pious; all depended upon our own exertions, and each result could only be brought about by our own simple and human energies, for the foundation was the natural.

Yet at times even this fertile source of enjoyment failed, and the dark spirit which haunted me in my first years would still occasionally descend upon my mind. I knew not how it was, but the fit came upon me in an instant, and often when least counted on. A star, a sunset, a tree, a note of music, the sound of the wind, a fair face flitting by me in unknown beauty, and I was lost. All seemed vapid, dull, spiritless, and flat. Life had no object and no beauty; and I slunk to some solitary corner, where I was content to lie down and die. These were moments of agony, these were moments in which, if I were spoken to, I had no respect for persons. Once I remember my father found me before the demon had yet flown, and, for the first time, he spoke without being honoured.

At last I had such a lengthened fit that it attracted universal attention. I would scarcely move, or speak, or eat for days. There was a general alarm. The Baroness fell into a flutter, lest my father should think that I had been starved to death, or ill-used, or poisoned, and overwhelmed me with inquiries, each of which severely procrastinated my convalescence. For doubtless, now that I can analyse my past feelings, these dark humours arose only from the want of being loved. Physicians were called in. There were immense consultations. They were all puzzled, and all had recourse to arrogant dogmas. I would not, nay, I could not, assist them. Lying upon the sofa, with my eyes shut, as if asleep, I listened to their conferences. It was settled that I was suffering from a want of nervous energy. Strange jargon, of which their fellow-creatures are the victims! Although young, I looked upon these men with suspicion, if not contempt, and my after life has both increased my experience of their character, and confirmed my juvenile impression.

Change of air and scene were naturally prescribed for an effect by men who were ignorant of the cause. It was settled that I should leave town, accompanied by my tutor, and that we should reside for a season at my father's castle.

From Contarini Fleming (1832)

BENJAMIN DISRAELI, Earl of Beaconsfield (1804–81), British politician and novelist, was born in London. As Chancellor of the Exchequer in 1866, he introduced and carried the Reform Bill. He was Prime Minister in 1868, and again 1874–76.

Felix Mendelssohn-Bartholdy

A LETTER FROM SWITZERLAND

TO CARL FRIEDRICH ZELTER

Secheron, September 13, 1822.

As I did not write to you again from Interlaken, dear Professor Zelter, I will continue the description of my journey from here at Secheron (an inn near Geneva). But I will make it briefer than in my last letter because I want to tell you something about the organs which, so far, I have had the chance to see, hear, and play on.

I closed my letter as we were about to start for our trip to the famous valleys of Lauterbrunnen and Grindelwald. Between Interlaken and the village of Lauterbrunnen we counted forty waterfalls which mostly roared down on the right side of the road and all headed for the White Lutschine, a wild mountain torrent coming from the smaller Grindelwald Glacier, halving the Lauterbrunnen valley and emptying itself into the Black Lutschine. Its icy waters spread a cool, almost cold temperature in the valley. Behind Lauterbrunnen the famous Staubbach cascade pours from a rock 800 feet high. But it is less imposing to look at than some other, smaller cascades; at least so it seemed to me, but maybe I was disappointed because I expected too much. We thought the Jungfrau was glorious as she peered down on us from behind another mountain, but we were to see her in still greater glory.

The next day we made the ascent of the Wengernalp and, accompanied by a fine rain, arrived at the cowherds' huts, which are built on the spot that gives the best view of the Jungfrau. From the highest crest to below the Wengernalp, thick snow covers the slopes. We saw several glaciers sparkling with a greenish light and we also saw avalanches fall; the Jungfrau towers more than 7000 feet above the huts. By the way, such a hut is not as picturesque as one is likely to imagine. It is built of sturdy grey pinelogs, cleverly fitted together. The thatched roof is protected from the blasts of wind by heavy rocks. It projects far beyond the house to give cover from the rain to a small area where the shepherds milk their cattle in bad weather. The floor of the cottage is bare earth, on which the hearth stands. It is difficult to get inside because the excavations, in which each of these huts is built, are so befouled by the cows that one can reach the door only by means of the stones and planks which the shepherds throw over the mire. A wooden partition divides this beautiful building into two parts. The part in front has one window and two doors. Here we sat down, one on a protruding board, another on one of those tiny stools which the shepherds use for milking, the third on a wooden block on which, behind him, the fourth stood, yelling to make himself heard: 'I want some bread too, I want some cream too!' The guides and porters retired into the back room, made a fire and gathered around it; now and then one of us joined them, in order to get warm, because it was very cold. One had cold feet, another cold ears, a third noticed that his nose was turning purple, and all of us were desperately hungry. Sometimes our lively conversation was interrupted by the thunder of the avalanches; then we all rushed to the window – those who were not pushed through the door – and a herd of reddish-brown pigs accompanied with sweet sounds the frightful noise of the avalanche.

As the room in the rear has no opening at all, it was pitch-dark, like a bag; and only the fire gave some light. On one side a ladder leads to the space where the shepherds sleep. This is under the roof, and its ceiling is so low that I could not stand upright in it. When at nightfall the cows have been milked, everybody crawls into the hay and vies in snoring with the oxen and the pigs which, I believe, also sleep in the huts. We cut a rather funny figure in such surroundings, and the food was funny too. To see in such huts shawls, lace-bordered neckerchiefs, and goodness knows what all these modish things may be called, was just as extraordinary as to eat the chocolate and candy which the ladies had brought, together with the shepherds' sour cream and cheese. And all that in sight of the glorious Jungfrau!

Now I apologise for having described so minutely the poetic chalets; but I had promised you such a description, and with this I have kept my word. Fanny has probably told you about the rest of our journey and, besides, I want to save a few things for when we come home. But I do want to tell you something about the singing of the Swiss.

First of all, the yodelling. I say 'first of all' because it is familiar throughout Switzerland and every Swiss knows how to yodel. It consists of notes which are produced from the throat and generally they are ascending sixths, for instance:

Certainly this kind of singing sounds harsh and unpleasant when it is heard nearby or in a room. But it sounds beautiful when you hear it with mingling or answering echoes, in the valleys or on the mountains or in the woods, and there, such shouting and yelling seems truly to express the enthusiasm of the Swiss people for their country. And when one stands on a crest early in the morning, with a clear sky overhead, and hears the singing accompanied, now loudly, now softly, by the jingling of cowbells from the pastures below then it sounds lovely; indeed, it fits perfectly into the picture of a Swiss landscape as I had imagined it.

Secondly there is the highly praised singing of the Swiss girls, which is especially indigenous in the Bernese Overland. Unfortunately I cannot say much about it that is good. True, they mostly sing in four parts, but everything is spoiled by one voice which they use like a flauto piccolo. For this girl never sings a melody; she produces certain high notes – I believe just at her discretion – and thus, at times, horrible fifths turn up. For instance, I heard:

this evidently should be:

without the top voice.

Otherwise they could be good singers, because they completely prove the saying: 'Cantores amant humores'. Four of them once put away twenty-four bottles of wine!

And thirdly something about the Swiss organs, as far as I got to know them. I was greatly pleased to find in the pastoral canton of Appenzell, one of the smallest in Switzerland, a tiny organ. I found one too in Zug, but in the worst possible condition. But it was delightful to make the acquaintance of Professor Kaiser in this same country-town. Our landlord introduced me to him. He has a good piano, the Haendel Suites and many of his fugues, and the Wohltemperiertes Clavier of Bach, and he loves both enthusiastically. In Bern I played on the organ in the Cathedral, a truly grand instrument with fifty-three stops, several sixteen-foot stops in the manual, a thirty-two in the pedal and eight bellows, which, however, leak, and often make the old organ sigh. Also two pipes of the 16 F Principal rattle together murderously. In Bulle, a small town in the canton of Fribourg, I found an excellent organ in very good condition. It has about twenty-eight stops, two manuals, and I found only one fault with it, that the pedal reaches only to high A; B and C are missing, so that nothing of Bach's can be played on it. All the stops worked, the instrument is in good condition, because Aloys Moser, who built it, is in Bulle. The man, who has recently completed his sixty-fourth work in Geneva, dresses like a peasant with his plain grey coat and his large shoes. The soft voices and the full organ are particularly fine.

We are proceeding today to Ferney where Voltaire lived, and thus I close, without forgetting Mr Heyse's greetings which he asked me to send to you.

F.M.

From Letters, *ed.* G.Selden-Gott (1945)

FELIX MENDELSSOHN-BARTHOLDY (1809–47), German composer and pianist, was born in Hamburg, son of a banker. Among his best-known works are the Violin Concerto, the Symphony in A Minor ('Scottish') and the incidental music to *A Midsummer Night's Dream*.

Karl Marx

School Report

CERTIFICATE OF MATURITY
FOR
PUPIL OF THE GYMNASIUM IN TRIER

Karl Marx, from *Trier,* 17 years of age, of *evangelical* faith, son of *barrister-at-law,* Herr *Justizrat Marx* in *Trier,* was *five* years at the gymnasium in Trier, and *two* years in the first class.

I. Moral behaviour towards superiors and fellow pupils *was good.*
II. Aptitudes and diligence. *He has good aptitudes, and in ancient languages, German, and history showed a very satisfactory diligence, in mathematics satisfactory, and in French only slight diligence.*
III. Knowledge and accomplishments
   1. Languages:
      a) In German, *his grammatical knowledge and composition are very good.*
      b) In Latin, *even without preparation he translates and explains with facility and circumspection the easier passages of the classics read in the gymnasium; and after due preparation or with some assistance frequently also the more difficult passages, especially those where the difficulty consists not so much in the peculiarity of the language as in the subject-matter and train of thought. His composition shows, in regard to material, a wealth of thought and deep insight into the subject-matter, but is often overladen with irrelevancies; in regard to language, he gives evidence of much practice and striving for genuine latinity, although he is not yet free from grammatical errors. In speaking Latin, he has acquired a fairly satisfactory fluency.*
      c) In Greek, *his knowledge and abilities, in regard to understanding the classics read in the gymnasium, are almost the same as in Latin.*
      d) In French, *his knowledge of grammar is fairly good; with some assistance he reads also more difficult passages and has some facility in oral expression.*
      e) In Hebrew . . . .
   2. Sciences:
      a) Religious knowledge. *His knowledge of the Christian faith and morals is fairly clear and well grounded; he knows also to some extent the history of the Christian Church.*
      b) Mathematics. *He has a good knowledge of mathematics.*
      c) In History and Geography *he is in general fairly proficient.*
      d) Physics [and nature study]. *In physics his knowledge is moderate.*
   3. Accomplishments.
      a) . . . .

b) . . . .
The undersigned examining commission has accordingly, since he is now leaving this gymnasium in order to study *jurisprudence*, awarded him the certificate of *maturity* and discharges him, *cherishing the hope that he will fulfil the favourable expectations which his aptitudes justify*.
Trier, *September 24, 1835*.

Royal Examining Commission
Brüggemann, Royal Commissioner
Wyttenbach, Director
Loers
Hamacher
Schwendler   *Küpper*
Steininger
                Schneemann

KARL MARX (1818–83), German political critic, was born in Trier, son of a Jewish lawyer who was forced to abandon his faith. He settled with his family in London in 1849, where he wrote the unfinished *Das Kapital*, the manifesto on which modern international communism is largely based.

Sarah Bernhardt

UNDERSTUDY!

An event, very simple in itself, was destined to disturb the silence of our secluded life and to attach me more than ever to my convent, where I wanted to remain for ever.

The Archbishop of Paris, Monseigneur Sibour, was paying a round of visits to some of the communities, and ours was among the chosen ones. The news was told us by Mother St. Alexis, the *doyenne*, the most aged member of the community, who was so tall, so thin, and so old that I never looked upon her as a human being or as a living being. It always seemed to me as though she were stuffed, and as though she moved by machinery. She frightened me, and I never consented to go near her until after her death.

We were all assembled in the large room which we used on Thursdays. Mother St. Alexis, supported by two lay sisters, stood on the little platform, and in a voice that sounded far, far off announced to us the approaching visit of Monseigneur. He was to come on St. Catherine's Day, just a fortnight after the speech of the Reverend Mother.

Our peaceful convent was from thenceforth like a bee-hive into which a hornet had entered. Our lesson hours were curtailed, so that we might have time to make festoons of roses and lilies. The wide, tall arm-chair of carved wood was uncushioned, so that it might be varnished and polished. We made lamp-shades covered with crystalline. The grass was pulled up in the courtyard – and I cannot tell what was not done in honour of this visitor.

Two days after the announcement made by Mother St. Alexis, the programme of the *fête* was communicated to us by Mother St. Sophie. The youngest of the nuns was to read a few words of welcome to Monseigneur. This was the delightful Sister Séraphine. After that Marie Buguet was to play a pianoforte solo by Henri Herz. Marie de Lacour was to sing a song by Louise Puget, and then a little play in three scenes was to be given, entitled *Tobit Recovering his Eyesight*. It had been written by Mother St. Thérèse. I have now before me the little manuscript, all yellow with age and torn, and I can only just make out the sense of it and a few of the phrases. Scene I. Tobias's farewell to his blind father. He vows to bring back to him the ten talents lent to Gabael, one of his relatives. Scene II. Tobias, asleep on the banks of the Tigris, is being watched over by the Angel Raphael. Struggle with a monster fish which had attacked Tobias whilst he slept. When the fish is killed the angel advises Tobias to take its heart, its liver, and its gall, and to preserve these religiously. Scene III. Tobias's return to his blind father. The angel tells him to rub the old man's eyes with the entrails of the fish. The father's eyesight is restored, and when Tobit begs the Angel Raphael to accept some reward, the latter makes himself known, and, in a song to the glory of God, vanishes to heaven.

The little play was read to us by Mother St. Thérèse, one Thursday, in the large assembly room. We were all in tears at the end, and Mother St. Thérèse was obliged to make a great effort in order to avoid committing, if only for a second, the sin of pride.

I wondered anxiously what part I should take in this religious comedy, for, considering that I was now treated as a little personage, I had no doubt that some *rôle* would be given to me. The very thought of it made me tremble beforehand. I began to get quite nervous; my hands became quite cold, my heart beat furiously, and my temples throbbed. I did not approach, but remained sulkily seated on my stool when Mother St. Thérèse said in her calm voice:

'Young ladies, please pay attention, and listen to your names and the different parts:

Tobit	Eugénie Charmel
Tobias	Amélie Pluche
Gabael	Renée d'Arville
The Angel Raphael	Louise Buguet
Tobias's mother	Eulalie Lacroix
Tobias's sister	Virginie Depaul.'

I had been listening, although pretending not to, and I was stupefied, amazed, and furious. Mother St. Thérèse then added. 'Here are your manuscripts, young ladies,' and a manuscript of the little play was handed to each pupil chosen to take part in it.

Louis Buguet was my favourite playmate, and I went up to her and asked her to let me see her manuscript, which I read over enthusiastically.

'You'll make me rehearse, when I know my part, won't you?' she asked, and I answered, 'Yes, certainly.'

'Oh, how frightened I shall be!' she said.

She had been chosen for the angel, I suppose, because she was as pale and sweet as a moonbeam. She had a soft, timid voice, and sometimes we used to make her cry, as she was so pretty then. The tears used to flow limpid and pearl-like from her grey, questioning eyes.

She began at once to learn her part, and I was like a shepherd's dog going from one to another among the chosen ones. It had really nothing to do with me, but I wanted to be 'in it.' The Mother Superior passed by, and as we all curtseyed to her she patted my cheek.

'We thought of you, little girl,' she said, 'but you are so timid when you are asked anything.'

'Oh, that's when it is history or arithmetic,' I said. 'This is not the same thing, and I should not have been afraid.'

She smiled distrustfully and moved on. There were rehearsals during the next week. I asked to be allowed to take the part of the monster, as I wanted to have some *rôle* in the play at any cost. It was decided, though, that César, the convent dog, should be the fish monster.

A competition was opened for the fish costume. I went to an endless amount of trouble cutting out scales from cardboard that I had painted, and sewing them together afterwards. I made some enormous gills, which were to be glued on to César. My costume was not chosen; it was passed over for that of a stupid, big girl whose name I cannot remember. She had made a huge tail of kid and a mask with big eyes and gills, but there were no scales, and we should have to see César's shaggy coat. I nevertheless turned my attention to Louise Buguet's costume, and worked at it with two of the lay sisters, Sister St. Cécile and Sister St. Jeanne, who had charge of the linen room.

At the rehearsals not a word could be extorted from the Angel Raphael. She stood there stupefied on the little platform, tears dimming her beautiful eyes. She brought the whole play to a standstill, and kept appealing to me in a weeping voice. I prompted her, and, getting up, rushed to her, kissed her, and whispered her whole speech to her. I was beginning to be 'in it' myself at last.

Finally, two days before the great solemnity, there was a dress rehearsal. The angel looked lovely, but, immediately on entering, she sank down on a bench, sobbing out in an imploring voice:

'Oh no; I shall never be able to do it, never!'

'Quite true, she never will be able to,' sighed Mother St. Sophie.

Forgetting for the moment my little friend's grief, and wild with joy, pride, and assurance, I ran up to the platform and bounded on to the form on which the Angel Raphael had sunk down weeping.

'Oh, Mother, I know her part. Shall I take her place for the rehearsal?'

'Yes, yes!' exclaimed voices from all sides.

'Oh yes, you know it so well,' said Louise Buguet, and she wanted to put her band on my head.

'No, let me rehearse as I am, first,' I answered.

They began the second scene again, and I came in carrying a long branch of willow.

'Fear nothing, Tobias,' I commenced. 'I will be your guide. I will remove from your path all thorns and stones. You are overwhelmed with fatigue. Lie down and rest, for I will watch over you.'

Whereupon Tobias, worn out, lay down by the side of a strip of blue muslin, about five yards of which, stretched out and winding about, represented the Tigris.

I then continued with a prayer to God whilst Tobias fell asleep. César next appeared as the Monster Fish, and the audience trembled with fear. César had been well taught by the gardener, Père Larcher, and he advanced slowly from under the blue muslin. He was wearing his mask, representing the head of a fish. Two enormous nut-shells for his eyes had been painted white, and a hole pierced through them, so that the dog could see. The mask was fastened with wire to his collar, which also supported two gills as large as palm leaves. César, sniffing the ground, snorted and growled, and then leaped wildly on to Tobias, who with his cudgel slew the monster at one blow. The dog fell on his back with his four paws in the air, and then rolled over on to his side, pretending to be dead.

There was wild delight in the house, and the audience clapped and stamped. The younger pupils stood up on their stools and shouted, 'Good César! Clever César! Oh, good dog, good dog!' The sisters, touched by the efforts of the guardian of the convent, shook their heads with emotion. As for me, I quite forgot that I was the Angel Raphael, and I stooped down and stroked César affectionately. 'Ah, how well he has acted his part!' I said, kissing him and taking one paw and then the other in my hand, whilst the dog, motionless, continued to be dead.

The little bell was rung to call us to order. I stood up again, and, accompanied by the piano, we burst into a hymn of praise, a duet to the glory of God, who had just saved Tobias from the fearful monster.

After this the little green serge curtain was drawn, and I was surrounded, petted, and praised. Mother St. Sophie came up on to the platform and kissed me affectionately. As to Louise Buguet, she was now joyful again and her angelic face beamed.

'Oh, how well you knew the part!' she said. 'And then, too, every one can hear what you say. Oh, thank you so much!' She kissed me and I hugged her with all my might. At last I was in it!

The third scene began. The action took place in Father Tobit's house. Gabael, the Angel, and young Tobias were holding the entrails of the fish in their hands and looking at them. The Angel explained how they must be used for rubbing the blind father's eyes. I felt rather sick, for I was holding in my hand a skate's liver and the heart and gizzard of a fowl. I had never touched such things before, and every now and then the nausea overcame me and the tears rose to my eyes.

Finally the blind father came in, led by Tobias's sister. Gabael knelt down before the old man and gave him the ten silver talents, telling him, in a long recital, of Tobias's exploits in Medea. After this Tobias advanced, embraced his father, and then rubbed his eyes with the skate's liver.

Eugénie Charmel made a grimace, but after wiping her eyes she exclaimed:

'I can see, I can see. Oh! God of goodness, God of mercy! I can see, I can see!'

She came forward with outstretched arms, her eyes open, in an ecstatic attitude, and the whole little assembly, so simple-minded and loving, wept.

All the actors except old Tobit and the Angel sank on their knees and gave praise to God, and at the close of this thanksgiving the public, moved by religious sentiment and discipline repeated, Amen!

Tobias's mother then approached the Angel and said, 'Oh, noble stranger, take up your abode from henceforth with us. You shall be our guest, our son, our brother!'

I advanced and in a long speech of at least thirty lines made known that I was the messenger of God, that I was the Angel Raphael. I then gathered up quickly the pale blue tarlatan, which was being concealed for a final effect, and veiled myself in cloudy tissue which was intended to simulate my flight heavenwards. The little green serge curtain was then closed on this apotheosis.

From My Double Life (1907)

SARAH BERNHARDT (1844–1923), French actress, was born Henriette Rosine Bernard, the illegitimate daughter of Judith van Hard, a Dutch Jewish courtesan, and Edouard Bernard, a French law student. Though she was baptised at the age of ten, she remained proud of her Jewish heritage.

Benjamin Farjeon

WAITING FOR FATHER

MRS. ROZELLA and Miriam were sitting up in expectation of the return of Mr. Rozella from the country; he had been absent five days, and was expected home at ten o'clock. The two younger children, Cecil and Clara, were abed and asleep.

The appointments of the room in which the mother and daughter sat denoted that the family were in good circumstances. The house, indeed, was one in which plenty reigned, and its guiding spirit was Mrs. Rozella, a gentle, kindhearted lady, under whose fostering care the children were educated and instructed in the right conduct of life. The ties which united the parents and children were of a peculiarly affectionate nature, each living for the other, as it were, and all instinctively uniting to make their home, what indeed it was, a home of love. Of all the memories of childhood there are none so sweet, so enduring, so beneficial. Harmony prevailed; there were no dissensions, no bickerings. The wife adored her husband, the children adored their father, and he contributed to their happiness by living at home the perfect family life, and keeping his business cares and anxieties sedulously in the background. In the esteem of the world they stood high; in cases of distress they were never appealed to in vain. Here again Mrs. Rozella was the guiding spirit; to the poor in her neighbourhood she was a ministering angel, and although her purse was liberally supplied by her husband, it was nearly always empty. So strong was her sympathy with suffering that it frequently clouded her judgement, and when she was challenged on this point she would answer, 'I am quite satisfied; the poor people were in want.' From the day of her marriage with the man she loved she had never known a pecuniary anxiety, and she was happy in the belief that her darling children were provided for. Miriam was thirteen years of age, Cecil eleven, Clara nine.

Miriam was the confidant of the whole family. Into her sympathising ears Cecil and Clara poured their childish troubles, and went away comforted. She was her mother's companion in missions of charity, and young as she was she gave continual evidence not only of the possession of a rare common sense, but of a strength and decision of character which argued well for her future. She possessed the faculty of making up her mind and acting upon it without needless argument, and after the thing was done and she spoke of it to her parents they invariably approved of it; and this approval did not spring solely from their love for her – which might easily have led then astray – but from the conviction that the thing she had done was right. The seeds of a strong self-reliance were implanted within her, and also – which was far better – the seeds of a firm faith in the goodness of God. She went to church with a devout heart, and prayed with all the earnestness and sincerity of one who was seeking the truth. While thus employed she presented a beautiful picture, her eyes luminous with the ecstasy of devotion, her face eloquent with impressive, absorbing prayer. Here was a fresh young soul wending its way ingenuously and trustfully in paths of purity, ignorant as yet of the deeper human problems of life, but unconsciously arming itself to grapple with them, in whatever shape they might present themselves.

At the present moment she was reading aloud *Paul and Virginia* in French, her mother occasionally correcting her accent. Mrs. Rozella was employed knitting socks for some poor people who had ample reason for blessing her name.

The reading and knitting were suspended by the striking of ten o'clock. Miriam closed her book, and Mrs. Rozella put her work aside and touched the bell. A maid answered the summons.

'Is supper laid, Anne?'

'Yes, ma'am.'

'Tell cook to send it up a quarter of an hour after Mr. Rozella arrives. He will be hungry.'

'Yes, ma'am,' said the maid, and retired.

Then there was silence in the room, the mother and daughter sitting in expectancy, listening to the sounds in the street. Every approaching vehicle caused them to start to their feet, and its rumbling past the door brought disappointment with it. By numerous signs, apparently insignificant, but pregnant with beloved meaning, it was made clear that the absent one's presence was a joy in the house of which he was master. Of the two, Miriam was the calmer.

'Do you remember, mother,' she said presently, 'the last time we were waiting for father? The train was half an hour late.'

'But that was quite exceptional, Miriam. He said it had very seldom happened before.'

'This may be exceptional, too.'

'It may be, dear.'

'It is only a quarter past ten. Shall I go on with *Paul and Virginia?*'

'Not aloud. I could not give my mind to it, and you might make a thousand mistakes without one being corrected. That would never do.'

'Do I make a thousand mistakes?' asked Miriam, with a smile.

'No dear. You are improving wonderfully, and your accent is fairly good. A few months in France would be a great benefit to you; that is what improved me so much. There – that is father's cab.' She listened and sighed. 'It has passed the door!'

'It would be delightful to go to France, mother.'

'I will tell you a secret, Miriam, only don't let Cecil and Clara know yet awhile; it would excite them. We are all going this year. Father has spoken of spending three or four days in Paris, and then travelling to a little village in Normandy, where we shall remain two months. That is to be our summer holiday.'

'Oh!' cried Miriam, in rapture; 'I shall dream of it – Paris! A little village in Normandy! I will draw it for you.' Her pencil was already busy. 'It is by the sea, of course.'

'Yes, dear,' answered Mrs. Rozella, smiling at Miriam's eagerness, 'it is by the sea. Father lived a whole year there when he was a young man, and is well acquainted with the neighbourhood – all the pretty spots and the lovely woods. Artists go there for pictures. We shall be very, very happy.'

'We are very happy here, mother. It seems ungrateful to be glad at leaving our dear old home.'

'It will be only for a short time. We shall come back to it better and stronger for the change.'

Miriam looked up apprehensively; the family doctor had paid several visits to the house lately.

'Are you ill, mother?'

'Not ill, dear, but not quite so strong as I could wish; the trip abroad will set me up. Let me see your drawing. How pretty it is! We'll show it to father presently; there's his cab at last!'

'No, mother, it has stopped on the opposite side.'

Mrs. Rozella went to the window and drew the blind; there was a moon, and the stars were shining. Miriam was right; the cab had stopped on the opposite side. The clock struck the half hour.

Miriam joined her at the window; she drew the girl close to her side, and they stood silent awhile. She dared not give utterance to what was in her mind, from a superstitious dread that spoken words might be prophetic.

There had been a frightful railway accident a week ago, in which lives were lost. What if there had been an accident to the train by which her husband was travelling home? She tortured herself by dwelling on the possibility, and sent up a mute prayer of supplication for his safety.

'Where are you going, mother?'

'To the street door. I will wait there for your father.'

Miriam accompanied her, and they looked up and down the street, eagerly watching each vehicle as it approached, their hearts now beating with joyful anticipation, now throbbing with disappointment. The elder lady's morbid anxiety had communicated itself to the younger, and Miriam also now began to fear that an accident had occurred. A distant clock struck eleven, and they clung to each other, their limbs trembling, as though some dread portent was conveyed in the sound. Their suffering was the more poignant because they could do nothing – nothing but wait!

'There may be an alteration in the trains, mother.'

'Your father would have told me. He is always very thoughtful.'

How slowly the time passed! Every moment was prolonged and charged with agonising import. At half-past eleven it seemed as if they had been standing at the door for hours.

'It is very chilly, mother. You will catch cold.'

'Bring me my hat and cloak, dear, and put on your own. I cannot go indoors.'

Leaving the street door ajar they paced the pavement, a few steps this way, a few steps that. A policeman came up, and asked if anything was the matter.

'No,' said Mrs. Rozella, in a tone of vague distress; 'we are waiting – waiting. You – you have not heard of any accident?'

'No, ma'am.'

'Do you hear, Miriam? He must have heard of it if there had been one.'

The policeman passed on, in a dubious state of mind. Anne came to the door, and Miriam answered her inquiry whether Cook was to stop up. Yes, if she did not mind; Mr. Rozella would be sure to arrive in a minute or two. Anne went down to the kitchen and the servants held a conversation as to the cause of the delay, speaking low, as was fitting in such circumstances.

'I had a brother killed on the railway,' said Cook.

'How awful!' exclaimed Anne.

Cook did not regard it in that light; it was a piece of family history to be proud of. It did not happen to everybody.

'I was just eleven at the time,' Cook continued. 'I shall never forget mother going down to indemnify him.'

'Identify,' corrected Anne, who had been better educated.

'What's the difference? He was killed on the railway, and I had a new black dress made.'

Midnight – and still no sign. Now and then Miriam drew her mother's cloak closer around her. Once she went up to the children's room to see if they were asleep. Mrs. Rozella's voice was choked with tears as she asked about them.

'Don't cry, mother; oh, don't cry! Father cannot be long now.'

'When he went away,' sobbed Mrs. Rozella, 'he had a presentiment. He ran back and kissed us all again. There was something on his mind – Oh, thank God! Here's the cab!'

It stopped at the house, and a man who looked like a railway official jumped off the box and opened the cab door. Mrs. Rozella sprang forward with open arms, and a world of love in her face. From the cab issued a gentleman gravely, and slowly. It was not Mr. Rozella.

'Doctor Richards!' cried Miriam.

'Yes my dear, yes,' said the doctor, and his voice shook.

'Oh, God!' gasped Mrs. Rozella.

He took her hand, and said, 'Come inside. I have something to tell you.'

She tore her hand away, and cried in agony, 'My husband! Where is my husband?'

'I am here at his request. Calm yourself, dear Mrs. Rozella. Come into the house – we cannot talk in the street. Be brave, be strong, for your children's sake!'

From Miriam Rozella (1897)

BENJAMIN FARJEON (1809–1903) was born in London but went to Australia and New Zealand after quarrelling with his parents. On his return to Britain in 1868, he became a prolific and successful novelist.

Sigmund Freud

CASE STUDY

I should like to give a single example of the way in which a childhood memory, which previously appeared to have no meaning, can acquire one as a result of being worked over by analysis. When I began in my forty-third year to direct my interest to what was left of my memory of my own childhood there came to my mind a scene which had for a long while back (from the remotest past, as it seemed to me) come into consciousness from time to time, and which I had good evidence for assigning to a date before the end of my third year. I saw myself standing in front of a cupboard ['*Kasten*'] demanding something and screaming, while my half-brother, my senior by twenty years, held it open. Then suddenly my mother, looking beautiful and slim, walked into the room, as if she had come in from the street. These were the words in which I described the scene, of which I had a plastic picture, but I did not know what more I could make of it. Whether my brother wanted to open or shut the cupboard – in my first translation of the picture I called it a 'wardrobe' ['*Schrank*'] – why I was crying, and what the arrival of my mother had to do with it – all this was obscure to me. The explanation I was tempted to give myself was that what was in question was a memory of being teased by my elder brother and of my mother putting a stop to it. Such misunderstandings of a childhood scene which is preserved in the memory are by no means rare: a situation is recalled, but it is not clear what its central point is, and one does not know on which of its elements the psychical accent is to be place. Analytic effort led me to take a quite unexpected view of the picture. I had missed my mother, and had come to suspect that she was shut up in this wardrobe or cupboard; and it was for that reason that I was demanding that my brother should open the cupboard. When he did what I asked and I had made certain that my mother was not in the cupboard, I began to scream. This is the moment that my memory has held fast; and it was followed at once by the appearance of my mother, which allayed my anxiety or longing. But how did the child get the idea of looking for his absent mother in the cupboard? Dreams which I had at the same time [as the analysis of this memory] contained obscure allusions to a nurse of whom I had other recollections, such as, for example, that she used to insist on my dutifully handing over to her the small coins I received as presents – a detail which can itself claim to have the value of a screen memory for later experiences. I accordingly resolved that this time I would make the problem of interpretation easier for myself and would ask my mother, who was by then grown old, about the nurse. I learned a variety of details, among them that this clever but dishonest person had carried out considerable thefts in the house during my mother's confinement and had been taken to court on a charge preferred by my half-brother. This information threw a flood of light on the childhood scene, and so enabled me to understand it. The sudden disappearance of the nurse had not been a matter of indifference to me: the reason why I had turned in particular to this brother, and had asked him where she was, was probably because I had noticed that he played a part in her disappearance; and he had answered in the elusive and punning fashion that was characteristic of him: 'She's "boxed up" ["*eingekastelt*"].' At the time, I understood this answer in a child's way [i.e. literally], but I stopped asking any more questions as there was nothing more to learn. When my mother left me a short while later, I suspected that my naughty brother had done the same thing to her that he had done to the nurse and I forced him to open the cupboard ['*Kasten*'] for me. I now understood, too, why in the translation of this visual childhood scene my mother's slimness was emphasized; it must have struck me as having just been restored to her.

From Complete Works Vol. VI, *tr.* under the editorship of James Strachey

---

SIGMUND FREUD (1856–1939), Austrian founder of psychoanalysis, was born in Freiburg. He was rescued after Austria had been overrun by the Nazis, and spent the rest of his life in Britain.

Ahad Ha-Am

Parental Choice

I was born on the 17th of Ab, 5616 [18th Aug., 1856], in the town of Skvire, one of the most benighted spots in the hasidic districts of Russia. In 5628 [1868] my father became tax-farmer of the village of Gapchitsa, near the town of Pohrbishtch, and on Friday the 30th of Sivan [20th June] in that year we moved from Skvire to the village. I was then twelve years old.

While we were still in Skvire I made good progress in my studies and was thought to show promise. In the village, with no companions of my own age and none of the amusements of childhood, I became a devoted student, and pored over the Talmud and the *Poskim* [decisions on points of Jewish law] day and night. At first I had the help of a *Melammed* [elementary school teacher], but after I had turned fifteen I studied by myself. I made such good progress that at the age of 16 or 17 I already had a reputation as a Talmudist and an expert in Jewish ritual law, especially marriage law; and the neighbouring Rabbis used to consult me on such questions. At this time I finished the whole Talmud, and my father celebrated the occasion by a large party, as was the custom in those days.

But at the same time I paid some attention to Hebrew grammar and the Bible as well, and I also read something of the philosophical works of the Spanish Jewish writers. All this reading was haphazard and piecemeal, without any guidance or teaching. The fanatics of the district in which I lived regarded these studies not only as useless, but as a dangerous poison. However, heaven prospered my father, and a rich man has many friends; so the hasidim respected me for my learning and piety, and overlooked my interest in philosophical literature. It was only the most important of them (like R. Sheftel Hurwitz of Berditchev, one of the leaders of the Sadagura community of hasidim, to which my father belonged) who sometimes ventured to argue with me about secular and religious studies when they came to our house to collect dues for one purpose or another. They fired at me familiar sayings of the ancient Rabbis, and anecdotes and quotations from our ethical and hasidic literature; I summoned to battle Maimonides,

Ibn Ezra and the other Jewish philosophers, in whom I was very well versed. The heated argument would go on until day-break, and in the end of course the engagement would be broken off with no decisive result.

On the 18th of Sivan, 5633 [13th June, 1873], at the age of 16, I married, or rather was married off by my parents. It was not their fault that I married so late. They had done their best. Two years before they had fixed on a girl of good family for me, and had arranged for the marriage to take place a year later; but there had been some difficulties on the bride's side, and in spite of all complaints and protests on our part, the wedding was postponed a further year.

The lady destined for me by heaven, or chosen for me by my parents, was the daughter of a man of great learning, R. Mordecai Zalman, grandson on his father's side of R. Menahem Mendel of Liubovitch, and on his mother's side of the Tsaddik R. Jacob Israel of Tshaski. The bride's father had died young, when he was a Rabbi in Zhitomir, during the plague of 5626 [1866], and she was afterwards brought up in the home of her maternal grandfather, R. Levi Isaac Zalmanson, who was Rabbi in Velizh.

This illustrious pedigree on both sides so dazzled my parents that they did not even go or send somebody to the bride's home to see that she was not blind or one-armed or anything of that sort. What greater honour could a hasid have than to become connected by marriage with such saintly men? My parents were unfortunately very vain and fond of display, and this weakness often stood in my way in after life. This time, however, luck was on my side. The young lady was neither blind nor one-armed, but was a normal Jewish girl, who had been strictly and religiously brought up and knew her prayers and all the other things that a Jewish girl has to know. And what more could one want?

From Essays: Letters: Memoirs, *tr.* and *ed.* Leon Simon (1946)

AHAD HA-AM (1856–1927), born Asher Ginsberg, leader of spiritual Zionism and Hebrew writer, was adviser to Chaim Weizmann in eliciting from Britain in 1917 support for a Jewish homeland in Palestine, where he spent his last years.

Shalom Aleichem

THE NIGHT OF HAKAFOTH

If I were Goethe, I would not describe the sorrows of young Werther; I would describe the sorrows of a poor Jewish lad who was madly in love with the cantor's daughter. If I were Heine, I would not sing of Florentine nights; I would sing of the night of *Simchath Torah*, when Jews make the rounds of *Hakafoth* and when young women and pretty girls mingle with the men in the synagogue – the one night when this is permitted. The women kiss the Scroll of the Law. They jump up and down, squealing in every key, 'Long life to you!' The answer is 'Same to you, same to you!'

An hour or two before the *Hakafoth* ceremony, the smaller children gathered in the synagogue and climbed upon the benches. Flags fluttered in their hands, flags topped with red apples in which candles were burning. But the apples were not redder than the cheeks of the children, and the candles shone no brighter than their eyes. The older boys strolled in the synagogue yard, and there the air was soft and clear, the sky star-studded, and one had the sensation that the whole world was enjoying a holiday. Even the silence was festive, and nothing dared to mar the holiness of this night, the night of the Rejoicing of the Law, when the Chosen People celebrated the heavenly gift of the Torah throughout the earth.

Did it matter that a peasant cart clattered by, raising a cloud of fragrant dust? Or that the post chaise rumbled past, breaking the stillness with the ting-a-ling of its bells? . . . The dust settled, the sound of the bell died in the distance, and the night remained as holy and as festive as before, for the holiday of the Rejoicing of the Law was being celebrated throughout the world. . . .

A black cat ran past on its soft, velvety paws; it cut across the synagogue yard and disappeared. A dog howled in a melancholy key and then was quiet. Yet the night remained holy, still festive, because this holiday of the Rejoicing of the Law reigned, and it was being celebrated everywhere.

It was easy to breathe in such clear air. One's heart almost burst with joy, and one's soul was light. . . . One felt proud – this was the night of the Rejoicing of the Law! Above was the sky, and God was there – your God, your heaven, your holiday!

'Children, they're starting the *Hakafoth*!'

They darted into the synagogue, but it was a false alarm. The men were still engaged in the evening prayer. Tzali, the cantor of the Cold Synagogue, stood at the altar with his two choir boys: one a swarthy lad with thick lips, the bass; the other a slender boy with a pale face, the soprano. The cantor, Reb Tzali, Tzali of the golden voice, was a tall, blond man with a nose hooked like a bull's horn. He had thin curly earlocks and a blond wavy beard that looked as if it had been tied to his face. Was it possible that this freak had such a handsome daughter? The cantor's daughter, you must understand, was *his* daughter, cantor Tzali was *her* father! . . . His daughter, he often boasted, was unique. There was only one trouble with her – she didn't want to get married. 'Anybody we suggest, she turns down. But, of course, that's just nonsense. When the right man comes along, she'll have to say yes. If not, we'll drag her to the wedding by her braids. And of course there's always a cane!' the cantor would say jokingly, flourishing his reed cane with its old yellow ivory knob.

And then at last the evening prayer was finished, but it was still a long way to the *Hakafoth*. Now they were intoning the hymn, 'Unto thee it was shown that thou mightest know that the Lord He is God. . . .' Stanzas of the hymn were being distributed among the most distinguished members of the congregation. Everyone recited his stanza, but each in a different key and with a different melody. Actually, the litany was the same the world over, but, since people have different voices and timbres and are a bit frightened of the sound of their own voices, the tune emerged not quite as expected, and the trills which should have come at the end of the stanzas were entirely lost.

The Cold Synagogue was large, wide, and lofty. It had no ceiling – just a roof; that was why it was called the 'Cold' Synagogue. The roof was painted sky-blue, but the color was somewhat too blue – in fact, it was almost green. The painter had evidently over-painted it and, besides, had painted the glistening stars a little too large. Each star was only slightly smaller than an apple; they looked rather like potatoes edged with gilt. Nor were they scattered haphazardly like the stars really are; they were painted in orderly rows and crowded together. An ancient candelabrum made of greenish yellow copper hung from the center of the ceiling, suspended by a long copper chain. The candlesticks hanging on the walls were also copper; they were all filled with candles, and every candle was lit. It was dazzling.

Where did all these men come from? All the women, girls, young men, and children? Sholom was visiting the Cold Synagogue for the first time, and he could not help thinking of the verse, 'How goodly are thy tents, O Jacob. . .' It was not easy to find a place. Happily, the beadle recognized him – why, wasn't he the son of Nahum Rabinowitz? Room must be made for him among the members of the congregation on the 'mirror' side!

What were they reading now? The noise and confusion were so great that neither the cantor nor the choir boys could be heard. In vain did everyone shout 'Quiet!' In vain did the beadle pound his fist on the table. Women were shouting, girls giggling, children squealing. . . .

Here was a little boy crying. 'Why are you crying, little boy?' Someone had knocked the apple off his flag and crushed it with his foot. What would he do without an apple? . . . A big boy, standing next to the child, grinned, showing all his teeth. The child's tragedy seemed to amuse him. This annoyed Sholom, and he asked angrily, 'What are you laughing at?' The lad replied, still showing all his teeth, 'That kid's weak in the head!' His answer irritated Sholom even more. 'Were you any brighter at his age?' The fellow stopped grinning. 'I really don't remember, but one thing I do know – I have more brains in my heel than you have in your head, even though you do go to the County School and are the son of Nahum Rabinowitz!' Had the son of Nahum Rabinowitz not been among strangers in a strange synagogue, he would have known what to do. But he managed to keep his temper. . . . Besides, through the terrific din, he heard the dear, familiar words with which the beadle invited the congregation to the rite of *Hakafoth*.

'The learned Reb Shimon Zeev, son of Reb Chaim Tzvi, the Cohen, is invited to honor the Torah!'

'The learned Reb Moshe Yaakov, son of Nahman Dov, the Levite, is invited to honor the Torah!'

Each man so honored received a Scroll of the Law with which he paraded around the synagogue.

And so the *Hakafoth* ceremony began. But where was the cantor's daughter? . . .

'Oh Lord! I beseech thee, save us. . . .' The first round had finished with the chorus 'Hai-da!' and with a dance. The beadle again called out in his hoarse voice, 'The learned Reb so-and-so is invited to honor the Torah. . . .' Thus ended the second round, the third, the fourth. . . . Each was followed by dancing and singing, and the cantor's daughter was nowhere to be seen!

Sholom could not sit still. He twisted and turned in his seat. Would he ever find her? Could she have deceived him so shabbily? Or had their tryst been discovered and had she been kept at home under lock and key? One could expect anything of Cantor Tzali, a man capable of pulling a girl by her braids and caning her! . . .

Apparently the beadle, noticing Sholom squirming in his seat and looking restlessly about, thought he must be eager to be called. Or perhaps it was one of the trustees who wanted to give Rabinowitz's son a treat. In any event, Sholom suddenly heard his name called. 'Sholom, the son of Manahem Nahum, is invited to honor the Torah!'

The blood rushed to his head. All eyes seemed to be fixed upon him. He felt as every young man feels when he is summoned for the first time to read from the Torah. Almost before he knew it, the beadle had brought a Scroll to him, and, standing among the others, he hugged the large Scroll in his arms. The procession had already begun. Cantor Tzali, at the head, sang, 'Helper of the poor, save us!' Women and girls crowded about to kiss the Scrolls, calling out, 'Long life to you!' It was strange to be treated with so much respect. The unexpected honor thrilled Sholom. He was very proud to be the only youth among men – and all because he was somebody. He was the son of Nahum Rabinowitz! . . . Suddenly someone kissed his hand. 'Long life to you!' He raised his eyes and saw the cantor's daughter, standing next to her friend. . . .

The heavens opened; angels descended singing hymns. They praised the world God had created – this good, beautiful world; praised the people He had created – good, kind people! Everything was so beautiful, Sholom wanted to weep, and his heart sang to the angels.

He was astonished and bewildered – instead of kissing the Scroll, she had kissed his hand. Had it been an accident? It could not have been! Her smiling eyes told him. He almost dropped the Scroll. He wanted to pause, to look again into her eyes, to say a word or two. . . . But he could not. He had to move on. The Scroll had to be passed to another. Only when he had reached the altar and returned the Scroll to the beadle was he able to glance back. But she was no longer there. Again he was in the procession, straggling after the men, but this time without a Scroll. His eyes searched for her everywhere, but she had disappeared. Perhaps it had only been an illusion. But he still felt the kiss on his hand. As he left the synagogue, he felt that he had wings; he was flying. . . . Angels were flying with him.

In the Big Synagogue, the ceremony was still going on. Father was in high spirits. Dressed in an old satin coat which was cracked at the seams, showing its yellow lining in places, he nevertheless looked noble and handsome. Lazar Yossel and Magidov stood beside him. Father smiled as he listened to them. 'Where have you been?' he asked Sholom, not angrily, but out of curiosity. 'In the Cold Synagogue,' Sholom replied, and boasted that his name had been called to honor the Torah. 'That was very nice of them!' Father said, pleased, and the superior sons-in-law teased Sholom. One of them asked whether he had been introduced to the Helper of the Poor. The other remarked, 'How could he have met the Helper there? It's only the Helper's grandson who's at the Cold Synagogue!' Everyone laughed. What a night that was! Such a night could only come during *Simchath Torah!*

From The Great Fair, *tr.* Tamara Kahana (1955)

SHALOM ALEICHEM, pseudonym of Shalom Yakov Rabinowitz (1859–1916), Yiddish author, was born in Pereyaslav, Russia, and established his family in Switzerland in 1906. He wrote more than forty volumes of novels, plays and stories, from a group of which was adapted the musical *Fiddler on the Roof. The Best of Shalom Aleichem* was published in 1979.

Israel Zangwill

SUGARMAN'S BAR-MITZVAH

The day of Ebenezer Sugarman's *Bar-mitzvah* duly arrived. All his sins would henceforth be on his own head, and everybody rejoiced. By the Friday evening so many presents had arrived – four breast-pins, two rings, six pocket- knives, three sets of Machzorim, or Festival Prayer-Books, and the like – that his father barred up the door very carefully, and in the middle of the night, hearing a mouse scampering across the floor, woke up in a cold sweat and threw open the bedroom window and cried, 'Ho! buglers!' But the 'buglers' made no sign of being scared, everything was still and nothing purloined, so Jonathan took a reprimand from his disturbed wife and curled himself up again in bed.

Sugarman did things in style, and through the influence of a client the confirmation ceremony was celebrated in 'Duke's Plaizer Shool.' Ebenezer, who was tall and weak-eyed, with lank black hair, had a fine new black cloth suit, and a beautiful silk praying-shawl with blue stripes, and a glittering watch-chain, and a gold ring, and a nice new Prayer-Book with gilt edges, and all the boys under thirteen made up their minds to grow up and be responsible for their sins as quick as possible. Ebenezer walked up to the reading desk with a dauntless stride and intoned his portion of the Law with no more tremor than was necessitated by the musical roulades, and then marched upstairs as bold as brass to his mother, who was sitting up in the gallery, and who gave him a loud smacking kiss that could be heard in the four corners of the synagogue, just as if she were a real lady.

Then there was the *Bar-mitzvah* breakfast, at which Ebenezer delivered an English sermon and a speech, both openly written by the Shalotten Shammos, and everybody commended the boy's beautiful sentiments, and the beautiful language in which they were couched. Mrs. Sugarman forgot all the trouble Ebenezer had given her in the face of his assurances of respect and affection, and she wept copiously. Having only one eye, she could not see what her Jonathan saw, and what was spoiling his enjoyment of Ebenezer's effusive gratitude to his dear parents for having trained him up in lofty principles.

It was chiefly male cronies who had been invited to breakfast, and the table had been decorated with biscuits and fruit and sweets not appertaining to the meal, but provided for the refreshment of the less-favoured visitors – such as Mr. and Mrs. Hyams – who would be dropping in during the day. Now, nearly every one of the guests had brought a little boy with him, each of whom stood like a page behind his father's chair.

Before starting on their prandial fried fish, these trenchermen took from the dainties wherewith the ornamental plates were laden, and gave thereof to their offspring. Now, this was only right and proper, because it is the prerogative of children to '*nash*' on these occasions. But, as the meal progressed, each father from time to time, while talking briskly to his neighbour, allowed his hand to stray mechanically into the plates, and thence negligently backwards into the hand of his infant, who stuffed the treasure into his pockets. Sugarman fidgeted about uneasily; not one surreptitious seizure escaped him, and every one pricked him like a needle. Soon his soul grew punctured like a pincushion. The Shalotten Shammos was among the worst offenders, and he covered his back-handed proceedings with a ceaseless flow of complimentary conversation.

'Excellent fish, Mrs. Sugarman,' he said, dexterously slipping some almonds behind his chair.

'What?' said Mrs. Sugarman, who was hard of hearing.

'First-class plaice!' shouted the Shalotten Shammos, negligently conveying a bunch of raisins.

'So they ought to be,' said Mrs. Sugarman in her thin, tinkling accents; 'they were all alive in the pan.'

'Ah, did they twitter?' said Mr. Belcovitch, pricking up his ears.

'No,' Bessie interposed. 'What do you mean?'

'At home in my town,' said Mr. Belcovitch impressively, 'a fish made a noise in the pan one Friday.'

'Well, and suppose?' said the Shalotten Shammos, passing a fig to the rear. 'The oil frizzles.'

'Nothing of the kind,' said Belcovitch angrily; 'a real living noise. The woman snatched it out of the pan and ran with it to the Rabbi. But he did not know what to do. Fortunately, there was staying with him for the Sabbath a travelling Saint from the far city of Ridnik, a *Chassid*, very skilful in plagues and purifications, and able to make clean a creeping thing by a hundred and fifty reasons. He directed the woman to wrap the fish in a shroud, and give it honourable burial as quickly as possible. The funeral took place the same afternoon, and a lot of people went in solemn procession to the woman's back-garden, and buried it with all seemly rites, and the knife with which it had been cut was buried in the same grave, having been defiled by contact with the demon. One man said it should be burnt, but that was absurd, because the demon would be only too glad to find itself in its native element; but to prevent Satan from rebuking the woman any more, its mouth was stopped with furnace ashes. There was no time to obtain Palestine earth, which would have completely crushed the demon.'

'The woman must have committed some *Avirah*,' said Karlkammer.

'A true story!' said the Shalotten Shammos ironically. 'That tale has been over Warsaw this twelvemonth.'

'It occurred when I was a boy,' affirmed Belcovitch indignantly. 'I remember it quite well. Some people explained it favourably. Others were of opinion that the soul of the fishmonger had transmigrated into the fish, an opinion borne out by the death of the fishmonger a few days before. And the Rabbi is still alive to prove it – may his light continue to shine! – though they write that he has lost his memory.'

The Shalotten Shammos sceptically passed a pear to his son. Old Gabriel Hamburg, the scholar, came compassionately to the raconteur's assistance.

'Rabbi Solomon Maimon,' he said, 'has left it on record that he witnessed a similar funeral in Posen.'

'It was well she buried it,' said Karlkammer. 'It was an atonement for a child, and saved its life.'

The Shalotten Shammos laughed outright.

'Ah, laugh not,' said Mrs. Belcovitch, 'or you may laugh with blood. It isn't for my own sins that I was born with ill-matched legs.'

'I must laugh when I hear of God's fools burying fish anywhere but in their stomach,' said the Shalotten Shammos, transporting a Brazil nut to the rear, where it was quietly annexed by Solomon Ansell, who had sneaked in uninvited and ousted the other boy from his coign of vantage.

The conversation was becoming heated; Breckeloff turned the topic.

'My sister has married a man who can't play cards,' he said lugubriously.
'How lucky for her!' answered several voices.
'No, it's just her black luck!' he rejoined; 'for he *will* play.'

There was a burst of laughter, and then the company remembered that Breckeloff was a *Badchan*, or jester.

'Why, your sister's husband is a splendid player,' said Sugarman with a flash of memory, and the company laughed afresh.

'Yes,' said Breckeloff. 'But he doesn't give me the chance of losing to him now, he's got such a stuck-up *Kotzon*. He belongs to Duke's Plaizer *Shool*, and comes there very late, and when you ask him his birthplace he forgets he was a *Pullack*, and says he comes from "behind Berlin." '

These strokes of true satire occasioned more merriment, and were worth a biscuit to Solomon Ansell, *vice* the son of the Shalotten Shammos.

From Children of the Ghetto (1892)

ISRAEL ZANGWILL (1864–1926), British novelist, was born in London of impoverished Russian immigrant parents. *Children of the Ghetto*, which won him an international reputation, was commissioned by the Jewish Publication Society of America.

Marcel Proust

THE ACTRESS

But if the thought of actors weighed so upon me, if the sight of Maubant, coming out one afternoon from the Théâtre-Français, had plunged me in the throes and sufferings of hopeless love, how much more did the name of a 'star,' blazing outside the doors of a theatre, how much more, seen through the window of a brougham which passed me in the street, the hair over her forehead abloom with roses, did the face of a woman who, I would think, was perhaps an actress, leave with me a lasting disturbance, a futile and painful effort to form a picture of her private life.

I classified, in order of talent, the most distinguished: Sarah Bernhardt, Berma, Bartet, Madeleine Brohan, Jeanne Samary; but I was interested in them all. Now my uncle knew many of them personally, and also ladies of another class, not clearly distinguished from actresses in my mind. He used to entertain them at his house. And if we went to see him on certain days only, that was because on the other days ladies might come whom his family could not very well have met. So we at least thought; as for my uncle, his fatal readiness to pay pretty widows (who had perhaps never been married) and countesses (whose high-sounding titles were probably no more than *noms de guerre*) the compliment of presenting them to my grandmother, or even of presenting to them some of our family jewels, had already embroiled him more than once with my grandfather. Often, if the name of some actress were mentioned in conversation, I would hear my father say, with a smile, to my mother: 'One of your uncle's friends,' and I would think of the weary novitiate through which, perhaps for years on end, a grown man, even a man of real importance, might have to pass, waiting on the doorstep of some such lady, while she refused to answer his letters and made her hall-porter drive him away; and imagine that my uncle was able to dispense a little jackanapes like myself from all these sufferings by introducing me in his own home to the actress, unapproachable by all the world, but for him an intimate friend.

And so – on the pretext that some lesson, the hour of which had been altered, now came at such an awkward time that it had already more than once prevented me, and would continue to prevent me, from seeing my uncle – one day, not one of the days which he set apart for our visits, I took advantage of the fact that my parents had had luncheon earlier than usual; I slipped out and, instead of going to read the playbills on their column, for which purpose I was allowed to go out unaccompanied, I ran all the way to his house. I noticed before his door a carriage and pair, with red carnations on the horses' blinkers and in the coachman's buttonhole. As I climbed the staircase I could hear laughter and a woman's voice, and, as soon as I had rung, silence and the sound of shutting doors. The man-servant who let me in appeared embarrassed, and said that my uncle was extremely busy and probably could not see me; he went in, however, to announce my arrival, and the same voice I had heard before said: 'Oh, yes! Do let him come in; just for a moment; it will be so amusing. Is that his photograph there, on your desk? And his mother (your niece, isn't she?) beside it? The image of her, isn't he? I should so like to see the little chap, just for a second.'

I could hear my uncle grumbling and growing angry; finally the man-servant told me to come in.

On the table was the same plate of marchpanes that was always there; my uncle wore the same alpaca coat as on other days; but opposite to him, in a pink silk dress with a great necklace of pearls about her throat, sat a young woman who was just finishing a tangerine. My uncertainty whether I ought to address her as Madame or Mademoiselle made me blush, and not daring to look too much in her direction, in case I should be obliged to speak to her, I hurried across to kiss my uncle. She looked at me and smiled; my uncle said 'My nephew!' without telling her my name or telling me hers, doubtless because, since his difficulties with my grandfather, he had endeavoured as far as possible to avoid any association of his family with this other class of acquaintance.

'How like his mother he is,' said the lady.

'But you have never seen my niece, except in photographs,' my uncle broke in quickly, with a note of anger.

'I beg your pardon, dear friend, I passed her on the staircase last year when you were so ill. It is true I only saw her for a moment, and your staircase is rather dark; but I saw well enough to see how lovely she was. This young gentleman has her beautiful eyes, and also *this*,' she went on, tracing a line with one finger across the lower part of her forehead. 'Tell me,' she asked my uncle, 'is your niece Mme. — ; is her name the same as yours?'

'He takes most after his father,' muttered my uncle, who was no more anxious to effect an introduction by proxy, in repeating Mamma's name aloud, than to bring the two together in the flesh. 'He's his father all over, and also like my poor mother.'

'I have not met his father, dear,' said the lady in pink, bowing her head slightly, 'and I never saw your poor mother. You will remember it was just after your great sorrow that we got to know one another.'

I felt somewhat disillusioned, for this young lady was in no way different from other pretty women whom I had seen from time to time at home, especially the daughter of one of our cousins, to whose house I went every New Year's Day. Only better dressed; otherwise my uncle's friend had the same quick and kindly glance, the same frank and friendly manner. I could find no trace in her of the theatrical appearance which I admired in photographs of actresses, nothing of the diabolical expression which would have been in keeping with the life she must lead. I had difficulty in believing that this was one of 'those women,' and certainly I should never have believed her one of the 'smart ones' had I not seen the carriage and pair, the pink dress, the pearl necklace, had I not been aware, too, that my uncle knew only the very best of them. But I asked myself how the millionaire who gave her her carriage and her flat and her jewels could find any pleasure in flinging his money away upon a woman who had so simple and respectable an appearance. And yet, when I thought of what her life must be like, its immorality disturbed me more, perhaps, than if it had stood before me in some concrete and recognisable form, but its secrecy and invisibility, like the plot of a novel, the hidden truth of a scandal which had driven out of the home of her middle-class parents and dedicated to the service of all mankind, which had brought to the flowering-point of her beauty, had raised to fame or notoriety this woman, the play of whose features, the intonations of whose voice, like so many others I already knew, made me regard her, in spite of myself, as a young lady of good family, her who was no longer of a family at all.

We had gone by this time into the 'study,' and my uncle, who seemed a trifle embarrassed by my presence, offered her a cigarette.

'No, thank you, dear friend,' she said. 'You know I only smoke the ones the Grand Duke sends me. I tell him that they make you jealous.' And she drew from a case cigarettes covered with inscriptions in gold, in a foreign language. 'Why, yes,' she began again suddenly. 'Of course I have met this young man's father with you. Isn't he your nephew? How on earth could I have forgotten? He was so nice, so charming to me,' she went on, modestly and with feeling. But when I thought to myself what must actually have been the rude greeting (which, she made out, had been so charming), I, who knew my father's coldness and reserve, was shocked, as though at some indelicacy on his part, at the contrast between the excessive recognition bestowed on it and his never adequate geniality. It has since struck me as one of the most touching aspects of the part played in life by these idle, painstaking women that they devote all their generosity, all their talent, their transferable dreams of sentimental beauty (for, like all artists, they never seek to realise the value of those dreams, or to enclose them in the four-square frame of everyday life), and their gold, which counts for little, to the fashioning of a fine and precious setting for the rubbed and scratched and ill-polished lives of men. And just as this one filled the smoking-room, where my uncle was entertaining her in his alpaca coat, with her charming person, her dress of pink silk, her pearls, and the refinement suggested by intimacy with a Grand Duke, so, in the same way, she had taken some casual remark by my father, had worked it up delicately, given it a 'turn,' a precious title, set in it the gem of a glance from her own eyes, a gem of the first water, blended of humility and gratitude; and so had given it back transformed into a jewel, a work of art, into something altogether charming.

'Look here, my boy, it is time you went away,' said my uncle.

I rose; I could scarcely resist a desire to kiss the hand of the lady in pink, but I felt that to do so would require as much audacity as a forcible abduction of her. My heart beat loud while I counted out to myself 'Shall I do it, shall I not?' and then I ceased to ask myself what I ought to do so as at least to do something. Blindly, hotly, madly, flinging aside all the reasons I had just found to support such action, I seized and raised to my lips the hand she held out to me.

'Isn't he delicious! Quite a ladies' man already; he takes after his uncle. He'll be a perfect "gentleman," ' she went on, setting her teeth so as to give the word a kind of English accentuation. 'Couldn't he come to me some day for "a cup of tea," as our friends across the channel say; he need only send me a "blue" in the morning?'

I had not the least idea of what a 'blue' might be. I did not understand half the words which the lady used, but my fear lest there should be concealed in them some question which it would be impolite in me not to answer kept me from withdrawing my close attention from them, and I was beginning to feel extremely tired.

'No, no; it is impossible,' said my uncle, shrugging his shoulders: 'He is kept busy at home all day; he has plenty of work to do. He brings back all the prizes from his school,' he added in a lower tone, so that I should not hear this falsehood and interrupt with a contradiction. 'You can't tell; he may turn out a little Victor Hugo, a kind of Vaulabelle, don't you know.'

'Oh, I love artistic people,' replied the lady in pink; 'there is no one like them for understanding women. Them, and really nice men like yourself. But please forgive my ignorance. Who, what is Vaulabelle? Is it those gilt books in the little glass case in your drawing-room? You know you promised to lend them to me; I will take great care of them.'

My uncle, who hated lending people books, said nothing, and ushered me out into the hall. Madly in love with the lady in pink, I covered my old uncle's tobacco-stained cheeks with passionate kisses, and while he, awkwardly enough, gave me to understand (without actually saying) that he would rather

I did not tell my parents about this visit, I assured him, with tears in my eyes, that his kindness had made so strong an impression upon me that some day I would most certainly find a way of expressing my gratitude. So strong an impression had it made upon me that two hours later, after a string of mysterious utterances which did not strike me as giving my parents a sufficiently clear idea of the new importance with which I had been invested, I found it simpler to let them have a full account, omitting no detail, of the visit I had paid that afternoon. In doing this I had no thought of causing my uncle any unpleasantness. How could I have thought such a thing, since I did not wish it? And I could not suppose that my parents would see any harm in a visit in which I myself saw none. Every day of our lives does not some friend or other ask us to make his apologies, without fail, to some woman to whom he has been prevented from writing; and do not we forget to do so, feeling that this woman cannot attach much importance to a silence which has none for ourselves? I imagined, like everyone else, that the brains of other people were lifeless and submissive receptacles with no power of specific reaction to any stimulus which might be applied to them; and I had not the least doubt that when I deposited in the minds of my parents the news of the acquaintance I had made at my uncle's I should at the same time transmit to them the kindly judgement I myself had based on the introduction. Unfortunately my parents had recourse to principles entirely different from those which I suggested they should adopt when they came to form their estimate of my uncle's conduct. My father and grandfather had 'words' with him of a violent order; as I learned indirectly. A few days later, passing my uncle in the street as he drove by in an open carriage, I felt at once all the grief, the gratitude, the remorse which I should have liked to convey to him. Beside the immensity of these emotions I considered that merely to raise my hat to him would be incongruous and petty, and might make him think that I regarded myself as bound to shew him no more than the commonest form of courtesy. I decided to abstain from so inadequate a gesture, and turned my head away. My uncle thought that, in doing so, I was obeying my parents' orders; he never forgave them; and though he did not die until many years later, not one of us ever set eyes on him again.

From Swann's Way, *tr.* C.K. Scott Moncrieff

MARCEL PROUST (1871–1922), French metaphysical novelist, was born in Paris of a Jewish mother and a Catholic father, and was all his life a semi-invalid. *Swann's Way* constitutes the first of his thirteen-volume work, *A la Recherche du Temps Perdu*.

William Rothenstein

COLLECTOR OF CURIOSITIES

In my first year [at Bradford Grammar School] I gained a prize, which I received from the hands of W. F. Forster, then Member for Bradford, and being an undersized lad, I got a round of applause. It was my only success – I never won another. The headmaster, known to generations of boys as 'Old Rusty', used to call out – 'Stand up, Sir. You will have to earn your living with your hands, you will never do it with your head!' Only in English History did I show any capacity. Happily there came to the school, early in my career, an admirable master, Arthur Burrell. Burrell knocked a hole, as it were, in the stale, drab walls of the schoolroom and let in the fresh air. He was an excellent reader, and encouraged us to read Shakespeare and other poets aloud for ourselves. He asked me often to his room, talked of books and authors, and encouraged my love for reading which, since my eyes gave me trouble, was discouraged at home. My brother and I shared a bedroom on the attic floor, and we were expressly forbidden to read in bed by gas light. My father would call up as he put out the lights on his way to bed, and at the sound of his voice we would spring out of bed and turn down the gas; but often, after hearing him shut the door of his room, we would turn up the gas again. Another practice of which I was guilty was saving the pennies I got for the daily school bun, to spend them on old books. There was a second-hand bookstall in the covered market where noble folios and quartos could be acquired for a few pence. I used my bun money and most of my pocket-money in this way, and spent much time copying the old prints I acquired, and often the title-pages too, which I thought beautiful. I was a voracious and undiscriminating reader, swallowing book after book, enjoying Harrison Ainsworth as much as Scott, and Talbot Baines Reed, Rider Haggard and Anstey as much as Dickens and Thackeray. But in youth nothing equals the joy of the theatre. No one, I thought, understood the subtlety of the actors as I did on the rare and rapt occasions when I went to the play. The first play, apart from the pantomime, which I saw was *Hans the Boatman;* a rubbishy play, no doubt, but wonderful to me. I saw Edward Compton and Kate Vaughan in *The School for Scandal*, when Compton as Charles Surface seemed all that was handsome, generous and manly; I was told too that he was in real life what he appeared to be on the stage. And I remember Mary Anderson as Galatea, and Barry Sullivan as Richard III; this must have been late in his life, for he belonged to the school of 'barn-stormers', and was born in 1828. I rather think he modelled himself on Hogarth's picture of Richard starting up from a couch, which later I saw at Saltaire. Then there was Hamilton's Panorama: painted scenes, showing many parts of the world, which moved slowly and continuously across the stage. One especially I remember, a scene representing Rotten Row, wherein Mr Gladstone was seen conversing with

Lord Hartington, with Mrs Langtry and other fashionable beauties near by. Gilbert and Sullivan operas came to Bradford as well, a delight to everyone, children and grown-ups. Above all I enjoyed the *Mikado*. Japan was then a remote and mysterious country; the dresses and characters were novel and fantastic, and, unmusical though I was, so tuneful were the songs I could even join in singing them at home. But I couldn't ever sing a bar in tune. My mother played the piano by ear, I believe quite brilliantly – her eyes were not good enough to read music – and my eldest brother and one of my sisters were musical. Frederick Delius, as a boy, used to play with my mother – his parents were friends of my parents – but this was during my childhood. Unfortunately, I was made to learn the violin, much against my inclination. My master used to say I would make the saints in Heaven swear; no doubt I did. I would cut the strings of the fiddle half through, so that one of them was sure to snap in the middle of my practising. Still, I was always a little hurt when the family groaned at my rendering of some mild sonata on my parents' birthdays. Happily I was able to convince them of the hopelessness of the pursuit, and I was allowed to give up torturing myself and others; and the language of the saints in Heaven became seemly again!

Having no taste for music, I never went to concerts; but I went, whenever I could, to the lectures at the Philosophical Society. Here I was able to see and hear great men from London, men like Andrew Lang and H.M. Stanley. Nothing excited me more. It is difficult for a Londoner to realise how cut off we were from art and literature, and how eventful a lecture was. I was all ears at these lectures. Often, when my father and others in the audience would suddenly laugh, I would fail to know why, and feel ashamed of not having laughed too.

Most of my school friends collected stamps; I had a passion for 'curiosities', and a set of book-shelves became my museum. My mother's sanitary sense was disturbed by the old books and other objects I brought home; happily I had Arthur Burrell's support, and so long as I did not keep my 'smelly old things' in my bedroom, my collection grew.

One day the local art master, to whom I confided my interest in old things, told me it was the sign of the artistic temperament. This remark made me glow all over, and I repeated it triumphantly on my return home. It was the first time I had heard the cliché; I considered it a final answer to my mother's disapproval.

From Men and Memories (1931)

SIR WILLIAM ROTHENSTEIN (1872–1945), British portrait painter, was born in Bradford. He was principal of the Royal College of Art 1920-35.

Helena Rubinstein

Mama's Beauty Cream

Coming as I did from a conservative European background, my attitude as an individualist – a girl who preferred to make it on her own rather than stay at home – was all the more unusual.

I was born in the early 1870s, in Krakow, Poland, on Christmas Day, the first child of Augusta and Horace Rubinstein. Before I was half-grown, I found myself the oldest of eight sisters. One brother died in infancy.

Krakow was, and still is, a medieval, almost feudal town, an intellectual and cultural centre. Here we were all brought up. We lived in a large old house near Rynek Square, close to the University. It was a house filled to overflowing with the overstuffed furniture of the nineteenth century, and the varied collections of a father who had a passion for papers and books. Oil lamps were used to light the rooms, and in winter we kept warm by the towering porcelain stoves which burned night and day.

My father was a strict, thoughtful man from a well-to-do family. When his own children began to arrive in rapid succession, he became a wholesale food broker, buying eggs from the local peasants and reselling them in quantity. He was not a very good businessman, and I remember recognizing this at an early age, and trying to figure out ways to help him. Mama was one of those fortunate women who, despite a child every year and the pressure of mounting economic problems, manage to grow more beautiful with each passing year. Her figure was slim and magnificent. I can see her even now, with her straight back, her tiny feet and wonderfully capable hands, wearing a simple black dress, with a white lace collar at the neck.

Mama's appearance was important to her. She had a neighbour come in and help her with her hair, and I would sit on a stool at her feet and beg her to allow me to have my hair done, too. Occasionally she would give way, and I learned the delight of having my own hair washed and then combed by hands that were deft and knowledgeable – my first salon experience.

My mother imbued her daughters with the philosophy of the times.

'Women influence the world through love,' she would tell us. 'Outer charm and inner beauty will give you the power to control your own lives and hold the love of the man you will marry.'

We would gather in the living-room, near the glowing stove. My mother would surround herself with her eight daughters: Helena, Paulina, Rosa, Regina, Stella, Ceska, Manka and Erna. Then in turn she would brush each head of hair, a hundred strokes, while we counted in chorus. We all had the same black, glossy, luxuriant locks, of which Mama was very proud.

Just how much beauty is God-given and how much is developed through a desire for it, no one can say. But I do know that my mother's beauty lessons, basic as they were, disciplined me in the daily ritual of beauty care which was later to become the ABC of my own simple philosophy. It was she who gave me the sense of confidence and self-fulfilment which can come from taking regular care of one's physical assets.

And then, the finger of fate . . . my mother's beauty cream.

A visiting actress friend, Modjeska, told her about it one day. The cream was made for her by a Hungarian chemist, Dr Jacob Lykusky, then living in Krakow. It was compounded, Modjeska said, from a mixture of herbs and essence of almonds, plus extracts from the bark of an evergreen tree. My mother was fascinated, insisted on meeting Dr Lykusky, and from then on, the Rubinstein household had a regular supply of the cream. In spite of the fact that she was quite old-fashioned, Mama encouraged all her daughters to use it. She would visit each of us at bed-time, and if we had been out in the wind or snow during the day, she would gently fingerprint a little of the cream on our cheeks.

'It will make you beautiful,' she would whisper, kissing us goodnight. 'And to be beautiful is to be a woman.'

It was, as I look back, an intensely feminine household, filled with gaiety, warmth, vanity and tantrums. As the eldest, I was learning, even at twelve, to take responsibility. My sisters called me 'The Eagle' because I ruled the nursery, high up under the eaves of the old house, with complete authority. I also served as interpreter and intercessor between the younger ones and our parents – excellent training for employee relations in later years. My mother, hard-pressed by her brood, relied on me. She put me in charge of the family linen, with full responsibility for keeping it clean and mended. . . .

Life in the Krakow Rubinstein household was quite different from family life today, in which teenagers exert so much influence over their world. My mother taught us all to knit and sew, and I was a great embroiderer. I could stitch a complex tablecloth in just a few days, and my skill must have been irritating to some of my contemporaries, for I have a hazy memory of one of my schoolmates cutting up my needlework out of sheer spite. As children of a large family we were loved, but we were not spoiled. And it never occurred to any of us to query our parents' judgement or to answer back.

I remember that a dancing-master lived next door to us, and he often gave dancing parties . . . with boys. Most of the other local girls attended, and one afternoon I decided to join them. In the midst of the party I was terribly embarrassed to have my father arrive, in high dudgeon, and remove me from the premises. I don't know whether it was because I was his eldest daughter, or perhaps the most impetuous, but he was over-protective of me to a fault. On the other hand, because he had no son, he would talk over his plans and projects with me, and since I was good at figures, he depended upon me to help him with his book-keeping. Once, when I was nearly fifteen, he was taken ill before an important business meeting. It was too late to cancel the meeting, which was to take place in a neighbouring town, and of course there was no such thing as a telephone in those days. I offered to go in his place, and after much talk and family consultation, I was allowed to go and speak for my father. Before I left the house, Mama whispered, 'Helenka, if you want to be smart, just listen and play dumb.'

The fact that I was able to bring off a very good deal was, I think, largely due to my youth and inexperience (and Mama's advice), which must have dumbfounded the others at the meeting. But my sense of triumph was a foretaste of what business achievement could mean.

On another occasion a wagon-load of eggs, ordered by my father, was delayed at the city gates because of a four-day religious holiday. The family counted heavily on the sale of the eggs, and if the authorities were to impound them in the summer heat, they most certainly would have gone bad. Taking matters into my own hands, I went off to see the city officials myself. With wiles, pleadings and tears, I told them of the family difficulties. The same afternoon the eggs were released.

Sometimes, taking things into my own hands had disastrous results. When I was about fifteen, I developed a hatred for the heavy, old-fashioned furniture in my room at home. One morning, when both my parents were away on a short holiday, I woke up with the brilliant idea of selling all the furniture in my room and using the proceeds for new, 'modern' furnishings. I had no idea of the affection my father had for the pieces that, to me, were just old dust-traps. Calling in a second-hand dealer, I disposed of the lot. Then I hurried to the shops and bought lots of shiny, new furniture. Delighted with the result, I felt sure that my father would be, too. Never will I forget the look on his face when he saw the room! He was almost too shocked for anger, but it was obvious that he was heartbroken. He went straight to the second-hand dealer and bought everything back! He would be pleased, I think, to know that the incident impressed me so strongly; to this day, I have never got rid of anything without long thought and expert advice.

From My Life for Beauty (1965)

HELENA RUBINSTEIN (1871–1965), beautician, businesswoman and philanthropist, was born in Krakow, Poland.

Chaim Weizmann

TIMBER

Motol was situated in one of the darkest and most forlorn corners of the Pale of Settlement, that prison house created by Czarist Russia for the largest part of its Jewish population. Throughout the centuries alternations of bitter oppression and comparative freedom – how comparative a free people would hardly understand – had deepened the consciousness of exile in these scattered communities, which were held together by a common destiny and common dreams. Motol was typical Pale, typical countryside. Here, in this half-town, half-village, I lived from the time of my birth, in 1874, till the age of eleven; and here I wove my first pictures of the Jewish gentile worlds. . . .

Like all Jewish boys I went to *cheder*, beginning at the age of four. Like nearly all *cheders*, mine was a squalid, one-room school, which also constituted the sole quarters of the teacher's family. If my *cheder* differed from others, it was perhaps in the possession of a family goat which took shelter with us in cold weather. And if my first *Rebbi*, or teacher, differed from others, it was in the degree of his pedagogic incompetence. If our schoolroom was usually hung with lines of washing, if the teacher's numerous children rolled about on the floor, if the din was deafening and incessant, that was nothing out of the ordinary. Nor was it anything out of the ordinary that neither the tumult nor the overcrowding affected our peace of mind or our powers of concentration.

In the spring and autumn, when the *cheder* was a tiny island set in a sea of mud, and in the winter, when it was almost blotted out by snow, I had to be carried there by a servant, or by my older brother. Once there, I stayed immured within its walls, along with the other children, from early morning till evening. We took lunch with us and consumed it in a short pause in the proceedings, often with the books still opened in front of us. On dark winter afternoons our studies could only be pursued by artificial light, and as candles were something of a luxury, and oil lamps practically unobtainable, each pupil was in turn assessed a pound of candles as a contribution to the education of the young generation. . . .

I did not relish the Talmudic teaching, but I adored that of the Prophets, for which I attended another *cheder*. There the teacher was humane and kindly, with a real enthusiasm for his subject. This enthusiasm he managed to communicate to his pupils, though here, too, school and surroundings were of the most depressing character. It is to this teacher, who became a lifelong friend of mine, that I am primarily indebted for my knowledge of the Hebrew Bible, and for my early and lasting devotion to Hebrew literature. He died in Poland not many years ago, and I was in correspondence with him till the end.

He was a man of the 'enlightened' type; that is, he had been touched by the spirit of the modernizing *Haskallah* (or Enlightenment) which was then abroad in the larger centres of Russian Jewry. Very surreptitiously he managed to smuggle into intervals in our sacred studies some attempts at instruction in secular knowledge. I remember how he brought into class, furtively and gleefully, a Hebrew text-book on natural science and chemistry, the first book of its kind to come into those parts. How this treasure fell into his hands I do not know, but without ever having seen a chemical laboratory, and with the complete ignorance of natural science which was characteristic of the Russian ghetto Jew, unable therefore to understand one scientific paragraph of the book, he gloated over it and displayed it to his favourite pupils. He would even lend it to one or another of us to read in the evenings. And sometimes – a proceeding not without risk, for discovery would have entailed immediate dismissal from his post – he would let us read with him some pages which seemed to him to be of special interest. We read aloud, of course, and in the Talmudic chant hallowed by tradition, so that anyone passing by the school would never suspect that we were not engaged in the sacred pursuits proper to a Hebrew school.

I have said that Motol lay in one of the darkest and most forlorn corners of the Pale of Settlement. This was true in the economic as well as in the spiritual sense. It is difficult to convey to the modern Westerner any idea of the sort of life which most of the Jewish families of Motol led, of their peculiar occupations, their fantastic poverty, their shifts and privations. On the spiritual side they were almost as isolated as on the physical. Newspapers were almost unknown in Motol. Very occasionally we secured a Hebrew paper from Warsaw, and then it would be a month or five weeks old. To us, of course, the news would be fresh. To tell the truth, we were not much interested in what was taking place in the world outside. It did not concern us particularly. If we were interested at all it was in the Hebrew presentation of the news. There were, from time to time, articles of general interest. No family in Motol could afford to subscribe to a newspaper regularly – nor would it have been delivered regularly. As it was, one copy would make the rounds of the 'well-to-do' families. When at last it reached the children it was in shreds, and usually illegible.

And yet Motol had two peculiar advantages, both deriving from its natural situation and its chief occupation, the timber trade. There was, in the Jewish population, a small layer which was more travelled than you would expect; and to some extent the effects of the general poverty were mitigated by the contact with nature.

My family was among the well-to-do, and it may help to give some idea of the standards of well-being which prevailed in Motol when I say that our yearly budget was probably seldom more than five or six hundred roubles (£50 or £60) in all. Even this income fluctuated widely, so that it could never be counted on with any degree of certainty. Out of it there were a dozen children to be clothed, shod and fed, and given a tolerably good education, considering our circumstances. On the other hand, we had our own house – one storey, with seven rooms and a kitchen – some acres of land, chickens, two cows, a vegetable garden, a few fruit trees. So we had a supply of milk, and sometimes butter; we had fruit and vegetables in season; we had enough bread – which my mother baked herself; we had fish, and we had meat once a week – on the Sabbath. And there was always plenty of fresh air. In these respects we were a great deal better off than the Jews of the city ghettos. . . .

The timber trade, the mainstay of Motol, played so large a part in our life, and is so closely bound up with my childhood and boyhood memories, that I must give it more than passing mention. To call even the more prosperous Jews of Motol real timber merchants would be somewhat of an exaggeration. They were at best subcontractors. But their connection with the basic trade of Motol did not give them any sense of security, for, as we shall see, it was hazardous and precarious in the extreme, and though it provided an all-year-round occupation, it was often far from providing an all-year-round income.

My father was what was called a 'transportierer.' He cut and hauled the timber and got it floated down to Danzig. It was a complicated and heart-breaking occupation. The forests stood on marshland, and except in times of drought and frost it was impossible to do any hauling. In the rainy seasons of spring and autumn the rivers overflowed, for there were no dykes and no attempt whatsoever at regulation. The rain came down and stayed there, till the summer dried it or the winter froze it. But sometimes it happened that between the rainfall and the dead of winter there intervened a heavy snowfall, which blanketed the soggy earth so that the frost could not penetrate. Unless a quick thaw intervened, and gave the following frost a chance to do its work, the forests and marshes remained impassable, and the season was ruined.

The cycle of work would begin in November, after the festival of *Sukkoth*, or Tabernacles. My father would set out for the heart of the forest, twenty or twenty-five miles away. His only communication with home was the sleigh road, which was always subject to interruption. He took along a supply of food and of warm clothing, and several bags of copper coins with which to pay the workers. We were never easy during father's absences in the forest, even during later years when my older brother Feivel went with him; for there were wolves in the forest and occasionally robbers. Fortunately there was, between my father and the fifty or sixty men he employed seasonally – *moujiks* of Motol and the neighbourhood – an excellent relationship, primitive, but warm and patriarchal. Once or twice he was attacked by robbers, but they were beaten off by his workmen.

It was hard, exacting work, but on the whole my father did not dislike it, perhaps because it called for a considerable degree of skill. It was his business to mark out the trees to be felled and he had to be able to tell which were healthy and worth felling. He had to supervise the hauling. The logs were roped and piled on the edge of the little river, to wait there for the thaw and the spring flood, which usually came between the festivals of *Purim* and Passover.

If the winter lingered we did not have father home for the Passover, for he could not leave to anyone else the responsible task of setting the timber afloat. When this happened it was a calamity which darkened the entire festival for us. But on the whole the thaw came in time, the stream broke up and flooded, and father would return on the last sleigh. He came home haggard, exhausted, and underfed; but it was an indescribably joyous home-coming. He brought the festival with him, as it were, and both would be with us for eight days.

After the Passover began the spring and summer work, the floating of the rafts to the sea. This too was a skilled and exacting occupation – really a branch of navigation. The rafts had to be fairly small to be able to negotiate the first streams; but they had to hold together strongly, against exceptional flood. The first job was to get them on the Pina and down to Pinsk, which they usually reached at *Shevuoth*, or Pentecost, seven weeks after Passover. There, instead of floating onward with the stream in a general southerly direction, which would have brought them to the Dnieper and the far-off Black Sea, the rafts were manoeuvred in the opposite direction through a canal which connected the Pina with Brest Litovsk on the Boug, the main tributary of the Vistula, which flows into the Baltic Sea at the port of Danzig.

Now Brest Litovsk was on the edge of the marshes, and from there on the Boug ran through sandy soil. The country became undulating, and less monotonous. But as the river was never looked after, never dyked or dredged, it formed sandbanks, especially in the summer. If the rafts consisted of oak, or were unskilfully piled up and drew too much water, they often stuck fast. Then there was nothing to do but wait, and bake in the sun, and pray for rain, or for a fresh flow from the head-waters of the Boug in the Carpathians. Meanwhile, days, perhaps weeks, would pass, and you watched your slender profits being eaten up by the delay; for though you included this hazard in the price, you could not make it high enough to cover every contingency.

Sometimes scores of rafts, floating easily, would be held up by one or two heavier rafts which were stranded. To get round them was a ticklish job, and you usually had to bribe the officials – the river police – to be allowed to do it. When at last you floated on to the wide Vistula you were faced with troubles of another kind. The rains and freshets which you welcomed on the Boug were often a bane on the Vistula. The waters became swollen and turbulent, and the rafts might be torn to pieces. Then you would tie up to the shore, and watch the flood, and wait for it to subside. At Thorn, which was German, everything changed. The river was regulated, order prevailed. From Thorn to Danzig it was a peaceful journey.

This description of river navigation is from my personal recollections, for when I was a schoolboy in Pinsk I used to spend much of my summers on the rafts. I had an uncle who was a great expert in this branch of the trade, and he would often take me on one of the journeys, which sometimes lasted for weeks. He used to have a very comfortable cabin, with bedroom and kitchen, on one of the rafts. He even had, as I remember, a mosquito net – an unheard-of innovation, though the air was sometimes black with insects. Those were jolly times for me. I did not go as far as Danzig, but got off on the nearer side of Warsaw, and took the train home.

The floating of the rafts lasted roughly from the Passover until the beginning of the great Jewish autumn festivals. Father would generally be back from Danzig for *Rosh Hashanah,* the New Year, and the Day of Atonement. Then, when the Feast of Tabernacles was past, and the heartache of collecting payments was over – and sometimes it wasn't – the annual cycle would begin again.

From Trial and Error (1949)

CHAIM WEIZMANN (1874–1952), Israeli statesmen, was born in Motol, near Pinsk, but was able to leave Russia to study in Germany and then to lecture in chemistry at Geneva and Manchester. He was President of the Zionist Organisation and, on the establishment of Israel in 1948, became its first President.

Leon Trotsky

THE LITTLE MUD HUT

For the first nine years of my life, I hardly stuck my nose outside my native village. Its name, Yanovka, came from the name of the landlord Yanovsky, from whom the estate had been bought. The old proprietor, Yanovsky, had risen from the ranks to a Colonelcy, had won the favour of the powers that be in the reign of Alexander II, and had been given the choice of one thousand acres of land on the uninhabited steppes of the province of Kherson. He built himself a mud hut thatched with straw, and equally crude farm-buildings. But his farming did not prosper, and after the Colonel's death his family moved to Poltava. My father bought over two hundred and fifty acres of land from Yanovsky and leased about four hundred more. . . .

My father's crops increased, as did the herds of cattle and horses. There was even an attempt to keep Merino sheep, but the venture was unsuccessful; on the other hand there were plenty of pigs. They wandered freely all over the place, rooted everywhere, and completely destroyed the garden. The estate was managed with care, but in an old-fashioned way. One measured profit or loss with the eye. For that very reason, it would have been difficult to fix the extent of father's fortune. All of his substance was always either in the ground, or in the crop above, or in the stocks on hand, which were either in bins or on their way to a port. Sometimes in the midst of tea or supper my father would suddenly exclaim: 'Come, write this down! I have received thirteen hundred roubles from the commission merchant. I gave the Colonel's widow six hundred, and four hundred to Dembovsky. Put down, too, that I gave Theodosia Antonovna one hundred roubles when I was in Elizavetgrad last spring.' That is about the way he kept his books. Nevertheless, my father slowly but obstinately kept climbing upward.

We lived in the little mud house that the Colonel had built. The straw roof harboured countless sparrows' nests under the eaves. The walls on the outside were seamed with deep cracks which were a breeding-place for adders. Sometimes these adders were mistaken for poisonous snakes, and boiling water from the samovar went into the cracks, but to no avail. The low ceilings leaked during a heavy rain, especially in the hall, and pots and basins would be placed on the dirt floor to catch the water. The rooms were small, the windows dim; the floors in the two bedrooms and the nursery were of clay, and bred fleas. The dining-room boasted a wooden floor which was rubbed once a week with yellow sand. But the floor in the main room, which was solemnly named the parlour, though only about eight paces long, was painted.

Yellow acacias, red and white roses, and in summer a climbing vine, grew around the house. The courtyard was not fenced in at all. A big mud house with a tile roof, which my father had built, contained the machine-shop, the main kitchen, and the servants' quarters. Next to it stood the 'little' wooden barn and beyond that the 'big' barn. Beyond that again came the 'new' barn. All were thatched with reeds. The barns were raised upon stones so that water trickling under them would not mould the grain. In hot or cold weather the dogs, pigs and chickens would take refuge under the barns. There the hens found a quiet place to lay their eggs. I used to fetch out the eggs, crawling in among the stones on my stomach; the space was too small for a grown person to squeeze into. Storks would nest every year on the roof of the 'big' barn. They would raise their red bills to heaven as they swallowed adders and frogs – a terrible sight! Their bodies would wriggle from their bills downward, and it looked as if the snake were eating the stork from the inside.

The barns, divided into bins, held fresh-smelling wheat, rough-prickly barley, smooth, almost liquid flaxseed, the blue-black beads of the winter rape, and light, slender oats. When the children played at hide-and-seek, they were allowed, on occasions when there were special guests, to hide in the barns. Crawling over one of the partitions into a bin, I would scramble up the mound of wheat and slip down on the other side. My arms would be buried to the elbows and my legs to the knees in the sliding mass of wheat, and my shirt and shoes, too often torn, would be filled with grain; the door of the barn would be shut, and someone, for the sake of appearances, would hang a padlock on the outside without snapping it, according to the rules of the game. I would be lying in the cool barn, buried in grain, breathing its dust, and listening to Senya V. or Senya J. or Senya S. or my sister Liza or someone else running about the courtyard, finding the others but not finding me, submerged in the winter-wheat.

The stable, the cowshed, the pigsty, and the chicken-house all stood on the other side of our dwelling. These were all made of mud and straw and twigs, somehow stuck together with clay. The tall well-sweep rose toward heaven about a hundred yards from the house. Beyond the well lay the ponds that watered the gardens of the peasants. The spring freshets carried the dam away every year, and it had to be rebuilt with earth and manure and straw. On the hill above the pond stood the mill – a wooden shed which sheltered a ten-horse-power steam-engine and two millstones. Here, during the first years of my childhood, my mother spent the greater part of her working hours. The mill worked not only for our own estate, but for the whole neighbourhood as well. The peasants brought their grain in from ten and fifteen miles around and paid a tenth measure for the grinding. In hot weather, on the eve of the threshing season, the mill worked day and night, and when I had learned to count and write, I used to weigh the peasants' grain and calculate the price of the grinding. When the harvest was over, the mill was closed and the engine went out to thresh. Later, a stationary engine was installed in a new stone and tile building. Our old mud house, too, was replaced by a large brick one with a tin roof. But all this happened when I had already reached my seventeenth year. During my last summer holidays, I used to calculate the distance between the windows, and the sizes of the doors for our new house; but I never could make the lines meet. On my next visit to the country, I saw the stone foundation being built. I never lived in the house itself. It is now used as a Soviet school. . . .

All my childish life is connected with the Colonel's mud house and the old sofa in the dining-room there. This sofa was veneered to look like red wood, and on it I sat for tea, for dinner and for supper. Here I played dolls with my sister, and here I would later read. The cover was torn in two places. The smaller hole was near the chair where Ivan Vasilyevich sat, the larger where I sat, next to my father. 'This sofa should have a new cover,' Ivan Vasilyevich used to say.

'It should have had one long ago,' my mother would reply.

'We haven't covered it since the year the Czar was killed.'

'But you know,' my father would justify himself, 'when one gets to that damned city, one runs here and there, the cab costs money, one is thinking all the time about how to get back quickly to the farm, and forgets all about what one came to buy.'

A rough, unpainted rafter stretched across the low ceiling of the dining-room, and on this the most varied objects found their resting-place: plates of provisions for safe keeping from the cat, nails, string, books, ink-bottles stoppered with paper, a penholder with an old rusty pen. There was no superfluity of pens at Yanovka. There were times when I made a pen for myself out of wood with the help of a table-knife, for copying horses out of old numbers of the illustrated magazine, *Field*. Up under the ceiling, where the chimney went out, lived the cat. There she raised her kittens, bravely jumping down with them in her teeth when it grew too hot up there. If a guest were tall he always hit the rafter with his head when he rose from the table, so that we had acquired the habit of pointing upward and saying: 'Mind your head!' . . .

In the springtime, the courtyard changed into a sea of mud. Ivan Vasilyevich would make a pair of wooden goloshes, or rather buskins, for himself, and I used to watch him with delight, striding along a foot above his usual height. In time the old saddler appears upon the scene. No one, it seems, knows his name. He is more than eighty years old and has served twenty-five years in the army of Nicholas I. Huge and broad-shouldered, with white beard and hair, he scarcely moves his heavy feet as he shuffles across to the barn, where his itinerant workshop has been installed. 'My legs are getting weak,' he has been complaining for the past ten years. On the other hand, his hands, which smell of leather, are stronger than pincers. . . .

After the hot, tense summer of the steppe is over, and its toilsome climax of reaping and harvesting has passed, comes the early autumn to take stock of a year's penal labour. The threshing is now in full swing. The centre of activity has moved to the threshing-floor beyond the sheds, a quarter of a mile from the house. A cloud of dust floats over the threshing-floor. The drum of the thresher is whining. Philip the miller, wearing glasses, is standing beside it. His black beard is covered with grey dust. The men are carrying in sheaves from the wagon. He takes them without looking at them, unties them, shakes them apart, and throws them into the thresher. At each armful the thresher growls like a dog with a bone. The straw-shaker throws out the straw, playing with it as it goes. The chaff pours out of a pipe at the side and is carried to the straw stack on a drag, with me standing on its wooden tail-board and holding on by the rope reins. 'Mind you don't fall!' cries my father. And down I go for the tenth time. I fall now into the straw, now into the chaff. The grey dust cloud thickens over the threshing-floor, the engine groans, the hulls get into one's shirt and nose and make one sneeze. 'Hey, Philip! not so fast!' warns my father from below, as the thresher growls too fiercely. I lift the drag. It slips out of my hands and falls with its whole weight on my finger. The pain is so intense that my head swims. I slip to one side so that the men shall not see me crying, and then run home. My mother pours cold water on my hand and bandages my finger, but the pain does not diminish. The wound festers during several days of torture.

Sacks of wheat now fill the barns and the sheds, and are piled in heaps under tarpaulins in the courtyard. The master himself often stands at the sieve and shows the men how to turn the hoop, so as to blow away the chaff, and how, with one sharp push, to empty the clean grain into a pile without leaving any behind. In the sheds and barns, where there is shelter from the wind, the winnower and the tare-separators are working. The grain is cleaned there and made ready for the market. . . .

Winter was a peaceful time in the country. Only the machine-shop and the mill were still really active. For fuel we burned straw which the servants brought in huge armfuls, scattering it along the way and sweeping it up after themselves. It was jolly to stuff this straw into the stoves and watch it blaze up. Once Uncle Gregory found my younger sister and me alone in the dining-room, which was filled with blue charcoal fumes. I was turning round and round in the middle of the room, not knowing where I was, and at my uncle's cry I fell in a dead faint. We often found ourselves alone in the house on winter days, especially during my father's absences, when all the work of the place fell on my mother. In the dusk, my little sister and I used to sit side by side on the sofa, pressed close together, wide-eyed and afraid to move.

A giant would come out of the cold outside into the dark dining-room, shuffling his huge boots, and wrapped in an enormous great-coat with a huge collar, and wearing a huge hat. His hands were encased in huge mittens. Large icicles hung from his beard and moustache, and his great voice would boom out in the darkness: 'Good evening!' Squeezed together in a corner of the sofa, we would be afraid to answer him. Then the monster would light a match and see us in our corner. The giant would turn out to be one of our neighbours. Sometimes the loneliness in the dining-room became absolutely unbearable, and then I ran out into the outer hall in spite of the cold, opened the front door, stepped out on to the big stone that lay on the threshold, and screamed into the darkness: 'Mashka! Mashka! Come into the dining-room!' over and over again. Mashka was busy with her own affairs in the kitchen, in the servants' room, or somewhere else. My mother would come in at last, perhaps from the mill, and light a lamp, and the samovar would be brought in.

We usually sat in the dining-room in the evening until we fell asleep. People came and went in the dining-room, taking or returning keys, making arrangements of various kinds, and planning the work for the following day. My younger sister Olya, my older sister Liza, the chambermaid and myself then lived a life of our own, which was dependent on the life of the grown-ups, and subdued by theirs. Sometimes a chance word of one of the elders would waken some special reminiscence in us.

Then I would wink at my little sister, she would give a low giggle, and the grown-ups would look absent-mindedly at her. I would wink again, and she would try to stifle her laughter under the oilcloth and would hit her head against the table. This would infect me and sometimes my older sister too, who, with thirteen-year-old dignity, vacillated between the grown-ups and the children. If our laughter became too uncontrollable, I was obliged to slip under the table and crawl among the feet of the grown-ups, and, stepping on the cat's tail, rush out into the next room, which was the nursery. Once back in the dining-room, it all would begin over again. My fingers would grow so weak from laughing that I could not hold a glass. My head, my lips, my hands, my feet, every inch of me would be shaking with laughter. 'Whatever is the matter with you?' my mother would ask. The two circles of life, the upper and the lower, would touch for a moment. The grown-ups would look at the children with a question in their eyes that was sometimes friendly but more often full of irritation. Then our laughter, taken unawares, would break out tempestuously into the open. Olya's head would go under the table again, I would throw myself on the sofa, Liza would bite her upper lip, and the chambermaid would slip out of the door.

'Go to bed!' the grown-ups would cry.

But we would not go. We would hide in corners, afraid to look at one another. My little sister would be carried away, but I usually went to sleep on the sofa. Someone would pick me up in his arms and take me out. Then I would perhaps give a loud yell, imagining, half-asleep, that I was being attacked by dogs, that snakes were hissing below me, or that robbers were carrying me away into the woods. The child's nightmare would break into the life of the grown-ups. I would be quieted on the way to bed; they would pat and kiss me. So I would go from laughter into sleep, from nightmares into wakefulness, and back into sleep again in a feather bed in the warm bedroom.

From My Life (1931)

LEON TROTSKY, Lev Davidovich Bronstein (1879–1940), Russian revolutionary and statesman, was born in Yanovka. After the 1917 revolution, he was Commissar for Foreign Affairs, and then Commissar for War during the civil war which ended in 1922. He was expelled by Stalin in 1929, and assassinated in Mexico.

Gertrude Stein

A Nineteenth-Century Girl

So I was five years old when we came back to America having known Austrians Germans and French French, and now American English, a nice world if there is enough of it, and more or less there always is.

Back to America and Baltimore where my mother's people came from, I do not know why but one is always proud of the places your people come from, you may never see them or perhaps never see them again as a matter of fact I did but nevertheless, that is where your mother came from and I suppose there is more meaning to that than where you were born particularly if you never saw it again there where you were born that is where I was born. In Allegheny Pennsylvania. Anything can be a dream, and in war it is more a dream than anywhere. Just now they have sent forty thousand people out of their homes in Marseilles, it is so real to me that it is a dream, not that I know any of them, if I did it would not be a dream but we were in Marseilles so much during the last war and that makes it a dream and in San Francisco when I was a child along the water front, the women of the town all of them came from Marseilles, and when I saw them in Avignon and Arles along the river front and at Marseilles they all seemed to be wearing the same wrappers, that is the kind of dressing gowns that they wore in San Francisco not far from Chinatown and that we used to see when we went to San Francisco with our parents, so that is what war is it is the inhabitants in geography.

A very nice kind of war was the Indian mutiny the Sepoy revolt. I always liked reading about that from Jules Verne on, it was such a satisfactory sort of war for the young, it could not be more satisfactory, there were so few killed and even very few wounded and everybody was a hero, and there were no crowds, Hindoos of course but no other crowds to confuse you. In a modern war there are no crowds because everybody is in it, so much so that there are no individuals, well that is something else, it is a queer life one leads in a modern war, every day so much can happen and every day is just the same and is mostly food, food and in spite of all that is happening every day is food, I had a friend who used to say Life dear Life, life is strife, life is a dear life in every way and life is strife in every way. The Germans say that war is natural peace is only an armistice that the natural thing is war, well that is natural enough because of course it is so, only when you have too much of it it is just as dull as peace, that is when you have had too much of it. And so I was a little girl in East Oakland California and of course one did have to find out that life although it was life there was death although there was death, and you had to find out that stars were worlds and moved around and that there were comets and that there was wind and rain, grass and flowers and birds and butterflies were less exciting in California, but most of all there were books and food, food and books, both excellent things. And then also and this is strange if you like but I was then already sceptical about Utopias, naturally so, I liked habits but I did not like that habits should be known as mine. Habits like dogs dogs have habits but they do not like to be told about their habits, and the only way to have a Utopia is not only to have habits but to be liked to be told about these habits, and this I did not like. I can remember very well not liking to be told that I had habits.

To come back to Shakespeare, Shakespeare which I read so much mostly the plays about wars, English kings and wars often said that nothing was anything that human beings had no meaning, that not anything had any meaning and everything was just like that. And it did worry me even when I was seven and eight not really worried me but it was there and then well not then but all the years I was grown up it was not like that and now when here in France when we all thought the young men were safe they are now all being taken away well it is like that, Shakespeare was right it is all just like that, even superstitions are all just like that, they mostly, said the very tall thirteen-year-old girl, they are always bad luck and then we all hope again, just like that, and although Shakespeare is right, we all do hope again.

Once upon a time the moon shone.

The visitor came.

The piano was struck that is the keys.

The ages although only differing between themselves and fifteen made them polite and complimentary, and no one is careless and if they are there is a loss.

War is never fatal but always lost. Always lost. And as they all said this, they knew that they meant what they said. Always lost.

And this brings me back to the time between eight and twelve when I read and read and in between I read all the historical plays of Shakespeare and all the other plays of Shakespeare and more and more this war of 1942-1943 makes it like that. The horrors the fears everybody's fears the helplessness of everybody's fears, so different from other wars makes this war like Shakespeare's plays. Rose d'Aiguy thirteen years old had just said that now having become superstitious because of course she has now become superstitious she notices that all the signs are bad signs, just like Macbeth just like Julius Caesar, the ides of March, and the general confusion, the general fear, the general helplessness, the general nervousness is just like all the kings, they are like that and they go on like that. The war 1914-1918 was not like Shakespeare but this war is the meaninglessness of why makes all the nothingness so real and when I read Shakespeare between eight and twelve, I suppose I was drowned in all that but naturally did not believe it or did I. Certainly not later when there was more meaning and more dread. But in Shakespeare there is no meaning and no dread, there is confusion and fear, and that is what is now here.

It was when I was between twelve and seventeen that I went through the dark and dreadful days of adolescence, in which predominated the fear of death, not so much of death as of dissolution, and naturally is war like that. It is and it is not. One really can say that in war-time there is death death and death but is there dissolution. I wonder. May that not be one of the reasons among so many others why wars go on, and why particularly adolescents need it.

It was a very long time between twelve and seventeen, between Shakespeare and the Boer war which was the first war I knew to be a war, a real war where a country that was a natural country was at war.

And in between there was religion, which too had to do with adolescence and with war. . . .

From babyhood to fourteen which is the beginning of adolescence, life is mostly taken up with slowly knowing that stars are worlds, that words are ways and that force is strength and that wiles are ways as words are, in other words that one is one and that the others can come to be with that one. That is what is most occupying from babyhood to fourteen, and during that time there are things like having apples given one to take home one for you and the other four for the other four and slowly one by one they are eaten until there is none, and there is the reason for eating the last one because since the other ones are eaten then of course there is no sense in keeping the last one, because then the story has to be told and why should it since after all all your life you can have it as remorse that it has been done. War is like that, it goes on like that it keeps going on like that and soon nobody has anything to eat that is nobody who does not take what does not belong to them and later although there is remorse the very last one has been eaten if not there has to be an explanation and if there is an explanation that does not help remorse nor does it help any one, remorse does not and not eating it does not, and so as I was then so am I now, and war, was not then but the feeling was just the same and eating was just the same in so many ways. A fish bone can even be a worry anything that can happen or has happened or has not happened can be a worry and that is what war is, and so what is the difference between life and war. There is none.

So then between babyhood and fourteen there are all these things, and romantic war with them, not to believe in but to dream.

Between babyhood and fourteen there was frequent change of scene. Modern wars all wars are like that, they go places, where they never heard of in many cases, and between babyhood and fourteen there had been so many changes of scene. And different ways of travelling about, and that also is like war. Just now all the young men of France have to go, they do not know where, some of them run away and when they run away they do not know where and a great many of them are taken away they do not know where and this is all as it was between babyhood and fourteen. Europe and America and railroad and water and stage coach and walking and horseback and in every there was no astonishment and that is the way war is.

I remember being very worried in reading, if anybody in the book died and did not have children because then nobody in that family could be living yet, and if they were not living yet how could they hear what was happening. This always bothered me from that time on until just now and now well now it does seem that the future is not important any more, the world has become so shrunken and it will never be different and so it does not mean much and there is no love interest, it is mostly parents who suffer, perhaps it was like that between babyhood and fourteen.

Dear Life life is strife Claribel used to say, but she did say dear life and in any way it is and she did say life is strife but is it.

It was all that between babyhood and fourteen, and it was the nineteenth century between babyhood and fourteen and the nineteenth century dies hard all centuries do that is why the last war to kill it is so long, it is still being killed now in 1942, the nineteenth century just as the eighteenth century took from the revolution to 1840 to kill, so the nineteenth century is taking from 1914 to 1943 to kill. It is hard to kill a century almost impossible, as was the old joke about mothers-in-law, and centuries get to be like that they get to be wearing like a mother-in-law. So as I was saying from babyhood to fourteen and of course longer much longer it was the nineteenth century and the wars civil domestic and foreign were nineteenth century wars, naturally enough.

Saint George and the Dragon, Siegfried and the dragon, anybody and the dragon, the dragon is always the century any century that anybody is trying to kill, and the worst of it all is that the one that says he is trying to kill the century that has to be killed is the last piece of the century that has to be killed and often the most long-lived, such as a Napoleon or a Hitler or a Julius Caesar the century has to be killed and they are the embodiment the most persistent end of it they are to live while really in its being killed they have to go, only nobody does tell them so, nobody and so they never do know, never do know.

However when I was a baby and then on to fourteen, the nineteenth century was full on.

In the nineteenth century, there was reading, there was evolution, there were war and anti-war which were the same thing, and there was eating. Even now I always resent when in a book they say they sat down to a hearty meal and they do not tell just what it was they ate. In the nineteenth century they often did. And in these days 1943 when eating well actually it is like prohibition one is so certain that one is never going to eat again that one is not greedy but one does eat everything well in these days you would imagine that you would not take pleasure in what the characters in a novel ate when they did eat, but one does enormously, well anyway the nineteenth century liked to cry liked to try liked to eat liked to pursue evolution and liked war, war and peace peace and war and no more.

When I was then I liked revolutions I liked to eat I liked to eat I liked to cry not in real life but in books and in real life there was nothing much to cry about but in books oh dear me, it was wonderful there was so much to cry about and then there was evolution. Evolution was all over my childhood, walks abroad with an evolutionist and the world was full of evolution, biological and botanical evolution, with music as a background for emotion and books as a reality, and a great deal of fresh air as a necessity, and a great deal of eating as an excitement and as an orgy, and now well just then there was no war no actual war anywhere.

In the nineteenth century there was nothing more exciting than climbing a high hill or a mountain and seeing the rain driving across a wide plain or valley with the sun following.

There was nothing more interesting in the nineteenth century than little by little realising the detail of natural selection in insects flowers and birds and butterflies and comparing things and animals and noticing protective colouring nothing more interesting, and this made the nineteenth century what it is, the white man's burden, the gradual domination of the globe as piece by piece it became known and became all of a piece, and the hope of Esperanto or a universal language. . . .

Between babyhood and fourteen years, it is hard to know whether it takes a long time or whether it does not and if it does any part of it is interesting but very little of it is recollecting, very little and so emotion is remembered, a few dimensions, and what is seen and any day.

Some days there are coincidences and some days there are none and when there are coincidences as there are coincidences that does make superstition and at any age, there is the same astonishment and the same belief, and between babyhood and fourteen there were coincidences and astonishment.

From Wars I Have Seen (1945)

GERTRUDE STEIN (1874–1946), American writer, critic and art collector, was born in Allegheny, Pennsylvania.

Bernard Baruch

COUNTRY BOY

As a child I was shy and sensitive, something of a mamma's boy. I always sat at Mother's right at the dinner-table, and I remember how fiercely I fought for this privilege. When I married, I asked my wife to sit where my mother would have sat – with me to her right.

When Mother taught us elocution, my brother Hartwig, who was two years older than I, displayed considerable talent. Eventually, in fact, he became an actor. But for me, getting up to recite was an agonizing ordeal. I have never forgotten one disastrous evening at Mannes Baum's house. Mother took me by the hand and, leading me to the centre of the room, urged, 'Now say something, dear.'

I was scared to death but started off in a singsong voice. So deeply etched in my memory is the incident that I can still quote the opening lines of the piece I was trying to recite. They were from 'Hohenlinden', by Thomas Campbell, a Scots poet:

> On Linden when the sun was low,
> All bloodless lay the untrodden snow;
> And dark as winter was the flow
> Of Iser, rolling rapidly.

I got no further than that when Father lifted a finger to the side of his nose and made a mimicking noise that sounded like:

A-toodle-dah!

That finished me. I rushed from the room, ran back to our house through the night, of which I was afraid, and cried myself to sleep.

In later years Father often told me how much he regretted his little joke. That episode nearly destroyed any hope I ever had of mastering the art of public speaking. For years afterwards I could never rise to my feet to say anything without remembering 'A-toodle-dah!' . . .

One autumn day, when I was about five or six, Harty and I were rummaging about the attic of our house. We were looking for a place to store the nuts which, like squirrels, we gathered every autumn. We came across a horsehide-covered trunk which looked promising. Opening it, we found Father's Confederate uniform. Digging deeper into the trunk, we pulled out a white hood and long robe with a crimson cross on its breast – the regalia of a Knight of the Ku Klux Klan.

Today, of course, the KKK is an odious symbol of bigotry and hate, reflecting its activities during the 1920s, when it acquired considerable power, particularly outside the South. I have good reason to know the character of the modern Klan since I was a target for its hatred. But to children in the Reconstruction South, the original Klan, led by General Nathan Bedford Forrest, seemed a heroic band fighting to free the South from the debaucheries of carpetbag rule. To my brother and me the thought that Father was a member of that band exalted him in our youthful eyes.

So intent were we in our examination of those garments that we did not hear Mother's footstep on the garret stairs. She gave us a mighty scolding and swore us to secrecy. It really was an important secret. The Klan had been outlawed by the Federal Government. Large rewards were offered for the conviction of its members, and spies were scattered through the South in an effort to discover who those members were. We came down from the attic feeling we had grown a foot taller.

Harsh as were the economic effects of the war, the political effects of eight years of carpetbag rule proved more galling and lasting. Even today, when the South is prospering, the carpetbag legacy of political and racial bitterness hangs on. The carpetbaggers maintained power largely through the control that they and their scallywag allies exerted over the vote of the Negro. This use of the ignorant Negro as a tool of oppression aggravated all the racial wounds and sores of slavery and the war. In the end it hurt the Negro most and probably set back progress in racial relations by a quarter of a century.

Through much of my childhood no white man who had served in the

Confederate Army was allowed to vote – while all Negroes could vote, even though few could write their names. Our state senator was a Negro, as was the county auditor and school commissioner – although at the county level never more than a third of the officials were Negroes. Still, the declared intention of the Black Republicans in Washington was to make this state of affairs perpetual. So oppressive was this that even a man like my father could write a fellow surgeon in the Confederate Army that death was preferable to living under such conditions. 'There is one recourse when all is lost. I mean the sword,' Father wrote in a letter which was quoted by Claude Bowers in *The Tragic Era*. 'What boots it to live under such tyranny, such moral and physical oppression when we can be much happier in the consciousness of dying for such a cause?'

The issue was to be decided by the contest for the governorship in 1876 between General Wade Hampton and the carpetbag incumbent, Daniel H. Chamberlain. I remember distinctly one Hampton mass meeting in Camden when barrels of resin were lighted at the street corners. There was a campaign chant in which we boys joined:

> *Hampton eat the egg,*
> *Chamberlain eat the shell,*
> *Hampton go to Heaven,*
> *Chamberlain go to Hell.*

The song was all the more appealing because that was the first time I was permitted to use the word 'Hell' with impunity. In later years Father told us many stories of how Hampton carried the election in the face of a preponderant black majority. One device was to distribute tickets to a circus that was playing out-of-town on election day. Another method was to beat the carpetbaggers at their own game by capitalizing on the Negroes' simplicity.

In those days a separate ballot box was assigned to each candidate. Most Negroes could not read the labels on the boxes but were coached to recognize the Republican boxes by their position in the line. With a crowd of Negroes around the polls, some Hampton man would fire a shot into the air. In the ensuing commotion, the Hampton and Chamberlain boxes would be switched. The Negroes would then be rushed up to vote as quickly as possible. As a result many dropped their ballots into Hampton's box.

On another election day, when I was about ten years old, Father was absent from home, either on professional or political business – probably both, for in those times there often was work for a doctor after a political rally. We heard a great din about the house. Mother became alarmed. She told Harty and me to get our guns. We got them – one a single-barrelled and one a double-barrelled muzzle-loader. Mother told us to load them and to take a position on the second-floor porch.

'But do not shoot,' she cautioned, 'unless I tell you to shoot.'

We stood there, our hearts pounding, each with a gun almost as tall as himself, watching the crowd of coloured people milling about the street. Drunk on cheap whisky, they were on their way to the polls or to a rally. I have a blurred memory of what happened next. I recall seeing a Negro fall from behind a tree. Suddenly everyone fled. We ran down to where the man lay to see what had happened. His head had been split as with an axe. Mother brought a basin of water and dressed the wound. I do not know what became of him, but he could not have lived long with his head as it was. Casualties of this nature were not uncommon, and it was the poor Negro who suffered most.

It was against the background of such happenings that we saw Father's membership in the Klan. That membership did not reflect any love of violence or any bitterness in his nature. Once Father was called to the deathbed of a scallywag Southerner. When Father came home he remarked that no friends or loving relatives had come to visit the dying man and how sad it was 'to see men made completely callous to the call of humanity by political differences.'

From My Own Story (1957)

BERNARD BARUCH (1870–1965), American financier and political adviser, was born in South Carolina.

Jacob Epstein

THE ARTIST'S EYE

My earliest recollections are of the teeming East Side where I was born.

This Hester Street and its surrounding streets were the most densely populated of any city on earth, and looking back at it, I realise what I owe to its unique and crowded humanity. Its swarms of Russians, Poles, Italians, Greeks, and Chinese lived as much in the streets as in the crowded tenements, and the sights, sounds, and smells had the vividness and sharp impact of an Oriental city.

Hester Street was from one end to the other an open-air market, and the streets were lined with push-carts and pedlars, and the crowd that packed the side-walk and roadway compelled one to move slowly.

As a child I had a serious illness that lasted for two years or more. I have vague recollections of this illness and of my being carried about a great deal. I was known as the 'sick one'. Whether this illness gave me a twist away from ordinary paths, I don't know, but it is possible. Sometimes my parents wondered at my being different from the other children, and would twit me about my lack of interest in a great many matters that perhaps I should have been interested in, but just wasn't. I have never found out that there was in my family an artist or anyone interested in the Arts or Sciences, and I have never been sufficiently interested in my 'family tree' to bother. My father and mother had come to America on one of those great waves of immigration that followed persecution and pogroms in Czarist Russia and Poland. They had prospered, and I can recall that we had Polish Christian servants who still retained peasant habits, speaking no English, wearing kerchiefs and going about on bare feet. These servants remained with us until my brother Louis, my older brother, began to grow up; and then with the sudden dismissal of the Polish girls, I began to have an inkling of sexual complications. My elder sister, Ida, was a handsome, full-bosomed girl, a brunette, and I can recall a constant coming and going of relatives and their numerous children. This family life I did not share. My reading and drawing drew me away from the ordinary interests, and I lived a great deal in the world of imagination, feeding upon any book that fell into my hands. When I had got hold of a really thick book like Hugo's *Les Misérables* I was happy, and would go off into a corner to devour it.

I cannot recall a period when I did not draw, and at school the studies that were distasteful to me, Mathematics and Grammar, were retarded by the indulgence of teachers who were proud of my drawing faculties, and passed over my neglect of uncongenial subjects. Literature and History interested me immensely and whatever was graphic attracted my attention. . . .

The many races in the East Side were prolific, children by hundreds played upon the hot pavements and in the alleys. Upon the fire-escapes and the roofs the tenement dwellers slept for coolness in summer. I knew well the roof life in New York, where all East Side boys flew kites; I knew the dock life on the East and West Sides, and I swam in the East River and the Hudson. To reach the river the boys from the Jewish quarter would have to pass through the Irish quarter, and that meant danger and fights with the gangs of that quarter; the children of Irish immigrants.

The Jewish quarter was on one side bounded by the Bowery, and this street at that time was one long line of saloons, crowded at night by visitors to the city, sailors, and prostitutes. As a boy I could watch through the doors at night the strange garish performers, singers and dancers; and the whole turbulent night-life was, to my growing and eager mind, of never-ending interest. I recall Steve Brodie's saloon with its windows filled with photographs of famous boxers, and the floor inlaid with silver dollars. A tour along the Bowery, for a boy, was full of excitement, and when you reached Chinatown, crooked Mott Street, leading to Pell Street, you could buy a stick of sugarcane for one cent and, chewing it, look into the Chinese shop windows, and even go into the temple, all scarlet and gilding, with gilded images. The Chinamen had a curious way of slipping into their houses, suddenly, as into holes, and I used to wonder at the young men with smooth faces like girls. Chinese children were delightful when you saw them, although no Chinese women were to be seen. Along the West Front, on the Hudson side, you saw wagons being loaded with large bunches of bananas, and great piles of melons. Bananas would drop off the overloaded wagons; you picked them up, and continued until you came to the open-air swimming baths with delightful sea water. I was a great frequenter of these swimming places, and went there until they shut down in November for the winter.

New York was at this period the city of ships of which Whitman wrote. I haunted the docks and watched the ships from all over the world being loaded and unloaded. Sailors were aloft in the rigging, and along the docks horses and mules drew heavy drays; oyster boats were bringing their loads of oysters and clams, and the shrieks and yells of sirens and the loud cries of overseers made a terrific din. At the Battery, newly arrived immigrants, their shoulders laden with packs, hurried forward, and it must have been with much misgiving that they found their first steps in the New World greeted with the hoots and jeers of hooligans. I can still see them hurrying to gain the Jewish quarter, and finding refuge amongst friends and relatives. I often travelled the great stretch of Brooklyn Bridge, which I crossed hundreds of times on foot, and watched the wonderful bay with its streamers and ferry-boats. The New York of the pre-skyscraper period was my formation ground. I knew all its streets and the water-side, I made excursions into the suburbs; Harlem, Yonkers, Long Island, and Coney Island I knew well, and Rockaway where I bathed in the surf. I explored Staten Island, then unbuilt on, and the palisades with their wild rocks leading down to the Hudson river.

Early on I saw the plastic quality in coloured people, and had friends amongst them, and later was to work from coloured models and friends, including Paul Robeson, whose splendid head I worked from in New York. I tried to draw Chinamen in their quarter, but the Chinese did not like being drawn and would immediately disappear when they spotted me. The Italian Mulberry Street was like Naples, concentrated in one swarming district. Within easy reach of each other, one could see the most diverse life from many lands, and I absorbed material which was invaluable.

At this time I was a tremendous reader, and there were periods when I would go off to Central Park, find a secluded place far away from crowds and noise, and there give myself up to solitary reading for the day, coming back home burnt by the sun and filled with ideas from Dostoyevsky's *Brothers Karamazov*, or Tolstoy's novels. Also I absorbed the New Testament and Whitman's *Leaves of Grass*, all read out of doors, amongst the rocks and lakes of the Park. It was only later I read the English poets, Coleridge, Blake, and Shelley, and still later Shakespeare. During my student days at the League, I would drop into Durand Ruel's gallery on Fifth Avenue, and there see the works of many of the Impressionist painters, which were not so sought after in those days. I saw splendid Manets, Renoirs, and Pissarros, and Durand Ruel himself, noticing my interest, gave me special opportunities to see pictures which went back to Europe and are now in the Louvre and National Gallery. I was very well acquainted at this time with the work not only of the American artists who were influenced by the Impressionists, but also with the works of the older men who now constitute the 'Old Masters' of America – Winslow Homer, George Innes, Homer Martin, Albert Ryder, and Thomas Eakins. The sincerity of these men impressed me, and my boyhood enthusiasms have been justified by time.

I began to feel at this period that I could more profoundly express myself, and give greater reality to my drawings by studying sculpture. I had been drawing and reading to excess, sometimes in dim light, and my eyes had suffered from the strain, so that sculpture gave me relief, and the actual handling of clay was a pleasure.

Naturally my family did not approve of all that I did, although they saw that I had what might be called a special bent. My turning to sculpture was to them mysterious. Later they could not understand why I did certain things, any more than do the critics who profess to see in me a dual nature, one the man of talent, and the other the wayward eccentric, the artist who desires to *épater*. What chiefly concerned my family was why I did things which could not possibly bring me in any money, and they deplored this mad or foolish streak in me.

They put it down to the perversity that made me a lonely boy, going off on my own to the woods with a book, and not turning up to meals, and later making friends with negroes and anarchists.

My grandmother on my father's side was a cantankerous old creature who swore that we children were going to the dogs, and were *goyim*, and she continued travelling between Poland and New York, as she declared she would not die in a pagan land; but – alas! for her wish – it was in New York she died.

My grandparents on my mother's side were a dear old couple, whose kindness and patriarchal simplicity I remember well. Every Friday evening the children would go to them to get their blessing. Before the Sabbath candles they would take our heads in their hands and pronounce a blessing on each one of us in turn. Then followed gifts of fruit and sweets. I was one of a large family, a third child, and my elder brother Louis was at all times sympathetic and helpful. Of my brothers, Hyam was an exceptionally powerful youth, a giant of strength, headstrong and with a personality that got him into scrapes. My sister, Chana, a beautiful, fair-haired girl, with a candid, sweet nature, was a great favourite of mine, and we often went out together. My father and mother in the evenings would lie in bed reading novels in Yiddish; my father would read aloud, and I often stayed awake listening to these extravagant romances. Saturday in the synagogue was a place of ennui for me, and the wailing prayers would get on my nerves, and my one desire would be to make excuses to get away. The picturesque shawls with the strange faces underneath only held my attention for a short while; then the tedium of the interminable services would drown every other emotion. Certainly I had no devotional feelings, and later, with my reading and free-thinking ideas, I dropped all practice of ceremonial forms, and as my parents were only conventionally interested in religion, they did not insist. I was confirmed at the age of thirteen in the usual manner, but how I ever got through this trying ordeal I cannot now imagine. The Passover Holidays always interested me for the picturesque meal ceremonies, and I remember my father, who was 'somebody' in the synagogue, bringing home with him one of the poor men, who waited outside to be chosen to share the Passover meal. These patriarchal manners I remember well, although there was about them an air of bourgeois benevolence which was somewhat comic. The earnestness and simplicity of the old Polish Jewish manner of living has much beauty in it, and an artist could make it the theme of very fine works.

From Let There Be Sculpture (1940)

SIR JACOB EPSTEIN (1880–1959), British sculptor, was born in New York. He was an outstanding modeller of heads in bronze, though some of his larger symbolic works caused controversy at the time.

Leonard Woolf

THE PULLING OF THE QUEEN'S DOCTOR'S NOSE

This looking back at oneself through middle age, youth, childhood, infancy is a curious and puzzling business. Some of the things which one seems to remember from far, far back in infancy are not, I think, really remembered; they are family tales told so often about one that eventually one has the illusion of remembering them. Such I believe to be the story of how as an infant I fell into a stream near Oban which I heard so often that eventually it became part of my memory. What genuine glimpses one does get of oneself in very early childhood seem to show that the main outlines of one's character are moulded in infancy and do not change between the ages of three and eighty-three. I am sure that my attitude to sin was the same when I lay in my pram as it is today when I sit tapping this out on the typewriter and, unless I become senile, will be the same when I lie on my deathbed. And in other ways when I can genuinely remember something of myself far off and long ago, I can recognize that self as essentially myself with the same little core of character exactly the same as exists in me today. I think that the first things which I can genuinely remember are connected with an illness which I had when I was about three. It was a very severe attack of scarlet fever which also affected my kidneys and in those days scarlet fever was a dangerous disease. I can remember incidents connected with the illness and I think they are genuine memories; they are so vivid that I can visualize them and myself in them.

The first is of a man coming into the room and applying leeches to my back. I insisted upon seeing the leeches and was fascinated by them. Twenty-five years later, one day in Ceylon during the rainy season, I was pushing my way through thick, wet grass in the jungle. I was wearing shorts and suddenly looking down I saw that my two bare knees were black with leeches. And suddenly I was back, a small boy of three, lying in bed in the bedroom high up in the Lexham Gardens house with the kindly man rather reluctantly showing me the leeches. I doubt whether in the intervening twenty-five years I had ever recalled the man with the leeches, but there in a flash the scene and the man and the leeches and my feelings were as vivid to me as the leeches on my knees, the gun in my hand, and the enveloping silence of the jungle.

When I look into the depths of my own mind (or should one say soul?) one of the characteristics which seems to me deepest and most persistent is a kind of fatalistic and half-amused resignation. I never worry, because I am saved by the feeling that in the end nothing matters, and I can watch with amusement and detachment the cruel, often undeserved but expected, blows which fate rains upon me. In another incident of my scarlet fever, which I think I do genuinely remember myself (though it became a family story), I seem to see this streak in my character already formed in the three-year-old child. At one moment my illness took a turn for the worse and I was, so it was said, upon the point of death. They called in Sir William Jenner, the Queen's doctor and a descendant of the Jenner who invented inoculation. He was a kindly man and I was fascinated by the shape of his nose. He prescribed a draught of the most appalling taste. I drank it down, but on his second visit – presumably next day – I sat up in bed with a second dose in the glass in my hand unable to drink it despite all the urging of my mother and Sir William. At last I said to them – according to my mother, with considerable severity – 'If you will *all* go out of the room, I will drink it.' I do not really remember that, but I do vividly remember the sequel. I remember sitting up in bed alone and the resignation with which I drank the filthy stuff, and the doctor and my mother coming back into the room and praising me. Sir William sat down on my bed and said that I had been so good that I would be given what I wanted. What did I want? 'A pigeon pie,' I said, 'with the legs sticking out.' 'You cannot,' he explained and his explanation was not unexpected by me, 'be given a pigeon pie with the legs sticking out just yet, but you will be given one as soon as you are quite well. But isn't there something – not to eat – which you would like now?' I remember looking carefully into his kindly old face and saying: 'I should like to pull your nose.' He said that I might, and gently, not disrespectfully, but as a kind of symbol or token, serious but also, I believe, deep down amused, I pulled Sir William Jenner's nose. . . .

My first experience of Weltschmerz, if that is what it was, must have come to me at the very early age of five or six. Behind the house in Lexham Gardens was a long parallelogram enclosed by the house on the north and on the other three sides by three grimy six-foot walls. It was a typical London garden of that era, consisting of a worn parallelogram of grass surrounded by narrow gravel paths and then narrow beds of sooty, sour London soil against the walls. Each child was given a few feet of bed for his own personal 'garden' and there we sowed seeds or grew pansies bought off barrows in the Earls Court Road. I was very fond of this garden and of my 'garden' and it was here that I first experienced a wave of that profound, cosmic melancholia which is hidden in every human heart and can be heard at its best – or should one say worst? – in the infant crying in the night and with no language but a cry. It happened in this way.

Every year in the last week of July or the first of August, the whole Woolf family went away for a summer holiday to the country. It was a large-scale exodus. First my mother went off and looked at houses. Then we were told that a house had been 'taken'. When the day came, six, seven, eight, and eventually nine children, servants, dogs, cats, canaries, and at one time two white rats in a bird-cage, mountains of luggage were transported in an omnibus to the station and then in a reserved 'saloon' railway carriage to our destination. I can remember country houses in Wimbledon, Kenley, Tenby, Penmaenmawr, Speldhurst, and Whitby which carry me back in memory to my fifth year. And I can remember returning one late, chilly September afternoon to Lexham Gardens from our holiday and rushing out eagerly to see the back garden. There it lay in its grimy solitude. There was not a breath of air. There were no flowers; a few spindly lilac bushes drooped in the beds. The grimy ivy drooped on the grimy walls. And all over the walls from ivy leaf to ivy leaf were large or small spider-webs, dozens and dozens of them, quite motionless, and motionless in the centre of each web sat a large or a small, a fat or a lean spider. I stood by myself in the patch of scurfy grass and contemplated the spiders; I can still smell the smell of sour earth and ivy; and suddenly my whole mind and body seemed to be overwhelmed in melancholy. I did not cry, though there were, I think, tears in my eyes; I had experienced for the first time, without understanding it, that sense of cosmic unhappiness which comes upon us when those that look out of the windows be darkened, when the daughters of music are laid low, the doors are shut in the street, the sound of the grinding is low, the grasshopper is a burden, and desire fails.

There is another curious fact connected with my passion among the spiders in the garden. Forty years later, when I was trying to teach myself Russian, I read Aksakov and the memories of his childhood. His description of the garden and the raspberry canes recalled to me most vividly my spider-haunted London garden and the despair which came upon me that September afternoon. I felt that what I had experienced among the spiders and ivy he must have experienced half a century before among the raspberries in Russia.

The second occasion on which I felt the burden of a hostile universe weigh down my spirit must have been when I was about eight years old. We had arrived in Whitby for our summer holidays and found ourselves in a large, new red-brick house on a cliff overlooking the sea. After tea I wandered out by myself to explore the garden. The house and garden were quite new for the garden was almost bare. Along the side facing the sea ran a long low mound or rampart. I sat there in the sunshine looking down on the sparkling water. It smelt and felt so good after the long hours in the stuffy train. And then suddenly quite near me out of a hole in the bank came two large black and yellow newts. They did not notice me and stretched themselves out to bask in the sun. They entranced me and I forgot everything, including time, as I sat there with those strange, beautiful creatures surrounded by blue sky, sunshine, and sparkling sea. I do not know how long I had sat there when, all at once, I felt afraid. I looked up and saw that an enormous black thunder cloud had crept up and now covered more than half of the sky. It was just blotting out the sun, and, as it did so, the newts scuttled back into their hole. It was terrifying and, no doubt, I was terrified. But I felt something more powerful than fear, once more that sense of profound, passive, cosmic despair, the melancholy of a human being, eager for happiness and beauty, powerless in face of a hostile universe. As the great raindrops began to fall and the thunder to mutter and growl over the sea, I crept back into the house with a curious muddle of fear, contempt, scepticism, and fatalism in my childish mind.

From Sowing (1960)

LEONARD WOOLF (1880–1969), British writer and publisher, was born in London. He was the husband of Virginia Woolf.

Sholem Asch

MY FATHER'S GREATCOAT

When I used to wake up in the middle of the night I would see, with eyes accustomed to the darkness, my father's sheepskin greatcoat, lying on the bench or hanging on its nail, and it would seem to me that it was a living thing and that it was trying to frighten me. There was a time when I used to draw the quilt over my head and tell myself repeatedly that after all it was only father's old sheepskin greatcoat pretending to be a monster; and having convinced myself that this was the case, I would say to myself: 'Now you can stick your head out from under the quilt.' But I didn't do anything of the sort. Conviction was one thing, courage another.

Actually that greatcoat gave me the feeling that it was a living thing, not only when father was wearing it, but when he had put it off for the night and hung it up on its nail. It was like father's shadow, or father's essence, detached from him, but not lifeless in detachment. There was something in the folds and shadows of the greatcoat which repeated all the gestures that father used to make; and when the greatcoat was hanging on the wall, long after father had gone to sleep, I – who had gone to sleep before father came home – could tell whether father had been sad or in good humour that evening, whether he had been harassed by an unpaid bill or delighted by an unexpected payment, whether he had been able to make the loan he needed or had been turned down ignominiously.

At certain times I would be aware that the greatcoat was growing older and greyer, like my father; the years were overtaking it, as they were overtaking him; and I would recall the days when the greatcoat was dark and glossy, just as my father had been. That was, of course, in the days of my early childhood, when my father was tall and erect, and had a black beard. I remembered, in particular, one evening. It was the last hour of the Sabbath, when the ceremony of the leavetaking from the Sabbath Queen was about to be performed. We were expecting guests; for it was the season of Chanukkah, the festival of the Maccabees, and we used to entertain then. But neither father nor the guests were there yet. There was an important meeting being held in the Rabbi's house. I refused to go to bed; I was excited by the festive atmosphere, by the expectation of guests. I sat on the floor spinning one of the tops which children are given for the festival of Chanukkah. Then at last father came, a whole host of Jews with him. Father was tall, erect, gay; his face shone; his beard was a glossy black; he was smoking a cigar. He had his greatcoat on, and the greatcoat was tall, erect, glossy; the collar flashed with newness, the hair of it bristled, as on a young, living animal; I was afraid of the hairs of the collar; I thought they would fly out at me. And when my father came near me, I shrank from the collar, and father laughed, and the greatcoat laughed with him. Then father took the greatcoat off and handed it to mother; and mother looked at it lovingly, and caressed it, and hung it on its nail. It was a very different greatcoat in those days.

It aged gradually; it accumulated the burden of the years. I remember a certain grey, dim morning; a milky light seeped in through the windows, which were covered with frost ferns. I was lying in mother's bed, and father was sitting at the table. He was studying by lamplight, or he was praying – his voice rose and fell in a pious chant. The light coming through the windows whitened, the frost ferns on the panes began to melt. Then father got up from the table and turned down the lamp, so that the room was steeped in half darkness. He went over to the wall, took down the greatcoat and sighed deeply. It was time to go out and earn his daily bread; and the earning of one's daily bread was a bitter and difficult task. And mother echoed father's sigh.

I looked at the greatcoat which father put on. It seemed to be depressed and worried, like father; it wasn't as young and gay as it had been in years past; the collar didn't flash, as of old, and the hairs didn't stand up stiffly and aggressively, threatening to fly out like arrows. They were lying wearily, as if they had had a bad night and looked forward to a bad day.

That must have been a weekday, because it was only on weekdays that father let the burden of the world oppress him. When Friday came, the eve of the Sabbath, the coat perked up, found its youth and gaiety again. When the Sabbath candles were shining on the table, next to the rich, white Sabbath loaves, and the wine flashed in the cut-glass decanter; when the house was warm, and the floor was strewn with fresh yellow sand, father would return from synagogue services; he would enter, wrapped in his greatcoat; and the greatcoat was refreshed and renewed, young and vigorous; the hairs stood up on the collar, they bristled aggressively, they threw back the gay candlelight, they radiated life and assurance. The coat was erect again; it confronted the world like a conqueror.

That was the way the greatcoat behaved all Friday evening and throughout the Sabbath. But as the Sabbath drew to a close, and the shadows gathered, and the time for evening prayer came; as mother chanted mournfully the woman's valedictory to the Sabbath Queen, 'God of Abraham and Isaac and Jacob,' and father, entering, gave the traditional greeting to his household, 'Good week,' while the candles were being lit, the greatcoat collapsed again; it wilted and surrendered; its age was back upon it; and it could not stand up, what with weariness and despondency.

I looked at the greatcoat as it hung on its nail; it was a sad, defeated and lonely greatcoat; it was no longer smooth, but all wrinkled, especially round the left arm, because father used to put his left arm to his brow whenever he was worried and did not know what to do next in the struggle for a livelihood; the greatcoat stooped, it almost had a hump; the collar was bedraggled, the great lapels were shapeless. Then I was not frightened at all; I was only filled with sadness and pity; and with remorse, too, because it seemed to me that the greatcoat was growing old and weary and hopeless on my account. It hung there on the wall worrying, calculating, wondering what it would do on the morrow and during the week to come, to provide me with bread. I was the cause of its wretchedness, I who had to eat every day. And it wasn't only my nourishment it worried about. There were other things. I was not a good boy. I did not take to my books as a good Jewish boy should; I hadn't the reverence one ought to have for the sacred lore of my people; I didn't behave with the piety that was expected of me. And what was going to 'become' of me? That question, 'What's going to become of him?' which I heard father and mother repeat so often, was eating into the greatcoat, too. It was for my sake that the greatcoat had to go out in all sorts of weather, in wind and rain and snow and frost; for my sake it had to stand for hours in the market-place, waiting for the peasants to bring their loads of wheat. I was so sorry for the greatcoat then that, when nobody was looking, I would go up to it, and caress its folds, which were like the folds on my father's face. I would pick up the sleeve, all wrinkled and weary, and pull it out from behind the coat – because it was always behind the coat, just like my father's arm, lying on his back as he walked up and down – and I would put it to my face and kiss it and console it.

The coat was something more than a coat; it served as a bedcover. That was true even in the years of its first glory. When winter came, when the nights had a burning frost in them and the ferns on the windowpanes never melted, father would take the coat off its nail and put it gently on mother's bed; that is, on *our* bed, because we little ones slept in mother's bed. That would happen only when mother was fast asleep, and didn't know what father was doing. But in the morning, when she woke up, mother would reproach father for humiliating the greatcoat like that, for reducing it to the status of a bedcover; all the more so because father, who used to get up before everybody else, would not go to the synagogue, where he could pursue his studies more comfortably, because all the books were there, but would sit at home, and study by lamplight, so as to leave the greatcoat on mother's bed as long as possible. And I, sleeping next to mother, would wake before her; and I would feel the cosy heaviness of the greatcoat; and then it didn't matter how sharp the frost was outside, I knew it couldn't get at me. I would put my hand out into the cold, and caress the greatcoat furtively; it was as though I were caressing my father's beard. Then I would fall asleep again, in the protection of the greatcoat, until father made a fire in the stove and the house warmed up.

As the years went by, the greatcoat became less greatcoat and more bedcover. It was heartbreaking to see the steady decline, the gradual loss of dignity. Once upon a time the greatcoat had been the glory of the family, our most distinguished possession. Now it was being relegated to the status of 'an old coat'; its place was among ordinary, outlived things, which could be put to any use. It had once stood alone, in unapproachable dignity; now its companions were cushions and quilts and ragged gaberdines. We were no longer proud of it. Father no longer put it on to show himself in the synagogue and Study House or among the peasants in the market-place. It no longer saw the light of day but was hidden among the bedclothes. It was mother herself who hastened the decline. She wouldn't let father put it on any more; she said she couldn't bear to think of him being laughed at by the people in the village. 'What will they think?' she said. Yes, she said it right in the presence of the greatcoat, and I saw the greatcoat shrink and almost blush, but it said nothing; it swallowed the insult in silence. It was hard to grow old.

And of course father had to get himself a new coat. It took a long time to persuade him to abandon the greatcoat; mother pleaded with him for years; and secretly she put away, coin by coin, a store from her house money, to get father a new coat. Till at last the tailor came, and measured father for a new coat, and the old greatcoat was definitely and permanently degraded to the rank of a bedcover, and it went to sleep its long sleep, by night on the bed, by day in the bedclothes closet.

It accepted its fate with silence and dignity, like an old, faithful house dog; it was glad that at least it could serve some purpose, that it did not eat the bread of charity, that there was enough fur left on it to make it useful as a cover; and if it could not serve the master of the house any more, it would serve his children.

And then a wonderful thing happened. The greatcoat which had died to this world as a greatcoat, was vouchsafed a resurrection! It was reborn, and entered into a second youth. And that happened when I reached my thirteenth year and was ready for induction into my duties and responsibilities as a son of Israel.

For a long time before the great day my mother had been worrying about a decent coat for me, in which I could present myself for the ceremony of my bar mitzvah. The time was again the festival of Chanukkah, when the winter covers the land. My mother worried, reckoned, counted the coins in her store, and could not reach a decision. And then, one day, when she was taking the bedclothes out of the closet, she saw light. For as she held the greatcoat in her hands her face brightened and she called out to my father:

'Don't you think we could cut this down and make a new coat for our Solomon?'

I could have sworn that the coat understood; for he seemed to hunch himself up, to hide the tattered and furless places; he tried ever so hard to put a new stiffness into the few hairs on the collar; all to prove that he could indeed be used, even in reduced and amputated form, for his original purpose. And my father answered:

'Perhaps we could.'

The next morning my mother took me by the hand, and with the rolled up greatcoat under her other arm, she went to see Mordecai the tailor.

I remember Mordecai the tailor clearly. He was a little man, with a little black beard in which were always tangled the white threads of his profession. He wore spectacles, not in order to see – for they were always either on the tip of his nose or at the top of his forehead – but for some mysterious reason which nobody understood. When we entered, and mother explained the reason for her visit, he shoved the spectacles from the tip of his nose to the top of his forehead, picked up the greatcoat and scrutinized it with great intentness, like a professor examining a patient. He turned it upside down, he looked at the collar, he fingered the chest, and now and again he frowned, and shook his head, as though the case were practically hopeless. Then he spread it out in front of him, and there the aged greatcoat lay, suppliant, as if pleading for its life. And all this time my heart was beating painfully, and I looked miserably at Mordecai and wanted to put in a kind word for the greatcoat. Mordecai scratched his head in perplexity, detached a couple of white threads from his beard, gazed on the greatcoat, and at last consented to perform the operation.

'We'll see what we can do,' was all he said, just like any cautious physician. And the old greatcoat almost started up with joy.

'Come here, you young rascal,' said Mordecai, and began to go through the ritual. He passed his tape round my chest, he tickled me under the armpits, so that I burst out laughing, and he took the measure of my length.

Every day for eight days I had to go to Mordecai the tailor, to have my measurements retaken and the new coat tried on. Every day I saw a new stage in the transformation and watched the greatcoat descending into the pit of death in order that it might be drawn up again into the world of the living.

On the ninth day, when I was to be inducted into manhood, I went to synagogue in the new coat; and my father's old greatcoat, in the fullness of resurrection, entered on its second life.

tr. Maurice Samuel

SHOLEM ASCH (1880–1957), Yiddish writer, was born in Kutno, Poland, and emigrated to America in 1914.

Stefan Zweig

THE SEDUCTIVE CITY

Until our fourteenth or fifteenth year we still felt ourselves perfectly at home in school. We made fun of the teachers and we learned our lessons with cold curiosity. But then the hour struck when school began to bore and disturb us. A remarkable phenomenon had quietly taken place: we, who had entered the *Gymnasium* as ten-year-olds, had intellectually outgrown the school already, in the first four of our eight years. We felt instinctively that there was nothing more of importance to be learned from it, and that in many of the subjects which interested us we knew more than our poor teachers, who had not opened a book out of personal interest since their own student years. But there was another contrast which became more apparent from day to day: on the benches, where no more of us than our breeches was sitting, we heard nothing new or nothing that to us seemed worth knowing, and outside there was a city of a thousand attractions, a city with theatres, museums, bookstores, universities, music, a city in which each day brought new surprises. And so our pent-up desire for knowledge, our intellectual, artistic and sensuous inquisitiveness, which found no nourishment in school, passionately yearned for all that went on outside of school. At first only two or three of us discovered in themselves such artistic, literary and musical interests, then a dozen, and finally nearly all of us.

For among young people enthusiasm is a kind of catching phenomenon. In a class at school it infects one after another like scarlet fever or measles, and while the neophytes, with childish, vain ambition, try to outdo each other as rapidly as possible in their knowledge, they lead each other on. It is therefore merely a matter of chance which direction these passions take: if there is a stamp collector in one class he will soon make a dozen as foolish as himself, and if three rave about dancers, the others will daily stand before the stage-door of the Opera. Three years after us came a class which was possessed with a passion for football, and before ours there was another that was wholly devoted to Tolstoy or socialism. By chance I entered a class in which my comrades were art enthusiasts; and this may possibly have been decisive for the development of my life. In itself this enthusiasm for the theatre, for literature and for art was quite natural in Vienna. The newspapers devoted special space to all the cultural events that took place in the city, and wherever we went, right and left, we heard the grown-ups discuss the Opera or the Burgtheater. The pictures of the great actors were on display in all the stationers' shops. Sport was still considered to be a brutal affair of which a student of the *Gymnasium* should rightly be ashamed, and the cinema with its mass ideals had not yet been invented. At home there was no opposition to be feared; literature and the theatre belonged to the 'innocent' passions, in contrast to playing cards or friendships with girls. Finally, my father, like all

Viennese fathers, had also been smitten with the theatre, and had attended the performance of *Lohengrin* under Richard Wagner with the same enthusiasm that we felt at the premières of Richard Strauss and Gerhart Hauptmann. For it was to be expected that we *Gymnasium* students should throng to each première; how ashamed we would have been before our more fortunate colleagues had we not been able to report every single detail on the morrow! Had our teachers not been completely indifferent, it would have occurred to them that on the afternoon of an important première – we had to stand in line at three o'clock to secure standing room, the only places available to us – two thirds of all the students were taken with some mysterious illness. With strict attention they would also have discovered that the poems of Rilke were stuck between the covers of our Latin grammars, and that we used our mathematics notebooks to copy the loveliest poems out of books which we had borrowed. Daily we invented new techniques for using the dull school hours for our reading. While the teacher delivered his time-worn lecture about the 'naive and sentimental poetry' of Schiller, under our desks we read Nietzsche and Strindberg, whose names the good old man had never heard. A fever had come over us to know all, to be familiar with all that occurred in every field of art and science. In the afternoon we pushed our way among the university students to listen to the lectures, we visited all the art exhibitions, we went in to the anatomy classrooms to watch dissections. We sniffed at all and everything with inquisitive nostrils. We crept in to the rehearsals of the Philharmonic, we hunted about in the antique shops, we examined the booksellers' displays daily, so that we might know at once what had turned up since yesterday. And above all, we read! We read everything that came into our hands. We got books from all the public libraries, and lent each other whatever we had been able to discover. But the café was still the best place to keep up with everything new.

From The World of Yesterday (1943)

STEFAN ZWEIG (1881–1942), poet, biographer and translator, was born in Vienna, but acquired British nationality in the 1930s.

Isaak Löwy

The Lure of the Theatre

For my devout Chassidic parents in Warsaw the theatre was naturally *trefe*, nothing less than *chaser*. Only at Purim was there a theatre, for then Cousin Chaskel stuck a big black beard on top of his little blonde goatee, put his caftan on back to front and played the part of a jolly Jewish pedlar – I could not turn my little childish eyes away from him. He was my favourite among all my cousins, his example left me no peace, and when I was scarcely eight years old I was already acting in the *cheder* like Cousin Chaskel. Once the Rabbi had gone, there was always a theatrical performance in the *cheder*, I was producer, stage-manager, in short everything, and the beatings I afterwards got from the Rabbi were also the hardest anyone got. But that did not bother us; the Rabbi beat us, but we went on thinking out other plays every day. And the whole year was all a hoping and praying: that Purim might come and that I might again see Cousin Chaskel dressed up. One thing I was resolved on – that as soon as I was grown up I would dress up and sing and dance every Purim too, like Cousin Chaskel.

But that people also dress up at other times than Purim and that there are many other artists like Cousin Chaskel was, of course, something of which I had no inkling. That is, until one day I heard from Isruel Feldscher's boy that there was really such a thing as a theatre where people acted and sang and dressed up, and every night, not only at Purim, and that there were several such theatres even in Warsaw, and that his father had several times taken him to the theatre. This news – I was about ten years old at the time – positively electrified me. I was seized with a secret, undreamt-of longing. I counted the days that must yet pass before I was grown up and would at last be allowed to see the theatre for myself. At that time I did not even know that the theatre was a forbidden and sinful thing.

Soon I discovered that the Grand Theatre was opposite the Town Hall, the best, the finest theatre in all Warsaw, indeed in the whole wide world. From that time on even the sight of the building from outside, when I went past it, positively dazzled me. But once when I asked at home when we were ever going to the Grand Theatre, I was shouted at: a Jewish child was not supposed to know anything about the theatre, it was not allowed, the theatre was there only for the Goyim and sinners. This answer was enough for me, I asked no more, but I had no more rest, and I was very much afraid that I was bound to commit this sin some time and, when I was older, would simply have to go to the theatre.

Once when I was going past the Grand Theatre in the evening after Yom Kippur, with two cousins, when there were a lot of people in the street where the theatre was and I could not turn my eyes away from the 'impure' theatre, Cousin Mayer asked me: 'Would you like to be up there too?' I said nothing.

Probably he did not like my silence, and he himself added: 'Now, child, there is no single Jew there – Heaven forbid! On the evening directly after Yom Kippur even the wickedest Jew does not go to the theatre.' But all I gathered from this was that although no Jew went to the theatre at the end of the sacred festival of Yom Kippur, on ordinary evenings all through the year plenty of Jews did go.

In my fourteenth year I went to the Grand Theatre for the first time. Little though I had learnt of the language of the country, still, by now I could read the posters, and there I read one day that *The Huguenots* was being performed. There had been talk of the Huguenots before this in the 'Klaus,' and besides, the play was by a Jew, 'Meier Beer' – and so I gave myself permission, bought a ticket, and that evening went to the theatre for the first time in my life.

What I saw and felt on that occasion is not relevant here, but for one thing: I came to the conclusion that the people there sang better than Cousin Chaskel and also dressed up much better than he did. And there was yet another surprise I got: I found I had long known the ballet-music from *The Huguenots*, the tunes were sung in the 'Klaus' on Friday evening to the Lecho Dodi. And at that time I could not make out how it was possible that people should be playing in the Grand Theatre what had for so long been sung in the 'Klaus.'

From that time on I went to the opera frequently. Only I had to see that I did not forget to buy a collar and a pair of cuffs for every performance and to throw them into the Vistula on my way home. My parents must not see such things. While I was soaking myself in *Wilhelm Tell* and *Aïda* my parents were lulled in the belief that I was sitting in the 'Klaus' over the folios of the Talmud and studying the Holy Scriptures.

Some time later I discovered that there was also a Jewish theatre. But however much I should have liked to go there too, I did not dare to, for it could have got round to my parents all too easily. However, I frequently went to the opera at the Grand Theatre, and later also to the Polish playhouse. In the latter I saw *The Robbers* for the first time. It very much amazed me that there could be such beautiful play-acting even without singing and music – I should never have thought it – and oddly enough I was not angry with Franz; perhaps it was he who made the greatest impression on me, and that was the part I should have liked to act, not that of Karl.

Of the boys in the 'Klaus' I was the only one who dared to go to the theatre. For the rest, however, we boys in the 'Klaus' had by that time fed thoroughly on 'enlightened books'; at that period I was for the first time reading Shakespeare, Schiller, and Lord Byron. Of Yiddish literature, however, all that found its way into my hands was the great detective-stories that America supplied us with in a language that was half German and half Yiddish.

A short time passed, it gave me no rest: there was a Jewish theatre in Warsaw, and I was not to see it? And so I risked it, staked everything on the throw, and went to the Jewish theatre.

That completely transformed me. Even before the play began I felt quite different from the way I felt among 'them'. Above all, there were no gentlemen in evening dress, no ladies in low-cut gowns, no Polish, no Russian, only Jews of every kind, in caftans, in suits, women and girls dressed in the Western way. And everyone talked loudly and carelessly in our mother-tongue, nobody particularly noticed me in my long caftan, and I did not need to be ashamed at all.

The play was a comedy with singing and dancing, in six acts and ten scenes: *Baal-Teshuva* by Schumor. They did not begin punctually at eight o'clock the way they did at the Polish theatre, but only about ten o'clock, and it did not end until long after midnight. The lover and the intrigant spoke High German and I was amazed that all at once – without having any notion of the German language – I could understand such excellent German so well. Only the funny man and the soubrette spoke Yiddish.

On the whole I liked it better than the opera, the dramatic theatre, and the operetta, all rolled into one. For first it was, after all, Yiddish; true, it was German-Yiddish, but still Yiddish, a better and more beautiful Yiddish; and secondly here was everything all at once: drama, tragedy, singing, comedy, dancing, all of them together – life! All that night I could not sleep for excitement, my heart telling me that I, too, must some day serve in the temple of Jewish art, that I must become a Jewish actor.

But on the afternoon of the next day Father sent the children into the next room, telling only Mother and me to remain. Instinctively I felt that here was a *Kasche* cooking up for me. Father did not sit down again; he kept on walking up and down the room; with his hand on his little black beard he talked, not to me, but only to Mother. 'You must be told: he becomes worse every day. Yesterday he was seen in the Jewish theatre.' Mother clasped her hands in horror. Father, quite pale, continued to pace up and down the room. My heart tightened, I sat there like a condemned prisoner, I could not bear to see the sorrow felt by my loyal, devout parents. Today I can no longer remember what I said then, I only know one thing, that after some minutes of oppressive silence Father turned his large black eyes on me and said: 'My child, think of this, it will lead you far, very far' – and he was right.

tr. Ernest Kaiser and Eithne Wilkin

ISAAK LÖWY (*fl. c.*1920) was a Yiddish actor and friend of Franz Kafka, among whose posthumous papers this transcribed account was found.

Mary Antin

WITHIN THE PALE

I do not know when I became old enough to understand. The truth was borne in on me a dozen times a day, from the time I began to distinguish words from empty noises. My grandmother told me about it when she put me to bed at night. My parents told me about it, when they gave me presents on holidays. My playmates told me, when they drew me back into a corner of the gateway, to let a policeman pass. Vanka, the little white-haired boy, told me all about it, when he ran out of his mother's laundry on purpose to throw mud after me when I happened to pass. I heard about it during prayers, and when women quarrelled in the market place; and sometimes, waking in the night, I heard my parents whisper it in the dark. There was no time in my life when I did not hear and see and feel the truth – the reason why Polotzk was cut off from the rest of Russia. It was the first lesson a little girl in Polotzk had to learn. But for a long while I did not understand. Then there came a time when I knew that Polotzk and Vitebsk and Vilna and some other places were grouped together as the 'Pale of Settlement,' and within this area the Czar commanded me to stay, with my father and mother and friends, and all other people like us. We must not be found outside the Pale, because we were Jews.

So there was a fence around Polotzk, after all. The world was divided into Jews and Gentiles. This knowledge came so gradually that it could not shock me. It trickled into my consciousness drop by drop. By the time I fully understood that I was a prisoner, the shackles had grown familiar to my flesh.

The first time Vanka threw mud at me, I ran home and complained to my mother, who brushed off my dress and said, quite resignedly, 'How can I help you, my poor child? Vanka is a Gentile. The Gentiles do as they like with us Jews.' The next time Vanka abused me, I did not cry, but ran for shelter, saying to myself, 'Vanka is a Gentile.' The third time, when Vanka spat on me, I wiped my face and thought nothing at all. I accepted ill-usage from the Gentiles as one accepts the weather. The world was made in a certain way, and I had to live in it.

Not quite all Gentiles were like Vanka. Next door to us lived a Gentile family which was very friendly. There was a girl as big as I, who never called me names, and gave me flowers from her father's garden. And there were the Parphens, of whom my grandfather rented his store. They treated us as if we were not Jews at all. On our festival days they visited our house and brought us presents, carefully choosing such things as Jewish children might accept; and they liked to have everything explained to them, about the wine and the fruit and the candles, and they even tried to say the appropriate greetings and blessings in Hebrew. My father used to say that if all the Russians were like the Parphens, there would be no trouble between Gentiles and Jews; and Fedora Pavlovna, the landlady, would reply that the Russian *people* were not to blame. It was the priests, she said, who taught the people to hate the Jews. Of course she knew best, as she was a very pious Christian. She never passed a church without crossing herself.

The Gentiles were always crossing themselves; when they went into a church, and when they came out, when they met a priest, or passed an image in the street. The dirty beggars on the church steps never stopped crossing themselves; and even when they stood on the corner of a Jewish street, and received alms from Jewish people, they crossed themselves and mumbled Christian prayers. In every Gentile house there was what they called an 'icon,' which was an image or picture of the Christian god, hung up in a corner, with a light always burning before it. In front of the icon the Gentiles said their prayers, on their knees, crossing themselves all the time.

I tried not to look in the corner where the icon was, when I came into a Gentile house. I was afraid of the cross. Everybody was, in Polotzk – all the Jews, I mean. For it was the cross that made the priests, and the priests made our troubles, as even some Christians admitted. The Gentiles said that we had killed their God, which was absurd, as they never had a God – nothing but images. Besides, what they accused us of had happened so long ago; the Gentiles themselves said it was long ago. Everybody had been dead for ages who could have had anything to do with it. Yet they put up crosses everywhere, and wore them on their necks, on purpose to remind themselves of these false things; and they considered it pious to hate and abuse us, insisting that we had killed their God. To worship the cross and to torment a Jew was the same thing to them. That is why we feared the cross.

Another thing the Gentiles said about us was that we used the blood of murdered Christian children at the Passover festival. Of course that was a wicked lie. It made me sick to think of such a thing. I knew everything that was done for Passover, from the time I was a very little girl. The house was made clean and shining and holy, even in the corners where nobody ever looked. Vessels and dishes that were used all the year round were put away in the garret, and special vessels were brought out for the Passover week. I used to help unpack the new dishes, and find my own blue mug. When the fresh curtains were put up, and the white floors were uncovered, and everybody in the house put on new clothes, and I sat down to the feast in my new dress; I felt clean inside and out. And when I asked the Four Questions, about the unleavened bread and the bitter herbs and the other things, and the family, reading from their books, answered me, did I not know all about Passover, and what was on the table, and why? It was wicked of the Gentiles to tell lies about us. The youngest child in the house knew how Passover was kept.

The Passover season, when we celebrated our deliverance from the land of Egypt, and felt so glad and thankful, as if it had only just happened, was the time our Gentile neighbors chose to remind us that Russia was another Egypt. That is what I heard people say, and it was true. It was not so bad in Polotzk, within the Pale; but in Russian cities, and even more in the country districts, where Jewish families lived scattered; by special permission of the police, who were always changing their minds about letting them stay, the

Gentiles made the Passover a time of horror for the Jews. Somebody would start up that lie about murdering Christian children, and the stupid peasants would get mad about it, and fill themselves with vodka, and set out to kill the Jews. They attacked them with knives and clubs and scythes and axes, killed them or tortured them, and burned their houses. This was called a 'pogrom.' Jews who escaped the pogroms came to Polotzk with wounds on them, and horrible, horrible stories, of little babies torn limb from limb before their mothers' eyes. Only to hear these things made one sob and sob and choke with pain. People who saw such things never smiled any more, no matter how long they lived; and sometimes their hair turned white in a day and some people became insane on the spot.

Often we heard that the pogrom was led by a priest carrying a cross before the mob. Our enemies always held up the cross as the excuse of their cruelty to us. I never was in an actual pogrom, but there were times when it threatened us, even in Polotzk; and in all my fearful imaginings, as I hid in dark corners, thinking of the horrible things the Gentiles were going to do to me, I saw the cross, the cruel cross.

I remember a time when I thought a pogrom had broken out in our street, and I wonder that I did not die of fear. It was some Christian holiday, and we had been warned by the police to keep indoors. Gates were locked; shutters were barred. If a child cried, the nurse threatened to give it to the priest, who would soon be passing by. Fearful and yet curious, we looked through the cracks in the shutters. We saw a procession of peasants and townspeople, led by a number of priests, carrying crosses and banners and images. In the place of honor was carried a casket, containing a relic from the monastery in the outskirts of Polotzk. Once a year the Gentiles paraded with this relic, and on that occasion the streets were considered too holy for Jews to be about; and we lived in fear till the end of the day, knowing that the least disturbance might start a riot, and a riot lead to a pogrom.

On the day when I saw the procession through a crack in the shutter, there were soldiers and police in the street. This was as usual, but I did not know it. I asked the nurse, who was pressing to the crack over my head, what the soldiers were for. Thoughtlessly she answered me, 'In case of a pogrom.' Yes, there were the crosses and the priests and the mob. The church bells were pealing their loudest. Everything was ready. The Gentiles were going to tear me in pieces, with axes and knives and ropes. They were going to burn me alive. The cross – the cross! What would they do to me first?

There was one thing the Gentiles might do to me worse than burning or rending. It was what was done to unprotected Jewish children who fell into the hands of priests or nuns. They might baptize me. That would be worse than death by torture. Rather would I drown in the Dvina than a drop of the baptismal water should touch my forehead. To be forced to kneel before the hideous images, to kiss the cross, – sooner would I rush out to the mob that was passing, and let them tear my vitals out. To forswear the One God, to bow before idols, – rather would I be seized with the plague, and be eaten up by vermin. I was only a little girl, and not very brave; little pains made me ill, and

I cried. But there was no pain that I would not bear – no, none – rather than submit to baptism.

Every Jewish child had that feeling. There were stories by the dozen of Jewish boys who were kidnapped by the Czar's agents and brought up in Gentile families, till they were old enough to enter the army, where they served till forty years of age; and all those years the priests tried, by bribes and daily tortures, to force them to accept baptism, but in vain. This was in the time of Nicholas I, but men who had been through this service were no older than my grandfather, when I was a little girl; and they told their experiences with their own lips, and one knew it was true, and it broke one's heart with pain and pride.

Some of these soldiers of Nicholas, as they were called, were taken as little boys of seven or eight – snatched from their mothers' laps. They were carried to distant villages, where their friends could never trace them, and turned over to some dirty, brutal peasant, who used them like slaves and kept them with the pigs. No two were ever left together; and they were given false names, so that they were entirely cut off from their own world. And then the lonely child was turned over to the priests, and he was flogged and starved and terrified – a little helpless boy who cried for his mother; but still he refused to be baptized. The priests promised him good things to eat, and fine clothes, and freedom from labor; but the boy turned away, and said his prayers secretly – the Hebrew prayers.

As he grew older, severer tortures were invented for him; still he refused baptism. By this time he had forgotten his mother's face, and of his prayers perhaps only the 'Shema' remained in his memory; but he was a Jew, and nothing would make him change. After he entered the army, he was bribed with promises of promotions and honors. He remained a private, and endured the cruellest discipline. When he was discharged, at the age of forty, he was a broken man, without a home, without a clue to his origin, and he spent the rest of his life wandering among Jewish settlements, searching for his family; hiding the scars of torture under his rags, begging his way from door to door. If he were one who had broken down under the cruel torments, and allowed himself to be baptized, for the sake of a respite, the Church never let him go again, no matter how loudly he protested that he was still a Jew. If he was caught practicing Jewish rites, he was subject to the severest punishment.

My father knew of one who was taken as a small boy, who never yielded to the priests under the most hideous tortures. As he was a very bright boy, the priests were particularly eager to convert him. They tried him with bribes that would appeal to his ambition. They promised to make a great man of him – a general, a noble. The boy turned away and said his prayers. Then they tortured him, and threw him into a cell; and when he lay asleep from exhaustion, the priest came and baptized him. When he awoke, they told him he was a Christian, and brought him the crucifix to kiss. He protested, threw the crucifix from him, but they held him to it that he was a baptized Jew, and belonged to the Church; and the rest of his life he spent between the prison and the hospital, always clinging to his faith, saying the Hebrew prayers in defiance of his tormentors, and paying for it with his flesh.

There were men in Polotzk whose faces made you old in a minute. They had served Nicholas I, and come back unbaptized. The white church in the square – how did it look to them? I knew. I cursed the church in my heart every time I had to pass it; and I was afraid – afraid.

On market days, when the peasants came to church, and the bells kept ringing by the hour, my heart was heavy in me, and I could find no rest. Even in my father's house I did not feel safe. The church bell boomed over the roofs of the houses, calling, calling, calling. I closed my eyes, and saw the people passing into the church: peasant women with bright embroidered aprons and glass beads; barefoot little girls with colored kerchiefs on their heads; boys with caps pulled too far down over their flaxen hair; rough men with plaited bast sandals, and a rope around the waist, – crowds of them, moving slowly up the steps, crossing themselves again and again, till they were swallowed by the black doorway, and only the beggars were left squatting on the steps. *Boom, boom!* What are the people doing in the dark, with the waxen images and the horrid crucifixes? *Boom, boom, boom!* They are ringing the bell for me. Is it in the church they will torture me, when I refuse to kiss the cross?

They ought not to have told me those dreadful stories. They were long past; we were living under the blessed 'New Régime.' Alexander III was no friend of the Jews; still he did not order little boys to be taken from their mothers, to be made into soldiers and Christians. Every man had to serve in the army for four years, and a Jewish recruit was likely to be treated with severity, no matter if his behavior were perfect; but that was little compared to the dreadful conditions of the old régime.

The thing that really mattered was the necessity of breaking the Jewish laws of daily life while in the service. A soldier often had to eat trefah and work on Sabbath. He had to shave his beard and do reverence to Christian things. He could not attend daily services at the synagogue; his private devotions were disturbed by the jeers and insults of his coarse Gentile comrades. He might resort to all sorts of tricks and shams, still he was obliged to violate Jewish law. When he returned home, at the end of his term of service, he could not rid himself of the stigma of those enforced sins. For four years he had led the life of a Gentile.

Piety alone was enough to make the Jews dread military service, but there were other things that made it a serious burden. Most men of twenty-one – the age of conscription – were already married and had children. During their absence their families suffered, their business often was ruined. At the end of their term they were beggars. As beggars, too, they were sent home from their military post. If they happened to have a good uniform at the time of their dismissal, it was stripped from them, and replaced by a shabby one. They received a free ticket for the return journey, and a few kopecks a day for expenses. In this fashion they were hurried back into the Pale, like escaped prisoners. The Czar was done with them. If within a limited time they were found outside the Pale, they would be seized and sent home in chains.

From The Promised Land (1912)

MARY ANTIN (1881–1949), American writer and lecturer, was born in Poland.

Anzia Yezierska

THE PROMISED LAND

Between buildings that loomed like mountains, we struggled with our bundles, spreading around us the smell of the steerage. Up Broadway, under the bridge, and through the swarming streets of the ghetto, we followed Gedalyeh Mindel.

I looked about the narrow streets of squeezed-in stores and houses, ragged clothes, dirty bedding oozing out of the windows, ash-cans and garbage-cans cluttering the sidewalks. A vague sadness pressed down my heart – the first doubt of America.

'Where are the green fields and open spaces in America?' cried my heart. 'Where is the golden country of my dreams?'

A loneliness for the fragrant silence of the woods that lay beyond our mud hut welled up in my heart, a longing for the soft, responsive earth of our village streets. All about me was the hardness of brick and stone, stinking smells of crowded poverty.

'Here's your house with separate rooms like in a palace.' Gedalyeh Mindel flung open the door of a dingy, airless flat.

'Oi weh!' my mother cried in dismay. 'Where's the sunshine in America?'

She went to the window and looked out at the blank wall of the next house. 'Gottuniu! Like in a grave so dark . . .'

'It ain't so dark, it's only a little shady.' Gedalyeh Mindel lighted the gas. 'Look only' – he pointed with pride to the dim gaslight.

'No candles, no kerosene lamps in America, you turn on a screw and put to it a match and you got it light like with sunshine.'

Again the shadow fell over me, again the doubt of America!

In America were rooms without sunlight, rooms to sleep in, to eat in, to cook in, but without sunshine. And Gedalyeh Mindel was happy. Could I be satisfied with just a place to sleep and eat in, and a door to shut people out – to take the place of sunlight? Or would I always need the sunlight to be happy?

And where was there a place in America for me to play? I looked out into the alley below and saw pale-faced children scrambling in the gutter. 'Where is America?' cried my heart.

My eyes were shutting themselves with sleep. Blindly, I felt for the buttons on my dress, and buttoning I sank back in sleep again – the deadweight sleep of utter exhaustion.

'Heart of mine!' my mother's voice moaned above me. 'Father is already gone an hour. You know how they'll squeeze from you a nickel for every minute you're late. Quick only!'

I seized my bread and herring and tumbled down the stairs and out into the street. I ate running, blindly pressing through the hurrying throngs of workers – my haste and fear choking each mouthful.

I felt a strangling in my throat as I neared the sweatshop prison; all my nerves screwed together into iron hardness to endure the day's torture.

For an instant I hesitated as I faced the grated window of the old dilapidated building – dirt and decay cried out from every crumbling brick.

In the maw of the shop, raging around me the roar and the clatter, the clatter and the roar, the merciless grind of the pounding machines. Half maddened, half deadened, I struggled to think, to feel, to remember – what am I – who am I – why was I here?

I struggled in vain – bewildered and lost in a whirlpool of noise.

'America – America – where was America?' it cried in my heart.

The factory whistle – the slowing-down of the machines – the shout of release hailing the noon hour.

I woke as from a tense nightmare – a weary waking to pain.

In the dark chaos of my brain reason began to dawn. In my stifled heart feelings began to pulse. The wound of my wasted life began to throb and ache. My childhood choked with drudgery – must my youth too die – unlived?

The odor of herring and garlic – the ravenous munching of food – laughter and loud, vulgar jokes. Was it only I who was so wretched? I looked at those around me. Were they happy or only insensible to their slavery? How could they laugh and joke? Why were they not torn with rebellion against this galling grind – the crushing, deadening movements of the body, where only hands live and hearts and brains must die?

A touch on my shoulder. I looked up. It was Yetta Solomon from the machine next to mine.

'Here's your tea.'

I stared at her, half hearing.

'Ain't you going to eat nothing?'

'Oi weh! Yetta! I can't stand it!' The cry broke from me. 'I didn't come to America to turn into a machine. I came to America to make from myself a person. Does America want only my hands – only the strength of my body – not my heart – not my feelings – my thoughts?'

'Our heads ain't smart enough,' said Yetta, practically. 'We ain't been to school like the American-born.'

'What for did I come to America but to go to school – to learn – to think – to make something beautiful from my life . . .'

'Sh-sh! Sh-sh! The boss – the boss!' came the warning whisper.

A sudden hush fell over the shop as the boss entered. He raised his hand. Breathless silence.

The hard, red face with pig's eyes held us under its sickening spell. Again I saw the Cossack and heard him thunder the ukaz.

Prepared for disaster, the girls paled as they cast at each other sidelong, frightened glances.

'Hands,' he addressed us, fingering the gold watch-chain that spread across his fat belly, 'it's slack in the other trades and I can get plenty girls begging themselves to work for half what you're getting – only I ain't a skinner. I always give my hands a show to earn their bread. From now on, I'll give you fifty cents a dozen shirts instead of seventy-five, but I'll give you night-work, so you needn't lose nothing.' And he was gone.

The stillness of death filled the shop. Each one felt the heart of the other bleed with her own helplessness.

A sudden sound broke the silence. A woman sobbed chokingly. It was Balah Rifkin, a widow with three children.

'Oi weh!' She tore at her scrawny neck. 'The blood-sucker – the thief! How will I give them to eat – my babies – my babies – my hungry little lambs!'

'Why do we let him choke us?'

'Twenty-five cents less on a dozen – how will we be able to live?'

'He tears the last skin from our bones!'

'Why didn't nobody speak up to him?'

'Tell him he couldn't crush us down to worse than we had in Russia?'

'Can we help ourselves? Our life lies in his hands.'

Something in me forced me forward. Rage at the bitter greed tore me. Our desperate helplessness drove me to strength.

'I'll go to the boss!' I cried, my nerves quivering with fierce excitement. 'I'll tell him Balah Rifkin has three hungry mouths to feed.'

Pale, hungry faces thrust themselves toward me, thin, knotted hands reached out, starved bodies pressed close about me.

'Long years on you!' cried Balah Rifkin, drying her eyes with a corner of her shawl.

'Tell him about my old father and me, his only bread-giver,' came from Bessie Sopolsky, a gaunt-faced girl with a hacking cough.

'And I got no father or mother and four of them younger than me hanging on my neck.' Jennie Feist's beautiful young face was already scarred with the gray worries of age.

America, as the oppressed of all lands have dreamed America to be and America *as it is,* flashed before me – a banner of fire! Behind me I felt masses pressing – thousands of immigrants – thousands upon thousands crushed by injustice, lifted me as on wings.

I entered the boss's office without a shadow of fear. I was not I – the wrongs of my people burned through me till I felt the very flesh of my body a living flame of rebellion.

I faced the boss.

'We can't stand it!' I cried. 'Even as it is we're hungry. Fifty cents a dozen would starve us. Can you, a Jew, tear the bread from another Jew's mouth?'

'You, fresh mouth, you! Who are you to learn me my business?'

'Weren't you yourself once a machine slave – your life in the hands of your boss?'

'You – loaferin – money for nothing you want! The minute they begin to talk English they get flies in their nose. . . . A black year on you – trouble-maker! I'll have no smart heads in my shop! Such freshness! Out you get . . . out from my shop!'

Stunned and hopeless, the wings of my courage broken, I groped my way back to them – back to the eager, waiting faces – back to the crushed hearts aching with mine.

As I opened the door they read our defeat in my face.

'Girls!' I held out my hands. 'He's fired me.'

My voice died in the silence. Not a girl stirred. Their heads only bent closer over their machines.

'Here, you! Get yourself out of here!' The boss thundered at me. 'Bessie Sopolsky and you, Balah Rifkin, take out her machine into the hall. . . . I want no big-mouthed Americanerins in my shop.'

Bessie Sopolsky and Balah Rifkin, their eyes black with tragedy, carried out my machine.

Not a hand was held out to me, not a face met mine. I felt them shrink from me as I passed them on my way out.

In the street I found I was crying. The new hope that had flowed in me so strong bled out of my veins. A moment before, our togetherness had made me believe us so strong – and now I saw each alone – crushed – broken. What were they all but crawling worms, servile grubbers for bread?

I wept not so much because the girls had deserted me, but because I saw for the first time how mean, how vile, were the creatures with whom I had to work. How the fear for bread had dehumanized their last shred of humanity! I felt I had not been working among human beings, but in a jungle of savages who had to eat one another alive in order to survive.

And then, in the very bitterness of my resentment, the hardness broke in me. I saw the girls through their own eyes as if I were inside of them. What else could they have done? Was not an immediate crust of bread for Balah Rifkin's children more urgent than truth – more vital than honor?

Could it be that they ever had dreamed of America as I had dreamed? Had their faith in America wholly died in them? Could my faith be killed as theirs had been?

Gasping from running, Yetta Solomon flung her arms around me.

'You golden heart! I sneaked myself out from the shop – only to tell you I'll come to see you to-night. I'd give the blood from under my nails for you – only I got to run back – I got to hold my job – my mother –'

I hardly saw or heard her – my senses stunned with my defeat. I walked on in a blind daze -- feeling that any moment I would drop in the middle of the street from sheer exhaustion.

Every hope I had clung to – every human stay – every reality was torn from under me. I sank in bottomless blackness. I had only one wish left – to die.

Was it then only a dream – a mirage of the hungry-hearted people in the desert lands of oppression – this age-old faith in America – the beloved, the prayed-for 'golden country'?

Had the starved villagers of Sukovoly lifted above their sorrows a mere rainbow vision that led them – where – where? To the stifling submission of the sweatshop or the desperation of the streets!

'O God! What is there beyond this hell?' my soul cried in me. 'Why can't I make a quick end to myself?'

A thousand voices within me and about me answered:

'My faith is dead, but in my blood their faith still clamors and aches for fulfillment – *dead generations whose faith though beaten back still presses on – a resistless, deathless force!*

'In this America that crushes and kills me, their spirit drives me on – to struggle – to suffer – but never to submit.'

In my desperate darkness their lost lives loomed – a living flame of light. Again I saw the mob of dusty villagers crowding around my father as he read the letter from America – their eager faces thrust out – their eyes blazing with the same hope, the same age-old faith that drove me on –

A sudden crash against my back. Dizzy with pain I fell – then all was darkness and quiet.

I opened my eyes. A white-clad figure bent over me. Had I died? Was I in the heaven of the new world – in America?

My eyes closed again. A misty happiness filled my being.

'Learning flows free like milk and honey,' it dreamed itself in me.

I was in my heaven – in the schools of America – in open, sunny fields – a child with other children. Our lesson-books were singing birds and whispering trees – chanting brooks and beckoning skies. We breathed in learning and wisdom as naturally as flowers breathe in sunlight.

After our lessons were over, we all joined hands skipping about like a picture of dancing fairies I had once seen in a shop-window.

I was so full of the joy of togetherness – the great wonder of the new world; it pressed on my heart like sorrow. Slowly, I stole away from the other children into silent solitude, wrestling and praying to give out what surged in me into some form of beauty. And out of my struggle to shape my thoughts beautifully, a great song filled the world.

'Soon she's all right to come back to the shop – yes, nurse?' The voice of Yetta Solomon broke into my dreaming.

Wearily I opened my eyes. I saw I was still on earth.

Yetta's broad, generous face smiled anxiously at me. 'Lucky yet the car that run you over didn't break your hands or your feet. So long you got yet good hands you'll soon be back by the machine.'

'Machine?' I shuddered. 'I can't go back to the shop again. I got so used to sunlight and quiet in the hospital I'll not be able to stand the hell again.'

'Shah! – Shah!' soothed Yetta. 'Why don't you learn yourself to take life like it is? What's got to be, got to be. In Russia, you could hope to run away from your troubles to America. But from America where can you go?'

'Yes,' I sighed. 'In the blackest days of Russia we had only a mud hut; not enough to eat and always the fear from the Cossack, but still we managed to look up to the sky, to dream, to think of the new world where we'll have a chance to be people, not slaves.'

'What's the use to think so much? It only eats up the flesh from your bones. Better rest . . . '

'How can I rest when my choked-in thoughts tear me to pieces? I need school more than a starving man needs bread.'

Yetta's eyes brooded over me. Suddenly a light broke. 'I got an idea. There's a new school for greenhorns where they learn them anything they want . . . '

'What – where?' I raised myself quickly, hot with eagerness. 'How do you know from it – tell me only – quick – since when –'

'The girl next door by my house – she used to work by cigars – and now she learns there.'

'What does she learn?'

'Don't get yourself so excited. Your eyes are jumping out from your head.'

I fell back weakly: 'Oi weh! Tell me!' I begged.

'All I know is that she likes what she learns better than rolling cigars. And it's called "School for Immigrant Girls."'

'Your time is up. Another visitor is waiting to come in,' said the nurse.

As Yetta walked out, my mother, with the shawl over her head, rushed in and fell on my bed kissing me.

'Oi weh! Oi weh! Half my life is out from me from fright. How did all happen?'

'Don't worry yourself so. I'm nearly well already and will go back to work soon.'

'Talk not work. Get only a little flesh on your bones. They say they send from the hospital people to the country. Maybe they'll send you.'

'But how will you live without my wages?'

'Davy is already peddling with papers and Bessie is selling lolly-pops after school in the park. Yesterday she brought home already twenty-eight cents.'

For all her efforts to be cheerful, I looked at her pinched face and wondered if she had eaten that day.

Released from the hospital, I started home. As I neared Allen Street, the terror of the dark rooms swept over me. 'No – no – I can't yet go back to the darkness and the stinking smells,' I said to myself. 'So long they're getting along without my wages, let them think I went to the country and let me try out that school for immigrants that Yetta told me about.'

So I went to the Immigrant School.

A tall, gracious woman received me, not an employee, but a benefactress.

The love that had rushed from my heart toward the Statue in the Bay, rushed out to Mrs. Olney. She seemed to me the living spirit of America. All that I had ever dreamed America to be shone to me out of the kindness of her brown eyes. She would save me from the sordidness that was crushing me I felt the moment I looked at her. Sympathy and understanding seemed to breathe from her serene presence.

I longed to open my heart to her, but I was so excited I didn't know where to begin.

'I'm crazy to learn!' I gasped breathlessly, and then the very pressure of the things I had to say choked me.

An encouraging smile warmed the fine features.

'What trade would you like to learn – sewing-machine operating?'

'Sewing-machine operating?' I cried. 'Oi weh!' I shuddered. 'Only the thought "machine" kills me. Even when I only look on clothes, it weeps in me when I think how the seams from everything people wear is sweated in the shop.'

'Well, then' – putting a kind hand on my shoulder – 'how would you like to learn to cook? There's a great need for trained servants and you'd get good wages and a pleasant home.'

'Me – a servant?' I flung back her hand. 'Did I come to America to make from myself a cook?'

Mrs. Olney stood abashed a moment. 'Well, my dear,' she said deliberately, 'what would you like to take up?'

'I got ideas how to make America better, only I don't know how to say it out. Ain't there a place I can learn?'

A startled woman stared at me. For a moment not a word came. Then she proceeded with the same kind smile. 'It's nice of you to want to help America, but I think the best way would be for you to learn a trade. That's what this school is for, to help girls find themselves, and the best way to do is to learn something useful.'

'Ain't thoughts useful? Does America want only the work from my body, my hands? Ain't it thoughts that turn over the world?'

'Ah! But we don't want to turn over the world.' Her voice cooled.

'But there's got to be a change in America!' I cried. 'Us immigrants want to be people – not 'hands' – not slaves of the belly! And it's the chance to think out thoughts that makes people.'

'My child, thought requires leisure. The time will come for that. First you must learn to earn a good living.'

'Did I come to America for a living?'

'What did you come for?'

'I came to give out all the fine things that was choked in me in Russia. I came to help America make the new world. . . . They said, in America I could open up my heart and fly free in the air – to sing – to dance – to live – to love. . . . Here I got all those grand things in me, and America won't let me give nothing.'

'Perhaps you made a mistake in coming to this country. Your own land might appreciate you more.' A quick glance took me in from head to foot. 'I'm afraid that you have come to the wrong place. We only teach trades here.'

She turned to her papers and spoke over her shoulder. 'I think you will have to go elsewhere if you want to set the world on fire.'

From *'How I Found America'* in Hungry Hearts (1920)

ANZIA YEZIERSKA (c. 1881–1970), critic and short story writer, was born in Warsaw, and emigrated to America with her family in the 1890s.

Sophie Tucker

THE PRICE OF PERSONALITY

Mr. Emerson, the music teacher at the Brown School, was talking to one of the grade teachers. As I passed by I heard him say: 'Sophie Abuza has personality.'

What was 'personality'?

I knew a lot of words that weren't in the spelling books, but most of those had only four letters. This was a new one to me. Going home from school I asked Dora Diwinski, who lived in our block and was my girl friend. But Dora was stumped too.

It began to look bad. After supper I asked Mama: 'What does "personality" mean?'

The word that was to make Dale Carnegie famous was beyond Mama. She had neither the English nor the patience to explain it.

'Personality, is it? What next? You should get to the dish-washing, and not fill your head with craziness.'

It wasn't that Mama was unkind or didn't love you that made her snap you up like that. All of us, even Moses who had now started to school, knew that. We knew if Mama was cranky it was because she was tired from standing in the kitchen all day. Her back ached and her feet were killing her. And she had worries. Phil and I, being the older ones, understood more about the worries.

The biggest worry was the card games that went on in the big room on the top floor. There was nothing in that room but an old round kitchen table that had some green pool-table cloth tacked over the top and a lot of battered chairs. Often the room would be filled with men in their shirt sleeves, the air thick with smoke and sour with the stench of stale beer and rotgut whisky. That was another of Mama's worries.

Papa wouldn't let any of us into that room, but you couldn't get him out of it so long as a game was going on. Upstairs, the pinochle sessions would run for four hours. One game, I remember, ran steadily for four days and nights. Poker games usually started on Saturdays and would last through till Monday or, if some players with real money came along, till Tuesday. When there was a big game on, the lines in Mama's forehead got deeper and deeper. Phil or I would be sent out to stand guard at the corner and keep an eye out for any strange coppers. We knew all the regulars on our beat, like Big Dan Ahearn. Big Dan was one of our best friends. We didn't have to worry about *him*.

It wasn't just the money Papa lost on the card games that made Mama sore. Most of all she hated the kind of people who often came to the house: hard-faced men, who talked out of the side of their mouths, bums, and pimps. Besides the restaurant, we ran a rooming house upstairs. A lot of fine travelling men and people in show business used to stay with us when their work brought them to Hartford. But Papa's card-playing customers were a different sort; they were the sporty set of the neighbourhood.

Without understanding all that was wrong I felt that the card games and the gamblers and their girls constituted a danger which Mama was terribly afraid of. I knew these goings-on made her angry. I could hear her scolding Papa at night in their room which was next to the one where Anna and I slept. I knew, too, that Papa's gambling kept us poor. If he had a run of good luck he would branch out, as when he took over the Boston Hotel on State Street. Then the luck deserted him, and pretty soon we were back in the old neighbourhood, and I was out on the corner with a wash boiler full of sweet corn to sell, a penny an ear.

Sometimes, during the summers, Papa would rent the soft-drink concession at Riverside Park where the crowds went on Saturdays and Sundays. That would be my job, opening the bottles of soda pop from the time the park opened in the morning till the cops chased the stragglers home. It was tough on the feet, but I loved it. I loved the crowds, out for a good time. I loved the bands. I was friends with the peanut man and the old Greek who sold popcorn and balloons to the kids.

It never occurred to me to be sorry for myself. I hated having to work in the restaurant when I wanted to be out playing with the other children in the block. But I accepted that, along with some of the other things that went on, as something that was unavoidable if you were poor. Everyone I knew had to work hard to get along, some at one trade, some at another. All around us were families going through terrible struggles. Poor as we were, Mama always managed to have something to give away to the ones who were worse off than we were. Scraps of food were carefully saved to carry to some woman whose husband was out of work and whose children would have gone to bed hungry but for Mama's charity. Old clothes that had passed from Phil to Moe, or from me to Anna, were repatched and darned and handed on to other children. Nothing was ever wasted or thrown away. Oftentimes a knock would come at the back door; and there would stand a woman with a shawl over her head, or an old man, bearded and long-haired under his black skullcap. There would be whispers, and then Mama would dig down into her petticoat pocket and bring out her worn leather purse. She would count out some silver or even a dollar or two to buy coal or medicine or to satisfy a landlord. A lot of the money I earned singing went that way. I turned the tips over to Mama as a matter of course and, true to her own nature, she used as little of them as possible for ourselves and as much as possible for those she considered really poor. That was another reason why she hated those card games upstairs. If Papa hadn't gambled away the earnings, she would have had more to give to the needy and desperate.

Knowing this, I used to try to think up ways of drawing more customers to the restaurant. I took to hanging around the stage doors of the three theatres in town, waiting for the actors to leave. I would go up to them and hold out one of our menus. 'Follow me,' I'd say, 'and I'll take you where you can get the best meal in town for the least money.'

When any of them did turn up at our place I took it as a personal triumph, and I would lay myself out to make them like it and come again. That was really how I started singing in the restaurant, hoping to draw more customers. None of our competitors offered entertainment with meals.

The show people were appreciative. They seemed to like my singing, especially when I would sing their own hits and try to mimic them. Some of the customers would give me a quarter, or even fifty cents. Once or twice it was as much as a dollar. They gave me their songs, too, writing down the words for me on a scrap of paper. I couldn't have read the notes if I had had them. And I had no need of them. I was born with a quick and true ear. The songs were the smash hits of those days. 'Wait Till the Sun Shines, Nellie', and 'On a Sunday Afternoon,' and another of Harry Von Tilzer's, 'I'd Leave Ma Happy Home for You'.

Some of the dimes I made singing in the restaurant went for seats for Dora and me at the Saturday matinées at Poli's Vaudeville Theatre, or at the Hartford Opera House. Among the vaudevillians our favourites were the Howard brothers, Willie and Eugene, and the Empire City Quartette, featuring Harry Cooper. All these used to come to our place to eat whenever they made Hartford.

Sometimes one of the companies of Jewish actors would come to Hartford for a one-night stand. Then they always came to our place to eat, and when we ran the hotel, they would stay all night with us. In the restaurant I waited on the great Jacob Adler, Mr. and Mrs. Boris Thomashefsky, Madame Lipsky, and that grand Jewish comedian, Margoulis. The thrill I got when I took an order from Bertha Kalich! She was my ideal Jewish artist. After she went on the English-speaking stage I never saw her except across the footlights. When I was in London in 1926 I went down to Whitechapel one night for a real Jewish meal and there in the restaurant was Madame Kalich. We had a long talk after I told her I was the little girl who used to carry the big plates of food in Abuza's Restaurant back in Hartford.

Jacob Adler and Boris Thomashefsky both tried to get my family to let me go with one of the Jewish companies. But I wasn't keen on it. I had seen how hard it was to make the Jewish plays a success even for one night. It used to be up to Papa to sell the tickets. Many times he was left, holding the bag, with hundreds of seats, meals, and sleeping rooms given free because of no business. I had noticed that this sort of thing didn't happen with the regular

American shows.

Going to shows with Dora taught me a lot of new songs and I began to work up business to go with them. Later I would try out some of the ideas I got from these shows on the customers in the restaurant and at the amateur concerts in Riverside Park where they gave prizes for the most popular acts. I was shy about going up on the stage in the park. I was nearly thirteen, and already I weighed one hundred and forty-five pounds. I was gawky and self-conscious. But Anna, who was pretty and dark, had a lovely singing voice. I didn't mind going on the stage to accompany her (with one finger). I thought, sitting on the piano stool, my size didn't matter. She and I carried off a lot of prizes.

Gradually, at the concerts I began to hear calls for 'the fat girl'. 'Let the fat girl do her stuff', and 'Give us the fat girl'. Then I would jump up from the piano stool, forgetting all about my size, and work to get all the laughs I could get. That was when I began to say to myself that maybe in show business size didn't matter if you could sing and could make people laugh.

That was what really started me thinking seriously about going in show business. I said to myself, suppose you could earn a living by singing and making people laugh, wouldn't that be better than spending your life drudging in a kitchen? I thought about Mama, and the years she had slaved at the stove and the sink. I knew I would do anything to get away from that. As the idea took hold of me I began to ask the actors who came to our restaurant how to get into show business.

Mama heard me, of course. Ever since I showed my first interest in the theatre she had been warning me to keep away from all that.

'Don't have anything to do with travelling men, or with show people. There are too many grifters and grafters among them. They have no real homes; no sense of responsibility. That kind don't care what they do on the road.' According to Mama, show people were no better than the gipsies who used to wander through Russia, thieving and making trouble – as well as music – in every village. She and Papa, to whom she confided her fears about me, took to watching me like hawks.

That spring everybody sang or whistled 'Bedelia'. The big girls had peek-aboo blouses. Mama wouldn't let me have one. 'A good girl don't go around showing everybody what she has got.' The shad started running up the Connecticut, and something else came stealing up the river valley with the warm April mists – something that gets you when you are nearly sixteen and big for your age.

I sat hunched up on the back stoop in the evening, after the kitchen work was done, and gave myself over to the luxury of thinking about Sophie Abuza.

In two months I was to graduate from school. Then what? I didn't seem any nearer my dream of getting into show business than I had been six months before, and Mama and Papa were set and determined that I should not make that dream come true. Mama was already talking about when I should get married. To her mind, marriage, having babies, and helping her husband get ahead were career enough for any woman. I couldn't make her understand that it wasn't a career that I was after. It was just that I wanted a life that didn't mean spending most of it at the cooking-stove and the kitchen sink.

'After you are through school,' Mama said, 'then you must look around for a good, steady young man and get married.'

I propped my elbows on my knees and my cheeks on my two clenched fists and considered the proposition. I didn't see how I was going to do any looking around when most of my time was spent in the restaurant, and Mama always discouraged me from making friends with the men customers. I had never been to a dance, or a picnic, or a straw ride. Always, I had to hurry home from school to help with the work. There were plenty of boys and girls in our neighbourhood and they were friendly with me. Just the same, when they would be starting out for some fun they never asked me to go along with them. It was only when I had some money – money I had earned singing, or even some I stole out of the restaurant cashbox – and offered to stand treat to sodas or seats at Poli's or at a circus or one of the patent-medicine shows that pitched their tents in the vacant lots on the edge of town, that I was popular. Popularity was so sweet I wasn't above stealing money from Mama to buy a taste of it now and then.

Something inside my chest gave a big, unhappy thump. More than anything in the world I wanted to be *wanted*.

From the house came Mama's voice calling: 'Sophie, Sophie. A customer is here. What are you sitting out there mooning at?'

I started to get up when I happened to look up the street and saw Louis Tuck coming. Louis lived just across from us. He was a wonderful dancer and had the reputation of being a 'card'. All the girls in the block were crazy about Louis. They used to hang around hoping he would ask them to go to the park to have a soda or something.

'Hello, Soph,' Louis said, and stopped by the fence.

'Hello,' I said back. I couldn't help smiling. Louis was so easy to look at. Maybe it was that that made Louis smile too.

'Listen,' he said, 'there's going to be a dance to-morrow night. How would you like to go?'

'With you?'

'Sure. Want to?'

'Sure,' I gulped. Still I couldn't believe my own ears. Louis Tuck asking *me*! To go to a dance with *him*! I was waiting for the catch.

'Okay,' said Louis. 'Be ready around nine.'

I nodded.

Mama's voice sounded again, nearer now. 'Sophie! Where are you, Sophie?'

'So long,' Louis said, and was around the corner before Mama opened the screen door.

'I'm coming,' I hollered, scrambling up. I still couldn't believe any of it had happened. And to me.

From Some of These Days (1945)

SOPHIE TUCKER (1884–1966), American singer and entertainer, regarded as 'the last of the red hot mommas', was born while her mother was en route from Russia.

Franz Kafka
A FILIAL VIEW

. . . . Your extremely effective rhetorical methods in bringing me up, which never failed to work with me anyway, were: abuse, threats, irony, spiteful laughter and – oddly enough – self-pity.

I can't recall your ever having abused me directly and in downright abusive terms. Nor was that necessary, you had so many other methods, and besides, in talk at home and particularly at business the words of abuse went flying around me in such swarms, as they were flung at other people's heads, that as a little boy I was sometimes almost stunned and had no reason not to apply them to myself too, for the people you were abusing were certainly no worse than I was and you were certainly not more displeased with them than with me. And here again, too, was your enigmatic innocence and inviolability, you cursed and swore without the slightest scruple about it, indeed you condemned cursing and swearing in other people and would not have it.

You reinforced abusiveness with threats, and this applied to me too. How terrible for me was, for instance, that 'I'll tear you apart like a fish', in spite of knowing, of course, that there was nothing worse to follow (admittedly, as a little child I didn't know that), but it was almost exactly in accord with my notions of your power and I saw you as being capable of doing this too. What was also terrible was when you ran round the table, shouting, to grab one, obviously not really trying to grab, but still pretending to, and Mother (in the end) had to rescue one, as it seemed. Once again one had, so it seemed to the child, remained alive through your mercy and bore one's life henceforth as an undeserved gift from you. This too is the place to mention the threats about the consequences of disobedience. When I began to do something you did not like and you threatened me with the prospect of failure, my veneration for your opinion was so great that the failure then became inevitable, even though perhaps it happened only at some later time. I lost confidence in my own actions. I was wavering, doubtful. The older I became the more material there was for you to bring forward against me as evidence of my worthlessness; gradually you began really to be right in a certain respect.

Once again I am careful not to assert that I became like this solely through you; you only intensified what was already there, but you did greatly intensify it, simply because where I was concerned you were very powerful and you employed all your power to that end.

You put special trust in bringing children up by means of irony, and this was most in keeping with your superiority over me. An admonition from you generally took this form: 'Can't you do it in such-and-such a way? That's too hard for you, I suppose. You haven't the time, of course?' and so on. And each such question would be accompanied by malicious laughter and a malicious face. One was so to speak already punished before one even knew that one had done something bad. What was also maddening were those rebukes when one was treated as a third person, in other words accounted not worthy even to be spoken to angrily: that is to say, when you would speak in form to Mother, but in fact to me, sitting there at the same time. For instance: 'Of course that's too much to expect of our worthy son' and the like. (This then produced a corollary in that, for instance, I did not dare to ask, and later from habit did not even really much think of asking, you anything directly when Mother was there. It was much less dangerous for the child to put questions to Mother, sitting there beside you, and to ask Mother: 'How is Father?' so guarding oneself against surprises.) There were of course also cases when one was entirely in agreement with even the worst irony, namely when it referred to someone else, for instance Elli, with whom I was on bad terms for years. There was an orgy of malice and spiteful delight for me when such things were said of her, as they were at almost every meal: 'She has to sit six feet away from the table, the great fat lump' and when you, morosely sitting on your chair without the slightest trace of pleasantness or humour, a bitter enemy, would exaggeratedly imitate the way she sat, which you found utterly loathsome. How often such things happened, over and over again, and how little you really achieved as a result of them! I think the reason was that the expenditure of anger and malice seemed to be in no proper relation to the subject itself, one did not have the feeling that the anger was caused by this trifle of sitting some way back from the table, but that the whole bulk of it was already there to begin with and only by chance happened to settle on this matter as a pretext for breaking out. Since one was convinced that a pretext would be found anyway, one did not bother particularly, and anyway one's feelings became dulled by these continual threats. One had gradually become pretty sure of not getting a beating, anyway. One became a glum, inattentive, disobedient child, always trying to escape from something and in the main to escape within oneself. So you suffered, and so we suffered. From your own point of view you were quite right when, clenching your teeth and with that gurgling laughter that gave the child its first notions of hell, you used bitterly to say (as you did only recently in connection with a letter from Constantinople): 'A *nice* crowd that is!'

What seemed to be quite incompatible with this attitude to your children was, and it happened very often, that you complained in public. I confess that as a child (though doubtless this was rather later) I was completely callous about this and could not understand how you could possibly expect to get any sympathy from anyone. You were so huge, a giant in every respect. What could you care for our pity, or even our help? Our help, indeed, you could not but despise, as you so often despised us ourselves. Hence I did not take these complaints at their face-value and looked for some hidden motive behind them. Only later did I come to understand that you really suffered a great deal because of your children, but at that time, when these complaints might in other circumstances still have met with a childish candid sympathy that would not have counted the cost but would have been ready to offer any help it could, to me they could only seem to be overemphatic means of drilling me and humiliating me, as such not in themselves very intense, but with the harmful accompanying effect that the child became used to not taking very seriously the very things it should have taken seriously.

Fortunately there were, I admit, exceptions to all these things, mostly when you suffered in silence, and affection and kindliness by their own strength ovecame all obstacles, and moved me immediately. Admittedly this was rare, but it was wonderful. For instance, when in earlier times, in hot summers, when you were tired after lunch, I saw you having a nap at the office, your elbow on the desk; or when you joined us in the country, in the summer holidays, on Sundays, worn out from work at the office; or the time when Mother was gravely ill and you stood holding on to the bookcase, shaking with sobs; or when, during my last illness, you came tiptoeing to Ottla's room to see me, stopping in the doorway, craning your neck to see me, and out of consideration for me only waved your hand to me. At such times one would lie back and weep for happiness, and one weeps again now, writing it down.

You have a particularly beautiful, very rare way of quietly, contentedly, approving smilingly, a way of smiling that can make the person for whom it is meant entirely happy. I can't recall it's ever having expressly been my lot in my childhood, but I dare say it may have happened, for why should you have refused it to me at that time when I still seemed blameless to you and was your great hope? For the rest, such friendly impressions in the long run brought about nothing but an increase in my sense of guilt, making the world still more incomprehensible to me.

From To My Father, *tr.* Ernest Kaiser and Eithne Wilkin

FRANZ KAFKA (1883–1924), Austrian writer, was born in Prague. His three existentialist novels were not published until after his death from lung disease, but had great influence on Western literature. The extract is from a letter to his father which he wrote in 1919, but never sent.

Emanuel Shinwell

NO TAILOR!

My father had many customers in the mining districts around Glasgow. Every Friday or Saturday I was sent with a parcel of suits to places like Cambuslang, Bellshill, Falkirk and Stirling to deliver them. I recall how on one occasion I had to take a parcel to the village of California, near Falkirk. This thrilled me because the name conjured up the picture of cowboys, gold prospectors and horses about which I had read in the various boys' magazines which came my way. It was a stiff climb of about two miles from Falkirk to the village. I found the house and delivered my parcel. While waiting for payment (this was most important because unless I got paid there and then there was doubt as to whether the customer would pay at all) I saw the mother of the household making up the 'snap' or 'piece' for her two sons who were about to go to the pit. It consisted of two thick slices of bread with cheese. On top of the cheese she spread marmalade. I had never seen this done before.

But I soon became tired of running errands for my father. When I was 12½ years old I got a job with the tobacco firm of Smith's, as a message boy, and later as van-boy. The pay was 5s. a week but sometimes I was lucky enough to get a small tip – it might be a penny or twopence. I shall never forget when on one New Year's Eve, on delivering a parcel of tobacco to a shop in Exchange Place, Glasgow, to my great surprise and joy the proprietor gave me a whole shilling. For many years afterwards whenever I passed the shop I recalled with much delight that notable occasion.

My father then conceived the notion that I should be trained as a tailor's cutter, so back to the workshop I went. It was simply of no use. I had no gift for the job. While I was being instructed my mind was on some story, perhaps a serial in one of the 'blood-and-thunders' I avidly read.

A variety of jobs followed. One was with a chair manufacturing firm at 6s. a week. Work started at 6 a.m., which meant getting up at 5 a.m. I remained there long enough to learn how to glue legs on a chair. One rosy prospect came at the Singer sewing machine factory at Kilbowie. I saw a foreman who promised me a job at the fabulous wage of 17s. a week. The fifteen-mile walk to and from the factory seemed to me to have been well worth while. To get this job I had simply walked out of my home that morning. Now came the realization that I dared not return. I met some chums and they collected 8d. between them so I could get a bed in a lodging house for the night. Then my mother, who had been searching the streets for me all day, came along – and home I went. The Singer job was off, and I was back in the family tailoring business.

The shop was in the East End of Glasgow. Many of our neighbours were Roman Catholics, but the customers included Irishmen from both the North and South. My father had a workroom at the back of the shop, and customers and friends would cram into it until long after working hours, talking and consuming many a pint of beer and glass of whisky which I had to bring from the pub at the corner.

My father sat on the fence as regards the arguments on Irish topics, with the result that both the Southern Irish and the Ulstermen respected and liked him. I listened with intense interest to arguments on topics which I did not understand and occasionally I intervened with my own views, much to the chagrin of my father who envisaged one customer or the other taking his trade elsewhere. The fact that virtually none of them ordered more than one cheap suit during scores of visits and time-wasting arguments did not affect him. The place was more like a club than a business, with consequent effects on the turnover and profits.

All too often customers would be out of work and then they borrowed money from my father, but they always paid it back. Sometimes I suspected that he borrowed money from them during his own bad patches. The good and the bad times were accepted with patient philosophy. I remember one man saying that 'he was never well when he ate too much but he was worse when he ate too little.' Another customer sometimes found he could not obtain the money to take his best suit out of pawn on Saturday, so on Sunday he would lean out of the window of his tenement wearing a boiled shirt but with his moleskin working trousers on. He wore the shirt to keep up appearances. There was nothing disgraceful to these folk about pawning their clothes every Monday but it was always expected that they would get them out in order to appear respectable on Sunday.

By the time I was fourteen the Boer question was the chief source of discussion. It even banished Home Rule from the scene, and by the time war broke out, a day or two before my fifteenth birthday, I was a fervid Tory, ready and willing to go to Africa and fight Kruger with my bare hands. Considering that the war was bitterly opposed by most Liberals and all Socialists it was not surprising that my father banished me from the workroom except on business at this period.

I soon found a better source of education: the Glasgow Public Library. As soon as my father's friends had effectively put a stop to further work I would hurry off and remain there until I was turned out at ten o'clock. The daring theories of evolution by Darwin I found absorbing reading, and I expanded my knowledge by reading such works of his as *The Origin of Species* and *Descent of Man*. On the same shelves were books concerned with similar scientific subjects of the day. I read works on zoology, geology, and palaeontology, for example, and was thereby encouraged to study the specimens of stuffed animals and birds, skeletons, rocks, and fossils in the Glasgow museums. I used to spend every Saturday afternoon testing myself on the knowledge I had gained from the verbose and serious works which were the forerunners of the popular scientific works of later years.

From Conflict Without Malice (1955)

LORD SHINWELL (1884–1986), British politician, was born in London, but spent much of his early life in Glasgow. He became a Member of Parliament in 1931, and after the Second World War served as Minister of Fuel, Secretary of State for War, and Minister of Defence.

Gilbert Frankau

CRACK SHOT

Far overshadowing my mother's distaste for dogs and cats was her abhorrence of music. In my twenties, I took her to a little music hall, long since swept away, at Monte Carlo, where a man demonstrated his skill as a marksman by picking out a tune on a piano with a repeating rifle.

'That,' observed she, 'is the only time I've ever seen a musical instrument treated as I'd like to treat all musicians.'

Accordingly – and although one, Henry Morris, secretary of the Royal Amateur Orchestral Society, who also practised the violin, even when our guest in the country, was among her greatest friends – she never forced me to thump scales from the ornamental Ascherberg upright which silently decorated the double drawing room at Weymouth Street.

Near this piano, high on a pedestal, backed by the heavy lace curtains which screened the front windows, stood a marble bust.

To that bust, and those curtains, an airgun presented by Henry Morris, and one wax vesta of the period, my childhood owed its release from a fear kept as secret as its tears over a story and its vivid dreams.

Before my brother Jack (actually registered under the inappropriate names 'Paul Ewart') was born in 1890, the domestic who shared my room would leave me alone as soon as I had asked for a blessing on my parents, implored God to insure my personal good behaviour and been put to bed.

All winter, there would be a fire in that room; and a terror in my childish imagination, lest dropping coals should set the house on fire. But the air-propelled vesta with the flattened base did that.

Buffalo Bill himself never shot more accurately. At maximum range – from the back windows overlooking the mews – the head of the match exploded on the very nose of the bust. Thence, it richocheted on to the lace curtains, which burst into immediate flame.

I ran from the room shouting. The parlourmaid rushed up from the basement. Five minutes – I imagine she must have rung the alarm on our

District Messenger call-instrument – brought the horses and the men in the helmets.

'Fire,' I must have said to myself when I subsequently surveyed the wreckage, 'is nothing to be afraid of. It can always be put out.'

Anyway, that particular fear went from me – and hardly ever returns.

From Self Portrait (1940)

GILBERT FRANKAU (1884–1953), British novelist, was born in London. His mother was an even more prolific writer, under the name of Frank Danby.

Humbert Wolfe

THE FANCY DRESS BALL

A triumph was achieved at the Mayor's Fancy Dress Ball for children given one glittering Christmas. Invitations for the three elder children had been received not without difficulty, for Martin, though a respected figure in commerce, had no municipal standing. While so much had been achieved it was almost certain that no opportunity would be afforded to Consola and Martin of conversing with the Mayor, still less of taking a glass of wine with him. This privilege would be reserved for such as Mrs. Hegstein, who, in spite of her name and her profile, was a member of the 'County' set – the set which ate dinner instead of supper in the evening, drank port out of decanters, sent their sons to Public Schools instead of the Grammar School, and in one or two cases had the personal acquaintance of a Baronet. It was not clear why Mrs. Hegstein was admitted to this exclusive circle. She was rich, childless and possessed of a very small and very clean fox-terrier, but there must or may have been other matrons in Bradford as fortunately circumstanced. On the negative side it had to be confessed that she was large, and dull and plain, and that her husband was, if anything, larger and duller and plainer. It is possible that he may have obliged some member of the great world financially, or it may have been that as a couple they could be safely invited anywhere because there was little fear that either would utter in the presence of their social superiors. Moreover, Mrs. Hegstein had as good a cook as any in the town and Mr. Hegstein the best cellar. Whatever the reason may have been they exchanged courtesies and invitations with the great almost on equal terms.

This naturally put Mrs. Hegstein in the happy position of being able to harass and affront her fellow Jewesses, who, burdened either by children or volubility, were strangers in Elysium. Before she had learned her place in this regard Consola had had the audacity to invite Mr. and Mrs. Hegstein to dinner. The boy was present at the composition of the letter written in

Consola's fine, sloping and Italian hand. Martin had suggested as a form, 'Dear Mrs. H., Would you and Mr. H. come to a little dinner that we are giving on the 20th.' But Consola wished to indicate with proud humility that she was aware that, though she was a beginner, one had to begin somewhere. 'Our rooms, compared with yours,' she wrote, 'are small, but we think that for once you will forgive that. It would be an honour as well as a pleasure if you could come, and Martin says that he and Mr. Hegstein might perhaps find a minute to talk privately about some Brazilian business – of which you and I cannot be expected to know anything.' (One may observe in passing that it had formed the sole topic of conversation at meals for some weeks past.) Kindly greetings concluded the note. 'There,' said Consola, raising her little head cheerfully, 'that makes everything spink and spank (her variant of spick and span) and Mr. Hegstein won't like to risk the deal.' She was wrong. Social position outweighed business advantage, or perhaps Mrs. H. overwhelmed her heavy adjunct. The reply was in about four lines, saying that Mr. and Mrs. H. so much regretted that they were already engaged. It was a direct rebuff and Consola bided her time.

Preparations for the ball were intensive. Consola was determined that her three should not only look lovely but should, if possible, attain the distinction of being noticed in *The Bradford Observer*. There was in the little drawing-room a large book on one of the ebony and ivory tables. The boy knew it well, because on one occasion he had spilt a vase of flowers on it. This, however, had not displaced Garibaldi's life from its place of honour. The frontispiece was a photograph of a fiercely-moustached man wearing a shirt open at the neck. Later in the book the same person appeared in uniform wearing a peaked shako, a belt and a sword. Consola, who could not be accused of any particular political interests, decided to have her own Garibaldi if only for a night. She set to work accordingly to compose the uniform for Oswald, who in due course marched up and down the house in full panoply, issuing what were understood to be the authentic military commands habitual with the Italian leader. It was not known how Oswald had learned Garibaldi's vocabulary, but the fact that he had was accepted with implicit confidence. Fanny with a cocked velvet hat, a short striped skirt and a most fascinating little barrel strapped to her side was a vivandière. A play called 'Under Two Flags' had supplied the original. The only thing the boy regretted was that there was nothing in the barrel, of which the bung was stuck down. The boy himself wore a little velvet jacket, a bright shirt, gay pants and stockings 'most villainously cross-gartered.' He was a Neapolitan fisher-boy and, glory of glories, had a little net slung over his shoulder. The net was to land strange fish.

The night arrived and the children, hugely bouncing, were inserted into the four-wheeler by the side of two resplendent parents. Martin looked, in retrospect, like a French Mayor presiding at a funeral, and Consola, in her tight bodice and her bustled skirt, like the pictures in *The Illustrated London News* that were pasted on the screen in the nursery. Nor when the boy remembered the beard that graced the chin of the Heir Apparent in those pictures could he find it in his heart to disapprove of his parents' appearance.

The cab trundled up to St. George's Hall transfigured with an awning and a red baize carpet. Two policemen stood at the door radiating benevolence – a most revolutionary display. Within were their two counterparts no less amiable and therefore no less disconcerting. Not even a whispered 'Pass along there' lent a touch of verisimilitude. It might be, however, that they were normal human beings in fancy dress. Past these paradoxes the children were conducted to the cloak-room, and shortly after Martin and Consola shepherded their bright fountains into the main hall. As Consola had feared their names, vaguely mispronounced, elicited no recognition from the Mayor, who shook them vaguely by the hand and wished the children a happy evening. The little group moved off in search of friends and partners, a difficult quest in a crowd of some two thousand persons.

The boy could not dance. He therefore sat for a time at his parents' side watching all the colours there are, and hearing all the happy laughter there is. He had, it seemed, a little the air of a miniature grown-up. For Mr. Clapham, the beau of the business world, came up to greet his chief with the phrase: 'Well, how are the three old people?' The boy liked being called an 'old people'. He had been trying to persuade himself that he didn't want to dance and that he didn't care for girls, especially girls in rotatory motion. Mr. Clapham, however, felt that something must be done for his amusement. 'May I take him to have an ice?' Consent was given and the boy, holding on to his rescuer's hand, was led up three flights of steps to a long buffet in one of the galleries. He was lifted and deposited on a high stool. He gasped at the sight of so many cakes and so much food. The most cakes he had ever been permitted to eat was four. He promised himself that twelve would be no more than his share of this plenitude.

Mr. Clapham was speaking to the large lady behind the buffet. 'Two small splits and large White Gee-gee's,' he was saying in a roguish voice. The joke – for it appeared to be a joke – went well with the barlady. 'Doesn't he drink his neat?' she inquired. 'No,' retorted the wit, 'very untidily.' 'Go on with you,' said the lady, pouring out one large whisky and digging an ice out of the pail. 'There,' she said to the boy, 'there's your tipple and mind it doesn't go to your little round head.' Both she and Mr. Clapham were hugely delighted, but the boy cared for none of these things. He had managed to get three chocolate cakes and a cream horn on to his plate, and no one had attempted to interfere with him. With the grave intentness of an adoring cherub he concentrated on his ice and cakes. He had a desperate hope that Mr. Clapham might be drawn away upon some grown-up activity. His hope was realized, Mr. Clapham had been claimed and led away by an aquaintance. The boy continued to eat with rapt intentness. The sound of voices, laughter and music was a pleasant background to this solitary feast. He asked no more of life, but life wished something more of him.

He became presently aware of a large male form occupying the stool next to his. He had reached his sixth cake and therefore, having beaten his record by two, was prepared to take an interest in the world at large. He turned his eyes and found himself the object of charmed interest on the part of the large gentleman, who was brilliantly wearing a gold chain round his neck, and who was entitled to wear it because he was no less a person than the Mayor. The boy did not clearly classify grown-ups, and he was unable to realize into what dazzling company he had strayed. The Mayor spoke. 'Don't you want to dance, little one?' he said. The boy didn't like being called 'little one'; there were numbers smaller than himself. He felt inclined to point this out to the old gentleman, but thought that this might lead to conversation, and thus interrupt his degustation of cakes. 'No,' he said briefly in his soft round voice. 'I like cakes.' The Mayor was delighted. This was a true Yorkshire boy who knew his mind in the true Yorkshire way. 'What's your name?' he asked, arresting the boy's attempt on his seventh cake. Grown-ups, he reflected, always asked your name. It saved time if you told them it all in one. 'Berto Wolff,' he replied, '4, Mount Royd, Manningham, Bradford, Yorkshire.' Again he had scored a palpable hit. 'Well,' said the Mayor, 'Berto Wolff, 4, Mount Royd, Manningham, Bradford, Yorkshire, I like your style. Have another ice with me.' He did. 'Your Worship,' said the waitress, 'he'll be sick. That's the third ice and seven cakes.' 'Six,' said the boy indignantly, 'and anyhow, I've eaten four – often.' 'Give the gentleman his ice,' he said. 'These men about town know where to stop.'

The boy's opinion of this person appreciated. He was prepared to converse. He explained that Oswald was the strongest boy in Bradford, that Fanny had torn one stocking and cried in the cab, that he wasn't really fat though people called him 'der dicke' and, above all, he took the view that if there were so many cakes about nobody would be any the worse off if he had twelve. The Mayor neglected his duties as a host to listen to the babble of the excited child, who looked more like a Romney portrait every moment. 'What's the net for?' he asked suddenly. 'For catching things,' and unpinning it from his shoulder he cast it – to his surprise – about the head of a lady who had apparently been standing behind him and the Mayor.

The lady was Mrs. Hegstein, who was proposing to exchange such compliments with the Mayor as became her station. It was, however, difficult to behave with dignity, when enmeshed in a net which was being tugged by a surprised and painstaking boy. Mrs. Hegstein exclaimed angrily and tried to move away. The boy clung tightly to his net which by this time had firmly entangled itself in combs and hairpins. He was anxious to get his net back, and he wished that the large lady would stand still. The Mayor, to his eternal discredit, in spite of heroic efforts, subsided into helpless laughter. Mrs. Hegstein, completely out of control, leaned forward to box the boy's ears – at which dramatic instant the net came away, Mrs. Hegstein's hair came down and Consola appeared. 'Oh!' said she, interposing herself between the outraged lady and her boy, 'how sweet of you to play with the child, but you shouldn't have let him pull your hair down even to please him. But I expect you don't often get a chance to play with children.' And then: 'O, Mr. Mayor, I didn't see you. Of course you know Mrs. Hegstein. She's devoted to children, which makes us all wish that she had some of her own. But I do hope

Berto hasn't been annoying you.' 'No,' said the Mayor, looking at Mrs. Hegstein's retreating back, 'he hasn't been annoying me.' Consola raised her radiant face to the already enchanted Mayor. 'Well,' she said, 'she was trying to hit him at his first party.' She didn't add that long ago Mrs. Hegstein had succeeded in hitting her at her first party. She didn't need to. Honours were easy.

From Now A Stranger (1933)

HUMBERT WOLFE CBE (1886–1940), British poet, critic, translator and civil servant, was born Umberto Wolff in Milan, and came to Bradford with his German father and Italian mother. As Deputy Secretary in the Ministry of Employment, he was responsible in 1939 for raising the two million men required for civil defence and auxiliary services.

Bethel Solomons

SABBATH RUGBY

Perhaps it is because my earliest childhood times were so happy that I have no very clear recollection of many particular incidents. My great pal of those days was Sophie, and my elder brother and sister were almost strangers to me, for they moved in their own circle of friendship.

I vividly remember being called to the window of the nursery, as a matter of urgency, so that I should not miss the extraordinary spectacle of a woman riding a bicycle. Never had I seen such a thing before, and the sight of a woman in bloomers was a talking point for days and gave me a great shock at the tender age of seven. It would take more than that to shock the children of the 'bikini' age!

Another early recollection is the fascination that the sight of the horse-trams passing our house held for me. I never tired of watching them go by. Later, it was my greatest treat to be taken by my father for a walk to Blackrock village, near the sea about four miles away, to have buns in the park and then return by tram.

Our nurse, Bridget, was a marvel. To me she was always old in appearance. Her digestion was troublesome, partly due to her bad teeth, but she was a marvel all the same. She taught us our early lessons and, what was more important, our manners. She was with us for many years. When she was in the forties, she married a guard on the railways. This man's first wife had been Bridget's greatest friend and, when dying, had insisted that she would swear to marry the guard and look after the several children. It was a tough assignment. Her job with us was a bed of roses compared to her subsequent life. I am glad to say that we were able to show our gratitude to her by making things a bit easier in her declining years.

I did not go to school until I was seven. Then I entered an establishment run by a Dr. Barnard in Leeson Street. I went to the kindergarten department under Miss Cahill. She was a little squat woman, but we all thought her so very beautiful. We worked like anything to get to the head of the class. The incentive was there, for the head child was allowed to kiss the good Miss Cahill at the beginning and the end of the day.

Dr. Barnard was a formidable character with a great black beard. His was a restless disposition and one hobby and interest followed another. While he confined his restlessness to the development of carpentry and such like things he did the school no great harm. The school was never a particularly good one, but it went from bad to worse, when Dr. Barnard decided to combine his schoolmastering with the work of a medical student. The number of lectures and medical cliniques he had to attend prevented him from giving more than nominal supervision to his livelihood.

Bullying was prevalent in the school in Leeson Street and Dr. Barnard was a mighty caner, although I never suffered from this.

When I look back on this period of my life I never can understand why my wise father left me at Barnard's until the numbers had diminished from more than a hundred to just three, on that happy day when this scholastic establishment closed its doors for ever. I think that it was from his highly-developed sense of loyalty. . . .

The great event of the year at Barnard's was the Annual Prize Day. I well remember, on one of these occasions, standing up a proud figure in a velvet suit to recite *Lochinvar*. It must have been something of an ordeal for the audience. . . .

The school athletic field was what is now Dartmouth Square which is surrounded by houses, and the boys could get there by going through the back of the school without touching the road. There was a cake shop a few minutes away and how proud I was in those days when the captain of football sent me to buy some pastry for his lunch.

When I was about thirteen, I was sent to St. Andrew's College which at that time was the most flourishing school in Dublin. It had been started some time previously by Presbyterians and they were lucky to get as their headmaster, W.W. Haslett. He had brought the number from scratch to between three and four hundred, when I went there. The first thing which struck me was the complete absence of the bullying which had been a predominant feature of Barnard's school. The next thing was that I felt I was being taught something worth learning, for the school had an excellent staff of masters. There was Haslett for Classics, Dowds and Ward for Mathematics, Johnston for English, Moscardi for French and Norminton for Science. Dowds and Monahan, who later became a bishop in Wales, were splendid teachers of football, and the teams were good.

I might well have gone to school in France. My two sisters were educated abroad and my parents were, at one time, making arrangements to send me away. Haslett, hearing this, rushed off to my father and expostulated: 'You can't send him to France, we want him for the Rugby team!' In spite of the fact that neither mother nor father had ever seen Rugby played at this time, they consented to allow me to remain at St. Andrew's College. Whether I lost by not acquiring a real proficiency in French or gained by having Ireland ingrained into me, together with some sound principles of work and some excellent teaching of Rugby, I have never finally decided. . . .

I enjoyed fully my days at St. Andrew's. I did fairly well at lessons but I am afraid Rugby was my real joy. When I was about thirteen it was discovered I might have possibilities and I was picked for an under-fourteen team. When I went home delighted with myself, my father dumbfounded me by saying I could not participate as the match was on a Saturday, the Sabbath. My mother was really a far more religious person than my father, but in spite of this she reasoned with him, saying: 'We are living in a Christian country, wait until we get to Palestine, then we shall not allow games on Saturday. But he can play.' And I did. My father was a very wise man and he listened to the counsels of my mother in everything in our happy home. And so my career in football started.

From One Doctor in His Time (1956)

DR BETHEL SOLOMONS (1885–1965), gynaecologist, was born in Dublin, and was Master of the Rotunda and a vice-president of the British College of Obstetricians and Gynaecologists.

André Maurois

'DISSENTERS, WITHDRAW'

There were two possible ways in which I could continue my studies, and between these my parents had to choose. They could put me in the Rouen Lycée as a boarder – it was thus that my Uncle Henry had prepared for the Polytechnique – or they could send me there each morning and have me return each evening. The daily trip would be tiring, for it would be necessary to take a train at six forty-nine in the morning, which meant getting up at a quarter to six, and at least two hours a day would be lost on the two trips. But my mother had an instinctive horror of my living away from home; and so, despite the fact that my health was not of the best, it was decided that I should return each evening to Elbeuf. There were, however, other young people, among them André Blin and one of Pastor Roehrich's sons, to accompany me. We were soon known at the Rouen Lycée as 'the Elbeuf train'.

Each morning – and in pitch darkness during the winter – with my schoolbag under my arm, I would walk through Elbeuf amid the labourers going to work. One could hear the machines in the factories slowly start to turn. The great glass windows would suddenly light up on the stroke of six-thirty. Presently in the smoky light of the railway compartment, seated on the dirty brown cushions, I would try to rehearse my lessons. How many verses have I recited between Elbeuf and Rouen! Even today I cannot think of those hideous stations, that charming countryside, those rivers and forests without seeming to hear the stanzas of *Polyeucte, La Jeune Captive, La Nuit de mai*, or perhaps: 'Sing, goddess, the wrath of Peleus' son, Achilles . . . '

The sequence of stations, their distance from one another, their odd, dissimilar names, formed a kind of musical phrase in my mind with a complex rhythm that I loved. First came Elbeuf-Rouvalets, a brief stop, a semi-quaver barely separated by a sigh from the point of departure. From there to La Bouille-Moulineaux was the longest run of the trip, an interminable interval punctuated by a noisy tunnel in the course of which one could shout without disturbing the other passengers: 'Eighteen-eleven! O year when the numberless nations . . . ' or: 'Waterloo, O mournful plain . . . ' Then came in quick, regular succession Grand-Couronne, Petit-Couronne, Grand-Quevilly, Petit-Quevilly, and finally Rouen. *Tac-tac . . . Tac-tac-tac-tac.* That was the rhythm of my childish thoughts on this daily morning trip, and when the exigent manoeuvres of a deputy resulted in establishing a station at Hêtre-à-l'Image in the middle of a wood, thus interrupting my longest interval by a short and wholly useless stop, it seemed to me that a strange and alarming dissonance had been brought into my life.

My first day at the Rouen Lycée was marred by a small but distressing incident that made so deep an impression that I should not consider it honest to omit it from this narrative. At that time it was the custom to begin the academic year by a mass called Mass of the Holy Spirit, celebrated in the beautiful chapel of the Lycée, which had once been a Jesuit college; the purpose of this mass was to invoke the benediction of the Holy Spirit upon the labours of the students. A few minutes before the ceremony the Head Usher called us together in the great courtyard and said:

'Dissenters, withdraw!'

The dissenters were the Protestants and the Israelites. About twenty Protestants and three or four Jews stepped out of the ranks.

'The others,' the Head Usher went on, 'will form in a column of twos and follow me into the chapel.'

There was the prolonged sound of tramping feet and the student body disappeared into a vaulted passage. Our little group remained alone beneath the trees, disconsolate and with nothing to say. From the nearby chapel rose the music of the organ magnificently played by my master Dupré, and the murmured responses. We strolled sadly beneath the chestnut trees of the courtyard. We felt no shame at being Protestants or Israelites, but we felt ourselves separated for an hour's time, on a solemn occasion, from a community which was, after all, our community, and we were unhappy, very unhappy, without knowing why.

Despite that one painful hour, I fell in love at once with my new school. The beautiful Court of Honour, framed by symmetrical grey buildings constructed by the Jesuits in the seventeenth century, the Latin inscriptions which ornamented the front of the sun dial and the pedestal of the statue of Corneille, the drum that rolled out from the head of the stairs at five minutes to eight, the ranks which immediately formed two abreast, this rigour, this discipline, gave me a joy I was to recapture later on with my regiment when we marched past the flag to the strains of a military band. Consciousness of belonging to a well-ordered group is an aesthetic pleasure which I believe musicians in an orchestra feel, as do students and soldiers.

At the end of a week our teacher, Monsieur Robineau, had us write a Latin composition. Thanks to Kittel, I knew how a Latin composition was made, and the text did not seem hard. Naturally I had no idea how I should rank in this class of forty students, none of whom I knew. A week later the headmaster, Monsieur Desfours, appeared to read the marks. It was a solemn moment. The Headmaster, corpulent, bearded, businesslike, entered with his high hat in his hand, followed by the Censor who held a large sheet of paper. The whole class rose.

'Greetings, Monsieur Robineau,' the Headmaster said majestically. 'Sit down, gentlemen . . . Your marks are as follows . . . '

And the Censor read:

'Latin composition . . . First: Herzog, Emile . . . '

The Headmaster stopped him:

'Ah! I take occasion to congratulate Monsieur Herzog. This is a triumph for the Petit Lycée of Elbeuf. Gentlemen of Rouen, here is a challenge to do your best.'

Those who had been the leaders of the class the preceding year began to regard me with exasperation. A curvature of the spine forced me to wear an iron corset which made my movements slow and awkward. This object of ridicule, my unfortunate scholastic triumph, the renewed interest in the *Affaire Dreyfus* combined, for a number of weeks, to make me the victim of a number of conscienceless and cruel boys. It was my first experience of anti-semitism. I suffered frightfully, not having met, up to that time, anything but tenderness at home and friendship at school. Life at the Lycée, which I admired so much, would have become insufferable if I had not found support from potent avengers.

These were a group of sporting characters, dirty and high-spirited, with buttonless waistcoats tied together by pieces of string, who called themselves the Morin family. Blot, a star forward in rugby, was Father Morin; Loustaunau, Bouchard, Godet, Pagny and Patin (whom the Morins called 'Pascaline') completed the family. We took our meals in a refectory, eight to a table. The Head Usher would say grace or, more accurately, he would mutter: 'Sancti amen . . . Sancti amen.' Then we would sit down. The Morins, seven in number, as soon as they saw that I seemed unhappy, requested the Usher to put me at their table; and since they were the best fighters in the middle form, their friendship, added to that of Abbé

Vacandard, chaplain of the Lycée, who enjoyed translating Cicero or Tacitus with me, quieted the brawlers.

From Memoirs, *tr.* Denver Lindley (1970)

ANDRÉ MAUROIS was the pseudonym of Emile Herzog (1885–1967), French novelist, essayist and biographer, who was born in Elbeuf of a family of industrialists which had recently moved from Alsace.

Jean Starr Untermeyer

A MAN
(to my father)

Often, when I would sit, a dreamy straight-haired child,
A book held gaping on my knee,
Watering a sterile romance with my thought,
You would come bounding to the curb
And startle me to life.
You sat so straight upon your vibrant horse –
That lovely horse, all silken fire and angry grace –
And yet you seemed so merged in him,
So like! At least my thoughts
Gave you a measure of that wildness.
And, oh, for many years you seemed to me
Something to marvel at and yet to fear.

But now I know that you resemble most
That growth in nature that you most revere.
You've taken on the likeness of a tree –
Grown straight and strong and beautiful,
With many leaves.
The years but add in richness to your boughs,
You make a noble pattern in the sky.
About your rugged trunk
Vines creep and lichens cling,
And children play at tag.
Upon your branches some will hang their load
And rest and cool while you must brave the sun.
But you put forth new life with every year,
And tower nearer to the clouds
And never bend or grow away.

I wonder what sweet water bathes your roots,

And if you gain your substance from the earth;
Or if you have a treaty with the sun,
Or keep some ancient promise with the heavens.

JEAN STARR UNTERMEYER (1886–1973), American poet, was born in Zanesville, Ohio. She also published a volume of reminiscences, *Private Collection* (1965).

Edna Ferber

DOWN THE MISSISSIPPI

There was no Jewish place of worship in Ottumwa. The five or six Jewish families certainly could not afford the upkeep of a temple. I knew practically nothing of the Jewish people, their history, religion. On the two important holy days of the year – Rosh Hashana, the Jewish New Year; and Yom Kippur, the Day of Atonement – they hired a public hall for services. Sometimes they were able to bring to town a student rabbi who had, as yet, no regular congregation. Usually one of the substantial older men who knew something of the Hebrew language of the Bible, having been taught it in his youth, conducted the service. On Yom Kippur, a long day of fasting and prayer, it was an exhausting thing to stand from morning to sunset in the improvised pulpit. The amateur rabbi would be relieved for an hour by another member of the little improvised congregation. Mr. Emanuel Adler, a familiar figure to me as he sat in his comfortable home talking with my parents, a quaint long-stemmed pipe between his lips, a little black skull-cap atop his baldish head as protection against draughts, now would don the rabbinical skull-cap, a good deal like that of a Catholic priest. He would open, on the high reading-stand, the Bible and the Book of Prayers containing the service for the Day of Yom Kippur; and suddenly he was transformed from a plump middle-aged German-born Jew with sad kindly eyes and a snuffy grey-brown moustache to a holy man from whose lips came words of wisdom and of comfort and of hope.

The store always was closed on Rosh Hashana and Yom Kippur. Mother put on her best dress. If there were any Jewish visitors in the town at that time they were invited to the services and to dinner at some hospitable house afterward. In our household the guests were likely to be a couple of travelling salesmen caught in the town on that holy day. Jewish families came from smaller near-by towns – Marshalltown, Albia, Keokuk.

I can't account for the fact that I didn't resent being a Jew. Perhaps it was because I liked the way my own family lived, talked, conducted its household and its business better than I did the lives of my friends. I admired immensely my grandparents, my parents, my uncles and aunt. Perhaps it was a vague something handed down to me from no one knows where. Perhaps it was something not very admirable – the actress in me. I think, truthfully, that I rather liked dramatizing myself, feeling myself different and set apart. I probably liked to think of myself as persecuted by enemies who were (in my opinion) my inferiors. This is a protective philosophy often employed. Mine never had been a religious family. The Chicago Neumann family sometimes went to the temple at Thirty-third and Indiana, but I don't remember that my parents ever went there while in Chicago. In our own household there was no celebration of the informal home ceremonies so often observed in Jewish families. The Passover, with its Sedar service, was marked in our house only by the appearance of the matzos or unleavened bread, symbolic of the hardships of the Jews in the wilderness. I devoured pounds of the crisp crumbling matzos with hunks of fresh butter and streams of honey, leaving a trail of crumbs all over the house, and though very little, I am afraid, of the tragic significance of the food I was eating or that weary heartsick band led by Moses out of Egypt to escape the Hitler of that day, one Pharaoh; or of how they baked and ate their unsalted unleavened bread because it was all they had, there in the wilderness. I still have matzoth (matzos, we always called them) in my house during the Passover, and just as thoughtlessly. Now they come as delicate crisp circlets, but they seem to me much less delicious than the harder, tougher squares of my childhood munching. Ours were not Jewish ways. My father and mother and sister Fan and I exchanged many friendly little calls with the pleasant Jewish families of the town – the Almeyers, the Adlers, Feists, Silvers, Lyons, living in comfortable well-furnished houses, conducting their affairs with intelligence and decorum, educating their children. They saw a little too much of one another. There was a good deal of visiting back and forth, evenings. At nine there would be served wine or lemonade and cake, a moment which I eagerly awaited. The Ferber speciality was a hickory-nut cake, very rich, baked in a loaf, for which I was permitted to crack the nuts and extract the meats. This was accomplished with a flat-iron between my knees and a hammer in my hand. The nuts went into the cake and into me fifty-fifty. Once baked, it was prudently kept under lock and key in the cupboard of the sitting-room desk, rather than in the free territory of the pantry.

My mother, more modern than most in thought and conduct, had numbers of staunch friends among the non-Jewish townspeople, and these enormously enjoyed her high spirits, her vitality, her shrewd and often caustic comment. She, too, was an omnivorous reader, so that when life proved too much for her she was able to escape into the reader's Nirvana. Certainly she was the real head of the family, its born leader; unconsciously she was undergoing a preliminary training which was to stand her in good stead when she needed it.

It is interesting (to me) to note that all this time I never wrote a line outside my school work and never felt the slightest urge toward original composition. But the piece-speaking went on like a house afire. I recited whenever I could. In school we had recitations every Friday afternoon, and a grand burst of entertainment at the end of each term and on that world-rocking occasion, the Last Day of School, in June. I was by this time a confirmed show-off and a chronic reciter. At the slightest chance I galloped to the front of the room and began my recitation, with gestures. My bliss was complete on those days when we went from room to room giving our programmes as visiting artists before an entire class of helpless listeners. To a frustrated actress like myself it is significant now to read a phrase that recurs again and again in that hastily scribbled line-a-day kept by Julia Ferber. Edna recited, it says. No comment, no criticism. Edna recited.

During the Ottumwa period my sister and I used to be taken to Chicago once a year, in the summer, to visit Grandma and Grandpa Neumann. By this time money was scarce, and we – my mother and the two of us – sat up all night in the coach. Children of six were allowed to ride free. I was bundled up in a shawl for a supposed nap, and told to make myself very small There I lay, trembling and sweating, until the conductor had passed on his ticket-collecting trip. He always looked exactly the same, though perhaps he wasn't. Perhaps he only followed the pattern of the Midwest American train conductor – grizzled, spectacled, brownish spots on the backs of his hands; an Elks and a Masonic emblem; service stripes on his sleeve; a worn, patient and rather benevolent face, strangely embittered by the pettiness, bad manners and vagaries of the American travelling public.

He would cast a doubting eye on the plump mound under the shawl. 'Looks like a big girl to me, ma'am.'

'She's big for her age.'

Which I undeniably was.

Always I watched and waited with enormous anticipation for the first glimpse of the Mississippi River. I can't explain why it held such fascination for me. Perhaps I had been impressed by what I had learned of it in school – three thousand miles long, tributaries, floods, currents, Mark Twain. For an hour before it was time to cross the great bridge that spanned the stream my face was pressed against the car window. With my own eyes I had seen its ruthless power reflected in the wild antics of our Des Moines River, its tributary. Every year, in the spring, we heard stories of the Mississippi's wild career, how it went berserk and destroyed farms and lives with a single lash of its yellow tail, or gobbled up whole towns in one dreadful yawning of its gigantic jaws. It was always a living thing to me. A monster. When we actually sighted it I eagerly knelt up at the window and watched it out of sight – its broad turbulent bosom, its swift current, its eddies, its vast width, like a mighty lake rather than a river.

The lowlands of Ottumwa, and especially the low-lying Main Street which embraced the chief business section of the town, frequently were flooded. I am here rather embarrassed to admit that I was quite old enough to have known better – such was the terror of the rivers in that part of the country – before I realized that the long laden trains of box-cars and flat-cars that crept and puffed so slowly and cautiously along the tracks by the side of the Des Moines River were not 'fraid trains, but freight trains.

It was because of these floods that I knew how rivers behaved. I saw bridges as they swayed, cracked, then, with screams of despair, were swept downstream in the flood. I saw houses tossing like toys in midstream, while sheep, cows, pianos, rocking-chairs, bedsteads, floated and bobbed by. People sat marooned on roof-tops as their houses took to the nautical life.

In the beginning chapters of the novel *Show Boat* there is a description of the Mississippi at floodtime. I found I did not need to consult books or ask old-timers to relate their river experiences. I just took my childhood memories of the Mississippi and the Des Moines at floodtime out of the back of my head where they had been neatly stored for so many years and pinned them down on paper.

It is a method every writer can use and one which all experienced writers do use. Sometimes (this may be scientifically disputed, but I believe it nevertheless) the memory goes back, back, beyond one's actual lifetime experience, into the unknown past. Most writers must have had the odd sensation of writing a line, a paragraph, a page about something of which they have had no actual knowledge or experience. Somehow, inexplicably, they know. It writes itself. Of course the everyday store-house method is merely a matter of having a good memory and a camera eye, with the mental films all neatly filed away for future development when needed. That is why, no matter what happens, good or bad, to a professional writer, he may count as just so much velvet. Into the attic it goes. This can better be illustrated, perhaps, by describing a shabby old yellow trunk kept in the storeroom of the Ferber household in my childhood. When you lifted the rickety lid there was wafted to you the mingled odour of moth-balls, lavender, faint perfumery, dyes, and the ghostly emanation peculiar to cast-off garments. Inside, the trunk foamed with every shade and variety of material. There were odds and ends and scraps and bolts and yards of silk, satin, passementerie, beads, ruchings insertion, velvet, lace, ribbon, feathers, flower trimmings, bits of felt, muslin. When my mother needed trimming for a dress or a hat for herself or for my sister Fannie and myself she merely dived into the old trunk, fished around in the whirlpool of stuffs, and came up with just the oddment or elegancy she needed.

From A Peculiar Treasure (1939)

EDNA FERBER (1887–1968), American novelist, was born in Kalamazoo, Michigan. Her novel *Show Boat* inspired the musical play of that name.

Sely Brodetsky

WHITECHAPEL GHETTO

One of the constant facts of our family life was that my father could never make a living. With all his Jewish and general knowledge he failed economically in London, as he had failed in the Ukraine. In the ghetto a man who could not make a living usually became a teacher. But my father realised that he hadn't the patience for teaching children. He tried dealing in cheap clothing, but his 'capital' was soon turned into debts that his customers owed him, and for the most part never paid. When we came to London he was the Shamas of a small synagogue in Princelet Street, with a salary of less than a pound a week. This synagogue was one of the oldest in Whitechapel, having been established in 1862. One of his duties was to go round collecting the weekly dues from the members. In those days membership of a synagogue, friendly society, Zionist organisation and the like cost a penny, twopence or threepence a week. Membership of the Burial Society of the Federation of Synagogues, which gave its members proper burial when they died, was twopence a week. The collector had special receipt books, marked according to the portion of the Torah ('Law' – the Pentateuch) read in the synagogues that week; he snipped off the appropriate receipt with a pair of small scissors.

My father was not a professional collector, but he had to do it for the synagogue. He was responsible for all the arrangements there. He got out the Scrolls of the Torah for the readings; he called up the congregants honoured to read a portion of the Torah; he had the wine ready for Kiddush. He was, of course, intimate with all this procedure.

The family had forgotten what the Ukrainian doctor had said, that I must not study. But I listened, and I picked up some of the Jewish knowledge that my father taught my elder brother. I soon persuaded my father to teach me to read Hebrew.

English education was compulsory; the London Educational authorities would have been very impatient with anyone who wanted them to exempt me because of something an Ukrainian doctor had said about my brain being unable to stand studying.

My brother and I went first to Hanbury Street Board School. One day a school inspector came to my class, Standard Two, and gave us a sum to do. The answer was six. The inspector asked: 'Six what?' There was no sensible reply till he reached me, and I said: 'Six numbers.' He was so pleased that he gave me sixpence for it. Of course my answer was as wrong as the others. It should have been 'Six of the particular things being discussed,' apples or fish or elephants or chickens. I wonder if the inspector realised afterwards that my answer, too, was wrong.

After a year or so we were admitted to the Jews' Free School. This was a very important institution. It was founded a century and a half ago, and was maintained largely by the Rothschild family, and by contributions obtained at periodical dinners. It was situated between Bell Lane and Middlesex Street, the famous Petticoat Lane. It bordered on the City of London. One entered the school from Whitechapel; the back was in the City. The school is now closed; it was hit by a bomb in the Second World War, and the district has also been largely deserted by the Jewish population for which it provided. Half a century ago it had about five thousand pupils, and was the largest school in the country. The educational authorities thought highly of it, and many of its pupils afterwards became distinguished and famous people. Among them were Israel Zangwill, Samuel Gompers, the American Labour leader, Sir John de Villiers, Barney Barnato and his cousin, Sir David Harris, the Kimberley pioneer.

One of the attractions of the school was that every pupil was given a suit of clothes and a pair of boots each year. It was important help for families like ours, struggling with poverty. The school gave a reasonable amount of Jewish education, far more than most children get today. But orthodox Jews found it inadequate, and supplemented it.

We were sent to the Brick Lane Talmud Torah, the most important orthodox Cheder in London, run by the orthodox Machsike Hadass Synagogue next door. Meanwhile the family increased, and our poverty with it. There were more mouths to feed, and no additional income. Then my father found that he could earn a little more money by doing spare-time work for cigarette manufacturers. He had to stick on a printed label with the name of the firm, the brand, and the number of cigarettes in the packet. They paid 1s. 3d. a thousand. I remember I was seven or eight when I helped my father in his work, adding perhaps another 6d. a week in this way to the family income.

After a few years my father became Shamas of the Sephardic Synagogue in New Court, Fashion Street. Sephardic did not in this connection mean Spanish origin. These were Ashkenazic Jews like the others, who had adopted small variations in the Ashkenazic Polish and German ritual from the Sephardim. . . .

In New Court, Fashion Street, there were two and a half synagogues, two proper synagogues and another in a private house. Whitechapel was a ghetto. New Court was the quintessence of the ghetto. Men coming from the synagogues walked about in New Court in their prayer shawls, and occasionally strayed like that into Fashion Street. It was the usual thing to put a table in the open air in the Court, bring out a scroll of the Torah from one of the synagogues, and read the prescribed portions, to give a number of people the chance to be 'called up'; especially on the New Year, on Yom Kippur, and particularly on Simchat Torah, when every male present must be called up.

There was a house attached to the Sephardic Synagogue for the shamas; so my family was elevated to living in a whole house. The house had only two rooms, but it was better than any of our previous residences; and we had privacy, where previously we had had other families living in the same house.

My father suffered much from the ignorance of his President, Wardens and other Honorary Officers. He strongly disapproved of the way in which they celebrated Simchat Torah. Some of them got drunk, and danced with the scrolls of the Torah; the children rushed about, making a noise; the women invaded the men's part of the synagogue, and on one occasion fireworks were exploded in the gallery, to demonstrate their love of God and their admiration for Moses. To my father everything was serious, especially religion. . . .

My general studies did not at first direct any special attention to me, though I shared largely in monitorial functions, even to the extent of taking some classes on behalf of the teacher; but this was mainly to hear whether the other boys knew the rivers, capes and bays of England by heart in their geographical order round the coast. I proceeded from standard to standard by the usual yearly advance.

My Jewish studies at the Brick Lane Talmud Torah attracted more attention. I began learning Talmud with Rashi's commentary when I was eight, and I soon proceeded to the Tossefot and other commentaries on commentaries. Of course I studied the Torah, the Prophets, Hebrew Grammar, etc.

A commentary on the 'public' services in the East End of London at that time is the fact that the teachers in the Talmud Torah had pails of water in the classroom, with the boys taking drinks in turn; those were the days of private ownership of water supplies, and the East End often had the water turned off for all but a couple of hours a day in the summer.

I became known as a Talmudist; and, when I was eleven, long-bearded Talmudists came to hear me 'learning' in Yiddish, using my hands and the Gemara tune in the long-established ghetto tradition. After a time a special teacher was engaged at the Talmud Torah for me personally: he was an excellent Talmudist who eked out a living by keeping a restaurant in addition to teaching; he often fell asleep in the middle of the lesson, and then I read books on shorthand, or German, which I kept hidden under the Talmud volume.

I enjoyed this because I liked learning things. The life I led was a ghetto life, for my school as well as my Talmud Torah were inside the area of ghetto Jewish life. Of course, we were surrounded by English life and, like so many other young people there, we spoke a gradually improving English among ourselves; but we spoke Yiddish to our parents and their friends. Yiddish was in fact my mother tongue. As I had a very effective Talmud teacher from Vilna when I was young – supported by a large wooden stick which was never used on the pupils – I changed my Yiddish pronunciation from the Ukrainian to his Lithuanian.

I remember Queen Victoria's Diamond Jubilee in 1897, four years after I came to London. The Jews of the East End rejoiced with everybody else. I was one of ten thousand children from the London schools who were taken to see a special ceremony connected with the Jubilee. We sat in Green Park, wore patriotic badges, and saw a ceremony in which the Queen participated, without understanding at all what was happening. . . .

A feature of Whitechapel life was the Shabbos-goy, the non-Jew who would do things in the house that a pious Jew could not do on the Sabbath. It is rather complicated, because it is forbidden to tell or ask a non-Jew to do it. A few had a maid, who knew her job; for most it meant hiring someone to light fires on the Saturday and put out lamps and candles on the Friday night. We could not afford anyone regular for twopence or threepence each Sabbath; so someone had to go out to look for one in the street. Sometimes a policeman would oblige, but it was hardly consistent with his duties. The greatest disaster was finding someone ready to oblige, who turned out to be a Jew; but this happened rarely. While out seeking a Shabbos-goy one Friday night I passed a public house, when a woman, quite drunk, staggered out, sat down on the kerb, saw me, and shouted: 'Bloody Jew! Go back to your own country.' She was not a Zionist, of course, but I had been attending the meetings for the first Zionist Society in Whitechapel, and I would have liked to go to my country. But there was then no country as yet for a Jew. Often our Shabbos-goy had difficulty with lighting a candle and making it stand in the candlestick. Candles had gone out of use with the discovery of gas, which was the main form of lighting at the beginning of the century. But sometimes the gas had not been laid on, and we used paraffin lamps. I often burned my hand through touching the chimney of the lamp long after it was out. Electric light was rare. Sometimes my father took me at night to Shoreditch Goods Station to see the electric arc lamps.

From Memoirs: From Ghetto to Israel (1960)

SELY BRODETSKY FRAS, FRAES (1888–1954), mathematician and leader of Zionism, was born in Olviopol, Ukraine, and came with his family to London in 1893. He was President, Board of Deputies of British Jews 1939–49, and President, Hebrew University 1949–52.

Marc Chagall

ONCE BITTEN

The years were passing by. It was time for me to begin imitating others, to resemble them.

And one fine day, I saw before me a kind of tutor, a little rabbi from Mohileff.

As though he had jumped out of my picture, or run away from a circus.

He had not even been sent for. He came of his own accord, the way the marriage-broker comes or the old man who carries away corpses.

'A season or two . . . ' he said to my mother.

How glib he is!

I look him straight in the face.

I already know that 'a' with a line below it makes 'o'. But at the 'a' I fall asleep; at the line I would like to . . . At that very moment the rabbi himself falls asleep.

How funny he is!

I would enter his class as promptly as a thunderbolt, and I would come home every evening with a lantern in my hand.

On Fridays he took me to the baths, making me lie down on a bench.

Birch twigs in hand, he would examine my body carefully, as if I were the Bible.

I had three such rabbis.

The first, a little bug from Mohileff.

The second, Rabbi Ohre (a nonentity, no memory of him).

The third, an imposing person who died early, Rabbi Djatkin.

He was the one who taught me that famous speech about 'tefillin' which I recited standing on a chair when I reached the age of thirteen.

I confess, I felt duty bound to forget the man less than half an hour later, or even sooner.

I think my first little rabbi from Mohileff had the greatest influence on me.

Just imagine, every Saturday instead of going bathing in the river, my mother sent me to study the Bible with him.

However, I knew that at that time (immediately after lunch) the rabbi and his wife were sleeping soundly in honour of the Sabbath, completely undressed. Just wait until he gets into his trousers!

Once, knocking on the closed door, I attracted the attention of the lordly dog, a bad-tempered, red old beast with sharp fangs.

He padded softly down the stairs and, pricking up his ears, came towards me and . . .

I do not remember what happened next. I remember being picked up at the main entrance.

My arm bleeding, my leg too.

The dog had bitten me.

'Don't undress me, just put some ice on here . . . '

'We must carry him home to his mother as soon as possible.'

That very day, that dog was hunted down by the police and it took them twelve shots to kill him.

That evening, I left for Petersburg for treatment, accompanied by my uncle.

The doctors declared I would die in four days.

Delightful! Everyone takes care of me. Every day brings me closer to death. I am a hero.

The dog was mad.

Going to Petersburg for treatment was very alluring.

I thought I might meet the Tzar in the street.

Passing the Neva, I had the impression that the bridge was hanging from the sky.

I forgot the dog-bite. It was a pleasure to sleep alone in a white bed, having yellow broth for lunch, with an egg.

It was a pleasure to stroll in the hospital garden; I thought I saw the Crown Prince among the well-dressed children playing there. I kept to myself, I did not play, I had no toys. I saw so many of them, such beautiful ones, for the first time.

They had never bought me any at home.

The uncle who had accompanied me advised me to take one of the abandoned toys quietly.

Adorable toy, it worried me far more than my angrily bitten arm.

But won't the little crown prince come and take it away from me?

The nurses smiled at me. Their smiles gave me confidence. But I always seemed to hear the sobs of the child who owned the stolen toy.

At last I recovered and left for home again.

I found the house full of finely dressed women and grave men, whose black shapes veiled the light of day.

A hullabaloo, whispering; suddenly, the piercing wail of a new-born child.

Mamma, half naked, is lying in bed – pale, with a faint pink flush. My younger brother had just been born.

Tables covered in white.

The rustle of holy vestments.

An old man, murmuring the prayer, cuts the little bit of skin below the baby's stomach with a sharp knife . . .

He sucks the blood with his lips and smothers the baby's wails and cries in his beard.

I am sad. Silently, beside the others, I munch the cakes, herrings, gingerbread.

From My Life, *tr.* from the French by Dorothy Williams (1965)

MARC CHAGALL (1889–1985), Russian surrealist artist, was born in Vitebsk, but after 1922 lived in France, spending the war years in America.

Isaak Babel

KARL-YANKEL

When I was a kid Jonah Brutman had a blacksmith's shop at Peresyp. There gathered horse-dealers, draymen, butchers from the city slaughter-houses. The blacksmith's shop was near the Balta Station. If you chose it as an observation post you could easily intercept peasants carting oats and Bessarabian wine to the city. Jonah was an easily-scared little man, but he had a palate for wine. In him dwelt the soul of an Odessa Jew.

In my time he had three sons at home. The father reached up to their waists. It was on the beach at Peresyp that for the first time I pondered the potency of the powers that dwell secretly in Nature. Three well-fed bitterns with crimson shoulders and feet like spades, the sons used to carry their skinny little father down to the water just like an infant in arms. Yet he and none other begat them, no doubt about it. The blacksmith's wife went to the synagogue twice a week, on Friday evening and Saturday morning. The synagogue was of the Hasidic persuasion, and there at Passover they used to dance themselves silly, just like Dervishes. Jonah's wife used to pay tribute to the emissaries sent out through the provinces of the South by the saddiks of Galicia. The blacksmith did not interfere in his wife's relations with God. After work he used to go off to a wine cellar near the slaughter-houses and there, sucking in the cheap wine, he would listen meekly to what was being talked of – politics or fat stock prices.

In strength and build the sons took after their mother. Two of them, when they grew up, went off and joined the partisans. The eldest was killed at Voznesensk. The second Brutman boy, Simon, went over to Primakov and joined the Red Cossacks. He was chosen commander of a Cossack regiment. From him and from a few other small-town lads grew that unexpected breed of Jews, the tough fighting men, raiders and partisans.

The third son inherited the blacksmith's calling. He is now working at the Gen plough factory in the old town. He has never married or begotten anyone.

Simon's children moved about with his division. The old woman needed a grandson whom she might tell about Baal-Shem, and she expected a grandson from her youngest daughter Polina. Alone of all the family, the girl had taken after little old Jonah. She was easy to scare, short of sight, tender of skin, and she had lots of suitors. Polina chose Ovsey Belotserkovsky – we could never understand why. Even more amazing was the news that the young people were leading a very happy married life. A woman's household is her own affair; outsiders don't see how the pots get broken. In this case the breaker of pots was Ovsey Belotserkovsky. A year after the wedding he sued his mother-in-law, Brana Brutman. Taking advantage of Ovsey's absence on an official mission somewhere, and of the fact that Polina had gone to hospital with mastitis, the old woman kidnapped her newborn grandson, carried him off to the little foreskin-clipper Naftula Gerchik, and there, in the presence of ten ruins, ten ancient and poverty-stricken old men, assiduous attenders at the Hasidic synagogue, the ceremony of circumcision was performed upon the infant.

All this Ovsey Belotserkovsky learned when he got back. Ovsey had his name down for admission to the Party. He decided to have a word with Bychach, the secretary of the Party organisation in the Imports and Exports Office.

'You have been morally defiled,' Bychach told him. 'You can't leave the matter as it is.'

The Odessa Prosecutor's Office determined to hold a public trial at the Petrovsky Factory. The little snipper Naftula Gerchik and the sixty-two-year old Brana Brutman found themselves in the dock.

In Odessa Naftula was just as much part of the town as the Duc de Richelieu's statue. Often he would pass our windows on Dalnitskaya carrying the worn and greasy midwife's bag in which he kept his simple appliances. Now he would pull from it a little knife, now a bottle of vodka and a piece of gingerbread. He would sniff the gingerbread before drinking, and when he had drunk he would start moaning prayers. He was redheaded, Naftula was, like the first redheaded man on earth. When he was doing his snipping he didn't drain the blood off through a little glass tube but sucked it away with his splayed lips, and his tangled beard got all blood-smeared. When he went out to the assembled guests he would be tipsy, his bear-eyes shining with merriment. Redheaded, like the first redheaded man on earth, he would nasally intone a blessing over the wine. With one hand he would tip the vodka into the hirsute, crooked, and fire-breathing pit of his mouth; in his other would be a plate. On it lay the little knife crimson with infant gore, and a piece of lint. When he was collecting his fee, Naftula would present this plate to all the guests, bump about among the womenfolk, roll on them, grab them by the bosoms, and yell so that the whole street could hear.

'Fat mommas,' the old man would yell, his coral eyes gleaming, 'bud little boys for Naftula, thresh wheat on your bellies, do your best for Naftula. Bud little boys, you fat mommas.'

The husbands would cast coins on his plate; the wives would wipe the blood from his beard with napkins. The courtyards of Glukhaya and Hospital Streets knew no lack of children: they seethed with them like river mouths with fish-roe. Naftula used to toddle about with his little bag just like a tax-collector. But Prosecutor Orlov put an end to his wanderings.

The Prosecutor thundered from the dais, endeavouring to prove that the little surgeon was the servant of a cult.

'Do you believe in God?' he asked Naftula.

'Let him believe in God who has won two hundred thousand,' returned the old man.

'Were you not surprised by the arrival of Citizeness Brutman at a late hour, in the rain, with a newborn child in her arms?'

'I am surprised,' replied Naftula, 'when a human being does something in an inhuman way, but when he just plays the fool, then I am not surprised.'

These answers did not satisfy the Prosecutor. The question of the little glass tube cropped up. The Prosecutor tried to prove that by sucking the blood with his lips the accused was exposing children to the risk of infection. Naftula's head, the clotted little walnut of his head, was now bobbing somewhere in the region of the floor. He was sighing, closing his eyes, and wiping his caved-in mouth with his little fist.

'What are you mumbling, Citizen Gerchik?' the President of the court asked him.

Naftula fastened his extinguished gaze on Prosecutor Orlov.

'The late Monsieur Zusman,' he said, sighing, 'your late poppa, had a head on him such as you wouldn't find anywhere else in the world. And, glory to God, he had no apoplexy when thirty years ago he summoned me to your circumcision. And now we see that you have grown up to be a big man in the Soviet land, and that Naftula didn't take with him, along of that little bit of nothing at all, anything that could later have been of service to you.'

He blinked his bear-eyes, shook his little red walnut, and fell silent. He was answered by big guns of mirth, thundering salvos of laughter. Orlov, born Zusman, waving his arms, was shouting something that the cannonade made it impossible to hear. He was demanding that it should go on record that . . . Sandy Svetlov, the columnist of the *Odessa News*, sent him a note from the press-box: 'Don't be a goat, Simon,' ran the note, 'slay him with irony, it's only what's funny that's fatal. Yours, Sandy.'

The courtroom was hushed when the witness Belotserkovsky was called in. The witness repeated his written testimony. He was a lengthy individual in riding-breeches and cavalry boots. According to Ovsey, the Tiraspol and Balta district Party committees had shown him perfect collaboration in the work of collecting quotas of oil cake. In the midst of the work he had received a telegram announcing the birth of a son. On consulting the chairman of the Balta committee, he had decided, in order not to interrupt the work, to limit himself to a telegram of congratulation, and had not reached home till two weeks later. Throughout the region sixty-four thousand pounds of oil cake in all had been collected. At his apartment, aside from the female witness Kharchenko, a neighbour, he had found no one. His wife had been taken to hospital, and the witness Kharchenko, as she rocked the child's cradle, which is an outmoded custom, was singing a lullaby. Knowing that the witness Kharchenko was addicted to drink, he had not considered it necessary to take in the words she was singing, but he was surprised to observe that she was calling the infant Yankel, whereas he had given instructions that his son was to be named Karl, in honour of our teacher Karl Marx. Upon unswaddling the child he had been confronted with the evidence of his misfortune.

The Prosecutor had a few questions. The Defence stated that it had no questions. The court usher led in the witness Polina Belotserkovsky. Staggering, she went to the bar. The bluish spasm of recent maternity twisted her face, on her forehead were drops of sweat. She cast a glance at the little blacksmith, dressed up with a bow and new boots as for a holiday, at the bronzed and grey-whiskered face of her mother. The witness did not reply when asked what she knew about the matter under consideration. She said that her father had been a poor man, had worked for forty years at the smithy by the Balta railway. Her mother had borne six children: three of them were dead, one was a Red Army commander, another was working at the Gen factory.

'My mother is very devout, as all can see. She always suffered from the knowledge that her children were not believers, and could not bear the thought that her grandchildren would not grow up to be Jews. You must take into account the sort of family my mother was brought up in. You all know the little town of Medzhibozh. The women there still wear wigs . . . '

'Tell us, witness,' a sharp voice interrupted her, and Polina was silent. The sweat drops on her forehead turned red, just as though the blood was oozing through her skin. 'Tell us, witness,' repeated the voice that belonged to the former advocate Samuel Lining.

If the Sanhedrin existed in our days, Lining would be at its head. But there is no Sanhedrin, and Lining, who learned to read Russian at the age of twenty-five, had in his fourth decade begun to write appeals to the Senate in no way differing from Talmudic treatises.

The old man had slept through the whole case. His jacket was covered with tobacco ash. He woke up at the sight of Polina Belotserkovsky.

'Tell us, witness,' clashed the fishlike row of blue teeth always on the verge of falling out, 'did you know of your husband's resolve to call the child Karl?'

'I did.'

'What name did your mother have him given?'

'Yankel.'

'And you, witness, what did you call your son?'

'I called him "sweetypie".'

'What was your motive in calling him "sweetypie"?'

'I call all children "sweetypie".'

'Let us continue,' said Lining. His teeth fell out. He caught them with his lower lip and thrust them back between his jaws. 'Let us continue. On the evening when the child was abducted to the abode of the accused Gerchik, you were not at home: you were in hospital. Is that correct?'

'I was in hospital.'

'At what hospital were you being treated?'

'On Nezhim Street, by Doctor Drizo.'

'Under treatment by Doctor Drizo?'

'Yes.'

'You are quite sure of that?'

'Why shouldn't I be?'

'I have a document to submit to the court.' Lining's lifeless face loomed above the table. 'From this document the court will perceive that at the period in question Doctor Drizo was attending the Paediatric Congress at Kharkov.'

The Prosecutor raised no objection to admitting the document.

'Let us continue,' said Lining, rattling his teeth. The witness leaned the full weight of her body against the bar, her whisper was scarcely audible.

'Perhaps it wasn't Doctor Drizo,' she said, lying on the bar. 'I can't remember everything, I'm worn out . . . '

Lining poked in his yellow beard with a pencil, rubbed his stooping back against the bench, and jiggled his false teeth.

When requested to present her Health Insurance card, the witness averred that she had mislaid it.

'Let us continue,' said the old man.

Polina passed her hand over her forehead. Her husband was sitting on the edge of a bench away from the other witnesses. He was sitting as straight as a poker, his long legs in cavalry boots gathered beneath him. The sun fell on his face, crammed with the crossbars of petty and cross-grained bones.

'I'll find the card,' whispered Polina, and her hands slithered from the bar.

At that moment an infant's yells rang out. Next door a child was weeping and groaning.

'What are you thinking of, Polina?' cried the old woman in a hoarse voice. 'The child's not been fed since morn, the child's yelling its poor little guts out.'

The Red Army men woke with a start and grabbed their rifles. Polina slipped lower and lower, her head jerked back and lay on the floor. Her arms flew up, threshed the air, and subsided.

'Recess,' cried the President.

Uproar exploded in court. The green hollows in his cheeks gleaming, Belotserkovsky stepped cranelike toward his wife.

'Feed the child!' people were shouting from the back rows, making megaphones of their hands.

'They'll do that,' replied a female voice from afar. 'No need of your help!'

'The girl's in it, you mark my words,' observed a workingman sitting next to me. 'Knows a lot more than she'll tell.'

'Family life, brother,' said his neighbour. 'Nocturnal goings on, dark goings on. At night they tie things up that you can't disentangle by day.'

The sun was shooting oblique rays through the courtroom. The crowd threshed about, breathing fire and sweat. Using my elbows, I made my way out into the corridor. The door of the clubroom was ajar, thence came the groanings and champings of Karl-Yankel. In the clubroom hung a picture of Lenin, the one in which he is speaking from the armoured car on the square at the Finland Station. The picture was surrounded by diagrams in colour produced at the Petrovsky Factory. Along the wall there were flags, and rifles in wooden stands. A working-woman who looked like a Kirghiz, her head bent, was feeding Karl-Yankel. He was a chubby little fellow of five months old, in knitted bootees and with a white tuft on his head. Sucked fast to the Kirghiz woman, he was rumbling, beating his nurse on the breast with his little clenched fist.

'The fuss he's making!' said the Kirghiz woman. 'Not everyone would be willing to give him suck.'

In the room there was also a wench of about seventeen in a red kerchief and with great knobbly cheeks like fir cones. She was busy rubbing Karl-Yankel's sanitary diaper dry.

'He'll be a military man,' said the girl. 'Just listen how he's yelling!'

The Kirghiz woman, pulling gently, drew her nipple from Karl-Yankel's mouth. The child started growling, and in despair jerked back his head with its white tuft. The woman uncovered her other breast and presented it to the little boy. He looked at the nipple with dull little eyes, and something gleamed in them. The Kirghiz woman gazed down at Karl-Yankel, squinting a dark eye.

'Why should he be a military man?' she asked, straightening the child's bonnet. 'He'll be an airman, you'll see, and fly about beneath the sky.'

In the courtroom the case had been resumed.

Battle was now being waged between the Prosecutor and the experts, who had insisted on reaching an evasive conclusion. The Social Plaintiff, half rising in his seat, was banging the desk with his fist. I could also see the first rows of the public: Galician saddiks, with their beaver caps on their knees. They had made the journey to be present where, it said in the Warsaw papers, the Jewish religion was on trial. The faces of the rabbis sitting in the front rows hung motionless in the dusty brown sunshine.

'Down with 'em!' cried a Young Communist who had forced his way right to the dais.

The battle flamed up more fiercely.

Karl-Yankel, fastening senseless eyes upon me, sucked away at the Kirghiz woman's breast.

From the window flew the straight streets trodden by my childhood and youth: Pushkin Street stretching itself along to the station, Little Arnautskaya jutting out into the park by the sea.

I had grown up on these streets, and now it was Karl-Yankel's turn. But they hadn't fought for me as now they were fighting for him: few were those to whom I had been of any concern.

'It's not possible,' I whispered to myself, 'it's not possible that you won't be happy, Karl-Yankel. It's not possible that you won't be happier than I.'

Tr. Walter Morison

ISAAK BABEL (1894–c.1940), Russian short story writer, was born in Odessa. His writings were suppressed in the 1930s, and he disappeared in 1939.

Schmuel Dayan

THE JOURNEY

There were several hundred Jewish families in Djeskov, in the Kiev region of the Ukraine in Russia. The houses were built of some kind of clay with wooden beams, and many of them were plastered and whitewashed. Their roofs were thatched with straw, renewed in places where it had grown brittle, giving them a striped appearance. The rows of houses were laid out in a rough sort of rectangle and in the open spaces between shops stalls had been erected. Thursday was market day, when the peasants came in from the surrounding countryside in their carts, laden with farm produce and handmade articles. The square was crowded with their horses, their foals, their pigs and their poultry. The air was full of strident noise, and the reek of pitch, resin and alcohol pervaded everything.

The Jews sold the peasants whatever they needed – fish, shoes, ribbons, coloured paper to decorate their houses, tools, farm implements, and clothes. In the evening, the peasants clambered unsteadily onto their carts, drunk, and made their way back to their villages. The Jews closed their shops, and the empty square resumed its usual state, looking like a deserted battlefield. The end of market day was also the end of any contact between the Jews and their non-Jewish neighbours except for the rare occasions when a horse-drawn carriage drove up to one of the bigger shops, bringing the wife of one of the local gentry. She would step down from her carriage and be received with a great deal of bowing by the shopkeeper and his assistants, who hurried to supply her wants.

In the main part of the town, behind the Jewish houses, the non-Jews lived in small, low houses set in gardens full of flowers and trees. Chickens scratched about and cackled, and cattle wandered about the fenced yards. The Jewish and non-Jewish areas were quite separate, although some brave Jews did mix with the non-Jews, transacting all kinds of shady business with them. These Jews were feared by other Jews, non-Jews and officials alike. There were some brothers, living with their mother, who were mixed up in all kinds of roguery. To their credit be it said, however, that whenever there was any sort of quarrel between Jews and non-Jews, they always came to the aid of their brethren. Jewish artisans lived in the lanes and side turnings, and they were a group on their own.

The old synagogue, a squat building, was in the main street, while the new prayer-hall was in a side lane. This was the headquarters of the progressive elements of the town, where the young men dressed in ordinary clothes and without side-curls. Here they used to gather and say their prayers quickly. Not for them the long drawn-out services of the synagogue, the glass of wine to celebrate a birth or a Bar-Mitzvah. The young lads came early and helped the Rabbi's wife to put the room in order before the service started. The young girls stayed at home scouring the pots and pans and polishing the candlesticks, while their mothers hurried to the market, handkerchiefs round their heads, and baskets in their hands. When the Sabbath came, quietness reigned and the only non-Jew to be seen in the Jewish quarter was the Sabbath-goy who turned out the lamps for a slice of chala (Sabbath bread) and a glass of Sabbath wine, raising his hat and accepting them gratefully. The table was covered with a clean white cloth, the chala laid out ready under a small coloured napkin. The men put on their long, black, shiny coats and wore a black sash tied round their waists. They would set out for the synagogue with slow, measured steps, their sons who were not yet Bar-Mitzvah carrying their prayer books and prayer shawls.

The cantor started the service, chanting with his prayer shawl draped over his head, and the congregation sang the responses. At the reading of the Law, a preacher would mount the rostrum and give a sermon. After prayers were over, everyone would leave the synagogue, busily discussing politics and Zionism. Everyone would go to one of the houses to drink a glass of wine to celebrate a wedding or some other joyful occasion, and then all of us would make our way home for Sabbath lunch, followed by a good sleep in the afternoon. While their parents slept, the children played. Some people went for a walk as far as the new railway which had been built near the sugar factory. Young men and girls also went walking there. There it was also that one heard Russian spoken by the intelligentsia – the doctor, the chemist, and the other professional men.

As the Sabbath began to draw to a close, sadness would steal into people's hearts and deep sighs would escape them. Another week was beginning, another week of hard work and worry about earning a living.

The bitterness of exile in the Diaspora showed itself in their eyes, and the same old question possessed their minds – 'Where shall I find rest?' . . .

My father, Avraham Dayan, was an unlucky man. When he was a child he had somehow got into the middle of a herd of cows and a bull had attacked him, breaking his leg, so that he always walked with a limp. He did not want to become a ritual slaughterer like his father, Pinhas, and deliberately threw the special slaughtering knife on the ground to break the blade and spoil it so that it could not be used. Instead he decided to become a business man. He went into partnership with someone, got deeply into debt, and had to wind up the partnership. He was left without a farthing and without any means of earning a living in Djeskov, so he and his family of eight went to Odessa.

He was an honest man and a lover of truth, was not obsequious, and fought against injustice. All he wanted to do was to set up as a shopkeeper so that he could be independent of other people's assistance, but he was dogged by misfortune and could not make a success of anything.

The family were grief-stricken when the two-year-old, the child of our parents' old age, died. I was only five then, and they sent me back to Grandfather's house. Eventually they all came back, and Father became a commercial traveller.

As for me, my heart was not in studying the Torah, the Holy Law. They sent me to cheder (Hebrew religious classes) but I did not learn very much, and at the age of thirteen became an assistant to my father, who used to travel round to the various merchants, selling them cloth. Father trusted me, and I also had an aptitude for business, so every Monday I used to go to the main city of the region, Oman, to buy the cloth our clients had ordered, returning a day or two later. I used to ride on one of the wagons laden with boxes, bales, sacks and barrels, which constituted our road haulage service. We would deliver the cloth on Thursday and send in our bills on Fridays. On Sundays we collected new orders. On Mondays, I would go off to Oman again, and so on.

I became a real commercial traveller, and Ivan the carter used to prepare a special place for me on his wagon on some soft straw. His horses were well fed and beautifully looked after, but he was always rather drunk.

My parents made me wear a black fur coat with an enormous collar, and a wide red sash round my middle. I was so muffled up inside the coat that no part of me was visible at all, and it was so big and heavy that I had to have help to take it off. In the pocket I kept our orders and the money for the cloth I had to buy to fill them.

I worked six days a week, but on Saturdays I needed some sort of spiritual sustenance. At home, even then, copies of *Hatzefira* and Zionist pamphlets could be found interspersed with the holy books which constituted our library. A Zionist preacher gave me a sermon in the synagogue. A Bund meeting was held in secret in the loft. After the Kishinev pogroms we studied Bialik's poems. The death of Herzl was a sad blow.

I was 16 years old, and began to wonder where my life was leading. I was surrounded by an atmosphere of depression and uncertainty. Everyone was talking about the non-Jews' hatred of us in the Duma. Then a few copies of *Hapoel Hatzair* came into my hands. Yosef Vitkin's articles opened my eyes. 'Our people is sick. Come to Palestine, where you are needed!' And there was a short article by Hararit, its theme going straight to my heart: 'Mule drivers, shepherds, you will be like Rabbi Akiva was!' Then and there I decided that I would help to build my country, my motherland. But how could I do it, and how could I get there? 'The land of the Jordan and Mount Hermon, of Jerusalem and the Cave of Machpela, and the Dead Sea'. I dreamed of all these places, but when I mentioned my ambition to the family they regarded it as a joke. Just the same, my resolve grew stronger, and the journey began.

In June 1908 I arrived off Jaffa in a Russian cargo ship, and my journey at an end, I transferred to a small boat. Before I had had time to collect my thoughts, the boat had completed its rocky passage, and I was put ashore in Jaffa. The sandy wastes all around, and the Arabs with their strange dress and guttural cries all added to my bewilderment. As I stood there my heart was filled with doubt and disappointment.

When my passport was taken from me and I was given a red form in exchange I realised that I had now come under the sway of a new authority – that of the fez and the strange writing on the form. It was an unhappy moment for me and for my companions, but our hearts were lightened by two fellow-

Jews who had come down to the shore to receive us. One was a representative of the Jaffa branch of the Odessa Committee and the other a hotel owner.

We followed them, a porter preceding us with our luggage slung across his shoulders. As we negotiated the dark twisting lanes of the town, camels passed us with their bells jingling. All around us donkeys were braying, and the air was full of smells. Veiled Arab women passed by, and over all could be heard the strident voices and rattling copper mugs of the cold drink sellers.

The scene changed suddenly as we came to a courtyard and passed through it into a large hall with rooms leading off on two sides. Tables and benches had been put up and ran the length of the hall with its latticed windows. All round us stood bearded men and youths, the hotel owner and his wife in their midst, asking us all kinds of questions and telling us what had been happening in Jaffa.

There had been riots there, they said, and showed us broken windows to prove it.

We set off for the Odessa Committee's office to see if there was any work. I had taken off my coat and was dressed Russian style in a black shirt buttoned up to the neck, and with a cord tied round my middle to serve as a belt. 'Russian', the Arabs called after me, as I made my way to the office. 'There is work at Petach Tikva', we were told.

My sister, meanwhile had been given a letter recommending her as an assistant to a tailor in Jerusalem, so we took her to the railway station and set off to find the diligence (stagecoach) to Petach Tikva. Our fellow passengers were well-dressed farmers, loaded with shopping they were bringing back from town. They spoke a different Yiddish from us.

The journey took three hours, and as there was no made-up road, the diligence often got stuck in the sand. We passed many black Beduin tents on the way, their owners standing beside them holding rifles and revolvers. The countryside was open, empty and wide, with the hills and villages of Judaea in the distance. Adjoining the settlement were citrus groves, vineyards, and almond plantations, surrounded by rows of cactus plants (the well-known prickly pear or sabra). Arabs, men and women, were walking about the paths in the groves, and from time to time a Jew would ride among them on a horse or donkey.

Then we saw the white houses of Petach Tikva.

The diligence stopped in the centre of the settlement and was immediately surrounded by a crowd of people wanting news and letters. Our baggage was put off at Shabetai Rabinowitz's workers' hostel, and we stood looking about us at the lively scene. Young men were dancing in the street and one of the new immigrants immediately took a violin out of his luggage, and began to accompany them. Soon we were drawn into the circle of dancers and that was our introduction and our induction to the workers of Petach Tikva.

From The Promised Land, *ed.* Yaël Dayan (1961)

SCHMUEL DAYAN (1891 – 1968) was a pioneer of co-operative settlement in Erez Israel.

Boris Pasternak

THE TRAIN

An express train was leaving Kursk station on a hot summer morning in the year 1900. Just before the train started someone in a black Tyrolean cape appeared in the window. A tall woman was with him. Probably she would be his mother or his elder sister. The two of them and my father discussed a subject to which they were all warmly devoted, but the woman exchanged occasional words with my mother in Russian, while the stranger spoke German only. Although I knew the language thoroughly I had never heard it spoken as he spoke it. And for this reason, there on a platform thronged with people, between two bells, this stranger struck me as a silhouette in the midst of bodies, a fiction in the mass of reality.

On our journey, nearer Tula, the couple reappeared, this time in our compartment. They talked about not being able to rely on the express stopping at Kozlovka-Zaseka, and they were not certain whether the guard would tell the engine-driver in time to pull up at the Tolstoys. From the talk following this, I concluded that they were on their way to Sophia Andreyevna, because she was going to Moscow for the symphony concerts, and she had been to see us not long ago – an endlessly important theme which was symbolised by the initials Count L.N. and played an obscure role in our family yet one discussed to saturation point, though without suggesting the personality of a man. It was seen too far back in childhood. His grey hair, afterwards renewed in my memory by the drawings of my father, Repin and others, had in my child's imagination long been assigned to another old man whom I saw more often and probably later – to Nikolai Nikolaevich Gay.

Then they said goodbye and returned to their own compartment. A little later the rushing embankment was suddenly held in check by the brakes. There was a glimpse of birch trees. The buffers snorted and knocked against one another along the whole stretch of railway track. With relief a cloud-piled sky tore itself from the whirlwind of singing sand. Skirting the grove, an empty carriage and pair, flinging itself forward as though dancing the *russkaya*, hopped up to meet the passengers who had just got down. The silence of a road-way which had nothing to do with us was yet disturbing momentarily, like a shot. It was not for us to stop here. They waved their handkerchiefs in farewell. We waved back. We could just see how the coachman with his long red sleeves helped them up, how he gave the lady a dust apron, and raised himself a little to adjust his belt and gather in the long tails of his coat. In a moment he would start. Meanwhile a bend caught us up, and the wayside halt, turning slowly like a page that has been read, vanished from sight. The face and the incident were forgotten, presumably forgotten for ever.

From Safe Conduct, *tr.* Beatrice Scott

BORIS PASTERNAK (1890–1960), Russian poet, novelist, dramatist and translator (of Shakespeare and Goethe), was born in Moscow, the son of a painter. His best-known work in the West is *Dr Zhivago*, banned in USSR, for which he was awarded the Nobel Prize in 1958: he was forbidden to accept it.

Sergei Eisenstein

IMAGE OF CRUELTY

In Petersburg Mama lives at Tavricheskaya Street Number 9. Main entrance through the courtyard. A lift. White marble fireplace downstairs. For me, it is always winter here: year after year I come here only at Christmas.

The fireplace is always burning merrily. A soft red carpet runs up the stairs. Mama's boudoir is upholstered in a light cream material. On a light background are scattered tiny pink wreaths. So with the draperies. The carpet – the same tone as the wreaths – is pale rose. The boudoir is also the bedroom. This is divided by two screens, hiding Mama's bedstead. The screens too are in rosebud crowns.

Many years later – already a student, already living permanently with Mama – I catch measles here for the second time. The windows are curtained. The sun beats through the blinds. The room is flooded with a bright pink light . . . Is it a fever?

Not only a fever: the lining of the blinds is also pink. The sun's rays, piercing through the lining, turn pink. The same pink light that shines through your fingers when you hold them up to the lamplight, or when, with closed eyelids, you turn your head toward the sun.

The rosy light merges with the fever and delirium of sickness.

Grandmother's bedroom – I remember being in it when very small – was all blue. Blue velvet on the low chairs and long blue draperies. Did Granny have a blue period? And Mama a pink one?

Now the draperies and furniture from Mama's boudoir spend the rest of their life in my summer home. The pink wreaths can hardly be seen. The upholstery is now gray. The velvet on the armchairs is torn in places, and the bottoms of the seats seem like jaws from which several teeth are missing.

The gray period?

When my mother lived among the furniture, the divans, settees, and sofas were strewn all over the books. More often than not they were yellow volumes published by Calmann-Lévy Books from the library of a lady of decisive and independent views.

Holding first place: *Nietzschéenne*, then the invariable *Sur la Branche* by Pierre de Coulevain, and, of course, *Demimondaine* by Bourget, relieving *Demi-Lumière* by Dumas fils.

I never looked inside those yellow covers. . . .

In the little divans and sofas I found two other books. I did look into these, and more than once, but with apprehension, with a certain excitement, even with . . . fear.

Those books I assiduously crammed between the back and the seat of the armchairs and divans. I covered them up with cushions, embroidered by Mama in the manner of 'Richelieu.' (Fretted drawings, parts of which are held together by means of a system of tiny straps. How many of such patterns I traced from journals for Mama! How many I later combined or created independently!)

I hid those books out of embarrassment, out of fear, because of what was in them, and because I wanted to make sure I could get at them when I wanted to. For there were many frightening things in *The Garden of Torture* by Octave Mirbeau and Sacher-Masoch's illustrated *Venus in Furs*.

These were the first examples of 'unhealthy desires' that fell into my hands.

And even though Krafft-Ebing came into my hands somewhat later, it is toward the first two books I still retain a feeling of sickly hostility.

Sometimes I wonder why I never play games of chance. I don't think it's from a lack of inclination. Quite the opposite. It is from my fear of being afraid. This fear came to me in childhood when I wasn't frightened of the dark but was afraid that if I awoke in the darkness, I should be frightened.

That is why I make a wide circle to avoid games of chance. I am afraid that if I touch them once, I should never be able to hold myself back.

In my mother's white rosebud boudoir, I feverishly followed the stock exchange reports when Mama decided to gamble on the exchange with a small sum of 'free' money.

Not in vain did I manage to evade the attraction of Mirbeau and Masoch. I came in contact with the alarming vein of cruelty much earlier through a living impression, a living impression from the cinema screen.

It was one of the earliest films I ever saw, no doubt produced by Pathé. The story took place during the Napoleonic Wars. In the house of a blacksmith was a military billet. The young wife of the blacksmith commits adultery with a young Empire sergeant. The husband finds out,. catches and binds the sergeant. Throws him in the hayloft. He tears off the soldier's uniform, baring his shoulders, and brands him with a red-hot iron.

I remember vividly the naked shoulder, a great iron bar in the muscular hands of the blacksmith, the black smoke and white steam rising from the charred flesh.

The sergeant falls senseless. The blacksmith brings a gendarme. Before them – a man lying unconscious with naked shoulders. On his shoulder – the brand of a convict.

The sergeant is arrested as an escapee and imprisoned in Toulon. The film's end is sentimentally heroic. The smithy is on fire. The former sergeant saves the wife of the blacksmith. As he does so, the 'brand of shame' disappears in his new burns.

Why does the smithy burn? Many years later? Does the sergeant save the blacksmith as well as the wife? Who pardons the convict? I have forgotten all that, but the scene of branding remains ineradicably in my memory to this very day.

In childhood it tortured me with nightmares. I imagined it at night. I saw myself either as the sergeant or the blacksmith. I caught hold of the bare shoulders. Sometimes they seemed to be mine, sometimes someone else's. It was never clear who was branding whom. For many years fair hair (the sergeant was blond) or black barrels and Napoleonic uniforms inevitably recalled that scene to my memory. Indeed, I developed a partiality for the Empire style.

To this day no sea of fire has swallowed the branding of the convict; no oceans of cruelty, which permeates my own films, have drowned the early impressions of that ill-starred film and the two novels on which it was undoubtedly based. . . .

Let us not forget that my childhood was passed in Riga, during the climax of the 1905 Revolution. And there are still so many more terrible and cruel impressions all around – the rampaging reaction and repression by Meller-Zakomelsky and his kind. Let us not forget this, all the more so because in my films cruelty is inextricably intertwined with the theme of social injustice and rebellion against it.

From Immoral Memories, *tr.* Herbert Marshall (1985)

SERGEI EISENSTEIN (1898–1948), Russian film director, was born in Riga, Latvia. His film *The Battleship Potemkin* (1925) revolutionised the art of the cinema, and led to *Alexander Nevsky* (1938) and *Ivan the Terrible* (1944).

Golda Meir

THE COSSACKS AND THE SWAMPS

The town that I remember was filled with Jews. Pinsk was one of the most celebrated centres of Russian-Jewish life and at one time even had had a Jewish majority. It was built on two great rivers, the Pina and the Pripet – both of which flow into the Dnieper – and it was these rivers that supplied most of the Jews of Pinsk with their livelihood. They fished, unloaded cargo, did porterage, broke the giant ice floes in winter and dragged the ice to huge storage cellars in the houses of the well-to-do, where they served to create cooling facilities all through the summer. At one time my grandfather, who was fairly well off compared to my parents, owned such a cellar to which neighbours brought their Sabbath and holiday dishes when it was very hot and from which they took ice for the sick. The richer Jews dealt in timber and in the salt trade; and Pinsk even had nail, plywood and match factories that were owned by Jews and, of course, gave employment to dozens of Jewish workers.

But I remember mostly the *Pinsker blotte*, as we called them at home, the swamps that seemed to me then like oceans of mud and which we were taught to avoid like the plague. In my memory, those swamps are forever linked to my persistent terror of the Cossacks, to a winter night when I played with other children in a narrow lane near the forbidden *blotte* and then suddenly, as though out of nowhere, or maybe out of the swamps themselves, came the Cossacks on their horses, literally galloping over our crouching, shivering bodies. 'Well,' said my mother later, shivering and crying herself, 'what did I tell you?'

Cossacks and the black bottomless swamps, however, were not the only terrors Pinsk held for me. I can remember a row of big buildings on a street that led to the river and the monastery that stood opposite the buildings on a hill. In front of it, all day, sat or lay numbers of wild-haired wild-eyed cripples who prayed aloud and begged for alms. I tried to avoid passing them, and when I had to I closed my eyes and ran. But if Mother really wanted to frighten me, she knew that all she had to do was mention the beggars and I would abandon all defiance.

Still, not everything could have been so fearful. I was a child, and like all children I played and sang and made up stories to tell the baby. With Sheyna's help, I learned to read and write and even do a little arithmetic, though I didn't start school in Pinsk, as I should have. 'A golden child, they called you,' my mother said. 'Always busy with something.' But what I was really busy doing in Pinsk, I suppose, was learning about life – again, chiefly from Sheyna.

Sheyna was fourteen when Father left for the States, a remarkable, intense, intelligent girl who became, and who remained, one of the great influences of my life – perhaps the greatest, apart from the man I married. By any standard, she was an unusual person, and for me she was a shining example, my dearest friend and my mentor. Even late in life when we were both grown women, grandmothers in fact, Sheyna was the one person whose praise and approval – when I won them, which was not easy – meant most to me. Sheyna, in fact, is part and parcel of the story of my life. She died in 1972, but I think of her constantly, and her children and grandchildren are as dear to me as my own.

In Pinsk, although we were so pitifully poor and Mother only barely managed (with my grandfather's help) to keep us going, Sheyna refused to go to work. The move back to Pinsk had been very hard on her. She had gone to a wonderful school in Kiev, and she was bent on studying, on acquiring knowledge and getting an education, not only so that she herself would have a fuller and better life but, even more, so that she could help to change and better the world. At fourteen, Sheyna was a revolutionary, an earnest, dedicated member of the Socialist-Zionist movement, and as such doubly dangerous in the eyes of the police and liable to punishment. Not only were she and her friends 'conspiring' to overthrow the all-powerful czar, but they also proclaimed their dream to bring into existence a Jewish socialist state in Palestine. In the Russia of the early twentieth century, even a fourteen- or fifteen-year-old schoolgirl who held such views would be arrested for subversive activity, and I still remember hearing the screams of young men and women being brutally beaten in the police station around the corner from where we lived.

My mother heard those screams, too, and daily begged Sheyna to have nothing to do with the movement; she could endanger herself and us and even Father in America! But Sheyna was very stubborn. It was not enough for her to want changes; she herself had to participate in bringing them about. Night after night, my mother kept herself awake until Sheyna came home from her mysterious meetings, while I lay in bed taking it all in silently – Sheyna's devotion to the cause in which she believed so strongly, Mother's overwhelming anxiety, Father's (to me, inexplicable) absence and the periodic and fearful sound of the hooves of Cossack horses outside.

On Saturdays, when Mother went off to synagogue, Sheyna organised meetings at home. Even when Mother found out about them and pleaded with Sheyna not to imperil us, there was nothing she could do about these meetings except nervously walk up and down outside the house when she got back on Saturday morning, patrolling it like a sentry so that when a policeman approached she could at least warn the young conspirators. But it wasn't only the idea that an ordinary policeman might swoop down at any moment and arrest Sheyna that so worried my poor mother. What really gnawed at her heart throughout all those months was the fear (always rampant in the Russia of those days) that one or another of Sheyna's friends might turn out to be an *agent provocateur*.

Of course, I was much too small to understand the reason for the arguments and tears and door-slammings, but I used to squeeze myself on to the flat top of our big coal stove (which was built into the wall) and sit there for hours on those Saturday mornings, listening to Sheyna and her friends and trying to make out what it was that they were all so excited about and why it made my mother cry so. Sometimes when I pretended to be engrossed in drawing or in copying the strangely shaped letters in the *siddur* (the Hebrew prayer book), which was one of the few books in our house, I tried to follow what Sheyna was so fervently explaining to my mother, but all I gathered was that she was involved in a special kind of struggle that concerned not only the Russian people but also, and more especially, the Jews.

From My Life (1975)

GOLDA MEIR (1898–1978), Israeli politician, was born in Kiev, Russia, and emigrated to America in 1906, and from there to Palestine in 1921. She was Prime Minister of Israel 1969–74.

Victor Gollancz

CHILDHOOD FEARS

I had lived, since the age of six in the one case and eleven or twelve in the other, with a horror, the sort of horror that goes about with a man and never leaves him, of two abominations – which I constantly visualised as happening here and now, and happening to me: poverty and war. I don't mean by this that I was *afraid* of them happening to me, though some fear of the kind, for all I know, may have been the real explanation: I mean that when I came up against them I immediately thought myself into them, imagined what I should be feeling if I were suffering them, and then imagined the other man in my own imagined shoes. It was war, and not poverty, that was my first horror. On a table in our drawing-room, by the piano, was a very large and very thick volume, bound in elaborately gilt buckram with broad bevelled edges, called 'Sixty Years a Queen': it had been issued in commemoration of the Diamond Jubilee, and was chock-full of pictures, on heavily coated 'art paper', illustrating events of the reign. I was looking through this book one day, round about my sixth birthday, when I came across a couple of pictures that faced one another: on the right-hand page was the Charge of the Light Brigade (at Balaclava) and on the left-hand page was the Charge of the Heavy Brigade. In one or other of them, I don't remember which, a man on horseback was slashing down with a sabre at another man's head, and the other man's head was – half off. I'm back again now, from half a century later, in the Elgin Avenue drawing-room; or not in the Elgin Avenue drawing-room, because as I looked *I* was the man with the head off, and the whole of me was an agony of pain and an obscene degradation. It was at this moment that my horror of war was consciously born; a horror that was then, as it has been ever since, a horror as of something that was in the same room with me, that was on the very table in front of me, that was outraging *me*, even though it might really be happening in China or Spain. And a horror not only of war; a horror also of violence, and of flogging, and of capital punishment, and of all the other unspeakable outrages that never fail to produce in me a feeling of personal contamination.

It must have been only a month or so after the Balaclava episode that I learned, I don't remember how, about guns. What appalled me immediately was that a man could be killed in a *second*. I said in my mind – my recollection is so clear that my mind might be saying it now – 'But how . . . how . . . *nothing*' (that is the way my childish thought formulated it: nothing, unreality, no purpose or meaning) 'how *nothing* that a man it's taken twenty years to make, with all the meals and the lessons and the getting up and the going to bed and the dressing and the walks and the being "brought up", can completely *stop* from a bullet *immediately*. What was the *point* of all the things *before* the bullet?' If I am not mistaken, Talleyrand, at a riper age, said very much the same.

My other horror, my horror of poverty, came later, when I was eleven or twelve. This was during my first term at St. Paul's. I used to get there by walking up Elgin Avenue to Westbourne Park station, and then taking the Metropolitan to Hammersmith. Just outside Westbourne Park, flanking the line on the left as you went westward, was a long row of houses, so miserable and squalid, so black and beastly and corrupt, that the idea of people actually living in them, actually getting up every day in them and having meals every day in them and going to bed every day in them, filled me with a sensation of loathing and despair. For at once I thought 'people like *me*'; at once I contrasted my own comfortable bed, and the curios my Aunt Minna had given me from the Sahara desert, and fires, and our little narrow garden, and lying on the sofa in the downstairs parlour on Saturday afternoons with a book and raspberry-jam sandwiches for tea – I contrasted all this with the dirt and the smell and the decaying fish-bones to which these other people, these people like me, these people who suddenly *were* me, were condemned. And just as it was the instantaneity, the all-over-in-a-secondness, that had appalled me in the case of the bullet, so it was the interminability, the never-to-be-over-at-allness, that appalled me in the case of my Westbourne Park houses. It is this aspect of the direst poverty – the utter lack of hope that it can ever end – that still seems to me the most awful thing about it.

You may think, my dear Timothy, that I was exaggerating, and that it was only by contrast with the palace in which I lived that these other houses struck me as so disgusting. No, I wasn't exaggerating. I didn't live in a palace: houses in Elgin Avenue weren't palaces, and my father was a small business man, midway between a jeweller with a shop and a petty wholesaler, whose income from a twelve-hour day varied from five or six hundred a year to an occasional thousand. And I was right about the Westbourne Park houses, I feel certain; for I 'looked into' similar ones when I was old enough to know how to go about such things, and confirmed my childish impressions.

Within a very few weeks I was to see the most disgusting poverty at even closer quarters. My parents were orthodox Jews, and it is 'forbidden' among such to ride, drive, or be driven anywhere from sunset on Friday evening, when the Sabbath begins, to sunset on Saturday evening, when it ends. You mustn't pedal a bicycle, or be driven by a horse, or go in any sort of car or train; if you want to get anywhere, you must walk.

This ban (to anticipate by a few minutes what I shall presently be saying in much greater detail) was one of those irrationalities that made me detest orthodox Judaism almost as soon as I was born. The thing, of course, had long since been nothing but a tabu, even at the time of which I am writing, and I imagine that the number of Jews who observe it today is comparatively negligible; but there's an explanation of sorts, if you go back far enough. God rested on the seventh day: men must do no work on it: but to manipulate a vehicle means work – your own, if you do the manipulating, or other people's, if they do. Therefore you may neither drive nor be driven. Now back in Biblical Palestine, or even in the ghetto, this had logic of a sort, granted the premises; for the entire community, more or less, being Jewish – the potential drivers as well as the potentially driven – no vehicle could proceed without somebody breaking the Sabbath. But the entire community was by no means Jewish in the England of the nineteen hundreds. The trains ran anyhow, on Saturday if not on Sunday, so if a Jew took a ride in one how possibly could he be committing an *avārah*? . . .

Now sunset gets earlier and earlier as the winter gets nearer and nearer; and I was in my first year at St. Paul's; and a Friday arrived; and school wasn't over till five; and Sabbath 'came in' at 4.50, or maybe 4.59; and riding was tabu; and from Hammersmith Broadway to Maida Vale is a distance of – heaven knows how many miles. These miles had to be walked, that Friday night and every Friday night till the days drew out, that year and every year until the year of my revolt. I was chaperoned by two much older boys, who of course were also Jews – otherwise they wouldn't have been walking – and who lived in my part of the world and knew the way. They were 'nibs' of eighteen or so, and one of them had already got a scholarship at Trinity, as you could tell from the mortar-board and gown in which he strode like a master down the corridor that led to the Eighth; and they were very stand-offish as they guided me those many Friday nights from Hammersmith to Elgin Avenue, forbidding me to speak unless spoken to, and keeping me ashuffle in their rear from the moment we set out till the moment, hours later, we arrived. Our way took us through a number of indifferent localities; but through a couple (the routes being alternative) which might almost have deliberately been put there to typify the 'two nations' into which the England of that day was as surely divided as it had been in Disraeli's. One of these localities was Kensington Palace Gardens, already known, I think, as 'Millionaires' Row': it stretched, a great noiseless carriage-way, with its own private gates and its line of what I had once heard described as domestic palaces, from Kensington High Street to the Bayswater Road. Flunkeys were at the entrance to guard it, in greatcoats of blue and chimney-pots braided with gold. The other locality was the neighbourhood of Latimer Road. I am not sure whether this was actually identical with the district nicknamed 'the Piggeries' or merely adjacent to it, nor whether 'Piggeries' was a term to be understood literally, with reference to some occupational tradition, or was just pejorative; but what I do know is that though I have been through many slums in the meantime that have made the sick saliva come dribbling into my mouth, I can think of none more hellish than the Latimer ones of nineteen hundred and five. Their beastliness was intensified for me, no doubt, by the drizzly coldness of the weather in which I traversed those November streets, and by the wretched dimness of the lighting that made of the darkness and night not the lovely things they are, but images of an evil half exposed. Hot sun can redeem anything. There are slums in Naples even viler, perhaps, than the vilest in the England of some fifty years ago; but the radiance of noonday somehow encloses and absorbs them, and half purges them of their misery.

Even worse than the walls and the windows of my Latimer houses, and the general aspect of the streets, was what I saw or half saw every now and again through an open doorway, spotty with sprawling children; and even worse than what I saw was what I imagined. I imagined the lavatories. Dirty and sordid lavatories have always obsessed me, and I still occasionally have nightmares about them. There are Freudian explanations for this obsession which seem reasonable to me; but I derive it in my own case from a visit to the lavatory on my very first day at St. Paul's, and the shock it gave my instincts for cleanliness and beauty. Through one of many doors in a row, with the paint flaking off them, you entered a cubicle of rather grimy roughcast, and sat down on a depolished seat. Below the hole in the seat was a trough of stale water, which ran undivided from the beginning of the row to its end. Lying in the water, or floating sluggishly down from higher up the stream, were lumps of ugly faeces, which emitted a mouldering smell. I didn't like it; I liked it so little that I preferred, during my whole time at St. Paul's, to endure agonies of restraint right up to the last possible minute, rather than visit the horrible *cabinetto*. (I must hasten to add that all this has long been changed, and that the lavatories at St. Paul's are now of quite exceptional beauty.) And I asked myself now, as I walked down Latimer Road on my Sabbath pilgrimage: if even at St. Paul's there are lavatories like that, what on earth must they be like in the Latimer Road? I was to find later on, when I was visiting a slum area in the North of England, that my imagination had been feebly inadequate.

So the horror of poverty and the horror of war, which together would be shaping my future, were already an inextricable part of me, the one when I was six and the other when I was twelve. But the two were accompanied by, or enclosed in, or perhaps took their life from, a less particularised, a more integral passion: a passion for liberty in every possible meaning of the word (so far as I then understood it), liberty for myself every bit as much as for every other living thing and for every other living thing every bit as much as for myself.

From My Dear Timothy (1952)

SIR VICTOR GOLLANCZ (1893–1967), British publisher, writer and campaigner, was born in London.

G.B. Stern

POTTED HISTORY

When we are children we learn history by quantities of little unrelated pictorial anecdotes, that adhere to memory with such obstinacy that no amount of scholarly research later on will ever quite dislodge them; small clear pictures in the bright colours of an illuminated missal, which Chesterton once called 'keyholes to Heaven and Hell'. In my weakness for making lists, I compiled a list of these the other day, inviting contributions from two friends who were spending the evening with me. Here is the result:

Woad, Druids and mistletoe.
Alfred and the Cakes.
Boadicea and the bleeding rods.
Phoenicians (tin and indigo dyes).
Winged hats and beaked ships.
Harold and Senlac and the arrow.
William Rufus and the other arrow.
Fair Rosamund and the Maze.
Henry II doing penance for Beckett.
King John at Runnymede. Simon de Montfort.
Bruce and the spider.
Wallace – 'Scots wha hae wi' . . . '
'Let the boy win his spurs', and that disgraceful exhibitionist the Black Prince on a pony, with the king of France mounted on a big white horse, riding captive beside him.
Richard II and Wat Tyler.
York and Lancaster roses, and a Kingmaker.
Queen Philippa and the Burghers of Calais.
Queen Eleanor who sucked the poison from somebody's wound. } (interchangeable)
Henry VIII had six wives.
Princes in the Tower, bobbed hair, black velvet tunics and tights, smothered by wicked uncle. Babes in the Wood.
Elizabeth on a white horse. Raleigh and the cloak. Drake and the Armada; beacons; we won. She never married(?).
Mary Queen of Scots. Pearls. Rizzio and being beheaded. And Hollywood (*no*, dear, Holyrood).
Edward VI and Lady Jane Grey, very clever and pale; studied Latin.
Charles II and the oak tree and the Orange girl. And being an awful long time a-dying.
Cromwell: 'Take away this Bauble'.
Nelson's 'Kiss me, Hardy'. Trafalgar. We won.
'Up, guards, and at 'em' on my pencil-box. We won.

Victoria – 'I will be good' and her Accession in a shawl and nightgown.
'Angels not Angles'. (Alternatively: 'Angles not Angels'.)
Perkin Warbeck and Lambert Simnel who became a scullion. And a cake.
Llewellyn and Bedgelert.
Butt of Malmsey that Clarence was drowned in.
A king who died of a surfeit of palfreys, or was it peaches dipped in the Wash?
'When did you last see your father?' ('Now let me see . . . Don't *hurry* me . . . I can only think properly when I'm not hurried. Was it Thursday? No, wait a moment, I'm wrong; I *did* see him Thursday, but he was sober; and I saw him again afterwards when he was carrying on in an awfully silly way, and tried to walk straight through a picture – yes, that one over there.')
Field of the Cloth of Gold.

And we neither knew nor cared what these historical people did in the intervals, when they were not doing or saying these little things.

The Field of the Cloth of Gold, vague and splendid, figured in that portion of history when Henry VIII was on the throne of England, Charles V on the throne of Spain, and Francis I on the throne of France. It was always a little surprising, at our Little Arthur's period of childhood, when we were taken for even a brief excursion across the Channel to any other history which was not English pure and simple (insular little beasts, but our teachers were to blame as well!). Later I learnt that Charles V was nephew-in-law to Henry VIII, and that Cardinal Wolsey craftily used the antagonism between Spain and France to make England arbiter between them; so that must have been when all those yards of expensive gold cloth were measured out and shipped across to decorate the conference with an illusion of grandeur and glory that our conferences nowadays most soberly lack.

Among other ostentatious gestures to impress his nephew-in-law, Henry sent him a gift of four hundred of his noble breed of mastiffs: 'Don't thank me, dear boy; I can easily spare them; plenty more at home.'

From Benefits Forgot (1949)

GLADYS BRONWEN STERN (1890–1973), British novelist, was born in London. *Tents of Israel* (1924), republished later as *The Matriarch*, was the first of six novels about the Rakonitz family.

Louis Golding

ADVENCHERS

I did not lisp in numbers, for I inherited from my father a clear articulation. He was a sacerdotal orator by profession, as well as a teacher, and I inherited from him also an almost ecstatic love of the Word for its own sake. The Word – the word is used not so much theologically as physiologically – meant almost the same thing to me written or spoken. I still do not see it without simultaneously hearing it. When I heard my father orating in dusking synagogues on Sabbath evenings, in a voice which still remains to me the loveliest, the most bell-like, of all remembered voices, despite our protracted internecine war, the words took shape before my five-year-old eyes. They were jets of water, they were stalks of grass, they were heavy paving-stones.

I composed a poem not long after, for it was inevitable I should soon be playing about with words on my own account. It was a good poem, spontaneous in feeling, revolutionary in technique, and it had actuality. It went:

> *He got a big smack*
> *and said he'd go back*
> *To school*
> *– The fool!*

I was proud of that poem. So was my mother. My father was indifferent to it. I am not sure whether I could read or write yet. It was carried about in my head as the minstrel carried his lays.

My first written poem was very literary and definitely inferior. It ran like this:

> *Alone I walked, I walked alone.*
> *My twitt'ring bird on high I heeded not.*
> *I heeded not my flower pompous grown,*
> *And at my twitt'ring little brook,*
> *I gazed not nor e'en gave a look*
> *Of fondling. . . .*

The spelling must have been less exact, but I have lost the original manuscript.

It was largely the intractability of that poem which turned me into a novelist. First of all there was the line, 'I gazed not nor e'en gave a look. . . .' It was as odious to look at as to listen to. I tried to adapt it one way and another, but it remained obdurate. Further, the poem stopped without coming to an end. It could not continue itself. I beat my head against a stone wall suspended in mid-air.

And then my sister, Janey, read me aloud a poem by another writer. It was called 'The May Queen.' That concluded my rout along two lines of attack.

In the first place I realised that no poet ever again could achieve such fluency and flexibility. In the second place it made me cry my eyes out. I despised myself. I said: if that is the effect of poetry, I've finished with it. I shall be a fireman or a millionaire or Dr. Saul in Cheetham Hill Road, but I shall be no poet.

I did not consciously make up my mind to be, on the contrary, a novelist, until I met a certain old lady in a tram. I may have considered her quite a nice old lady, till she addressed me as 'little man.' 'And now, little man,' she said, 'what are *you* going to be when you grow up?'

I resisted violently the temptation to stick my tongue out at her. And this I did by concentrating on the subject she had propounded, a subject which had only vaguely occupied me before. What, after all, was I going to be when I grew up? And then suddenly the decision crystallised. I knew in that moment there was nothing else I wanted to be, or was capable of being. 'I'm going to be an aufor.' 'Aufor' definitely mean 'novelist.' I had had quite enough of being a poet, as I have said, for the time being.

'And what are you going to write?' asked the old lady.

My reply was instantaneous. 'Circus tales. And school tales.' And then, as if I was aware that those were not the highest achievements of authorship, I qualified: 'But wiv a moral!'

It may be as a result of my reaction from that early avowal, that I have never consciously saddled my more mature works with a moral, and that I have never attempted either a circus tale, or a school tale, with or without a moral.

My first attempt in fiction followed not long after. I suppose that its diction and form were dictated by the boys' magazines I was still reading avidly, in which there was always a busy traffic in the market-place during school playtimes: I mean such stalwart weeklies as the *Marvel*, *Pluck*, the *Union Jack*, the *Boy's Friend*, some of which survive to this day, I believe.

My first novel, then, was entitled: *The Advenchers of Three on Bludy Island*. The three were the captain, the engineer, and the cabin-boy, on the model of the triune heroes of my magazines. The novel plunged *in medias res* with a promptness and vividness which I have sought in vain to emulate in more mature endeavours in fiction. It opened, like *The Tempest*, in the midst of a howling storm. Thunder crashed. Lightning spat. Waves roared sky-high. And at the very heart of the storm a ship was seen driving inevitably against the rocks. I remember the unction with which I conceived and set down the word 'inevitably.' I reported it both to my mother, who was as pleased with it as I, and to Miss Brown, my teacher, who had one of her attacks of stomach-ache, and was less impressed.

But there were one or two climaxes to come. In the crash against the inevitable rocks, the ship foundered with all hands, except for the captain, the engineer, and the cabin-boy, who, amid the seething ruin, managed hastily to rig up a raft. But, alas, hardly an hour later, the undiminished seas washed the cabin-boy overboard. The storm raged for six days and nights and then, on the seventh, miraculously subsided. The tropic sun shone in a cloudless sky. Thereupon the captain and the engineer busied themselves with a fishing-rod and a length of twine which they had fortunately salvaged from the wreck along with certain other equipment. The line was cast. 'And what were they fishing for?' I remember the oratorical question vividly, and the triumphant reply? 'They were fishing for a human life.' In an hour or two there was a jerk on the line. The cabin-boy was hooked. He was lifted to the surface and placed on the raft. Artificial respiration was applied to him, and three-quarters of an hour later he opened his eyes again with a gentle sigh. He was in perfect condition, excepting for the fact that a shark had bitten off his left calf. . . .

On reflection I am wrong in saying that I did not attempt a school novel. The successor to the *Advenchers of Three on Bludy Island* was a chapter, but only one, of the Advenchers of another Three, this time at St. Marylebone. The heroes were the son of a fox-hunting squire, of an Argentine rancher, and of a Jewish financier. I only remember the name of the third. It was Rothschild. I was at particular pains to point out that the fortunes of Rothschild Père were made not by sharp dealing but by honest labour. There must have been a note of tendentiousness in that insistence, so that, within those limits, there was a moral to that tale. The story collapsed under the pyramid of Master Rothschild's impossible virtues. I did not attempt a financier again till I evoked a certain Smirnof, many years later, and he was only half a Jew.

The first phase of my novelistic career ended when I was about ten or eleven with an Alpine-climbing novel. But I had climbed so few Alps that my narrative petered out for want of material. I was not sorry. I had been reading Shelley and Edgar Poe rabidly for some time, particularly Edgar Poe, and under this compulsion I returned to my first love, poetry.

I still engaged publicly in the practice of prose. I had moved to the Southall Street Elementary School, where they taught French, and there was hope, therefore, that I might win a scholarship to the Manchester Grammar School. A Mr. Ashworth was the teacher of Standard Seven, and I owe more than I shall ever be able to estimate to his sympathy and his swift intuition. I wrote essays for him, which gave him more pleasure than they gave the class. He read them aloud and discovered virtues in them which I had not suspected, and which embittered my class-mates. I had not even intended them, for I had grown contemptuous of prose. Night after night, for long hours after midnight, to the crepitation of black-beetles between the wall and the wall-paper, I wrote long labial melancholy poems. I share a vanity common to most writers. I, too, am convinced that no poems since the invention of writing were as bad as my early love-poems. They were all about maidens called Laremia, Lenoria, Loramia. Loramia was a frequent maiden.

> *Loramia was a winsome maid,*
> *Loramia was my bride.*
> *She left me for a stranger's smile*
> *And she crossed the ocean wide*
> *– Loramia, cruel, cruel!*

By this time I had won my scholarship to the Manchester Grammar School. I remember a forlorn attempt to publish a volume of poems in collaboration with the first of my literary friends, Maurice Samuel, who subsequently became a novelist and orator of note in the United States. I remember the exquisitely tactful way in which John Lewis Paton, my most-beloved High Master, tackled the situation. He made the agony of the failure just bearable. I was driven into a poetry more mournful and horrific than before:

> *Zarda's plains are stained, alas!*
> *Woe betide, ah woe betide!*
> *Green before, now red the grass!*
> *Ah! Woe betide!*

It went on like that for a good many stanzas, with the substitution for 'Woe betide,' of 'Lackaday,' 'Welladay,' and 'Woe is me.' Woe was me for quite a long time to come, till the High Master induced the editor of *Ulula*, the school magazine, to print a poem by a writer who somewhat crudely disguised his identity under the pen-name 'Gholedynge.' I ran from school to Harris Street that day carolling blithely, waving the little blue sheet like a banner. My mother gave me a dish of whinberries in sour cream. She was proud of her small poet.

I was destined not to read to her many more of my poems. Some months later she became seriously ill, and almost before we realised it was not she who was scouring her brasses or cooking the Sabbath dinner, it was clear she would be dead in a week or two. I said to myself fiercely: 'I will make her death bearable by writing a great poem about her life and death.' And long nights after she died, I sat up to make her lovely for ever in octosyllabic couplets. It was a lengthy poem, but the grief was longer. I managed to make the circumstances of her death less desolate by exteriorising them and giving them precise shape, in my first novel, *Forward from Babylon*.

From The World I Knew (1940)

LOUIS GOLDING (1895–1958), British novelist and author of *Magnolia Street* (1932), was born in Manchester.

Bud Flanagan

THE RUNAWAY

I took my usual halfpenny that morning from my mother. She gave me one every day to spend at school. I'm sorry to say she didn't see me again for a very long time. I had saved a few shillings and decided to walk to Southampton. The traffic was practically nil, and there were no hitch-hikers in those days. I used up my cash on food and somewhere to sleep.

In Southampton, broke but eager for adventure, I found the Seamen's Home, where they asked a shilling a night for a bed. I hadn't a penny. Perhaps, I thought desperately, they might need a call boy at the local theatre. Meanwhile, I wandered off in the direction of a park, thinking that if I couldn't find a job, I could always sleep on the grass. It was summer, anyway.

My thoughts went back to my parents, trying to imagine what their feelings were. I hadn't been home for nearly a week. In a panic I thought that the school truant man must have called.

Right opposite the park was a theatre with a queue all round it. My hopes rose, and I started looking for the Stage Door. In I went, and out I came. They already had a call boy. The posters outside were no help in finding someone on the bill I knew. It was a musical comedy. I had never seen one, but knew it was mostly singing. Suddenly, it struck me that singing might be a good way to make enough for a bed. Why not sing to the queue of people around the theatre waiting to go in? They called it busking, and it took nerve. Singing in the theatre is a 'doddle' compared with singing in the streets. Anyway, it was the park or the Seamen's Home.

I started to sing Dora Lyric's 'My Boy' and followed that up with her other song. I had no cap with me and held my hand out timidly, and in no time took three shillings in copper and a silver threepenny bit.

As the queue started to move, a policeman was coming towards me. I was quickly away, heading for the Seamen's Home, where I paid for and booked a bed for the night. The air was thick with the nasal twang of Liverpool, certainly one of the most difficult dialects to understand, but I kept my ears well open.

It didn't take me long to find out the ways and means of getting a ship; a Union card wasn't necessary then; all you had to do was see a man at the Home, tell him you wanted a ship, and leave the rest to him.

Next morning I decided to put my name down, and while waiting in the crowd, heard nearly everyone say they were either stewards or seamen. I decided to put a different trade down from the others, otherwise I might be there for years. 'Name?' asked the man. 'Wayne,' I said nervously. I didn't want to be caught now, and the police must be looking for me.

'What are you?'

'Electrician,' I said and told him I was seventeen. I started to walk towards the docks and looked at the big ships. Today, it's very hard to get into the docks without passing the policeman at the gates, but at that time you could walk through and wander at your will.

I saw them all – the *St. Paul*, the *Minnesota*, the *New York* and the *Majestic*, a one-funnel boat. 'Look for the "Blue Peter",' one of the lads told me, 'and you will know if she is sailing today.' It was explained to me that it was a white flag with a blue square in it. If only I could get on that ship I could be off that day!

Back at the Home, the man who had taken my particulars called me over to his window and asked if I had ever been to sea. I hesitated. 'If you haven't, it doesn't matter,' he said kindly. 'Only, you have no clothes with you.' My heart started to sink. 'Anyway,' he said, 'you sail on the *Majestic* today. Here's a card. Go to so-and-so's shop at the gates. They'll fit you out with whatever you want and dock it off your first wages. Then take the card and see the chief electrician. Good luck.'

I thanked him and was off in a jiffy, stepping jauntily through the dock gates and over to the shop. I gave the man the card, signed some papers and received three shirts, two pairs of electricians' dungarees, some hankies and a kitbag. Then over to the S.S. *Majestic* which looked as big as St. Paul's Cathedral.

The sailor at the foot of the gangway gave me the okay, and I went aboard. I found the second electrician, a very pedantic Scotsman, who asked me one or two questions about my age and experience. He kept mumbling something about my being a bit young to know too much, but at last took me to the fo'c'sle and showed me my bunk, one of about thirty. He told me to put my gear on the deck, get my working clothes on, and report to him as soon as I was ready.

I put on my dungarees, which were new and a bit too big, and swished along to the electricians' store-room. Very soon a chap asked if I was the electricians' mate, and I followed him in. Two cabins had been knocked into one. It was full of what I thought was junk – bits of lamps, insulating tape and so on all over the place. Again I was asked if I had ever been to sea. This time I told the truth, and was given two electric light bulbs and told to take them to a cabin on A deck and replace two which were not working.

In high spirits I went along to the cabin. My first job was easy – putting new lamps in sockets. I soon found A deck and a door which was open with quite a crowd inside. I knocked, and half a dozen fuzzy voices shouted, 'Come in.' They nearly all had a glass of champagne in their hands. I went in and the steward, who was waving a bottle of wine, told me to see to the two lamps. As I started to reach for the old ones, the ship's siren sounded three times and nearly frightened the life out of me. There was a lot of kissing and farewells, and in a few minutes we were on our way to America.

I couldn't resist seeing the boat leave, so I walked on deck with a screwdriver in my hand to make believe I was on a job. Slowly the dockside slid away as we moved out into Southampton Water. I was soon jerked out of dreamland by a sharp tap on the shoulder and told to stop admiring the scenery and do some work.

The second electrician pointed to a big bit of machinery that was lying on the bench and told me to rewind it. I did not know what it was and couldn't even lift it, let alone rewind it. I looked for the handle, probed it clumsily with a screwdriver, hoping for inspiration, when the third electrician came in. 'What the hell are you doing?' I told him I had orders to rewind this thing. 'Ever rewound one before?' I said 'No,' and without thinking added, 'I don't even know what it is.'

That did it! From the store to the galley or kitchens can't be more than a few hundred feet, but it was like the Last Mile for me before I was confronted with the Chief Electrician, who cursed me for making him sail with a man short. I cried like a baby, thinking it was the end of the trail, but got no sympathy from any of them.

At last the Chief left and returned with another man in gold braid but no hat. He looked me over sourly and snapped, 'Get your gear from your quarters and report to my office immediately.'

We stopped before a door marked Chief Steward. The third knocked and a gentle voice told us to enter. My deception on this trip was nothing new; it happened every time the ship sailed. Another steward came in and led me away along corridors, passages, through doors, and at last to some steep stairs which dropped to a very large fo'c'sle with bunks two high. I was taken to the far side, shown a bunk on top, and told to leave everything there. Where to now, I wondered.

Back we went to the chief steward's office, where a man, definitely a cook, gave me a sharp once-over and told me to follow him.

At last we came to the galley. Wow, the size of it! Steam hissed and water roared on all sides. There were dozens of men dressed in white hats, white trousers and jackets with aprons, and slippers on their feet. I was shown to a large sink with an open porthole above it. The voices of the cooks were echoing through the huge kitchens, together with the clatter of pots and pans and the scraping of mechanical potato peelers. It was fascinating, but very hot. A pile of pots and pans stood on the side of this huge sink, and I was told to go ahead and wash them. This is going to be too easy, I thought, feeling much brighter.

We were not yet out of the Channel when I started to wash those pots and pans. I grinned to myself, thinking that I had been promoted from electrician to galley slave in the time it took the liner to pass the Isle of Wight.

The ship had sailed at 3 p.m. and the cooks were preparing dinner for the first, second, third and steerage passengers. There must have been two thousand aboard including the crew, which meant a lot of cooking and thousands of pans to clean. There were six of us just washing pans and pots, ladles and other utensils.

I was washing for the first-class cooks, which was unlucky for me because they used far more than those needed by the second, third and steerage.

About 7.30 that night, I felt first the dip and roll of the ship. It was only slight, but it was there. Now, if ever there is a cup given for the world's worst sailor, I would win it easily. I even became seasick when my Mother took me to Margate on the *Royal Sovereign*, an old sidewheeler that sailed down the Thames. To this day when I hear a band playing, 'Life on the Ocean Wave', I'm nearly away with it. I imagine that smell of engine room and new paint, and I can really be seasick.

However, roll, bowl or pitch, I had to wash those pots and pans. The smell of the food didn't help, and when you have a large pan to wash, with bits of fat, pork or grease sticking to it, something has to go, and I went. I was violently sick in the kitchen sink. One of the other washers came over, consoled me or tried to, and told me to lie down for a while. He would take over.

I made my way to the bow of the ship and in my dungarees, wet and greasy by now, climbed into my bunk and tried to sleep. I couldn't. Some men were playing cards; someone was mucking about on the mouth organ, and another was plucking a mandolin. After about an hour, the chap below came in and started to undress to get into his own bunk. He saw me, said hello, and we began to talk. He too was in the kitchens and confided that he was jumping ship in New York.

It was a shock at 5.15 next morning when we were awakened by a sailor yelling 'Rise and shine for the White Star Line. Show a leg; get out of bed.' I was lost for a moment or two, then became quite enthusiastic. I wasn't seasick and I didn't have to shave; I was too young.

At 6.30 work really started. It was the breakfast dishes we had to clean, and I had spoken too soon about not being seasick. I have never seen so much or such a waste of good food. Instead of waiting for an order for breakfast from the passengers, the cooks fried grosses of eggs in large trays and cooked hundreds of rashers of bacon, sausages, and mountains of fried potatoes. Rows and rows of trays were handed to me and, as soon as I saw and smelled the eggs and bacon, I was off again. It was many months before I could force myself to look at, let alone eat, a fried egg, bacon or sausage.

It went on the same way for six or seven days. Six in the morning until three, and then a rest till 6.30 p.m. And on again till 10 p.m. The lad in the bunk below, whose name I can't recall but I know he was a nephew of the lightweight champion, Matt Wells, had it all worked out about getting off the boat in New York as soon as he could. By the time we docked, I knew it all by heart.

He was going to some relations uptown in New York. Although I also had some cousins and uncles, I wasn't going to them, thinking the police would be after me for running away at my age.

The sun was high and hot as we passed the Statue of Liberty. A haze hung low over Manhattan, making it seem as if molten steel was being cooled in water. I had finished the luncheon dishes and was free just as the ship was docking. I had changed into a clean white shirt and my English trousers and watched the stewards taking off the hand luggage. It was our plan to grab two suitcases, carry them ashore into the huge shed and then walk out through the gates.

Dressed only in white shirts and pants would give the impression that we were coming back. It never occurred to us that we might need a jacket. We wanted to get off as soon as possible. The steerage passengers were being taken to Castle Garden or Ellis Island, and most of the policemen were busy with them. We looked over the side of the ship and only a few stood by the customs shed with one or two others at the gates. We had arranged that, if possible, we would pick up the suitcases of anyone starting with 'A' or 'B' which would take us to the far end and make it easier to get out without being noticed.

The passengers' hand luggage was littered over the deck near the gangway. We were dressed as nearly as possible like the rest of the stewards. We soon spotted a large black 'B' painted on white paper and, near it, about six suitcases. We nodded to each other and went out, picked up two of the smaller cases, and walked down the gangway to the customs shed.

'B' was right down at the end and we made our way to the large sign. Nobody took the slightest notice of us. A woman suddenly shouted, 'Steward, over here'. I put the cases down where she pointed, and she handed me a dollar. Imagine it! A dollar! My friend also put his cases down and together we went to the gates. I was really nervous now and we approached the policeman with my heart thumping. He nodded to us and grunted something about 'a good trip'. Then we were through the gates and out into West Street.

It was very hot and nearly every man was coatless. We made as if to cross to the corner saloon in case the cop was watching us, but quickly ducked up a side street. At last, we were free and in New York. But what slums we were walking through! Dirty kids galore, screaming and shouting and splashing at fire hydrants. Frowsy women with children in arms sitting on the steps or being suckled. Every house had a rusty fire escape which ran down the front of it and each floor had a little iron platform on which men were lying asleep or just sprawling unshaven in their trousers and singlets.

It was my first impression of New York and a sad shock. Hanbury Street, Spitalfields, was like the Mall in comparison. It was Dockland, and I saw the same scene repeated years later all over the world. The poor seem to congregate where the rich big ships come to rest.

From My Crazy Life (1961)

BUD FLANAGAN (1896–1968), born Weinthrop, British comedian, achieved international fame with his partner, Chesney Allen, and was later the leader of the Crazy Gang.

S.N. Behrman

Blighted Passion

My memory of all these summer twilights merges into a haze of warm felicity. But one of them I remember singly and vividly, since, as a gloomy German philosopher has said, we remember most clearly those things that have hurt us. On this particular evening I had been for a swim in Lake Quinsigamond, had dallied in Elkind's and had stolen a ride on the Providence Street car, intending to drop off in front of my house. But the conductor was absent-minded and I hung on till we got to the top of the hill. Lovers Lane looked especially inviting and I walked along for a bit under the great elms that met overhead. The silence was murmurous; the diamond light reflected from the leaves of the arching elms in green facets. I thought about my mother waiting for me with supper, turned back and started down the hill. I knew how she worried whenever I went to the lake. For a moment I hurried, but then I slowed down again. The immediate images, the teeming plans for the evening, were too compelling. I might go back to the lake for another swim – it had been brought up as a possibility that very afternoon. Someone might take me canoeing. Perhaps Morton Leavitt would be working in his father's shoe store, in which case Ada Summit, the siren of the hill, might be free. She might walk up Lovers Lane with me. The possibilities were dazzling. There was the night itself – a mystery that came from nowhere and under cover of which life took on a new coloration, a new shape, a new promise. Swimming in the lake at night was in a heightened category of experience, compared to swimming in it in the day time.

Next week would be the Fourth of July. The Maccabees Club next door to our house would be giving its annual party. Perhaps Ada Summit would come with me. A daring scheme formed in my mind: 'Ask Ada Summit!' I was passing South Street. My Aunt Ida was sitting on her front piazza. She waved and called to me: 'Spooning in Lovers Lane?' I nodded; it wouldn't do to tell Aunt Ida that I had been solitary. The abiding passion of her life centred in romance and its crystallisation in marriage. Her piazza on South Street gave her a special vantage point; she could watch the young couples walking hand in hand, making their way towards the paradise of Lovers Lane. From her piazza she took the amorous pulse of the hill, and spotted prospects for her passionate avocation of match-making.

It was getting darker. The girls, more dutiful than I, had already had their suppers and were at the posts. The Providence Street mothers looked at the world from their balconies; their daughters surveyed it from the white-painted posts in the front yards. The more opulent of the triple-deckers (ours was not one) had little yards in front of them right up to the sidewalk. In the centre of these yards were white-painted posts. Originally, probably, they were hitching posts; horses were not unfamiliar neighbours then. Against these posts the girls would lean, waiting for their steadies, or merely waiting. Several girls greeted me. They inquired whether I had had my supper. I had to say no; I remembered my waiting mother and hurried on. What were they doing later? They weren't sure. It was hazarded that we might see each other.

Then I saw Ada Summit. She was at her post. She gave me a ravishing smile. I stood before her, my heart beating.

'I was just thinking, Ada,' I heard myself saying. I couldn't go on with it; I felt it was the wrong moment.

'What?' said Ada invitingly. 'What were you thinking?'

'I was wondering . . .'

'What?'

'Who you're going to the Maccabees dance with . . .'

'That,' said Ada provocatively, 'is for me to know and for you to find out!'

I felt a fool and had a quick, throbbing sense of failure. I went down the hill. My mother was standing in front of our house, tense with anxiety. So was I – about Ada.

Although, for some reason of pride, she always denied it, we all of us knew that Ada did have a steady. He was Morton Leavitt. Morton had the inside track. Morton was better off than the rest of us; Morton had spending money. He was a dandy and a card. He went away for vacations. He had been to Old Orchard Beach in Maine. He received travel folders. He had heard of Bermuda and talked airily of going there. He was good-looking and a snappy dresser – the Beau Brummell of the hill. Because, I suppose, of some excessive functioning of the salivary glands, there was always a slight foam at the corners of Morton's lips. The rest of us, who were very jealous of him, applied to him the sobriquet of 'Spit' Leavitt. Even this he took as a kind of accolade. 'Spit Leavitt made it,' he would say of himself in terse summary of an anecdote of conquest.

Morton's hold over Ada Summit was complete. It amused Morton to demonstrate his power over Ada by allowing the rest of us, her unsuccessful lovers, to take her out occasionally when he had to work evenings at his father's shoe store on Harding Street – 'The Shoe Mart' – during a holiday rush: or when he had what he would refer to mysteriously as 'another engagement.' He once gave me a nickel to take Ada to the Nickelodeon on Park Street, where the first silent pictures were playing. Afterwards, I had to deliver her back to Morton at the shoe store. Sometimes he would allow one of us to hold Ada's hand. He would take out a gold watch with an elaborately interwoven monogram of his initials on the case, and say: 'Like to hold Ada's hand? Give him your hand, Ada, and let him hold it for a minute.' Demurely, a little embarrassed, but smiling, Ada would offer her hand. Morton would stand, like a timekeeper, while you held Ada's hand. It was a kind of dispensed *droit du seigneur*, a demonstration to the world, as far as Ada was concerned, of Morton's power of total recall.

There was a devotional cult, among us small fry on Providence Street, for what we called 'out-of-town' girls. An out-of-town girl automatically had overwhelming glamour simply because she didn't live in Worcester.

One June day there came into our midst a very unusual and heralded out-of-town girl, Miss Sawyer of Toronto. This was in itself noteworthy because Toronto was in Canada, which made Miss Sawyer the first foreign visitor to Providence Street. Moreover, she was a banker's daughter. With us the word 'banker' was a synonym for a man of wealth beyond computing. Miss Sawyer and her father were to be house guests of the Wolfsons; Miss Sawyer's father was coming to look over Mr Wolfson's comb factory with a view to refinancing and expanding it. The particular Fourth of July party after the arrival of Miss Sawyer of Toronto was memorable, packed with sensation.

The Maccabees was a social organisation which actually had its own clubhouse next door to where we lived. It was a club organised by the older businessmen on the hill: my brother, Willie Lavin, and the rest were junior members. I hadn't the faintest idea what Maccabees were; it was not till many years later that I had reason to suspect that the founders of the club next door were not the original Maccabees. The earlier Maccabees, I was to discover, were a doughty crew who excelled in feats of arms. The Worcester ones were non-belligerent. They had officers whose terms lasted a year. The newly elected officials were inducted on the Fourth of July. They made speeches. After the oratory, there was ice-cream and soft drinks and dancing in the light of the Japanese lanterns that were strung among the pear and apple and cherry trees. The trees were in full leaf and beneath them, under the Japanese lanterns, were long wooden trestles set out with refreshments. Inside the clubhouse a pianist and a banjoist were playing 'On a Sunday Afternoon,' 'Moonlight Bay,' 'Take Me Out to the Ball Game,' and other popular songs of the time. My crowd, the small fry, tried to infiltrate these parties and act like Maccabees.

On this particular Fourth of July, the lovely Myra Ellender, with whom the older set was in love as my set was in love with Ada Summit, came up and greeted me. She made me promise her a dance, which was generous of her, as I was a very uncertain dancer. I saw several girls and chatted with them, but I was miserable because they were not Ada. Ada, I was sure, would, of course, soon appear with Morton Leavitt. And suddenly I saw Ada; she was sitting wanly under a tree. She was, amazingly, alone. I went up to her and asked where Morton was. She shook her head miserably, but said nothing.

The music struck up, and I asked Ada to dance. She nodded listlessly, still without saying anything, and I walked with her into the clubhouse. The floor was densely crowded, which was a relief to me, because I was limited in manoeuvre. I wedged Ada into the swirl. After a few minutes, she asked me abruptly if I'd mind if we sat it out. As I led her off the floor to the rows of chairs ringed around the wall, I saw what she had just seen. Morton, grinning confidently, was leading Miss Sawyer on to the dance floor.

Willie Lavin, who, for some reason, had always taken a deep interest in me, sidled up to us. I had confided to Willie my passion for Ada. It had always irked Willie that I, whom he considered worthy to enter into deep discussions of large questions with him, whom he had encouraged to be a pianist, a debater, a philosopher, a puzzle-contest winner, and even a writer, should take second place with Ada Summit to a character like Morton Leavitt, whom he looked down upon as a Philistine and a shoe salesman, with what he contemptuously referred to as 'superficial values.' Strolling with me under the Japanese lanterns, he now gave me a heart-to-heart talk. The incident with Miss Sawyer, he said, was a godsend. It must reveal to Ada what a materialist, opportunist, will-o'-the-wisp Morton Leavitt was. Miss Sawyer, he understood, would be resident among us for two weeks. These two weeks presented me with a golden opportunity. It was the moment to rush in for the kill. By devoting myself to Ada for a fortnight, by allowing her to look deep into the cool depths of my character, I would make her, he ventured to say, wonder what she could ever have seen in a shallow fellow like Leavitt. 'Why,' he said, cracking his knuckles, a little idiosyncrasy of his, 'I can well imagine a situation where Ada will thank her lucky stars that this incident happened, where she will look on Miss Sawyer's arrival as an act of Providence.'

Suddenly, Willie took me by the arm and swerved me towards one of the windows of the clubhouse. He pointed to Miss Sawyer; she was abnormally tall; her somewhat pelican-like head bobbed over the other dancers. 'Look at her!' he commanded. 'Imagine giving up a beautiful girl like Ada for *that*! I will go so far ās to say that Toronto or no Toronto, banker's daughter or no banker's daughter, Miss Sawyer is as homely as a hedge fence!' I gasped at such a heresy about an out-of-town girl and, moreover, a banker's daughter. When I looked at Miss Sawyer again, through Willie's eyes, I saw that there was something in what he said. That did it. I went back inside and sat by Ada, emboldened.

There followed a delirious two weeks when I occupied the proud and throbbing status of being Ada's steady. She was sweet. She was willing to see me every night, to go everywhere with me: canoeing; dancing in White City, the pleasure-dome on the lake; walking with me in Lovers Lane, or just sitting with me on her porch, on the warm summer evenings, watching the passing scene on the hill. Of course all this was very expensive. Taking Ada to the lake meant the additional cost of streetcar fare. When I went with my crowd, we always walked, but you couldn't expect Ada to walk. Then, canoes were expensive. Willie financed me.

One Saturday during these two weeks, I got the idea that I must take Ada to Rebboli's. Rebboli's was a fine confectioner's on Main Street. The moment I arrived with Ada I was aware of Miss Sawyer, looming up towards the crystal chandelier that hung from the centre of the atelier. Morton sat possessively beside her. As we passed their table, Morton half rose; but Ada moved straight on. She cut him dead. Somewhat in a dither, conscious of moving uncertainly through a thick ambush of amorous intrigue, I piloted Ada to a table at the back. Somehow, the presence there of Morton and Miss Sawyer put a blight on this costly rendezvous. Somehow, although Ada had indeed been mine for two weeks, the relationship was never secure. Things hadn't gone quite as Willie predicted. Ada was adorable and kind, but she was abstracted. I felt increasingly that I was living on borrowed time.

I heard myself saying to Ada: 'I suppose, after Miss Sawyer goes back to Toronto, you'll take up with Morton again.'

'You needn't worry about that,' Ada said tensely. 'I never want to see Morton again. I hate him!'

That afternoon, when I took her home, Ada unaccountably pleaded with me to save the following Tuesday night for her. I promised, of course, but I was bewildered by her request because I was seeing her every night anyway. The next day, though, the gossips of our crowd shed some light on it. Miss Sawyer was returning to Toronto on Tuesday. I thought then that I saw the reason for Ada's insistence about seeing me Tuesday, and the conclusion I reached was not cheering. Ada had known that Miss Sawyer was leaving; she had divined that on that night Morton would be free and might ask to see her. She had not been able to rely on her own strength or pride to refuse, and she wished to have an engagement with me in order to be able to say that she was busy. My heart sank. The intensive and costly courtship was a failure; Willie, the *éminence grise* of the manoeuvre, had under-estimated Morton's power; to Ada, evidently, Morton's values were anything but superficial!

My dates with Ada between then and Tuesday were agonising; there was no joy in them for either of us. On Tuesday night, however, I went to her house at the appointed time. I walked into the living-room and there was Morton. He was sitting on the sofa with Ada. Ada looked happy for the first time since the arrival of Miss Sawyer. As for Morton, he was in wonderful fettle; he jumped to his feet and beamed at me like a welcoming committee. He took out his gold watch to note the time. 'Like to hold Ada's hand?' he said. 'Forty-five seconds?'

From The Worcester Account (1954)

SAMUEL NATHANIEL BEHRMAN (1893–1973), American writer of stage comedies and short stories, was born in Worcester, Massachusetts.

Groucho Marx

LUCKY DATE

My precarious financial status had, up to the age of twelve, been the single uncomplicated problem of my life. But a new dimension was about to be added – and boy, oh boy, was I ready for it!

Love is a many-splendoured thing. I don't quite know what this means, but song-writers have to make a living, too. I suppose it means that love is all-important. It's a word that is difficult to contain in any specific mould. Today the word 'love' is flung around so carelessly that it's almost meaningless. One man will say, 'I love Cheddar cheese'; a girl will say, 'I love Paris in the spring'; a boy will say, 'I love the way Mickey Mantle swings from both sides of the plate'; and someone will sing, 'I love to see the evening sun go down.' This character is probably a burglar. The word 'love' should be confined to just one subject – the relationship between a male and a female, a man and a woman, a boy and a girl.

Anyway, love hit me when I was twelve. I was still in short pants, but tiny hairs were beginning to sprout from my upper lip. A young girl lived in the flat above ours and she, too, was twelve. She had 'a good shape.' In addition to her shape, she had a number of light-brown curls that fell pleasantly around the back of her neck, and teeth as even as the kernels on a good ear of corn. By some careful manoeuvring on my part, she invariably encountered me in the hallway as she climbed the stairs to her flat.

I had been saving my pennies and nickels for some time, and I finally had accumulated enough of a bank-roll to invite her to go to Hammerstein's Victoria vaudeville theatre. I had never been there, but I had heard about it. I had seventy cents saved up and I had it all measured out. Two tickets in the second balcony, fifty cents . . . car-fare both ways, twenty cents . . . total: seventy cents.

We could have walked, but we lived on East Ninety-third Street and the theatre was on West Forty-second. It was January, the days were short and the weather was giving a pretty good imitation of Lapland.

Lucy looked charming, and I looked handsome, as we disembarked from the street-car in Times Square. But there was a fly in the ointment. The fly was a push-cart vendor. He was parked in front of the theatre, hawking coconut candy at a nickel a bag. True to her sex, Lucy spied the push-cart and murmured that coconut candy was her favourite confection – what did I intend to do about it? I did what every sucker has done all his life when beauty demands something. What this beauty didn't know was that her casual request for candy had knocked my carefully budgeted bank-roll sky high and ruined the afternoon before it had begun.

We sat in the second balcony, far, far above the stage. The performers all looked like midgets and the sounds they emitted were barely audible from our perch. Louder than the actors' voices, however, was the steady crunch of the coconut candy as each piece slid gracefully down the fair Lucy's gullet. Perhaps she was too wrapped up in the show to offer to share the candy, or perhaps she assumed that I had diabetes and, being madly in love with me, didn't want to endanger my health. Whatever the reason, she ate every bit of it, crumbs and all.

I was rather upset at Lucy's greediness, but I had a problem that made me forget even the candy I didn't get. As I searched my pockets hopefully, I still found only one lonely nickel nestling there. Living was cheap in those days, but it wasn't so cheap that two passengers could ride home on a street-car for one nickel.

The performance was finally over. We left the theatre in silence. As we walked into the street we encountered both darkness and a raging snowstorm.

Today I feel terrible about this, but remember, I was only twelve, it was bitter cold, and Lucy had gobbled up every piece of the candy. Furthermore, if she hadn't forced me into buying the candy, there would have been ten cents left – enough for both of us to ride home on the street-car.

In spite of all these convincing arguments I still had some honour. I turned to her and said, 'Lucy, when we started out for Hammerstein's Theatre I had seventy cents, enough for the theatre tickets and car-fare. I hadn't planned on candy. I didn't want candy. *You* wanted candy. If I had known you were going to want candy, I would have held off inviting you for a few more weeks. As it is, I have only one nickel left. Remember, Lucy, *you* had the candy, and you know I have every right to ride home and leave you to walk. But you know I'm mad about you and I just can't do that without giving you a fair chance. Now listen carefully. I'm going to toss this nickel in the air. You call 'Heads.' If it falls heads you get to ride home. If it's tails I ride home.'

The gods were with me. It was tails.

The female of the species has always baffled me, and I have always regarded them as a race apart. For some curious reason, Lucy never spoke to me again. The next time she saw me, she cut me dead. Had she been carrying a knife, she would have used that, too.

Well, this was the end of my first romance, and, incidentally, my seventy cents. However, I believe it had one distinction. It was probably the only love affair in history that perished for the lack of a nickel.

From Groucho and Me (1959)

JULIUS HENRY (GROUCHO) MARX (1890–1977), American actor and comedian, was born in New York City. With his younger brothers he formed the Marx Brothers, whose films included *A Night at the Opera*.

Dorothy Parker

FULFILLMENT

    For this my mother wrapped me warm,
    And called me home against the storm,
    And coaxed my infant nights to quiet,
    And gave me roughage in my diet,
    And tucked me in my bed at eight,
    And clipped my hair, and marked my weight,
    And watched me as I sat and stood:

That I might grow to womanhood
To hear a whistle and drop my wits
And break my heart to clattering bits.

Dorothy Parker (1893–1967), American writer and wit, was born in New York, the daughter of a Jewish father and a Scottish mother. *The Collected Dorothy Parker* was published in 1973.

Harriet Cohen

Overtures

Passengers in the omnibus trundling down Finchley Road in north-west London were often to see a small girl, holding an enormous music case, talking to a military-looking gentleman with iron-grey moustachios; both were so deeply absorbed in their conversation that those in the know, for there were many musical people living in Hampstead at that time, came to the conclusion that the mighty Sir Edward Elgar was propounding nothing less than *The Art of Fugue* to the little student. The truth is that the great man was telling me what he thought would win the 2.30 race that day: for I was that little girl.

The Public Library, from which our fantastic family borrowed all those books, was at the bottom of the street where Tobias Matthay lived, and I used to drag myself up the hill regularly, heavily weighed down by music and books, to have lessons with his sister Dora and an odd one with Mr Matthay himself. Netherhall Gardens – where Sir Edward Elgar and his family resided in Severn House, called after his beloved Severn River in his native Worcestershire – was a turning half-way up this hill. After the lesson my black-stockinged legs would stray to the home of this god as if drawn by a magnet. Cold and rain did not deter me, and I hung about the house until one day I dared to go up to Sir Edward and ask for his autograph. After that I still haunted the street and accompanied him on the bus several times – he would be going to lunch at one of his clubs, possibly with actor friends of whom he had many, and I to the Royal Academy of Music in Marylebone Road. Sometimes I spied that handsome Roman profile from the garden of Sir Landon Ronald's home in Maida Vale. This brilliant conductor was one of the most enthusiastic admirers of Elgar's music, and as a young person I was in the Queen's Hall to hear him give the finest performance of *Falstaff* that anyone had ever heard. It is nice to recall that it was at a musical party given at his home near Maida Vale that I first played in front of Sir Edward Elgar. 'Ha! Grown up at last, I see!' and Sir Edward cast a pleased and twinkling glance over my first long frock, as with a courtly bow he brought me a glass of wine saying, 'Champagne to match a champagne-coloured silk.' I had not known that I was going to be asked to play and my fingers were icy cold. I was trembling as Sir Landon led me to the piano while Sir Edward stationed himself behind me. . . .

I learned, when a very young girl, that Elgar was passionately devoted to animals; a feeling we shared. The cherished photo of him on my piano is with his dog Marco. When I last saw them together in a garden at Hereford Marco was his shadow. Elgar cried when he told me what he suffered over the carnage of the horses in the First World War. '*My* horses' he used to call them. In the whole of my life I can say that he was the only one who understood to the full my perhaps extreme, even exaggerated love for animals. As a friend, Elgar was supremely loyal and full of loving kindness. Of course, as I grew older I could see that he had come to regard me as an attractive young woman and not just the dear little girl of Severn House days. Although he was a very shy man, he always seemed to be surrounded by one or two lovely ladies. I remember Bernard Shaw saying to me once, pretending to be jealous, 'I am very huffy: Elgar finds you far too beautiful for my liking – he calls you "The Nymph".'

The only time I remember meeting Lady Elgar was at the gate of Severn House. She was obviously amused at my devotion and said: 'You have got yourself a little page, Edward.' . . .

Arnold Bax told me that I must have been about fifteen when he first set eyes on me in the concert hall of the Academy. He said I was too busy making faces at members of the orchestra to notice when he came in with Mr Corder. Frederick Corder, who used to play Wagner to me by the hour (he even forgave me for preferring Moussorgsky) told me that Bax had said to him at this concert 'Who is that elf of a creature with the little white face?' and that he had replied 'Oh, she is a jewel of a girl – she's just the person to play your new works.'

From A Bundle of Time (1969)

HARRIET COHEN (1901–67), British pianist, had her public debut at Queen's Hall, London, in 1914, and was a virtuoso by the time she was twenty. She was also active in supporting the Jewish cause in Israel.

Solly Zuckerman

The Laws of Gravity

My parents were among the poor relations of the family. Occasionally my mother took in paying guests to tide us over the bad times, and I used to suspect that my uncle more than once had to bail my father out when matters were not going well. In retrospect, I can see my father as someone totally uninterested in business, and happy only when he was sitting down with a book. But I also now realise that relatively speaking we were not all that poor. We had coloured servants, and if we were poor, so were most of the other white people around us. The world of the diamond and gold magnates, of the Abe Baileys and the Solly Joels; the world of the Barney Barnatos and of Cecil Rhodes, might have been on some other continent or some other planet. I can still remember my utter astonishment when, soon after arriving in London, I was on the top deck of an open bus going along Southampton Row and saw a white woman washing down her front steps. It was the first time I had ever seen a European doing such a menial task. White women in the kitchen, yes; but scrubbing steps — that was totally different.

It was impossible not to feel that my quiet father and my bustling extrovert handsome mother were hardly suited to each other. He was a retiring character and while mainly self-educated, read continuously but with little critical sense. It was through him that I was introduced to the writings on evolution of Darwin, Haeckel, Tyndall and other giants of the nineteenth century. I still have some of the Rationalist Press paperback reprints of their works which he bought from 'Perry & Co., Cash Book Warehouse'. I cannot think who else Perry & Co. catered for in Cape Town. My father was also very much interested in the life of Christ, and shortly before he died he sent me a privately-printed tract which he had written to spell out the message that Christ had not died on the cross, but was still living in an everlasting spiritual trance somewhere in India where, as a youth, he had acquired from the yogis and other masters of Indian culture his great wisdom, and the power to perform miracles. He had long been obsessed with the subject because of the charge that the Jews had been indirectly involved in the death of Jesus, and his good-bye present to me when I left South Africa at the end of 1925 had been a translation of a German life of Christ.

In spite of this interest, and even though he observed the Jewish 'high holidays', I would think my father was more an agnostic than a religious man. He once tried to tell me that such belief as he had in God derived from Spinoza, and that there was no personal God. To my childish mind he made God seem like some tank of spiritual fluid in the sky, ready to perfuse all mankind. There was an occasion when he took me, a small boy, on a slow train journey to a village near Cape Town. Soon after the train started, the only other man in our compartment handed my father a small pamphlet.

Presumably in order not to be outdone, my father passed him a small book which he had started to read. This was soon returned with the remark 'I don't understand any of this'. To which my father replied 'Nor do I understand this', and returned the pamphlet. I asked in a whisper what the pamphlet was about. 'Oh about God', was his reply. My own agnosticism, which was certainly established by my early teens, is perhaps not surprising.

I saw my father only twice after I left South Africa. The first time was during a visit I made there four years later. He wished me to know that my mother's badgering had become unbearable and that he wanted to disappear. I cut him short – I was embarrassed to be told what I already sensed. The second time was in 1939, just before the outbreak of war, when he and my mother were passing through London on their way back to South Africa from an overseas visit which had included the Palestine of those days. So my picture of him is as I saw him up to my twentieth year, when he was in his mid-fifties, and although he lived for nearly thirty more years, I knew less and less what he was really like. We hardly ever corresponded.

There was nothing mystical about my mother's interests. She would complain about my father's lack of ambition and business success, and was always immersed in one or other public cause: first the suffragettes, and then ending up as one of the more prominent Zionists of South Africa. Once I returned home from school to find a party of people being addressed by Sarojini Naidu, at the time Gandhi's most famous woman disciple. My mother was also very keen on our cultural education. I was made to take lessons on the violin and, when I reacted by showing no interest in that instrument, on the piano. When Cape Town got its first symphony orchestra, we had to become subscribers; but going to concerts became more of a penance than a pleasure. Not until I had left South Africa did the musical interest which she had succeeded in suppressing start to emerge. As a child I was also made to take Hebrew lessons, in a small class to which I went for a short time after school. This also soon became a penance, and then a terror. No boy could have been less popular than I was, and when we left the teacher's home at the end of the hour-long lesson, I would invariably be set upon and beaten by the other boys, who taunted me with being a milksop. I was sent an obituary notice which appeared in a newspaper on my mother's death (she too was in her eighties), and I remember being surprised to read of her as a selfless social worker, or words to that effect – I still see her only as an overpowering taskmaster. . . .

Apart from the uncles whom I have mentioned, there was another, who, I seem to remember, was often the worse for drink. There were two aunts whom I particularly liked. One was my 'rich' uncle's wife, Aunt Dinah, an elegant woman who died when I was in my early teens. She helped to introduce me to the world of novels. She had made a scrapbook of a mass of newspaper cuttings about Oscar Wilde's trial, which she felt that I should read. The other aunt was my mother's sister Martha, who lived in a small town in the Karoo where her husband had a general store, and an ostrich farm nearby. In those days it took a day and a night's railway journey to reach them, but from time to time I was taken there for a holiday. I remember Aunt Martha mainly because she would tell me that I was 'the best boy of all the girls', a remark which I took as a major piece of praise.

If I found my mother a taskmaster, she, I suppose, must have found me an unresponsive child. I mostly walked alone, and sometimes did odd things. One evening when on holiday at a small seaside resort near Cape Town where we had rented a small house, I put myself to bed and was found to be fully clothed under the bedclothes. I had worked it out that it was silly to undress at night only to have to dress again next morning. I never tried that again. If birds could fly, so could I – so flapping my arms as I jumped off a small ledge, I defied the laws of gravity, and then had to have my scalp stitched. That was not the only time when as a child I defied those laws, and suffered mild concussion as a result. I hated learning to read, and still recall the torture of being made to struggle through Ballantyne's *Coral Island*. But once I had overcome an initial reluctance, I found myself wanting to open books, provided I chose them myself, and discovered the joy of reading illicitly at night by the light of a secreted candle. I also found pleasure in collecting books, even as a boy. For a time Henty was my passion, and I responded to his stories, as no doubt did all his young readers, not only by sharing the adventures of his heroes, but also by being proud that South Africa was part of an Empire that had spread across the whole world. I discovered that lead piping could be melted in the flame of a candle, and that the strange shapes the molten drops took as they fell into a bowl of water were those of animals and people. And I remember my puzzled humiliation when I demonstrated the experiment to a boy whom I had told of my discovery, and who looked at me strangely and went off laughing. I was believed to be 'delicate' because after the extraction of a milk-tooth I had once bled as though I were a haemophiliac. I must have been even more of a nuisance when the reaction to my music lessons took the form of a swelling of my finger joints. A tentative diagnosis of bone tuberculosis led to my being taken away from school for a couple of months. The whole thing was, in modern parlance, psychosomatic, but it got me off my music lessons. During this self-generated school holiday I wandered into a small second-hand bookshop and bought for a few pennies what turned out to be a first edition of Edmund Burke's *Enquiry into the Origin of our Ideas of the Sublime and Beautiful*. Why I should have wanted this book at the age of twelve years or so I cannot think, but I did not part with it till years later, long after I had settled in England.

From From Apes to Warlords (1978)

BARON ZUCKERMAN of Burnham Thorpe (1904–), British scientist, was born in Cape Town, and came to Britain as a Rhodes Scholar. He was Scientific Adviser, Combined Operations HQ 1939–46; Chief Scientific Adviser to the Secretary of State for Defence 1960–66; President, Zoological Society of London 1977–84.

Isaac Bashevis Singer

THE YOUNG PHILOSOPHER

We starved at home. Bitter frosts raged outside, but our stove wasn't lit. Mother lay in bed all day and read her books of morals – *Duty of the Heart, The Rod of Punishment, The Good Heart*, and occasionally the aforementioned *Book of the Covenant*. Her face was white and bloodless. She, too, sought the answers to the eternal questions, but her faith remained firm. She didn't cast a speck of doubt upon the Almighty. Mother argued with my older brother: 'It isn't the Creator's fault. He wanted to give the Torah to Esau and Ishmael but they rejected it.' My brother asked: 'Were you there?' He denied the concept of free choice. There was no such thing as free will. If you were born into a Jewish house, you believed in Jewishness; if you were born into a Christian home, you believed in Jesus; if you were born a Turk, you believed in Mohammed. He said to Mother: 'If someone abducted you as a child out of your father's house and raised you among Gentiles, you'd keep on crossing yourself, and instead of the Jewish books you'd be reading the history of the Christian martyrs now.'

Mother grimaced at this blasphemy and said: 'May the Almighty forgive your words.'

'There is no Almighty. Man is an animal like all animals. This whole war is on account of oil.'

This was the first time I had ever heard such words. Oil, of all things? All the time we had lived in number 10 we had used oil or kerosene in our lamps. Now that we lived in number 12 we used gas. It seemed incredible that Germany, Russia, England, and France should fight over such a filthy thing as oil, but my brother soon explained it.

Mother heard him out and said: 'They only need an excuse to fight. Today they fight over oil; tomorrow it'll be over soap or cream of tartar. The fact is that they are evildoers and the evildoer wants to commit evil. All he needs is an excuse.'

'When the Jews had a country, they fought, too. The whole notion of the "chosen people" isn't worth a row of beans. We're the same animals as all the others. We have our share of swindlers, fakers, and charlatans.'

'It's all because of the accursed Exile.'

I didn't know myself with whom to agree – I loved them both deeply – but it appeared that my brother was right. Whatever home one was raised in, that was the faith one accepted. The home hypnotized people like that hypnotist Feldman described in the newspapers. That which Feldman did in a minute the home did gradually. If you heard day in and day out that there is a God, you believed in God. If you raised children to believe that everything resulted from evolution, they would believe in evolution. But which was the truth? I, Isaac, or Itchele, from Krochmalna Street, wouldn't let myself be hypnotized by anybody. I had to consider everything on my own and come to my own conclusions! I realized by now that reading popular books on science wouldn't reveal the secret of the world to me. Kant and Laplace were men, too, not angels. How could they possibly know what had happened millions and myriads of years ago? Since one cannot dig a pit seven miles deep and see what goes on beneath the earth, how could they know how the universe had formed? It was all supposition or plain guesswork. Both the cabala and the astronomy book spoke of presences that existed forever, but I couldn't for the life of me conceive of such a thing. If God or the fog had existed forever, this would mean that you could take a wagonful of pencils and write the number of years these presences had existed and it still wouldn't be enough. The fact was that you couldn't write this total with all the pencils in the world on all the paper in the world. In the book on astronomy it stated that space was without limit as was the number of heavenly bodies. But how could something stretch on without an end? On the other hand, how could time have a beginning? What was *before* the beginning? And how could space have a limit? I spoke of this to my brother, and he said: 'Your questions have to do with philosophy, not with science, but you can't find the truth there either.'

'Where can you find it?'

'The real truth was never known, it isn't known, and it will never be known. Just like a fly can't pull a wagon of coal or iron, our brain can't fathom the truth of the world.'

'In that case, what's to be done?'

'Eat, drink, sleep, and if it's possible, try to create a better order.'

'What kind of order?'

'One in which the nations stop slaughtering each other and people have work, food, and a decent place to live.'

'How can this be done?'

'Oh, there are all kinds of theories.'

My brother waved his hand. He himself was in deep trouble. He was hiding from the Russian military authorities. He lived under a false passport listing a different name and different place of birth. He was living in some unheated studio of a sculptor and starving along with the rest of us. He risked his life every moment, since deserters were shot. Mother cried her eyes out as she prayed to God that no harm befall him. Although I doubted the existence of God, I, too, prayed to Him (whenever I forgot that I was a heretic). After all, you couldn't be sure about such things.

My brother left after a short visit, but before leaving, he glanced out the window to see that no military patrols were roaming about. I began to pace to and fro like a caged beast. How could you live in such a world? How could you breathe when you were condemned to never, never know where you came from, who you were, where you were going? I looked out the window and saw a freight wagon of sacks drawn by a skinny nag. I compared myself to this creature that pulled a load without knowing what it was or where it was going or why it had to strain so. My brother had just now advised me, like Ecclesiastes, to eat, drink, and sleep, but I had nothing to eat and it wasn't even easy to drink a glass of water, since our water pipes had frozen. No matter how I covered myself at night I still felt cold. The mice in our apartment were apparently starving, too, since they grew ever bolder in their desperation – they even leaped over our beds. Well, and how would I go about creating a better order? Should I write a letter to Nicholas II or to Wilhelm II or to the English King that it didn't pay to go to war over oil? Hadn't Malthus said that wars and epidemics were useful – actually vital to man's existence?

My brother had mentioned the philosophers, and although he said that I could learn nothing from them, they had to know something, after all. Otherwise, why were they called philosophers? But where did one get such a book? I could have asked my brother, but first of all, he seldom came home now, and secondly, he often forgot what I asked him for and it took him weeks to remember. But I had to learn the answer right now! I began to rummage among my brother's papers, and I found what I wanted – a book from Bresler's Library listing its address somewhere on Nowolipki Street. Now I was ready to launch the biggest adventure of my life – namely, I resolved to go to this library and try to get a book out on philosophy. It was my feeling that my brother had probably already read this book and that it was high time he brought it back. A few times cards had come from the library demanding from my brother that he bring back books that were overdue. I would therefore take this book back and ask for another in its stead, one on philosophy. It was true that if my brother found out what I had done, he might grow terribly angry and might even slap me for going where I didn't belong. But what was a slap compared to the joy that a book on philosophy would grant me? I burned with the urge to read what the philosophers had to say about God, the world, time, space, and, most of all, why people and animals must suffer so. This to me was the question of questions.

I took the book and started off toward Nowolipki Street. It was freezing outside. The Germans had pushed so close to Warsaw that I could hear their cannonfire in the streets. I pictured to myself how a thousand soldiers died from every shot. Freezing blasts blew, making my nose feel like a piece of wood. I had no gloves, and the fingers of the hand holding the book had become stiff. I was terribly afraid they would yell at me at the library or make fun of me. Who knows? My brother might even be there. I raced against the wind, and a voice within me shouted, 'I must learn the truth! Once and for all!'

I went inside the library and, for a moment, saw nothing. My eyes grew bedazzled and my head spun. 'If only I don't faint!' I prayed to the forces that guided the world. Gradually the dizziness subsided, and I saw a huge room, actually a hall stacked with books from floor to the astoundingly high ceiling. The sun shone in through the windows casting a bright wintery light. Behind a wide counter stood a corpulent man – bareheaded, beardless, with longish hair and a mustache – who placed paper patches on the margins of a book. For a long time he didn't look up, then he noticed me, and his big black eyes expressed a kind of amiable surprise.

He said: 'What do you say, young fellow?'

I savoured the title 'young fellow.' It was a sign that I was already half grown.

I replied: 'I brought back my brother's book.'

The librarian stuck out his hand and took the book. He stared for a long time at the inside of the cover and knitted his brow. Then he asked: 'Israel Joshua Singer is your brother?'

'Yes, my older brother,' I replied.

'What's happened to him? It's a year since he took out this book. You're not allowed to keep a book longer than a month. A pretty big fine has accumulated. More than the deposit.'

'My brother is in the Army,' I said, astounded over my own lie. It was obviously either my way of justifying my brother's failure to return the book or a means of drawing sympathy to myself. The librarian shook his head.

'Where is he – in the war?'

'Yes, the war.'

'You don't hear from him?'

'Not a word.'

The librarian grimaced.

'What do they want – those savages? Why do they drag innocent victims into their murderous wars?' He spoke half to me, half to himself. He paused a moment, then said: 'Your brother is a talented young man. He writes well. He paints well, too. A talent. A born talent. Well, and you obviously study at the study house, eh?'

'Yes I study, but I want to know what goes on in the world, too,' I said. I had the feeling that my mouth was speaking of its own volition.

'Oh? What do you want to know?'

'Oh – physics, geography, philosophy – everything.'

'Everything, eh? No one knows everything.'

'I want to know the secret of life,' I said, ashamed of my own words. 'I want to read a book on philosophy.'

The librarian arched his brows.

'What book? In what language?'

'In Yiddish. I understand Hebrew, too.'

'You mean, the sacred language?'

'My brother read the *Ha-tzephirah*, and I read it, too.'

'And your father let you read such a heretical paper?'

'He didn't see.'

The librarian mulled this over.

'I have something about philosophy in Yiddish, but a boy your age should study useful things, not philosophy. It'll be difficult for you and it'll serve no practical purpose.'

'I want to know what the philosophers say about why people must suffer and how the world came about.'

'The philosophers don't know this themselves. Wait here.'

He went to search among the books and even climbed a ladder. He came down with two books and showed them to me. One was in Yiddish, the other in Hebrew.

He said: 'I have something for you, but if your father should see them, he'd tear them to pieces.'

'My father won't see them. I'll hide them well.'

'When you take out books from a library, you have to leave a deposit and pay for a month in advance, but you probably haven't a groschen. All right, I'll take the chance, but bring them back when you're finished. And keep them clean. If you bring them back in time, I'll find something else for you. If a boy wants to learn the secret of life, you have to accommodate him.'

The librarian smiled and marked something down on cards. He handed me the books, and I barely restrained myself from kissing his hand. A great surge of affection swept over me toward this good person along with the desperate urge to read what was written in these books.

From Love and Exile (1984)

ISAAC BASHEVIS SINGER (1904–), Yiddish writer, was born in Radzymin, Poland, and in 1935 he emigrated to New York, where his brother had already arrived. He was awarded the Nobel Prize for Literature 1978.

Arthur Koestler

OVERBAKED BEANS

The year was 1914-15. The outbreak of the First World War had ruined my father's business in Budapest; we had given up our flat and moved to Vienna. From then on we never again had a permanent home.

The first station in our nomadic wanderings was a boarding-house called Pension Exquisite; it was, and probably still is, on the fifth floor of an old building in the heart of Vienna, facing St. Stephen's Cathedral. One afternoon, at a time when the conflict between my parents was at its height, I was left alone in our rooms in the Pension. I was depressed, and thought that the glow of some coloured candles which my mother had bought, would create a pleasant change of atmosphere. I lit them, put them on the window sill and, becoming absorbed in my reading, forgot all about them – until one of the candles fell into a waste-paper basket and set it alight. I tried to extinguish the flames by waving the basket in the air; and when the flames grew too hot, hurled it against the gauze curtains. The room, like every self-respecting boarding-house of the period, was richly draped with velvet and plush, and the fire spread rapidly. I was too frightened of being punished to call for help, and tore in a frenzy at the burning curtains in the thickening smoke. The next thing I remember is waking up on the bed of Fräulein Schlesinger, a French teacher who lived in the boarding-house and with whom I was very much in love. My parents' return coincided with the arrival of the fire brigade; some three or four rooms facing the Cathedral were gutted before the fire was brought under control. I was not punished, not even in disgrace; the heroic dimensions of my misdeed had evidently transcended the limits of any possible retribution.

Not long after this event, I was again reading in my room one lonely afternoon when suddenly there was a loud report, and a hard object hit me on the back of the head, knocking me momentarily unconscious. A big can of tinned beans which had been standing on the radiator cover had exploded, presumably under the effect of fermentation. The elaborately far-fetched nature of this further catastrophe made the inmates of the Pension Exquisite regard me as a boy endowed with somewhat awe-inspiring potentialities, and I was much sought after for table-lifting seances, a popular pastime in those days.

From Arrow in the Blue (1952)

ARTHUR KOESTLER (1905–83), writer and political prisoner, was born in Budapest, and came to Britain in 1940.

Lilian Hellman

THE FIG TREE

There was a heavy fig tree on the lawn where the house turned the corner into the side street, and to the front and sides of the fig tree were three live oaks that hid the fig from my aunts' boardinghouse. I suppose I was eight or nine before I discovered the pleasures of the fig tree, and although I have lived in many houses since then, including a few I made for myself, I still think of it as my first and most beloved home.

I learned early, in our strange life of living half in New York and half in New Orleans, that I made my New Orleans teachers uncomfortable because I was too far ahead of my schoolmates, and my New York teachers irritable because I was too far behind. But in New Orleans, I found a solution: I skipped school at least once a week and often twice, knowing that nobody cared or would report my absence. On those days I would set out for school done up in polished strapped shoes and a prim hat against what was known as 'the climate,' carrying my books and a little basket filled with delicious stuff my Aunt Jenny and Carrie, the cook, had made for my school lunch. I would round the corner of the side street, move on toward St. Charles Avenue, and sit on a bench as if I were waiting for a streetcar until the boarders and the neighbors had gone to work or settled down for the post-breakfast rests that all Southern ladies thought necessary. Then I would run back to the fig tree, dodging in and out of bushes to make sure the house had no dangers for me. The fig tree was heavy, solid, comfortable, and I had, through time, convinced myself that it wanted me, missed me when I was absent, and approved all the rigging I had done for the happy days I spent in its arms: I had made a sling to hold the school books, a pulley rope for my lunch basket, a hole for the bottle of afternoon cream-soda pop, a fishing pole and a smelly little bag of elderly bait, a pillow embroidered with a picture of Henry Clay on a horse that I had stolen from Mrs. Stillman, one of my aunts' boarders, and a proper nail to hold my dress and shoes to keep them neat for the return to the house.

It was in that tree that I learned to read, filled with the passions that can only come to the bookish, grasping, very young, bewildered by almost all of what I read, sweating in the attempt to understand a world of adults I fled from in real life but desperately wanted to join in books. (I did not connect the grown men and women in literature with the grown men and women I saw around me. They were, to me, another species.)

It was in the fig tree that I learned that anything alive in water was of enormous excitement to me. True, the water was gutter water and the fishing could hardly be called that: sometimes the things that swam in New Orleans gutters were not pretty, but I didn't know what was pretty and I liked them all. After lunch – the men boarders returned for a large lunch and a siesta – the street would be safe again, with only the noise from Carrie and her helpers in the kitchen, and they could be counted on never to move past the back porch, or the chicken coop. Then I would come down from my tree to sit on the side street gutter with my pole and bait. Often I would catch a crab that had wandered in from the Gulf, more often I would catch my favorite, the crayfish, and sometimes I would, in that safe hour, have at least six of them for my basket. Then, about 2:30, when house and street would stir again, I would go back to my tree for another few hours of reading or dozing or having what I called the ill hour. It is too long ago for me to know why I thought the hour 'ill,' but certainly I did not mean sick. I think I meant an intimation of sadness, a first recognition that there was so much to understand that one might never find one's way and the first signs, perhaps, that for a nature like mine, the way would not be easy. I cannot be sure that I felt all that then, although I can be sure that it was in the fig tree, a few years later, that I was first puzzled by the conflict that would haunt me, harm me, and benefit me the rest of my life: simply, the stubborn, relentless, driving desire to be alone as it came into conflict with the desire not to be alone when I wanted not to be. I already guessed that other people wouldn't allow that, although, as an only child, I pretended for the rest of my life that they would and must allow it to me.

I liked my time in New Orleans much better than I liked our six months apartment life in New York. The life in my aunts' boardinghouse seemed remarkably rich. And what a strange lot my own family was. My aunts Jenny and Hannah were both tall, large women, funny and generous, who coming from a German, cultivated, genteel tradition had found they had to earn a living and earned it without complaint, although Jenny, the prettier and more complex, had frequent outbursts of interesting temper. It was strange, I thought then, that my mother, who so often irritated me, was treated by my aunts as if she were a precious Chinese clay piece from a world they didn't know. And in a sense, that was true: her family was rich, she was small, delicately made and charming – she was a sturdy, brave woman, really, but it took years to teach me that – and because my aunts loved my father very much, they were good to my mother, and protected her from the less wellborn boarders. I don't think they understood – I did, by some kind of child's malice – that my mother enjoyed the boarders and listened to them with the sympathy Jenny couldn't afford. I suppose none of the boarders were of great interest, but I was crazy about what I thought went on behind their doors.

I was conscious that Mr. Stillman, a large, loose, good-looking man, flirted with my mother and sang off key. I knew that a boarder called Collie, a too thin, unhappy looking, no-age man, worked in his uncle's bank and was drunk every night. He was the favorite of the lady boarders, who didn't think he'd live very long. (They were wrong: over twenty years later, on a visit to my retired aunts, I met him in Galatoire's restaurant looking just the same.) And there were two faded, sexy, giggly sisters called Fizzy and Sarah, who pretended to love children and all trees. I once overheard a fight between my mother and father in which she accused him of liking Sarah. I thought that was undignified of my mother and was pleased when my father laughed it off as untrue. He was telling the truth about Sarah: he liked Fizzy, and the day I saw them meet and get into a taxi in front of a restaurant on Jackson Avenue was to stay with me for many years. I was in a black rage, filled with fears I couldn't explain, with pity and contempt for my mother, with an intense desire to follow my father and Fizzy to see whatever it was they might be doing, and to kill them for it. An hour later, I threw myself from the top of the fig tree and broke my nose, although I did not know I had broken a bone and was concerned only with the hideous pain.

I went immediately to Sophronia, who had been my nurse when I was a small child before we moved, or half moved, to New York. She worked now for people who lived in a large house a streetcar ride from ours, and she took care of two little red-haired boys whom I hated with pleasure in my wicked jealousy. Sophronia was the first and most certain love of my life. (Years later, when I was a dangerously rebellious young girl, my father would say that if he had been able to afford Sophronia through the years, I would have been under the only control I ever recognized.) She was a tall, handsome, light tan woman – I still have many pictures of the brooding face – who was for me, as for so many other white Southern children, the one and certain anchor so needed for the young years, so forgotten after that. (It wasn't that way for us: we wrote and met as often as possible until she died when I was in my twenties, and the first salary check I ever earned she returned to me in the form of a gold chain.) The mother of the two red-haired boys didn't like my visits to Sophronia and so I always arrived by the back door.

But Sophronia was not at home on the day of my fall. I sat on her kitchen steps crying and holding my face until the cook sent the upstairs maid to Audubon Park on a search for Sophronia. She came, running, I think for the first time in the majestic movements of her life, waving away the two redheads. She took me to her room and washed my face and prodded my nose and put her hand over my mouth when I screamed. She said we must go immediately to Dr. Fenner, but when I told her that I had thrown myself from the tree, she stopped talking about the doctor, bandaged my face, gave me a pill, put me on her bed and lay down beside me. I told her about my father and Fizzy and fell asleep. When I woke up she said that she'd walk me home. On the way she told me that I must say nothing about Fizzy to anybody ever, and that if my nose still hurt in a few days I was only to say that I had fallen on the street and refuse to answer any questions about how I fell. A block away from my aunts' house we sat down on the steps of the Baptist church. She looked sad and I knew that I had displeased her. I touched her face, which had always been between us a way of saying that I was sorry.

She said, 'Don't go through life making trouble for people.'

I said, 'If I tell you I won't tell about Fizzy, then I won't tell.'

She said, 'Run home now. Goodbye.'

And it was to be goodbye for another year, because I had forgotten that we were to leave for New York two days later, and when I telephoned to tell that to Sophronia the woman she worked for said I wasn't to telephone again. In any case, I soon forgot about Fizzy, and when the bandage came off my nose – it looked different but not different enough – our New York doctor said that it would heal by itself, or whatever was the nonsense they believed in those days about broken bones.

From An Unfinished Woman (1969)

LILIAN HELLMAN (1905–84), American dramatist and screenwriter, was born in New Orleans. Her *Collected Plays* was published in 1972.

Ruth Michaelis-Jena

Under the Weimar Republic

News of the armistice came on 11th November. Nothing was quite as before, and school continued to be in a somewhat confused state. Apparently orders were given to change the angle of much of the teaching, but naturally there were no new textbooks yet. Many lessons had to be improvised, and depended on the individual stand each teacher took towards the situation. The word democracy was bandied about, and everybody clung to it, as to a life-raft in rough waters. A special subject, *Bürgerkunde*, instruction in citizenship, was introduced, and an eager young teacher tried to set out the aims of the brand-new German Republic: liberty and goodwill were written in large letters, and war was outlawed. The end of an epoch, in fact.

Daily life was difficult, with strikes, and shortages of almost everything, and a growing clandestine market kept going by people known as *Schieber*, who 'pushed' goods in order to make an excessive profit. Things became more and more expensive, a great worry in a household depending on a fixed income. Many of my father's foreign investments were 'frozen' or even useless as a result of the war. Strict savings had to be introduced, and when our good Marie married a returned soldier, she was not replaced. Mother now worked with a daily woman only. My dresses and coats were made from clothes sent by my Dutch cousins. Our family had a long connection with Holland, and these relatives were to prove good and helpful friends in those hard years. Through them I had a unique experience.

Though no passports for foreign travel were available to German adults, more and more *Kriegskinder*, children under fourteen, who had suffered in the war years, were sent for holidays to neutral countries. This travel was arranged through organisations like the Quakers – who also provided extra food for thousands of children – or through personal contacts. One of my classmates had been to Scandinavia, and had come back with tales of peace and plenty. It was to be my turn now. A cousin had made preparations for me to spend a couple of months in Holland. I had never quite overcome the weakness caused by my long illness two years earlier. Special leave from school was obtained, and one fine summer's morning my cousin collected me in an elegant dark-blue Packard complete with smart chauffeur. The farewell was a little tearful as I had never been away from my parents for any length of time. However, excitement soon took the upper hand, and I gave myself completely to the new and thrilling experience. For the first time I crossed a frontier, and after the German customs, we soon reached the Dutch maréchausée men, looking well-fed, and in much better uniforms than their German counterparts. They waved us on, and gave the 'war child' a big smile.

The weeks that followed were like a dream. I was given a room on the first floor of my cousin's handsome house. Large glass doors opened on to a big square balcony, the roof of the garden-room below. The garden with flowers, lawns and fruit trees, stretched a long way down till it met the gardens of the houses in a street running parallel with ours. At seven o'clock each morning a maid in a cotton dress and white apron came in to draw the curtains, open the balcony doors, and let me enjoy the view. I was served with hot chocolate, and told to rest for another hour or two. Then came breakfast with the family which included cheese, eggs and cold meats, foods I had almost forgotten about, and some I had never seen before, like Dutch honeycake and delicious currant bread. Relations vied to make me strong and happy, and there was a succession of outings and parties. The family owned a farm outside the town, and there we went on hot afternoons by carriage or car, to lounge, to take tea in the open, help with berry picking, or play tennis which I was taught. At weekends we went further afield, and I saw much of the northeast of Holland: picturesque towns and villages, windmills, canals, big flower markets, and men and women wearing *klompjes*, the traditional wooden clogs.

Above all else I lived in a country which had not known war, and where there was great prosperity. Sometimes I found it all a little overwhelming, and in spite of all the comfort and luxury I occasionally longed for home and my parents. I felt from their regular letters that they, too, were missing me.

At the end of two months – we were to leave on a Monday morning – the door bell suddenly rang latish on Sunday night. To everybody's amazement there stood my mother. She had longed for me badly, and impatiently had set out by train to see if a frontier official would give her permission to enter Holland just for one night. She had succeeded, and our joy was great. She was given a huge meal which she could not really enjoy after all the severe rationing.

Next morning we all left by car, laden with presents of food, and I was wearing my first pair of new shoes, a fact I was immensely proud of. For years I had had nothing but shoes handed down to me from someone or other. I had put on several stone, and my hair had gone back to its normal thickness and shine. I was grateful yet happy and anxious to get home. Two months' separation from my father and mother, in a new and foreign country, had changed me in some strange way.

Physically and mentally I was different.

Childhood was over. The journey to Holland was a watershed. The thirteen-year-old child was growing into a young woman of almost fourteen.

In some ways life at school had also changed. Equality for women was much talked about, influenced possibly by echoes from revolutionary Russia, and now propagated by German Marxist writers. Women were to take a more active part in society. To be prepared for their new role, they must receive an education equal to that of boys. Even our half-comprehending minds became filled with new and exciting ideas.

Science gained greater importance in our curriculum. Fortunately for me who just scraped through mathematics and science subjects, the arts held their place with the teaching of the history and appreciation of art as important subjects. We were encouraged to form and express opinions and write essays on topics which appealed to us. I had developed a great liking for the Italian Renaissance painters, and I happily spent long hours with Vasari's *Lives of the Italian Painters*. The book's story-telling style brought the period very close, and I eventually wrote an essay full of definite views on the painters and the Renaissance as a whole.

Teachers no longer addressed us by the familiar *Du*, but used the formal *Sie*, though still with our first names. This meant a lot to us, showing, as it did, that we were no longer considered 'children'. To be called *gnädiges Fraülein* in some shop or other, was honey to my ears. I so desperately wanted to be grown-up.

Clothes were a great hindrance to this ambition. With material and money – prices kept rising – in very short supply, we just had to go on wearing clothes as long as they would hang together. I remember crying my eyes out when I had to go to a party dressed in an old blouse, white with blue sailor's collar; quite smart at one time, but now, I thought, beneath contempt.

Again help came from our good relations in Holland. On every visit they brought bundles of new clothes. Old they may have been to them, they were treasure-trove to me and a few friends who benefited from the largesse. I was never good at sewing, but I enjoyed sitting evening after evening unpicking dresses, suits and skirts. In the end my mother booked a week with the home-dressmaker. Much sought after, she was a very genteel lady, commanding respect from everybody. She only worked, it was said, for 'good families', and she did work well. When eventually the appointed date came along the *Fräulein* would arrive complete with her small sewing machine and a clean white overall to put over her neat dress. My mother had the 'sewing room' ready, with a large table for cutting and boxes of thread of all colours, cotton and silk. All week Mother was prepared to be the dressmaker's assistant, doing the hand-finishing, bits of embroidery or decorative stitching which might be required. By the time I came home from school, they would be well established, and with some luck I could try on their first 'creation'. It was astonishing what marvellous clothes could be made from cast-offs. I achieved my great desire: a 'tailor-made', a handsome little suit, a symbol then for being 'grown-up'. Navy-blue it was, with a pale-blue silk shirt tucked into the skirt. . . .

Among the Dutch 'seconds' there was a left-over piece of blue and pink printed crêpe de chine which made a longish Russian-type smock. Worn over my blue skirt, this became my first evening outfit, and I was proud of it. Something to wear in the evening had now become important as passion for the theatre was growing with me and my friends. Everybody then dressed for the occasion. In fact, visits to the theatre were social events. Though our pocket-money would only stretch to seats high up in the gallery, we hurried in the interval to the foyer below, to see and perhaps be seen. Some slightly older boys, with whom we had a nodding acquaintance, had reached the independence of earning money of their own. They could afford the luxury of the dress circle and we enjoyed being seen by them in our finery. We used our scant resources to buy the cheapest seats as often as possible. Our tastes were catholic: the German classics, Shakespeare, Molière, Strindberg and Ibsen in translation, Gerhart Hauptmann, Wedekind and, of course, Toller and the early Brecht caught our imagination. We identified with the characters, particularly in modern plays, questioned and even accused the past, in favour of a stirring present and what we liked to think of as a 'fabulous future'. Yet, romance still had a grip on us, and we were thrilled by the gaiety of *Die Fledermaus* and *The Merry Widow*, while *Lilac Time*, the sentimental story of Schubert's life, made us shed copious tears.

In spite of the many worries of our elders, to us, the young, life in the new Weimar Republic seemed good. We felt the excitement of a fresh beginning. And to be young and fully experiencing the advent of a new epoch was important, at least that is what we thought. . . .

The study of languages was steadily gaining in importance, a step nearer to becoming 'European'. I had always liked French and English, and now devoted more and more time to acquiring a degree of fluency. Father with his very good knowledge of languages was a wonderful companion in my quest. We arranged for me to spend an hour every evening in his study, aiming at speaking one evening only English and the next French.

During these evenings a curious little incident happened to which, I believe, I owe my capacity of having stayed all through life a one or two cigarettes-a-day woman.

The slightly older and hence very superior-feeling brother of a schoolmate of mine kept boasting that he enjoyed smoking. He came in one day when his sister was spending the afternoon with me, and grandly supplied us with a cigarette each. He then dared us to smoke them at once. We had just lit them, and were awkwardly puffing and coughing when my father came home from a walk. To put it mildly, we were thunderstruck. However, all Father said quite casually was, 'Carry on, I hope you won't be sick.'

Next day when I entered his study for our conversation hour, he asked how I had enjoyed the smoke. 'It's fine,' I answered, with more boast than truth, after which Father pointed to a small metal box on his desk, filled with Turkish cigarettes. He was a pipe smoker with the occasional cigar after dinner, but kept cigarettes for his visitors. I had for long been fascinated by the tin box in which these cigarettes were packed, less for its contents than the coloured picture of an Oriental market on its slightly rounded lid. It had all the magic of the Arabian nights.

Now Father opened the lid, saying, 'Please take one,' and with a gallant gesture lit my cigarette, adding, 'as for me, I have nothing against smoking, within reason, that is. But what I do not want you to do, is smoke in secret.' After that the tin box was offered to me every evening. The nightly cigarette became a pleasant ritual in the same way a glass of half wine, half water, with dinner had been since infancy.

From Heritage of the Kaiser's Children (1984)

RUTH MICHAELIS-JENA (1905–   ) was born in Detwold and came to Britain in 1934 where, until her marriage to a Scot, she continued her career as a bookseller.

Meyer Levin
ESCAPE

My dominant childhood memory is of fear and shame at being a Jew. We lived on Racine Avenue in the notorious Bloody Nineteenth ward of Chicago. It was so known because it was the scene of a political vendetta between Italian ward chiefs. And it was at that time the incubating ground for the gunmen of Chicago's later gangster era.

Before I was born, the ward had been an Irish neighborhood, and in the classic pattern of deterioration in American cities, the Irish had moved on and been supplanted by Jews, the Jews were being supplanted by Italians, who were in turn to vacate the slums to Negroes before the area was at last cleared for a housing project.

My father was a tailor, with a hole-in-the-wall shop near the old Dearborn Station, downtown; he did pressing and mending, and a little buying and selling of used clothing, work-tools, and odds and ends possessed by South State Street derelicts. He worked twelve hours a day, and invested his savings in real estate. At that time, he had overextended himself in buying a three-story brick house containing twelve small flats, on Racine Avenue. Thus, we were landlords.

But as the Jews moved away and rents dropped there was an endless debate as to whether to allow the flats to stand vacant in the hope of keeping up the quality of the building, or whether to rent to Italians and deteriorate the property. Worried discussions of mortgages, first, second and even third mortgages, reverberated into the dark little children's bedroom while our parents sat discussing finances in the kitchen. Though we were landlords, though my father 'had his own business,' we somehow felt that we were worse off than the poorest of the tenants, we were janitors as well as landlords, and our living was always on the edge of peril and collapse.

And in the same way that, as landlords, we felt superior and inferior to our tenants, so we feared and yet somehow felt superior to the dagos and wops who were engulfing us, who had swarms of babies, and whom we considered dirty.

We children believed ourselves to be smarter than the wops. Yet they seemed more American. For though the Italians were immigrants just like our own parents, their children already seemed to have a native right over us, a right to call us sheenie and kike which had overtones of degradation far beyond anything associated with wop or dago. Perhaps we knew that there was something particularly inferior about being a Jew through all the tales we absorbed in childhood, of how the lives of our parents had been in the old country. From our earliest consciousness, we absorbed these tales of our people being kicked around and browbeaten by drunken goyim, and we therefore knew that with our people, in no matter what country they lived, it had always been as it was with us – we were a despised people. While we could yell back at the dagos and wops, we knew from the beginning that our epithets only applied to their old people, who were immigrants and who had green peppers and funny smelly sausage strings hanging in their grocery stores, but the children, we knew, would have nothing to be ashamed of when they grew up, they wouldn't be wops and dagos. We would still be Jews.

This unthought-out realization must have been in us from the start, to make us feel somehow inferior to them. And then, we were plain afraid of them. Going to school each day was like running the gauntlet. By each house, the Italian kids might be laying for us with stones or knives. – I'll cut your nuts off you lousy little sheenie.

On Racine Avenue, our side was still Jewish, but the Italians faced us from across the street. From our house to the corner we felt nearly safe, but once we turned into Taylor Street on the way to Andrew Jackson school, we were in entirely Italian territory. The first place of refuge was a friendly Italian's grocery store where a hunchbacked boy would serve us with penny pickles out of a barrel. Then, after peering out to make sure the coast was clear, we would scuttle the rest of the way to school.

Actually, though we lived under constant derisive taunts and promises of beating, and though occasionally stones were thrown and knives flashed, I don't remember being assaulted, and recall instead that in my only fight I was the physical aggressor.

One morning as I was on the way to school some kid started shouting sheenie at me; I rushed at him in sudden rage, and to my own astonishment, knocked him down. I ran away, and for days afterward I was terrified that he would be laying for me with his gang.

I was a bookish child of the sort considered typically Jewish, and I shrank from physical encounter. It was certainly a monumental rage that overrode my fear. I suppose it may be said that I have been repeating this pattern all my life, raging at being called or fancying I was being called a sheenie. In all my life I never again struck anyone, until last year when I hit a man under provocation curiously associated to the sheenie cry, for that man was a Jew. I shall come to the incident in its place.

There were only a handful of Jewish children left in our class, for by the time we reached the upper grades the Bloody Nineteenth was virtually all-Italian. After school, we few boys went to a Hebrew class in the old and deserted Jewish People's Institute that still functioned in the neighborhood.

One day, after coming home from Hebrew class and gym, I sat down at the kitchen table and wrote a story, passionately, in a little notebook resting on the oilcloth. After supper there was an unusual atmosphere of well-being in the flat. My father was home rather early from his store. My mother had polished the stove that afternoon: it shone, and a kettle steamed. Suddenly, standing with my back to the stove, I felt called upon to communicate to the family that I would be a writer. I opened the notebook and recited, rather than read, the story to them:

There was an innocent man who had been jailed, and he broke out of prison and hid in the tonneau of a passing car in order to get to the city to prove his innocence. There was a beautiful blonde American girl driving the car.

Many years later it appeared to me that there were obvious unconscious meanings in this little story. Wasn't the jail the restricted precinct of Jewish life to which we were innocently confined? I would break out, and in my childish fantasy, I would be carried in the womb of a car driven by an American girl, to be delivered to the great city where I would establish my guiltlessness.

Thus, in my later interpretation, I was seeking an escape from my Jewishness in order to prove to the world that it was no crime. In the symbols of the fantasy, I wished for rebirth.

At the time, my simple adventure story evoked a family debate. My mother and father were aware that the fundamental goal of Jewish family life was for the son to become either a lawyer or a doctor. However, they said, they would not try to influence me or hold me back from any path I chose. They would try to help me. But, my mother worried, could one make a living as a writer?

I appealed to my father, as being in contact with the outside American world. Writers made fortunes, I pointed out. Especially since the invention of movies. Writers made fortunes because everybody bought their books, and then the movies paid them again for using their stories. (How I had already come to this knowledge is a mystery.)

Although I sensed that my parents still hoped I would study medicine or law as a safety career, my nine-year-old self understood that they were too timid to advise me because they felt that even an American child knew better than a pair of immigrants about the way of the world. All through childhood I sensed, and resented, this terrible shame and inferiority in my elders; they considered themselves as nothing, greenhorns, Jews.

Some months after my declaration of vocation I wrote a poem. I was then in eighth grade, a prodigy. My favorite class was the printshop; I suppose I had a notion that I could print my own works when I grew up.

The instructor called me Minsk, and with an amused tolerance for my zeal, he sometimes permitted me to stay after school, and to attempt color printing.

My great ambition was to use the shop's three-color border of leaves and berries, and to get the red berries to register perfectly on the ends of the stems. I had so little knowledge of nature that I didn't know this was a holly border, but I knew it had something to do with Christmas, and I was a little dubious as to whether I had a right to touch such an item.

One of my uncles was marrying, and I wrote a poem for the wedding and decided to print it myself; for this, the teacher permitted me to use the three-color border. I still recall the poem's concluding couplet:

> . . . and when once more the earth turns round,
> Behold, a newborn infant on its ground.

I set up the poem in Old English and got the border printed perfectly. The wedding was to take place at a hall on the corner of Racine Avenue and Taylor Street, and I knew there was a high point in such a festivity when the master of ceremonies stopped the music, and read out telegrams of congratulation. That was when my poem would be read.

But when we reached the wedding hall, I realized that in my excitement I had forgotten to bring along my present. It was locked up in the printshop at school.

There, from the first – even when I myself was the publisher – I seemed to have difficulty in reaching my audience. It is intriguing to wonder whether I didn't forget my gift because of an unconscious feeling that what I did there in the American school printshop, with the Christian holly border, somehow couldn't be brought together with my life amongst my own people. Perhaps the conjecture is farfetched: perhaps I am forcing an adult pattern of thought back upon my childhood.

From In Search (1950)

MEYER LEVIN (1905–81), American novelist, Jewish historian and journalist, was born in Chicago.

Kenneth Hart

THE HALL, HAMPSTEAD

'Big boys,' Mr. Montauban's deep voice echoed through the hall, 'stand: turn; go along;' and the big boys filed out to their class-rooms. 'Little boys, stand: turn; go along.'

I followed those in front of me, and on the staircase met with my first set-back. This would never do, I thought. There were no hand-rails here: there could only be one way for me to go up; and I put one hand on one wall of the not very wide staircase, the other on the other, and charged ahead like a young war-horse.

'Hi, what are you doing? Get out of the way! Oh, he's lame, you chaps. Oh, sorry.'

All in one breath it seemed to come: and it put matters on a proper footing at once. From that very day I began to learn how to allow my schoolfellows always to pass, and yet to use the walls for support: and, as at the other schools, there was never the slightest hint of unkindness or even of impatience.

By the end of my first week at school I had settled very happily into its routine. To my intense gratification, also, I acquired in the playground popularity of an unusual kind. I had already achieved what was for me considerable speed. I had no idea of what I looked like: but I was soon to have an excellent notion. In a moment, as it seemed, the playground all around me was filled with laughing, merry boys walking with stiff side-to-side movements, their arms circling and jerking. Why, I thought, they're imitating me! How nice of them to think it worth while doing that!

'You don't mind, do you?' asked a particularly pleasant and kind boy, whose last wish would have been to hurt anyone's feelings.

'Of course I don't,' I answered, and forthwith sallied round the playground with them.

Idiosyncracy fared less well with far-seeing Mr. Montauban. 'Look here, old chap,' he said, patting my shoulder after I had treated him to a particularly bad exhibition of 'jumping' when he had raised his voice to another boy, 'you mustn't be so "nervy".' The admonition, however, was quite ineffective: and, undeterred in his brave efforts to rid me of a trouble which was causing me acute misery, he said 'I'm going to startle you deliberately; and you're jolly well not going to jump: see?'

I did 'see'. How could I not? But – still I 'jumped': and Mr. Montauban, realizing that I was trying my utmost, said no more.

The school's Christmas concert was to take place in December at the end of term and Mr. Montauban had decided that I, too, should be in it. Of course I could not take part in the procession on to the raised platform, since several steps without a handrail had to be mounted: and I was plainly told to wait until one of the masters lifted me on to it. Yet, at a rehearsal, when the procession was over and all the boys were on the platform, there was I among them, though no-one had lifted me.

'*Hart*,' roared Mr. Montauban, his laughing eyes showing how much he appreciated my perseverance, notwithstanding the disobedience, '*will – you – wait – until – you – are – lifted – up?*'

The concert itself included the singing by one of the masters of the Negro ditty, 'Ain't yer comin' out, my Juliet?' This feature pleased Aunt Emily as little as had my precocious (and faithfully accurate) imitation of it at home as soon as I had heard it at rehearsal. For myself, however, I felt that my first term at The Hall had ended well.

One subject Mr. Montauban taught to every form and, as I learned nearly forty years later, would allow no other master to teach – namely, Scripture. He had his own vastly entertaining way of teaching it. Recounting the quarrel of Saul and the young David, he promptly set the words 'Saul hath slain his thousands and David his ten thousands' to a lilt resembling a five-finger exercise, a device intended solely as a mnemonic. On my presenting it at home, however, Aunt Emily took an unfavourable view of it. Undismayed, I gave her in due course Mr. Montauban's next aid to memory, this time directed to the reign and activities of King Solomon and the building of the temple. Probably very few boys would have forgotten that Hiram was King of Tyre. Mr. Montauban, however, was not taking chances and, calling in aid the name of a well-known firm of children's outfitters, bid us remember that '*Hi*ram was the King of *Ty*re' by remembering that '*Hy*ams sold *at*tire'. On that Aunt Emily proclaimed roundly that, however many suitable methods there might be of teaching Holy Writ, this was not one of them – an opinion in which, taking a long view, I have never concurred.

At the beginning of the next term, in January, 1911, I walked into the form room, overbalanced and sent my books cascading on to the floor.

The new master looked round. Tall, scholarly, steel-rimmed *pince-nez* balanced precariously on aristocratic nose, he saw at once how things were with me.

'Give him a hand,' he said quietly to a boy standing near: and on those four words Mr. Wilfred Herbert Copinger and I were to build a friendship ended only by his death in 1949.

The form was the Third and Mr. Copinger took us for French. What appeal his method would have made at home I never discovered, for, warned by the reception accorded to Mr. Montauban's efforts, I never expounded it there.

'That' he would say with dignity to a budding linguist whose strong points did not include orthography 'is not the way to spell "soeur". This' putting pen to paper 'is the way to spell it. D'you see, soeur?'

Merrier than even his charmingly atrocious punning was his practice of incorporating any and every interruption into what he happened to be saying at the moment. Thus, a mathematical demonstration to the fourth form, during which someone knocked at the door just a moment before a boy handed to him a ruler for which he had asked, emerged as 'A plus B over C plus D is equal to come in, and P minus Q into X minus Y is equal to thank you.' All this with a perfectly grave face and with instant reproof for overmuch hilarity.

Like Mr. Montauban Mr. Copinger was a skilled psychologist and, as with Mr. Montauban, his approaches to tribulation were all his own. As swiftly as he had understood my plight amid the shower of books did he realize the effect on me of the sudden raising of the voice.

'Sorry, Hart,' was his greeting of the inevitable 'jump', sometimes without even looking at me. He never said anything more, never commented or even questioned: and I realized at once that here was one who understood how deep was the distress that this trouble caused me – understood, too, that the best thing for me was to set me at ease and say as little as possible.

Early in 1911 Aunt Emily entered me for the primary examination in piano playing at the Royal College of Music. Ordinarily that could not be called ambitious for a child of eleven and I myself had never even thought of my condition as a hindrance to piano-playing, although I could not use the pedals. The examiner, however, set me wondering.

'I have a note against this name,' he said as we entered, 'Slight muscular contraction in hands and arms.'

The immediate effect of this observation on me was that I did not hear Aunt Emily's answer, if any, or notice when she left the room. I went straight to the piano, opened my music and played what I had been told that I would have to play. Then I closed the piano, took my music, rose and made for the door.

'Good bye,' said the examiner.

'Good bye,' I answered as a mere afterthought, it never even occurring to me to wonder whether I ought to have said it first.

In the result of the examination I quite genuinely had no interest whatever. Even when, some weeks later, Aunt Emily told me that I had passed with distinction, I did not so much as answer – at any rate relevantly. Had colloquial English then boasted any equivalent of 'so what', I should probably have used it, or at least thought it. As it was, with sudden, pointless recollection, I asked 'What did he mean by "slight muscular contraction in hands and arms?" I'm' – with remembrance equally sudden of a crude observation made at a children's party years before – 'a little cripple, aren't I?'

'Don't you ever let me hear you use that word again,' snapped Aunt Emily. 'No, you're not. You have spastic muscles and that's all. Remember that.'

My success greatly impressed the visiting teachers of piano-playing at The Hall, at whose request I played one of the pieces, with much more pleasure than I had done before the examiner.

'Well,' said one of the teachers, 'now I know why you got distinction.'

I myself had not the least idea why, nor did what happened in the following year increase understanding.

'I'm going to take you to play to Mr. Moor,' announced Aunt Emily early in 1912, without saying either what 'Mr. Moor' was or why I should be taken to play to him.

'Play what?' I asked.

'Those pieces you've been learning: and you're going to show him how you can sing music at sight and can listen to chords played on the piano and say what the notes are.'

I was still unenthusiastic. Who was 'Mr. Moor' and, anyway what was the whole beastly thing about?

During the long journey to 'Mr. Moor' I had ideas. Surely I had been this way before: and – didn't I know that building?

'Look here,' I said, 'have you sent me in for another Royal College exam?'

'Yes,' for once losing her self-assurance, 'I have.'

'But,' I went on, in astonishment, 'without telling me anything about it? And wouldn't you have told me at all if I hadn't asked you just now?'

She was thoroughly disconcerted, and was silent as we walked into the building. I determined to do my best, though Heaven alone knew what was to happen to the piano-playing part of it. With sight-singing and chords I might be able to do something.

In the examination room, also, things did not begin too well. Presumably by some last minute substitution, 'Mr. Moor' gave place to 'Dr. Richards', who speedily proved very charming. As before, Aunt Emily went out of the room at once. I sat down at the piano. Dr. Richards set before me some very simple melodies to sing, gave me (quite needlessly) 'the key' on the piano and bid me 'go ahead'. This I did with a lack of hesitation that astonished me as much as it did him. He smiled, did not comment.

Came now piano-playing, which I scrambled through as best I could, feeling that I had been placed at a bad disadvantage.

Still he did not comment.

'Ear-training now,' he said with a smile, indicating a chair which was turned away from the piano. 'Come and sit here.'

He played a chord.

'That's the key of G. Got that in your head?'

'Yes.' I had needed all my self-control to refrain from telling him as soon as he played it that I knew that it was G. Even now I had all I could do not to say 'I knew that at once'.

Dr. Richards played quite a complicated chord.

'What are those notes?'

I rattled them off at a speed that made my sight-singing seem like snail's pace. He said nothing, played more chords – and I repeated the performance.

When Aunt Emily collected me he faced her with blank amazement: and when, in due course, I was found merely to have 'passed' in piano-playing, with 100 marks out of 150, that was amply compensated for by my having 'got distinction' in sight-singing and ear-training with 139.

And still I could not feel any enthusiasm for music.

From A Spastic Wins Through (1955)

KENNETH HART (1905–74) was Legal Correspondent of the *Jewish Chronicle*.

Josephine Kamm

Lunch at Grandfather's

During our early childhood, my sister Margaret, my junior by fourteen months, and I had the happiest relationship with both parents. Mother was loving, endearing and understanding; Father was wise, affectionate and full of fun. I was not yet five when he persuaded Mother to borrow from her sister a pair of knickerbockers belonging to her younger son. Dressed in these and a jersey of my own, with my short curly hair parted at the side, my father and I walked hand-in-hand to the nearby school hall. He left me just inside the entrance with instructions to look carefully at what went on. All I remember was a number of men posting slips of paper into a large tin.

When my father emerged he was chuckling. 'You didn't see any other little girls or ladies, did you?'

'No, I didn't.'

'That's because they wouldn't have been allowed in. But, by the time you're grown up, I'm sure they will be.'

Father was a keen supporter of Women's Suffrage and, had he lived, would have been delighted at the eventual outcome.

Almost immediately after our outing an event occurred which might well have put paid to my chances of voting. I developed acute appendicitis and had an emergency operation on the kitchen table. Just when I seemed to be recovering an abscess formed and a second operation was necessary. The trained nurse who had been engaged remained a member of the family for two months. Mother described this episode in one of the poems she later contributed to the *Morning Post*:

> . . . There came a day
> When pain, the spectre, snatched you from your play.
> Bewildered, fever-flushed,
> You moaned and fought for breath. The house was hushed.
> We watched you, racked with fear,
> Until the danger passed . . .

While I was ill I told my father that I was going to ask God to make me better. This placed him in a quandary. Since petitionary prayer was considered unethical, how could he explain that, while I might pray for help to bear the pain, I might not ask to be cured? He compromised by assuring me that God would understand and that my nightly prayer, 'God bless Daddy and Mummy . . . God bless me and help me to be a good girl', would suffice.

Mother, meanwhile, turned to more mundane matters. 'Eat up your nice milk puddings; they'll stick your tummy together.' I complied although everything I ate reeked of the sickening smell of chloroform.

It had been hard on Margaret that so much attention was focused on me but she was a sensible, stoical child who accepted the inevitable with equanimity. (Rivalry between us was mostly confined to our extreme youth. Once, when we still shared a double pram, we were alone in the garden for a few minutes when one of the maids, who had been watching from a window, rushed upstairs, calling frantically: 'Madam, Madam, come quickly; one of them's bitten the other!')

Soon after my recovery Margaret and I and our nurse went to stay with Mother's sister and her family. We enjoyed the company of our cousins, the walks on Primrose Hill, our first visit to the Zoo. But before long I began to feel home-sick and was relieved when our aunt told us it was time to leave. 'You must promise to be good,' she warned, 'and do nothing to worry Mummy.'

At home we found Mother dressed in unfamiliar black, her normally smiling face, pale and pinched. Seating us on either side of her on the drawing room sofa, holding each of us tightly by the hand, she began to speak in an infinitely sad voice. 'We've all got to try to be very brave now because Daddy isn't with us.'

'Has he gone for a holiday?' If he had I wondered why she wasn't with him. Mother shook her head.

'When's he coming back?' queried Margaret.

'I'm afraid he isn't coming back.'

'Not ever?'

'No, my darlings, never.' She went on speaking but, if she mentioned Heaven, we didn't hear. We were too stunned to absorb anything more until her final words: 'So, you see, we must always remember how much we loved him.'

Although I realised superficially that I mustn't expect to see him again, for weeks to come I fancied I heard his footsteps on the stairs, his cheerful voice calling: 'How are my chickabiddies this evening?' And long after we had reluctantly accepted the fact of his death we continued to miss him. Emotionally we clung to Mother. Each time she left the house we were terrified that she wouldn't return; each time we misbehaved we remembered our aunt's stern warning and felt guilty. As for Mother, she did her utmost to conceal her anguish by making us feel how much we meant to her.

On the practical side, we moved to much smaller premises, with a nurse and a cook-general in place of a staff of four. Financially, Mother was now more or less dependent on her father-in-law. In return for his help – and because he suspected we were not receiving enough religious instruction – he insisted that Margaret and I should lunch at his home every Saturday. On the way, escorted by our nurse, we called on our maternal grandmother, Granny Marx, who lived in a Jewish boarding-house nearby. She was a stout, warmhearted widow, genuinely interested in our childish doings, and it was a joy to be with her. (During my late twenties I was to see a portrait of the unfortunate Eleanor Marx who so closely resembled Mother's eldest sister that I enquired if there could possibly be a family connection. Mother, a lifelong Tory, confessed that, while we were not of course directly descended from Karl, we were in fact related.)

Our visit over we walked with dragging feet to our paternal grandparents' spacious but gloomy house. Grandpa Hart, son of poor East End parents, had emigrated to Australia as a boy of fifteen, made good, returning to settle in London's Maida Vale and a prosperous career in the City. However hard we tried we children couldn't rid ourselves of the suspicion that our commanding, white-moustached, white-whiskered grandfather, alternately benign and irascible, was a replica of God. His wife was the daughter of Moses Angel, also the son of poor East End parents, who had been befriended by a philanthropic patron and well enough educated to become, first, part-time editor of a Jewish newspaper and teacher at the Jews' Free School, and then, at the age of twenty-three, headmaster of the school, where he remained until his death.

Naturally Grandpa walked to and from synagogue on Saturday mornings. We had been begged by Mother to try to make conversation or, at least, to ask intelligent questions. I hadn't been forgiven for letting slip the news that we ate bacon at home, 'Because Mummy thinks it's good for us', when I enquired: 'Have you been to synagogue this morning, Grandpa?' He made me repeat the question twice before replying: 'No, of course not; can't you see it's raining?' At that moment the parlourmaid, standing respectfully at his elbow, was murmuring: 'Cabbage or cauliflower, Sir?' To this he answered, just loud enough for me to overhear: 'None of your speeches!'

While Grandpa was slightly deaf, poor Grandma was totally blind as a result of diabetes and had grown increasingly silent and withdrawn. She had a living-in companion who helped her in every way, even cutting up her food and holding her hand as she prodded at the pieces. Grandma had never seen us and, owing partly to her habitual melancholy, there was little rapport between us. Once, as we thankfully left the house, Margaret declared: 'Granny Marx is *my* granny; Grandma Hart's yours.' Angrily I turned to Mother, who happened to be with us that day, for support. She was laughing, her first spontaneous sign of amusement since our father's death; and so, instead of quarrelling, Margaret and I laughed with her.

After his usual homily on an Old Testament theme, Grandpa, if in a genial mood, would tell us a story. He described, for instance, how, travelling steerage, he had sailed to Australia. 'I had all my belongings in one bundle. It was taken away from me and I never saw it again till we arrived.' Smiling, he added: 'I had only the clothes I stood up in, so I washed my shirt every single night. There wasn't much left of it by the end, I can tell you.'

'We're going to the seaside soon,' I volunteered when we had expressed polite amazement.

'We shall be there at the same time, staying in a Jewish hotel. You two will spend most of the day on the beach, paddling in the sea and building sand castles. We'll wave every morning when we go for our walk along the front.' He kept his word. After calling and waving energetically he would lift Grandma's arm and point it in our direction so that she, too, could wave.

On our return home the Saturday visits we so much dreaded were resumed. What we quite failed to appreciate was that, however trying they were for us, they must have been almost as trying for our grandparents.

JOSEPHINE KAMM (1905–   ), novelist, biographer and writer of books for children, was born in London.

Roy Welensky

WATCHER OF THE DEAD

I learned to say *kaddish* phonetically, for my mother, who died when I was eleven. That was the first occasion, too, on which I attended synagogue. She was an Afrikaner, called Aletta Ferreira, but she was known as Leah after she was converted to Judaism (by Dr Hertz, Chief Rabbi of the British Empire), so that she could marry my father. He was born between 1843 and 1847 – we are not sure of the exact year – in a village in Russian Poland. His most vivid memory of his early days was during the cholera epidemic of 1853, when he helped his father to cart the Jewish dead to burial each day before sunset, as tradition required. One late afternoon, hurrying to get to the cemetery on time, with the body of a man named Hertz, they felt the vehicle slowing down. My grandfather turned to look behind, and realised that the corpse was sitting up. All he could think of to say on the spur of an unexpected moment was, 'Hertz, are you all right?' The corpse did not answer. What had happened was that the shroud had got wound round one of the wheels of the carriage, pulling the body upright!

At that time young men were liable to be forcefully conscripted into the Czar's army by roving bands of Cossacks, and allowed to return to their families only after twenty years, if they survived. To avoid being high-jacked himself, my father, when he was seventeen, chopped off the top of his right index finger. Shortly after that, he prudently left the country. He travelled about Europe for a while, and then emigrated to America, where he spent ten tough, hectic years, on one occasion in the West being robbed and having his throat cut, and being left for dead. Then, hearing that diamonds could be picked up in the streets of Kimberley, he went to South Africa. Unfortunately, by the time he got there, Rhodes's companies had introduced the illicit diamond-buying laws, and he was too late. So he went into ostrich feather trading instead. He walked to Rhodesia from Pietersburg in 1894. My mother followed him by ox-waggon to Bulawayo in 1895, with their six children.

I was the youngest of thirteen children in all, some of the others of whom I never even knew. My mother ruled the household with a rod of iron, though I found the world a much harsher place when she died. I was the only one left at home, then, and my father and I lived in two rooms, which was all we had left of the old house which had been converted from part of a block of offices. I was never aware of hardship, only of poverty, but that didn't worry me much. Other children got presents and had toys. I learned to accept it as a fact of life that I got no presents, but I made my own make-believe toys from clay that I gouged out of the banks of the Makabuse River. My brother and I swam naked in the river with youngsters of all shades. There wasn't much colour-feeling, then. My nickname in the area became 'King of the Kids', as I led a gang of Pioneer Street boys, several of whom were black.

My father was a watcher for the Jewish community, performing the ritual of sitting with the dead, so that the corpse was never left unattended. I used sometimes to take him his dinner at the mortuary. On one occasion, the body was of a man we had known. When I had given my father his soup, he asked me, 'D'you want to have a look at him?'

'No, Dad,' I said. 'I've seen him before, when he was alive.'

'Roy, you're not afraid, are you?' he said.

'No, Dad.'

My father looked at me for a while.

'That's right,' he said. 'It's not the dead ones you've got to watch, it's the live buggers you must keep an eye on.'

The old man was a brilliant linguist, who knew nine or ten languages, though he never got round to being able to read or write English, and spoke it with a pronounced American drawl. He would read to me from the Hebrew scriptures, translating them as he went. Otherwise, though I was always conscious that I was a Jew, I had no religious instruction; nor did I ever hear my parents discuss religion. There were two kinds of school, in those days: the good private schools for children whose parents could afford fees, and the Free School, to which I went. The head, and only male teacher in the school, was a Welshman called Jones. He walloped my backside regularly, but he also instilled in me a love of music, which has been with me ever since, and for which I have always been grateful.

I left school before I was fourteen, and got myself a job, as clerk to an auctioneer, Ikey Cohen, at £5 a month. I was a voracious reader, and one day he caught me at my regular practice of reading a book I had picked out from his second-hand stock. He looked at them, and said: 'All right. You can take home any book you like, when we close for the night. But you must bring it back in the morning.' There was a tremendous choice, there, of things to read, and that single experience did more towards my limited education than anything else. I was particularly fond of novels – Walter Scott, Conan Doyle, Fenimore Cooper, in particular –, but I read anything and everything, including books that I would find heavy-going even today. After eighteen months of that, I joined the Grand Parade Mine – it was a mica enterprise – and though I was only fifteen, they put me in charge of the stores. I was treated like a man, as I was big and tough, and would fight almost anyone. My brothers had been keen on boxing, but my interest in the sport had really begun because I didn't like being called 'Fatty'. I *was* fat, but after I took up boxing, people left me alone! I became a professional boxer for a time. I really hoped it would lead to a great career. . . . But at least it taught me how to keep my temper!

RT HON. SIR ROY WELENSKY PC CMG (1907–   ) was born in Salisbury, and became heavyweight boxing champion of Rhodesia. He was Prime Minister and Minister of External Affairs 1956–63.

Leo Rosten

A BOOK WAS A BOOK

A good book makes my nostrils quiver. In all other respects, I like to think I am a clean, wholesome American boy. The memory of Lou Gehrig brings a lump to my throat; a well-shaped limb brings a gleam to my eye; but a good book makes my nostrils quiver.

It is not that my nostrils are especially quiverable. They quiver because, for reasons you soon shall hear, a book triggers the most delicious associations in my mind between reading and (of all things) pickles. Dill pickles.

'*Dill* pickles?' you echo. 'What on earth do books have to do with pickles?' I'm glad you asked that.

In my youth, I lived on the west side of Chicago. It offered all who inhabited that rough-and-tumble section of the city the vitality of life: crowds, noise, challenge, conflict, camaraderie, sidewalk poets, alley crooks, frontstep seminars – plus the priceless dream of someday moving to a nicer neighborhood. This is a life and a dream that my children, raised in antiseptic California and genteel Connecticut, have been cruelly deprived of.

In those days, the Chicago public library used to establish outposts of civilization in depositary branches scattered around the city. The closest depot from which I could get free books was located at the rear of a seedy stationery store near Kedzie Avenue on Twelfth Street, which no campaigns by civic improvementeers could get us to call 'Roosevelt Road.' The man who ran the stationery store received a fee, I suppose, for the use of the dreariest twenty square feet of his premises.

To the golden, magical promise of that stationery store I would race in breathless excitement from George Howland school several afternoons a week. Neither hail nor fire nor pestilence, nor even Chicago's weather, could slow me down. I ran to my Eldorado in order to pick up such books as might hae been deposited there, ear-marked for me, by a truck from the central library in that far-off sector of wealth and lake-front we called Downtown.

To order a book, under the neighborhood depositary system, you first consulted a card catalogue at the rear of the stationery (or dry goods, candy, novelty) store. On a slip of coarse brown paper, with the majestic words CHICAGO PUBLIC LIBRARY printed on top, you wrote your name and address, and then, in the columns provided, listed the call numbers of the books you wanted to get.

All the brown slips from all the depositary branches went to the central library, where the slaves who toiled in the stacks would go down the lists of numbers. If the first number on your list was not on the shelves of the stacks, the cellar gnomes would draw a contemptuous line through that number and proceed to the next. Since I could never be sure that the books I most yearned for would be available, I soon learned to list ten, twenty, even thirty numbers. The faceless lackeys at Michigan and Randolph never would send thirty books, of course, or even twenty, or even ten. They usually meted out no more than two to a customer. In any case, several days after listing my numbers on those library slips, I would race back to the stationery store for the treasures I might have drawn in this strange lottery.

Now the Lord, as we all know, doth move in mysterious ways. In my case, I think He received a special celestial pleasure in afflicting the guys in the stacks with astigmatism or hallucinations whenever they got to the brown slip on which I had so carefully, so legibly, so lovingly printed the numbers of the books I most coveted.

For instead of receiving, say, number 712.8T, a piece of glory I could rattle off in my sleep as *Dave Porter in the Philippines*, I would get instead, say number 912.8T, which is *The Prickle-Edged Flora of the Lower Sudan*, or 782.8R, a racy gem entitled *Aunt Polly's System for Tatting Antimacassars*, or even 742.5B, a dandy little thriller about the drainage problems of the Mosquito Coast. (The Mosquito Coast is that strip of Honduras and Nicaragua I hope to hell I never see.)

Well, a man going mad from thirst is not likely to reject a bottle of wine because of its vintage; I, a book-starved lunatic of no discrimination whatsoever, read any book that fell into my hot little hands. I would be bitterly disappointed, of course, to discover that I had been gulled once more, that the malevolent cabal downtown had not sent me a single book out of the thirty immortal numbers I had listed – books by the great Burt L. Standish, the peerless Frank Packard, the masterly Sax Rohmer, the incomparable Joseph Altsheler. But if I was to be denied the joy of chortling over the antics of *The Red-Headed Outfield*, or cliff-hanging on the exploits of Dr. Fu Manchu, or cheering that matchless modern Robin Hood, Jimmy Dale – then, by heaven, *The Prickle-Edged Flora of the Lower Sudan* it would be. And it was.

Between my passion to read anything and the statistical aberrations of the pixies in the library's nether regions, I managed to stuff my mind with information about as odd, exotic, pointless and useless as you are likely to find in the brain-pan of any bibliophile of my generation. It is not that I have a particularly retentive memory: I am not even blessed with the kind of mentality that latches on to simple facts like my bank balance, or the name of my daughter's latest suitor, or when it was my wife told me to be sure and turn off the oven. It is just that through some perverse arrangement of cells my brain seizes with joy upon such bits and pieces of culture as these:

Nicolas Lancret left 780 paintings.

Sirutel is a river in Rumania. (I'll bet you thought it was a syrup that provides 'stomach regularity' – Leturis spelled backward.)

In Borneo, they call 1.36 pounds of anything a Catty.

The sawfly often is wingless.

The Esopus Creek Dam is 252 feet high.

In 1905, our Secretary of the Navy was a man named Bonaparte – Charles J. Bonaparte, to be exact.

I have spent my life walking around with junk like that in my head, hoping that one of these days someone will come right out and ask me how many gametes are in a zygote, or in what year the Diet of Worms convened, or who played third base for the infamous Black Sox. I sometimes dream of dazzling beautiful duchesses in Mayfair with just such nuggets of knowledge – tossed off, need I say, with the most casual of airs and the most memorable aplomb. At dinner parties on Park Avenue I sometimes smile inscrutably as I drop the name of Ethelred the Unready into the table talk, or the diameter of the rose window at Chartres, or the great, undying name of Bonehead Merkle – but no one seems to care about erudition any more. In fact, people tend to draw away from me when I ruminate aloud about Philander Smith College, which you probably didn't know is in Little Rock.

I have learned to enjoy these things just for themselves. It enlivens many a solitary walk for me to chuckle to myself over the sudden recollection that it was in 1811 that Tecumseh, that noble Shawnee, decided to make a stand against the white man, or that 'monoecious' denotes the presence of *both male and female flowers on the same plant.*

My experiences at that stationer's shop, so many years ago, taught me (apart from such nonsense) that there are rare and wonderful surprises to be found in the random. The book picked up to browse in, the side street taken just because you feel like it, the bus ride to no place in particular, the pedestrian stopped with a question to which you already know the answer ('How do I get to Fort Knox?') – in these random encounters with the unknown I have often found unexpected and delightful rewards.

I sometimes think that in exchange for the priceless treasures it supplies, every library ought to set aside one day a year for Random Reading. Everyone who comes into the library on Random Day would be invited to reach into a huge barrel filled with books, pull out a volume at random – and read it. I should like to be on the committee that chooses the masterpieces, neglected by passing fads and debased tastes, that would go into those barrels.

Barrels. That brings me back to pickles, from which I have strayed. Why does a good book make my nostrils quiver? Because whenever I left the stationery store, my eyes and mind glued to whatever book I had not ordered, there would be wafted into my nostrils a most pungent and provocative smell

– a whiff of garlic and dill. I can't be sure whether the pickle barrel from which it came was concealed behind the stationer's counter, to satisfy some secret, shameless appetite of his, or whether that ambrosian scent came from the grocery store next door. But what does it matter? Just give me a good book and a pickle, or an olfactory facsimile of same, and I am in heaven. Even the gross deadweight tonnage of Liberia's tankers cannot intrude on my ecstasy.

LEO ROSTEN (1908–), American author, screenwriter and political scientist, was born in Lodz, Poland. As a novelist, he created the character of Hyman Kaplan.

Irene Mayer Selznick
I HAD A LITTLE LAMB . . .

It would have been more dramatic to arrive in California in midwinter and feel the contrast as Mother had, but never was there a more wide-eyed passenger than me sitting in the open part of the observation car of the Chief, taking in every single sight as though it were going to disappear forever, the continuing and mounting wonder of it. We got off at the various stations, long stops where some of the passengers had their meals at the Fred Harvey Houses while we explored each town. By the time we got to Albuquerque, which was an hour stop, we were seasoned sightseers. I might never see those towns again, because they went by in the middle of the night when you were going East and I might never go to California again. I also spent a lot of the time playing cards with my father. There were no likely prospects around, so he decided he would make me into a worthy opponent at two-handed pinochle.

Some months earlier my father had signed a second star, a girl named Mildred Harris. As an 'under-age' bride, she had just married a reluctant, even unwilling, Charlie Chaplin, and was therefore to be billed as Mildred Harris Chaplin, a name not to Mr. Chaplin's liking, for which I do not blame him. Mildred Harris was sending her car to welcome us to California.

When we got to the station, there was Mrs. Chaplin herself, and we were agog. Waiting was a Marmon tonneau limousine, the closed back of which was upholstered in a soft, pale fabric and boasted a cut-glass vase containing a single rose. This wasn't a make-believe world, this was fairyland.

As we neared our house, the splendor of which we could hardly imagine, I held my breath. Then there it was, our anticlimax – not too elegantly located, and with a most unprepossessing exterior of brown-stained shingle. It was called a bungalow. It didn't even have a front hall, and was furnished in a somewhat desolate fashion. Mother said it was probably splendid upstairs.

We soon retreated to the living room and Edie and I sat huddled in silence. We had read too many movie magazines. My father persuaded us outside in the back to marvel at the varied fruit trees, which lifted the gloom momentarily. So this was California! Pleasant Street had looked like a palace compared to this.

I never did know whether this house was the faulty judgement of whomever my father had delegated to choose it, or whether it deliberately reflected his determination that he would keep a low profile and that the family would not 'go Hollywood' – an understatement that was to be further emphasized. . . .

Our only grandeur was that we were to go to a private school, the Hollywood School for Girls. The Brookline schools had a long tradition of high standards, but the public schools of Hollywood made my parents uneasy. This school had no pretensions whatsoever; clearly it was a jerry-built place run on a shoestring. It had some rooms for boarders; everything else was ramshackle – some unlikely scattered shacks and a few oversized crates. The excuse was that it was an 'outdoor' school. The entire high school was contained in a one-room building, one side of which folded out, but that did not make it an outdoor school. From time to time Mother reminded them that they were supposed to hold classes in the sunshine, which is where she intended Edith to be.

Nevertheless, it was only about a mile from our house, and besides it was the only private school in Hollywood. What impressed Mother was that there were trees and flowers, riding and tennis, and what gave it the seal of approval was the presence of the de Mille girls. Actually, the school not only educated the de Mille children, it appeared to be dominated by their parents (William de Mille with a small 'd,' the intellectual brother, and Cecil DeMille with a big 'D,' glamorous and more successful.) Cecilia, to whom horses were all-important, seemed to account for the riding class. Tennis was probably attributable to the William de Milles.

Rarely can there have been a more heterogeneous group of girls than those who had landed there. Most of them were new or temporary residents (but then so was practically everybody else in Southern California), except for a few socialites-to-be. There was a small handful who later recrossed my path, such as Jean Harlow and Joel McCrea, who was the only boy in the high school apart from Harriet Beecher Stowe's nephew. Douglas Fairbanks, Jr., in a long-standing joke, claims we were there at the same time, but we both know better, because he was there much earlier. We've adapted it to 'We practically went to school together.'

Then there was my art teacher, who also taught French, named Edith Spare, a remarkably talented young woman whom I didn't meet again for many decades, when she was the celebrated designer Edith Head. I tried to reminisce with her about the old days, but she denied the whole thing. Oh well. The only continuing relationship was with Agnes and Margaret de Mille, even after they left to live in New York.

Other girls' fathers went to the office, but mine went to the studio. That was a pretty stunning phrase, except for the fact that the studio wasn't even in

Hollywood. Where was it? It was at the Selig Zoo! Where was the Selig Zoo? It was at Eastlake Park, near the wrong end of Pasadena, of all places. Colonel Selig had a zoo because he had animals, and he had animals because he had made movies with them, and there had to be some use for these animals when he wasn't using them or renting them out. And to use them he needed a small studio and considerable land, which was cheaply available in a remote part of southeastern Los Angeles. My father could lease space there because by this time it was more zoo than studio.

The locality did not detract from the thrilling privilege of seeing a movie being made in a real studio, though we were laden with prohibitions. Children did not belong in studios. We were to be practically invisible. Moreover, there was not to be a word out of us; even a sneeze would have been reprehensible. It was as though sound pictures were already in.

The new climate did have an effect on Dad after all, because one Sunday we stopped at a rabbit farm and he bought me a pair of rabbits. I recall the elaborate hutch built at the studio, and I was to 'take the responsibility.' Feeding, cleaning. My mother was afraid we were going to be overrun with rabbits; my father couldn't wait for the litter. The excited expectancy was exceeded only by the growing disappointment when nothing happened. The explanation was simple: they were the same sex. All that big hutch for nothing.

About this time my father thought it would be nice for me to have a baby lamb. He knew it was unwise, but he said he found the image of me going to school followed by the lamb irresistible. Inasmuch as I already had rabbit duties in the back of the garden, I might as well take on the lamb, who was called Lammikin. The poor little thing was a couple of weeks old, of uncertain gender, and could hardly stand up. I had to warm milk and feed it from a bottle several times a day, including the middle of the night.

At first I adored the lamb, which promised a good deal more action than the rabbits, who were pretty dull. At least it sometimes followed me around in the garden. But there was no future in the lamb, which didn't enjoy going along Franklin Avenue to school. It was even more impractical for the neighbors, because as it got older its voice got lustier, and the baaa, baaa, baaa rent the air through the night until the police were sent for. Finally I tried making it a household pet; I took it upstairs onto my bed one morning, where it made a dubious contribution. In June we went East, and Lammikin spent the summer at the Selig Zoo. After that it couldn't be retrieved because it was indistinguishable from the other lambs, sheep by then! . . .

Celebrities abounded, but my father would have no part of them. Edie and I found this attitude disenchanting. Here we were in golden California, surrounded by tantalizing personalities, and my father said nothing doing. There were not as yet many substantial citizens in filmland, and he didn't approve at all of the kind the industry had attracted. Frowning on their ways, he hoped in time to find more serious film-makers from whom he could learn, and meanwhile he sought to make his connections with the downtown establishment. And he was as disinclined as ever to get involved socially, except for limited relationships with those people connected with his company, and with those he valued from the past when they came West to visit.

It was a quiet family life: early dinner and to bed. An hour of sleep before midnight. . . .

However, one social occasion in our first year there sticks in my memory for the wrong reasons.

We were invited to Sunday lunch at Anita Stewart's house. I now not only knew a movie star, I was about to eat at her table. And she lived right next door to Cecil DeMille himself! But a cloud hung over the event for me in the shape of four little words . . . and a gift. Mother felt we must bring something, not come empty-handed, and settled on a big box of chocolates. So far so good. But it had to be presented . . . presented by me. Me, why me? And I was to hand it to her on arrival with those four words. Something told me it was dead wrong.

The arrival was a mess. Amidst greetings and coats, I stood holding a hot potato which no one seemed to notice. Lugging the candy, I couldn't shake hands or get out of my coat. Then silence, and all eyes were focused on me. Finally the dreaded words came out. With burning cheeks and downcast eyes, I mumbled, 'Sweets to the sweet,' and hoped nobody really heard it. I obeyed, but only just.

I'm still embarrassed.

From A Private View (1983)

IRENE MAYER SELZNICK (1907–), daughter of film-magnate Louis B. Mayer and wife of the producer David O. Selznick, was born in New York City, and became a notable theatre producer.

David Daiches

THE TWO WORLDS

What was my father's relation to *his* father? My grandfather migrated to England while my father was still a student, to become rabbi of an orthodox Jewish congregation – the Beth Hamedrash Hagadol – in Leeds, and from that time on my father regarded Britain as his true home. He already knew English perfectly, and after a few years in England spoke it perfectly, while my grandfather never mastered more than the merest rudiments of the language. He and my grandmother represented for me a picturesque old world in which I was not really at home. My father mediated between their world and my own, translating my grandfather's Yiddish (my grandmother could speak English) and trying to interpret the behaviour of an Edinburgh schoolboy to the old man; yet I had the feeling that my father, for all his tremendous sense of family pride and loyalty and for all the great mutual affection between him and my grandfather, was not altogether happy in seeing us in this old world atmosphere. He looked forward, to a Judaism no less orthodox but less involved with the memories of the Ghetto. We went rarely to see our grandfather. I may be quite wrong, but I have a suspicion that my father preferred to keep us apart.

The house in Leeds where my grandfather lived was one of a row of small nineteenth-century brick dwellings, all exactly alike, in which a number of *nouveau* middle-class hangers-on of the Industrial Revolution had once proclaimed their precarious gentility. The street had a run-down look when I knew it, and it was inhabited by very small business men or by miscellaneous oddities of firm respectability but moderate means. It was the kind of street one can see today in any British industrial town, shabby and tired looking, but determinedly decent. Behind the front door of any one of its houses one expected to hear thick Yorkshire accents proclaiming phrases out of J. B. Priestley or Eric Knight.

But number 6 was different. The brass plate read, in letters almost too worn to be legible, 'Rabbi J. H. Daiches' – the 'J' should have been 'I' as it stood for 'Israel', but my grandfather considered the letters 'I' and 'J' interchangeable – and if you pushed open the gate and went up the narrow path that skirted the tiny apology for a front garden to the front door you were aware of approaching the entrance to a very different world from that of industrial Yorkshire. It was, one might say, an emanation which seemed to be coming out of the house, a smell perhaps, a feeling, an atmosphere. And if you entered and went through the dark bead curtain into the small entrance hall and smelled the mingled odour of cigar smoke and Jewish cooking you had left Yorkshire very far behind.

My grandfather as I knew him was a benevolently patriarchal figure with twinkling eyes and a white beard. Only recently an old man who had known him in his prime told me that in his younger days in Poland he had been known for his neat clothes and well-groomed appearance, and that he had given scandal to the orthodox by sending his children (my father and my uncle) to secular non-Jewish schools and universities. Between afternoon and evening services (*'minchah'* and *'ma'arev'*) at the synagogue he would go for a walk with a certain Christian civic official, with whom he would converse in Russian – a habit which caused much shaking of heads among the older people. This new light on my grandfather came as an astonishing revelation to me, who had always considered him as belonging to a Ghetto world of Jewish piety and Jewish isolation. But evidently he too was a pioneer in his day, and tried to reconcile tradition with progress.

I saw no sign of that as a child, however. I had to watch my every movement in my grandfather's house, in case I unwittingly offended against his sense of what was proper Jewish behaviour. I could never leave my head uncovered for a moment, for example. At home we always covered our heads to pray, and to say grace before and after meals, but we were never expected to keep our heads covered continually. My father wore a black skull cap when receiving members of his congregation in his study, but as the years went by he developed the habit of keeping it in his pocket throughout much of the day and diving hastily for it when the bell rang. In his father's presence he wore it continually. I remember once, seeing the two of them together in my grandfather's house, thinking how young and *modern* my father looked beside the white-bearded older rabbi. Yet at home in Edinburgh I had so often thought my father old-fashioned in manner and dress, with his black frock-coat, stiff shirt front and bow tie, and his rather formal eighteenth-century English.

In the house at Leeds the slightest daily activity seemed to partake of ritual. The great stone kitchen in the basement, where my grandmother presided amid rows of shining copper vessels, was like something out of Grimms' fairy tales, and even the dining-room, with its long narrow table running up the length of the room and its black horsehair sofa on one side (how the horsehair used to scratch my bare legs!) seemed more than a dining-room to me. My grandfather used to shuffle in in his carpet slippers before dinner and take his place at the head of the table, where there was laid out for him a special little cloth on which were a bottle of cognac, a plate of sliced pickled herring, and a loaf of dark rye bread. He would fill himself a tot of brandy and drink it off at a gulp; then he would cut a slice of bread and eat it with the herring; and then his special cloth with everything on it was removed and the meal proper (which my grandfather hardly touched) could start. I would watch this ritual with pure admiration from my place on the horsehair sofa (which was placed along one side of the table, so that we children could sit there, side by side, when having our meals: I suppose we must have been propped up on something, but I don't remember that). Together with the admiration went a sense of the mystical strangeness of it all. Once, when I was almost grown up, I ventured to remark that I, too, liked pickled herring. My grandfather expressed the utmost astonishment and passed me the plate, and would not take anything himself until I had eaten rather more than I really wanted.

When I was a child I knew no Yiddish except the occasional word, referring to some aspect of daily Jewish practice, which had found its way into our ordinary discourse, and an occasional phrase such as 'Ich vaiss nisht' ('I don't know'). It was only after I had learned German, in my last years at school, that I acquired any degree of facility with the language, and even then such Yiddish as I spoke was more German than Yiddish. (It is significant that my father took an interest in and encouraged my learning of German, but took no steps whatever to help me learn Yiddish.) When I conversed with my grandfather, which was not often, we used simple Hebrew until I was in my 'teens, when he spoke in his native Yiddish and I replied in my Germanised form of the language. Lionel and I also used to write occasional letters to our grandfather in Hebrew. Most of them were expressions of thanks for a birthday present (generally a pound note) and I still remember the typical opening of such letters (I am transliterating roughly the Ashkenazi pronunciation): *'Hin'ni nowsein es towdosi be'ad ha'matonoh shai-sholachto li'* – 'Behold I send my thanks for the gift which you have sent me.' Later on, when I had read some of the Hebrew letters of Ahad Ha'am, I would vary this opening with elegant locutions learned from him, such as: *'Kabail no es towdosi . . .'* – 'Receive I pray thee my thanks . . .' and I learned too, also from Ahad Ha'am, a fine opening with which to begin a letter that should have been written some time ago. It began 'Forgive, I pray thee, that on account of my abundant business I have delayed writing until now. . . .' The phrase, beginning as it did with the familiar penitential phrase *s'lach no*, reminded me of the service of the Day of Atonement: and it did not seem altogether improper to address my grandfather in those terms. Yet his conversations with me violently contradicted the impression of an aloof patriarchal character with which I could not help associating him in general. He had a great fondness for low jokes. I knew that he was the world's leading authority on the Jerusalem Talmud (to be distinguished from the more popular Babylonian Talmud), and that he had produced a noble edition of it with a large Hebrew commentary surrounding a tiny island of original text; so I naturally expected words of profound wisdom to fall from his venerable lips. Instead, he would inquire whether I went to the bathroom in order to drink brandy or smoke cigars secretly, or he would suggest that the sixty-five-year old charwoman was pining for me to take her to the pictures.

I would come into his study to find him stroking his beard and poring over a huge Hebrew tome, looking the very quintessence of rabbinic grandeur. I was prepared for him to throw a question at me concerning my Hebrew knowledge and had even got up one side of a long dialogue in that language on which I was ready to embark if only he would give me the opportunity. But when I appeared he would close his book, ask me to bring him a cigar from the cupboard (like my father, he would smoke nothing but the choicest Havanas, which he got as presents from members of his congregation), and proceed to make joking or teasing remarks about kilts and bagpipes, or about girls, or clothes, or other unrabbinical subjects. Yet as soon as I left the room he was at his book again, and I could see him through the window from the back garden, with his hand on his beard and his head nodding gently, reading and meditating.

He lived in what seemed to me an almost feudal fashion. His salary must have been quite small, and in any case when I knew him he had, I believe, virtually retired, but he had retainers who would come and see him and bring cigars or a bottle of brandy or an occasional duck or chicken. He had absolutely no money sense. My grandmother ran the financial affairs of the household, and when she died a not very efficient elderly couple came to live with him and look after things. Every time I visited him he would want to present me with a large cheque, and had to be restrained by my father or some other watchful grown-up. He was quite capable of giving me a cheque for much more than he had in the bank, for I don't think he ever knew how much he had in the bank – or indeed exactly what a bank was supposed to do.

My impression is that, at least in his later years, much of his income was paid in kind, and he had little occasion to handle money.

From Two Worlds: an Edinburgh Jewish Childhood (1957)

DAVID DAICHES (1912–   ), British academic, critic and historian, was born in Leeds, the son of a rabbi. He was professor, Cornell University 1945–51, and Professor of English, University of Sussex 1961–71.

Ralph Glasser

SOAP BOY

He repeated, parrot fashion, a piece of conventional wisdom of the slums: 'You must have a trade in your hands. With a trade you can go anywhere!'

A trade lifted you above the common labourer.

Two weeks later, on my last day at school, the headmaster said to me: 'Pity. You should go to university. You would do well there, but still ... I understand.'

He knew there was no chance, and probably knew why too. Not that the specific reason mattered. Of the boys I knew, none remained at school after fourteen.

And then my father took me to a barber shop in Gorbals Street, and I started being a soap boy. The ritual was simple but strict. You ushered the customer to the wooden armchair, clicked its ratchet-held neck rest to the correct height, spread a white sheet over him and tucked its top edge into his shirt collar, and then spread a small towel like a bib under his chin. Then you applied shaving soap to his face with a bushy bristle brush, spread the soap and lathered it into the skin with a massaging action of the fingers and hand. The barber then stropped his cut-throat razor with brisk back and forth strokes on a length of leather that hung from the back of the chair and, to the accompaniment of breezy chatter, shaved the customer. 'Soap boy!' he would call, 'Ready now!'

You applied hot towels and cleaned up all the flakes of soap round the edge of the shaved area of the face, combed the man's hair, smartly whipped away the bib towel and the sheet, and turned and called the next customer.

I felt miserable having to touch these beery, bristly faces, but I tried to be stoical. One day, somehow, I would escape.

Perhaps father sensed my feelings. Perhaps he wanted to test me further. One evening, after only a few days at the barber shop, he said:

'An intelligent boy like you should learn the trade in no time. Come, I'll sit here and you can practise shaving me.'

He pulled one of the battered wooden chairs away from the kitchen table and sat in it and put a towel round his neck and I soaped his face. Then he stropped his open razor and handed it to me, the concave hollow ground blade shining like bright silver. I took the razor, held it as I had seen the barber do so, between thumb and forefinger on the haft of the blade, the other fingers steadying it by resting on the little curved tail that projected behind the guard, and drew back the loose skin under his chin to make the first, grazing, upward stroke. I hesitated.

'Come on!' he barked. 'Don't just stand there like that. It's easy!'

Tears came again, and I could hardly see. Quickly I put the razor down on the kitchen table. 'I can't do it, father. I – I am afraid I – I'll cut you!'

I could not bring myself to say why I had to put the razor down quickly. But I could see that *he* knew. I was afraid I would cut his throat.

I knew I could not do that. I also knew that with that scalpel-sharp blade in my shaking hand the risk was there, and I dare not take it. Forces worked within me, shaking me with their rebellion against what he had done to me. Knowing that he had fought in vain against his destiny, I felt an enervating fear that I too might fail, indeed that he was bequeathing a similar destiny to me, insisting that I too should not rise above it.

He did not meet my eyes. Without saying a word he took the towel from under his chin, stood up, turned the chair round and tucked it once again under the flap of the kitchen table, took the razor, a fine German one and a prized possession, and carefully cleaned it in his own special fashion. He spread a handkerchief across his left hand and held it taut across the cushion of flesh at the base of the thumb, held the rounded butt edge of the hollow blade on it and slid the blade over it from butt side to the hair-thin edge, then swivelled it over on to its other face and slid it back again across the fabric; back and forth, back and forth, in a smooth, rhythmic, hypnotic motion, intent, absorbed, almost tender, as if he caressed a loved one. Then he held it up to the light and twisted it back and forth, inspecting it for specks of dust on the fine edge, and the blade glittered with a vibrant mirrorlike sheen, as if it answered him in a private communion, as the magic sword Durendal might silently have spoken to its heroic master. Then he folded the blade into its ivory guard and placed it gently in the shaped blue velvet cushion in its slender leather case and closed it.

At last he turned to me, the jaws tight, and spoke with a softness that I knew meant suppressed anger: 'All right. You won't go back to that barber's tomorrow. You'll come with me and learn to be a presser. You won't have to be afraid you'll cut someone's throat *that* way.'

From Growing Up in the Gorbals (1986)

RALPH GLASSER (1915–), British development consultant and applied economist, was born in Leeds, but brought up in Glasgow.

Bud Schulberg

SAMMY'S STAND

Three weeks before Sammy's thirteenth birthday Papa came in too upset to eat.

'Tonight when I come out of *schule* the Rabbi wants to talk to me. "Max, my heart is like lead to tell you this," he says, "but your son Samuel cannot be *Bar-mitzvah*. He never comes to *cheder*. He does not know his *Brochis*. The *melamud* says he knows no more about the *Torah* than a *goy*."'

'*Oi weh!*' Papa cried. 'That I should live to see the day when my own flesh and blood is not prepared to become a man.'

'Aw, what's that got to do with becomin' a man?' Sammy said. 'Just a lotta crap. I been a man since I was eleven.'

'Oh, Lord of Israel,' Papa said, 'how can You ever forgive us this shame? That I, a man who went to synagogue twice every day of his life, should have such a no-good son.'

'Yeah,' Sammy said. 'While you was being such a goddam good Jew, who was hustlin' up the dough to pay the rent?'

'Silence, silence!' Papa roared.

'I guess I gotta right to speak in this house,' Sammy said. 'For Pete's sake I'm bringin' in more money 'n you are.'

'Money!' Papa cried. 'That's all you think about – money, money –'

'Yes, money, money,' Sammy mimicked. 'You know what you c'n do with your lousy *Bar-mitzvah*. It's money in the pocket – that's what makes you feel like a man.'

The day that Sammy was to have been *Bar-mitzvahed* Papa went to the synagogue and prayed for him as if he were dead. He came home with his lapel ripped in mourning. He would have liked to lock himself in all day because he couldn't face the shame of it. But it was a weekday, and on weekdays he was just an extension of his pushcart.

People saw him push his cart through the street with his eyes staring dumbly at nothing. The driver who hit him said he sounded his horn several times, but the old man did not seem to hear.

When he was carried upstairs to his bed Israel and Mama sat there crying and watching him die.

Afterward, Israel didn't know what to do, so he went up on the roof to look at the stars. He found Sammy there smoking a butt.

'Is it over?' Sammy said when he saw his brother.

Israel nodded. He had not really broken down yet, but the question did it. He cried, deep and soft, as only Jews can cry because they have had so much practice at it.

Israel was eighteen, but now he was a little boy crying because he had lost his papa. Sammy was thirteen, but he was a veteran; he had learned something that took the place of tears.

When Israel realized that he was the only one crying he became embarrassed and then angry.

'Damn you, why don't you say something?' Israel said. 'Why don't you cry?'
'Well, what's there ta say?' said Sammy.
'At least, can't you say you're sorry?'
'Sure,' Sammy said. 'I'm sorry he was a dope.'
'I oughta punch you in the nose,' Israel said.
'Try it,' Sammy said. 'I bet I c'n lick you.' Sammy sat there dry and tense. 'Aw, don't work yourself into a sweat,' he said.

'Sammy,' Israel pleaded, 'what's got into you? Why must you go around with a chip on your shoulder? What do you have to keep your left out all the time for?'

'Whatta you take me for, a sap like you?' Sammy said. 'You don't see me getting smacked in the puss.'

'But we aren't fighting now,' Israel said.

Israel was right about not knowing Sammy. There were no rest periods between rounds for Sammy. The world had put a chip on his shoulder and then it had knocked it off. Sammy was ready to accept the challenge all by himself and this was a fight to the finish. He had fought to be born into the East Side, he had kicked, bit, scratched and gouged first to survive in it and then to subdue it, and now that he was thirteen and a man, having passed another kind of *Bar-mitzvah*, he was ready to fight his way out again, pushing uptown, running in Israel's cast-off shoes, travelling light, without any baggage, or a single principle to slow him down.

From What Makes Sammy Run (1941)

BUD SCHULBERG (1914–   ), American novelist and screenwriter, was born in New York City.

Howard Fast

MY FATHER

I was never surprised to find that my father had been something else in his time that I had ever dreamed of; I suppose the only thing he had never been was rich. He told me once that for two years or so, he had been gripperman on the cable cars – that is until they decided to do away with cable cars in New York entirely. It surprised me less that he had been a gripperman – something I had never heard of before – than that there had ever been cable cars in New York City; but he explained that there were in the old times, running south from Forty-Second Street, on Seventh Avenue, I believe.

Years later, in San Francisco, I spent the better part of a day riding the cable cars up Nob Hill and Telegraph Hill and all the other hills and little valleys that make San Francisco like no other city on earth; and for hours I watched the gripperman handle his three long levers with grace and competence, a wonderful survival of a world that is no more.

So there it was, and my father had been a gripperman. He had large, beautiful and strong hands, and he was superbly muscled, lean and hard to the day of his death, and always from the beginning of memory, I remember those hands. They were the hands of a working man; they were his rock and his foundation, and all he ever had in the world were those two hands.

I am not completely certain of what work he did first. He went to work at the age of eleven, as I did, but he talked little of the work he did before he was seventeen years old. I think he worked in a stable in downtown New York – that was in the 1880s – curried horses, cleaned wagons, but there were many other things too.

In those times, man and boy too worked a twelve-hour day, and fourteen hours often enough, and when my father was fifteen years old he went into a sweatshop and worked from seven in the morning until eight at night. He was of a generation of working people to whom laughter and joy came hard and uneasily, and I will never forget the glad excitement of his face when he did laugh, the sunshine breaking through, and the wonderful pleasure that I and my brothers knew because he was laughing.

There was a time when he had been on strike for seven months and then, when the strike was broken, laid off for longer than I care to remember, and the burden of support for the family, of eating and drinking and paying some of the rent, so we would not be put out on the street, fell upon my older brother and myself.

I was twelve then, and we had a newspaper route which brought in ten dollars a week for the work of both of us, and it meant that on Sundays we had to rise at three in the morning, in the cold darkness of night, dress, and drag our aching, over-used bodies to the collating station. My mother was long dead, and my father was father, mother, and guardian angel to three small boys – with never enough to feed them or clothe them or to overcome his guilt at being able to do neither.

The only compensation was that strange communion of working people which bound us together, and on those Saturday nights he would rise a half hour before we did, prepare breakfast, wake us gently, help us to dress, feed us breakfast and watch us go – all with that silent anguish in his face that only the poor know, and having once seen, the poor can never properly forget.

I never really believed that my father had ever been young, and when he talked of his youth, I always felt that he was describing a third person. There are some people who remain young and clad in youth until the day they die, even though they live to be eighty, but my father was not one of them, although there was youth enough in his body, his stride, and his amazing strength. He had the arms of a blacksmith, and they came from his years as an iron-worker.

In those days, just at the turn of the century, there was a great vogue in New York – and in other American cities too, I suppose – for wrought iron. Not only were the new-fangled fire-escapes built to a large extent of wrought iron, but it was used ornamentally on stoops, horse-cars, wagons, for iron railings to guard open cellars, and in a hundred other ways. Much of this iron-work was wrought in the hot forge, over charcoal fires with hammer and bellows and the strong arm of the smith, who was called in this trade, a *monger* – a method of working iron as old as man's knowledge of iron. The iron sheds were on the lower East and West Sides, near the rivers, and the race of mongers were akin to the smiths who shoed the thousands of horses and the wheelwrights who repaired the thousands of iron wagon-wheels.

My father told me how as a boy he would rather be in an iron shed than in paradise, and how he would take his sandwich and can of beer in his lunch hour, squat in the open side of an iron shed, and glory in the roaring flames, the hiss of the bellows, and the mighty clang and clamor of the hammers.

He began as an apprentice of the lowest rank, a boy who ran errands, dragged iron bars, and made endless trips to the nearby saloon for beer to quench the smith's raging thirst. Then he became a tongs-boy, permitted to hold and move the metal as the smith worked, and finally, a full-fledged smith in a leather apron, with his own hammer to beat and subdue the red hot iron.

But even if the type and method of working iron had not gone out of existence, he would have broken himself on the anvil; and in later years until I finally learned, I often puzzled why a man of his wit and skill could never depend on anything but his own two hands. With the end of the wrought iron industry, he became a tinsmith, but the use of tin for troughs and sinks and roofing had its own short day, and inevitably he gravitated toward the one industry in New York that increased steadily, and became a cutter in a garment factory. He had to learn a new trade, and he learned it well – and in between these three, how many others? I watched him work as a journeyman painter, and I worked with him once on a plumbing job, myself clumsy and incompetent next to his incredible hands. He had a store of patience that was inexhaustible, and his temper was as long as the time between sunrise and sunset. Only the manner of training a dollar to work for him and increase itself was unknown to him.

My mother died when I was a little boy, leaving my father with the overwhelming task of raising three small boys. I suppose we were just as poor before my mother died, but she somehow had the skill to draw a mask over the naked face of poverty, and this my father alone could not do. Work as he would, twelve and fourteen hours a day, he still could not feed us and clothe us; and he gave away our childhood the way millions of working class fathers in so many lands gave away the childhood of their children. My older brother went to work when he was twelve, myself when I was eleven – the beginning of an ache, a weariness, a tiredness that came not only out of work done, but out of play and gladness passed by. Possibly it was then that my father became old; he had to sell our youth, just as his own was sold, and his face became gray and tired, the life gone out of it.

I live in a time now when in my country the word *socialism* is far from popular, and *communism* little better than an epithet, but until I was sixteen years old, I don't think I had ever heard those words, or if I had, that I was in any particular way conscious of their meaning. I knew that *Bolshevik* characterized a variety of obscenities, made plain to me by the rotogravure supplements in the Hearst newspapers, but the wild riot of rapine, starvation and murder therein described was sufficiently apart from my own experience for me to be unconcerned to any large degree.

I was then working as a messenger for the New York Public Library for the fine wage of twenty-two cents an hour – at a time when so many had no wages at all, and it was one of a dozen jobs I drifted in and out of, in spite of my father's pleas that I learn a decent trade; but I liked books, being around them, handling them, reading them – and I read everything and anything, so long as it had the shape of a book and told a story for me to escape into. It was at this time that a librarian put into my hands George Bernard Shaw's *Intelligent Women's Guide to Socialism and Capitalism*.

She had no wish to subvert me; she was someone who became interested in me when I once happened to remark that late at night I occupied myself in writing stories, and when I gave her some to read, she observed that none of them were about my own orbit of experience. I tried to explain, and found myself explaining that I had no manner of understanding or power to understand my own orbit of experience. So she gave me one or two short pieces to whet my appetite, and the book to satisfy it.

I didn't like the title; the title embarrassed me. I was just turning seventeen years old, but I was a man in the earning of my daily bread, in the battles I had fought for my own survival, in the blood and filth and hardness I had encountered in my own jungle of street and work, in the profanity that marked my rich gutter speech, in my extensive if lopsided knowledge of the facts of life and biology – and I wondered what I could learn from a book earmarked for 'intelligent women.'

That night I learned. I began the book that night, at the kitchen table, the heart of family life and work, with my father and my two brothers beginning to doze opposite me, and then I went on reading after they had gone to sleep, and I read until there was light in the morning sky, with the world dancing and leaping in circles for the first time with a glint of reason breaking through the insanity of how I lived and was, and where I had come from and where I was going.

Yet it was not George Bernard Shaw, not the kindly librarian who turned my mind from the 'righteous paths' and turned me forever into an enemy of class oppression and class injustice; it was not they alone who showed me that my poverty of body and mind, my physical and mental hunger, my ragged clothes and broken shoes were not simply personal bereavements, visited upon me by some crafty fate, but rather the price I paid for belonging to that great and mighty factor in modern history called the *working class* – no, it is not easy to 'subvert,' as our present day Neanderthalers call it; no, it was life that did the 'subverting,' and Shaw, of ever beloved memory, only took the senseless hate and resentment and directed it to paths of understanding, reason and creation.

Yet I could never convince my father, my wonderful, strong, wise and patient father, whose hands were gifted with magic, whose heart was big and strong beyond breaking – who, in a curious way, was the best the working class produces; and who always, always belittled himself to justify his own poverty. How deeply it had been hammered home in him that the race was to the strong, the good, the best! – so deeply that he could never admit that we inhabited anything but the best of all possible worlds. Only he had failed.

Only, I say that he had not failed. He gave me a worker, before my eyes and that way until I die. The bitter, endless arguments we had about the system and its meaning, those were nothing against himself who was the largest argument of all, teaching me just in his being.

And he wanted me to be a writer, and without him I would not have been a writer. He, who could barely read and write, would sit silent and even awe-stricken, night after night, as I sat with sheets of paper, making stories – which I then read aloud to him and to my brothers. They were very poor stories, pathetically poor, but I became a writer because the three people who listened each night to what I had written knew that they were not bad stories, but miracles because words were written at all. It wasn't that my father's literary judgement was poor; it was because his wisdom went far deeper than any matter of literary judgement.

It was shortly before he died that I published my novel, *The Last Frontier*, in which I wrote the dedication, 'To my father, who taught me to love, not only the America that is past, but the America that will be.' My father was already an old man, older than his years, worked out and used up, and very sick, and he wondered how I had meant what I wrote – for all the pleasure it gave him. For, as he said, he knew so little of the America that was past and was so deeply troubled concerning the America that would be.

I couldn't explain to him that in himself, he was the America that would be; and I think that of all my angers in so many angry years, the longest lasting is that he, who was so splendid in so many ways, should have been robbed of that most precious of possessions: pride in and knowledge of the generation of millions like himself who had built with their strong hands what was best and truest in the America of the past.

From The Last Supper (1955)

HOWARD FAST (1914–), American novelist (he has also written thrillers as E.V. Cunningham), dramatist, screenwriter and historian, was born in New York City.

Larry Adler

EXPULSION

When I began at grade school No 60 in Baltimore I found that I had very bad eyesight. Although I could read books all right I couldn't see the blackboard clearly. I was taken for an eye examination and had to be held down by force to have eyedrops inserted. I couldn't bear anything approaching my eyes. I was short-sighted and the glasses I had to wear from then on got me the usual nickname: Four Eyes.

One day a kid at that school tried to take my marbles away from me. Another kid, a bigger one called Reese Whittemore, came along, made the first kid give me back my marbles and told me that if I was bothered again, I should come to him and he'd beat the shit out of anybody who picked on me.

It figures that the big boy, my rescuer, was a hero to me and, when he let me into his gang, it was like winning the Manliness Medal. When I was nineteen I read that Reese Whittemore had been executed in the electric chair in Maryland for murder. Had I stayed in the gang, I might have been in on the job that ended in murder and an execution. But I went on the stage when I was fourteen.

At the Sha'arei T'filoh Synagogue, on Auchentoroly Terrace (don't we have great names in Baltimore?), I went every Friday evening and Saturday morning to sing in the choir. At the end of the high holidays each choir boy was given a gold watch and chain. One night, after the synagogue service, while walking back home (I wouldn't even ride a bicycle on *Shabbos* I was that religious) I heard some exciting piano music as I was passing a house. I walked up the steps to the porch – all houses in that part of Baltimore had porches – and looked in. A boy, about my age, was playing four hand duets with a lady. I don't know how long I stayed there, fascinated, until suddenly my left ear was gripped hard by the lady.

'Vot you doing hot here?' she asked.

I explained (not easy when your ear is grabbed) that I was listening to the music.

'So? Den dunt stand hotside like tremp, com heen.' Still gripping my ear she led me into the drawing-room and sat me in a chair, after which I heard Schubert, Schumann and Tchaikovsky. The boy was Shura Cherkassky, who had just come from Russia and spoke no English, the lady was his aunt. She invited me to play with Shura the next day but it was difficult because we couldn't talk to each other. He had a sensitive face and a mane of black, bushy hair.

A few months later Shura gave a solo recital at the Lyric Theatre, which was Baltimore's concert hall. He played his own piece, *Prelude Pathétique* and, though Shura has forgotten it, I can still play it on the piano.

I was deeply jealous of Shura, despite our friendship. Here he was, just a year or two older than me, giving a recital. I couldn't match that. Zadie took Shura's success to heart. He said to Dad: 'Look at Shura Cherkassky, only twelve years old and already giving concerts. And look at Lawrence, ten years old and what has he accomplished? Nothing!'

I didn't like being made to feel a has-been at ten and I resented Zadie for making me look small.

After Junior High I went to study the piano at the Peabody Conservatory of Music at Mount Vernon Place in Baltimore. I was never a good student. I tried really hard to do what teacher said, but it just wasn't in me. For the students' recital, which was obligatory after two terms, I prepared a Grieg waltz, based mainly on my imitation of Rachmaninoff's recording. I was nearly twelve by that time and it seemed to me that my interpretation compared quite favourably with that of the Master.

The supervisor, big tits and pince-nez, called my name and, as I sat at the piano, said: 'And what are we going to play, my little man?' Goddammit, *we* weren't going to play *anything*, I was, and I didn't like being patronized. To hell with the Grieg waltz. I went into a stride version of *Yes, We Have No Bananas*, glaring at tits and pince-nez to the cheers of the other students. She stopped me after about twelve bars. 'That will do. We have heard *quite* enough.' She sent me to my seat and later my parents got a letter saying, in effect, don't send him back. I was expelled and it is still a unique distinction.

My parents then arranged private lessons with Miss Virginia Fore, but the practising got no better. My friend Earl Steinberg was also learning the piano and he hated practice as much as I did. The year before I'd become interested in hypnotism, because I'd read that Rachmaninoff, in a depression that was ruining his music, was cured by hypnotic treatment under A. Moll, to whom he dedicated his *Second Piano Concerto*. I tried hypnotising Earl and made piano-practising out to be more fun even than girls. From then on Earl did indeed practise and actually seemed to like it. I tried auto-hypnosis, but it didn't work.

From It Ain't Necessarily So (1984)

LARRY ADLER (1914–), American mouth organist and writer, was born in Baltimore but now lives in Britain. He has played as soloist with the New York Philharmonic, and Vaughan Williams and Malcolm Arnold are among those who have composed works for him.

Herman Wouk

The Purple Suit

Mom decided that a Townsend Harris yoxen was entitled to his first suit with long pants; so she took me to the cloak-and-suit district on the Lower East Side, where Pop bought his clothes. Clothes were cheaper there, and especially cheap at Michaels', a store directly under the rumbling El. A dark noisy repulsive location, but because the rent was so low, Mr. Michaels could cut his prices to the bone. Not that he did, unless he had to. The first time I saw myself in a three-way mirror, in long trousers drooping around my ankles, I did get a thrill, but it soon wore off. Mom had me putting suits on and off for an hour while she haggled. Soon I was yearning for Mom to pick a suit, any suit, and get us out of there. To me a suit was a suit, and those bombinating elevated trains were giving me a headache.

Then Mom spied the purple suit off by itself on a high rack. She asked about it. Mr. Michaels warned her that it was too dear; jacket, vest, two pairs of pants plus a pair of kneepants; too much material, a line he was discontinuing because customers wouldn't pay the price. Never mind, Mama wanted me to try it on. So he took it down, and I trudged into the narrow dressing booth and got into the suit. Seeing myself in the three-way mirror, I was not pleased. I had no sense of style whatever, but even I could see that it swam on me, and that the color was disagreeable: bold dark purple stripes on a dull purple background.

'It's too big,' Mama said.

'You don't expect him to grow?' asked Mr. Michaels, a plump pale bald man, with big sorrowful eyes.

Mom felt the material.

'Iron,' said Mr. Michaels. 'Steel. He will never wear it out, he can't.'

On this point Mr. Michaels was not just talking. The suit lasted like chain mail. It must still exist somewhere and some unlucky kid must be wearing it.

Mom reluctantly nodded. She did know material, and she recognized the texture of eternity between her fingers. 'How much?'

'Missus, you don't want this suit. It costs too much,' said Mr. Michaels, sizing her up carefully with his grieving eyes. But he named a price. Mama offered him about half. Mr. Michaels groaned, and proposed to give her the suit as a present. He had a heart condition, he said, the suit was the last of the line, and she was welcome to it. He didn't have the strength to discuss her offer seriously, it wasn't worth risking another coronary attack.

Mama stood her ground. Half.

Mr. Michaels came down about a dollar. Mama went up about a dollar. The gap remained wide. Long dickering ensued, mostly shouted over train noise, while I stood staring at three images of myself, comparing my two profiles to pass the time. Finally, wincing and clutching at his chest, Mr.

Michaels gasped that to end the matter, he would make one last offer; and he came down another dollar.

'All right, David,' said Mom, 'take off the suit and let's go home.'

I headed for the booth, the pants slopping over my shoes. Mr. Michaels began to cry, and to beg Mom to take the suit as a gift. I mean he cried real big tears out of those sad eyes, mopping them with a handkerchief. It was a very upsetting sight. To console him I said, 'Anyway, it doesn't matter. I don't like the color.'

'The color? What's wrong with the color?' sobbed Mr. Michaels. 'It's a beautiful color. All the college boys are wearing that color.'

'Take off the suit, David,' Mama said.

'Do me a favor, David,' Mr. Michaels wept, grasping my elbow. 'Come and look at the color by daylight. It's a very sporty color.' He led me outside. There wasn't much daylight under the El, but the suit if anything looked worse. There were two sets of purple stripes, I now discerned, one fainter than the other, making for a very muddy effect.

'I don't like stripes,' I said.

'WHAT?' he wailed, for a train was crashing by overhead.

'I HATE STRIPES,' I screamed.

Mama was now in the doorway. 'You wait here,' she shouted at me. 'I'm going to get Morris Elfenbein.'

Mr. Michaels didn't have much color in his face, but whatever was there faded away. His jaw dropped, his melancholy eyes bulged, and he said in a plaintive voice, 'Elfenbein? Why Elfenbein? Missus, I beg you, never mind Morris Elfenbein.'

But Mom marched off around the corner.

'You're wrong about the stripes, sonny,' said Mr. Michaels, as we went back into the store. 'Stripes are the latest fashion. Nothing but stripes. Take the suit, don't take it, but if you want to be real collegiate, you want stripes.'

He sat down at a shabby desk and wrote in an account book, drying his eyes. I perched myself on a box, for walking around in those dragging pants was hazardous. So a little time and a couple of trains passed, and Mama returned with Morris Elfenbein.

I knew the man very well, from all the synagogue trustee meetings that had taken place in our home. He was also our main holiday *ba'al t'fila*, lay cantor. On Yom Kippur, when Morris Elfenbein, with his silver-collared prayer shawl framing his head, his voice cracking with emotion, his face red with strain, his tall sturdy body swaying far up and down, poured out in the old minor mode that great Psalm

> *Lift up your heads, ye gates,*
> *And let the everlasting doors open*
> *And the King of Glory will come in!*

I tell you, you didn't have to know what the Hebrew meant to be stirred to your bones. He was terrific.

He was terrific now, too, but this was a different Morris Elfenbein;

different from the rousing lay cantor, and different, too, from the worrisome synagogue trustee. Morris Elfenbein entered Mr. Michaels's shop like a matador; erect, eyes flashing, shoulders back, the champion ready for the supreme act, the hour of truth, the kill. As dramatic, as exciting, and as somber was the demeanor of Mr. Michaels, as he rose to encounter Morris Elfenbein. Mr. Michaels was a brave bull, who knew his time had come; but he faced the sword with defiant grace, head down, eyes tragic, his bearing uncowed as he waited for the blow. It was pure ritual, and seeing the scene now in my mind's eye, I almost hear the phantom crowd noise die away to a hush, and the matador music sound forth, even over the crashing of the elevated train.

The contest was short, fierce, and mostly in rapid cloak-and-suit Yiddish. I could barely follow the words. The question of whether or not I liked the purple suit dropped from view. Of course I was going to get and wear that purple suit. When Morris Elfenbein entered the arena, there was only one possible outcome. The suspense and the thrill lay only in his skill at weakening his adversary, and his timing of the final thrust. Mama watched the master perform with her face aglow. Down, down, a dollar, and a dollar, and then half a dollar, came Michaels's price. These men were both well-off merchants, you realize. The money gap had shrunk to very little, and anyway there was nothing in it for Elfenbein. They were zestfully playing out a contest as old as the ziggurats of Babylon, and as fresh as the bagels being vended outside on Canal Street. Michaels, as he sank to his knees, so to speak, had almost lost his sad look. His eyes glittered with the exalted despair of the end.

'He's being ridiculous,' said Elfenbein to my mother at last, with a wonderful hitch of his broad shoulders, a fantastic flourish of both hands, and a three-quarter turn to the door that was pure bloody poetry. 'I'm going back to my store. Take your son home.'

'All right, Elfenbein.' The sword was in to the hilt, and Michaels gave up the ghost with a noble groan at Elfenbein's back. 'I'll take it.'

On the instant, Elfenbein turned and struck hands with Michaels, who still looked tragic, yet sheepishly amused, like Hamlet when he rises for a bow after being slain. He stayed in character to shake his head dolefully at Mama and tell her she was getting the bargain of her life, but by the time he accepted her check and wrapped up the suit he was all smiles. I suspect he had waited years to get rid of that suit, and was a very happy man; but at any rate he got bottom dollar for it. Morris Elfenbein saw to that.

From Inside, Outside (1985)

HERMAN WOUK (1915–), American novelist and dramatist, was born in New York City. His fourth novel, *The Caine Mutiny* (1951), written out of his war experience, won the Pulitzer Prize for Fiction.

Saul Bellow

'LIKE MY OWN BOY'

After the age of twelve we were farmed out in the summer by the old woman to get a taste of life and the rudiments of earning. Even before, she had found something for me to do. There was a morning class for feeble-minded children, and when I had left Georgie in school I reported to Sylvester's Star Theatre to distribute handbills. Grandma had arranged this with Sylvester's father, whom she knew from the old people's arbor in the park.

If it got to our rear flat that the weather was excellent – warm and still, she liked it – she would go to her room and put on her corset, relic of when she was fuller, and her black dress. Mama would fix her a bottle of tea. Then in a chapeau of flowers and a furpiece of tails locked on her shoulder with badger claws she went to the park. With a book she never intended to read. There was too much talk in the arbor for that. It was a place where marriages were made. A year or so after the old atheist's death, Mrs. Anticol found herself a second husband there. This widower traveled down from Iowa City for just the purpose of marriage, and after they were married the news came back that he kept her locked a prisoner in his house and made her sign away all rights of legacy. Grandma did not pretend to be sorry; she said, 'Poor Bertha,' but she said it with the humor she was a crackerjack at, as thin and full of play as fiddle wire, and she took much credit for not going in for that kind of second marriage. I quit thinking long ago that all old people came to rest from the things they were out for in their younger years. But that was what she wanted us to believe – 'an old *baba* like me' – and accordingly we took her at her word to be old disinterested wisdom who had put by her vanity. But if she never got a marriage offer, I'm not prepared to say it made no difference to her. She couldn't have been so sold on *Anna Karenina* for nothing, or another favorite of hers I ought to mention, *Manon Lescaut*, and when she was feeling right she bragged about her waist and hips, so, since she never gave up any glory or influence that I know of, I can see it wasn't only from settled habit that she went into her bedroom to lace on her corset and wind up her hair but to take the eye of a septuagenarian Vronsky or Des Grieux. I sometimes induced myself to see, beyond her spotty yellowness and her wrinkles and dry bangs, a younger and resentful woman in her eyes.

But whatever she was after for herself, in the arbor, she wasn't forgetting us, and she got me the handbill job through old Sylvester, called 'the Baker' because he wore white ducks and white golfer's cap. He had palsy, this the joke of his making rolls, but he was clean, brief-spoken, serious in the aim of his bloodshot eyes, reconciled, with an effort of nerve that was copied straight into the curve of his white horseshoe of mustache, to the shortness of his days. I suppose her pitch with him was as usual, about the family she was protecting, and Sylvester took me to see his son, a young fellow whom money or family anxiety always seemed to keep in a sweat. Something, his shadow business and the emptiness of the seats at two o'clock, the violinist playing just for him and the operator in the projection box, made it awful for him and misery to come across with my two bits. It made him act tough. He said, 'I've had kids who shoved the bills down the sewer. Too bad if I ever find out about it, and I have ways to check up.' So I knew that he might follow me along a block of the route, and I kept watch in the streets for his head with the weak hair of baldness and his worry-wounded eyes, as brown as a bear's. 'I've got a couple of tricks myself for any punk who thinks he's going to pull a fast one,' he warned me. But when he believed I was trustworthy, and at first I was, following his directions about rolling the bills and sticking them into the brass mouthpieces over the bells, not fouling up the mailboxes and getting him in dutch with the post office, he treated me to seltzer and Turkish Delight and said he was going to make a ticket-taker of me when I grew a little taller, or put me in charge of the popcorn machine he was thinking of getting; and one of these years he was going to hire a manager while he went back to Armour Institute to finish his engineering degree. He had only a couple of years to go, and his wife was after him to do it. He took me for my senior, I suppose, to tell me this, as the people at the dispensary did, and as often happened. I didn't understand all that he told me.

Anyway, he was just a little deceived in me, for when he said his other boys had dumped bills down the sewer I felt I couldn't do less either and watched for my chance. Or gave out wads to the kids in George's dummy-room when I came at noon to fetch him at the penal-looking school built in the identical brick with the icehouse and the casket factory which were its biggest neighbors. It had the great gloom inside of clinks the world over, with ceilings the eye had to try for and wood floors trailed with marching. Summers, one corner of it was kept open for the feeble-minded, and, coming in, you traded the spray of the icehouse for the snipping, cooing of paper-chain making and the commands of teachers. I sat on the stairs and divided the remaining bills, and when class let out Georgie helped me get rid of them. Then I took him by the hand and led him home.

Much as he loved Winnie, he was scared of strange dogs, and as he carried her scent he drew them. They were always sniffing his legs, and I carried stones to pitch at them.

This was the last idle summer. The next, as soon as the term was over, Simon was sent to work as a bellhop in a resort hotel in Michigan, and I went to the Coblins' on the North Side to help Coblin with his newspaper route. I had to move there, for the papers came into the shed at four in the morning and we lived better than half an hour away on the streetcar. But it wasn't exactly as though I were passing into strange hands, for Anna Coblin was my mother's cousin and I was accordingly treated as a relative. Hyman Coblin came for me in his Ford; George howled when I left the house; he had a way of demonstrating the feelings Mama could not show under ban of the old woman. George had to be shut up in the parlor. I sat him down by the stove and left. Cousin Anna wept enough for everybody and plastered me with kisses at the door of her house, seeing me dog-dumb with the heartbreak of leaving home – a very temporary kind of emotion for me and almost, as it were, borrowed from Mama, who saw her sons drafted untimely into hardships. But Anna Coblin, who had led the negotiations for me, cried the most. Her feet were bare, her hair enormous, and her black dress misbuttoned. 'I'll treat you like my own boy,' she promised, 'my own Howard.' She took my canvas laundry bag from me and put me in Howard's room, between the kitchen and the toilet.

Howard had run away. Together with Joe Kinsman, the undertaker's son, he had lied about his age and enlisted in the Marine Corps. Their families were trying to get them out, but in the meantime they had been shipped to Nicaragua and were fighting Sandino and the rebels. She grieved terribly, as if he were dead already. And as she had great size and terrific energy of constitution she produced all kinds of excesses. Even physical ones: moles, blebs, hairs, bumps in her forehead, huge concentration in her neck; she had spiraling reddish hair springing with no negligible beauty and definiteness from her scalp, tangling as it widened up and out, cut duck-tail fashion in the back and scrawled out high above her ears. Originally strong, her voice was crippled by weeping and asthma, and the whites of her eyes coppery from the same causes, a burning, morose face, piteous, and her spirit untamed by thoughts or the remote considerations that can reconcile people to awfuler luck than she had. Because, said Grandma Lausch, cutting her case down to scale with her usual satisfaction in the essential, what did she want, a woman like that? Her brothers found her a husband, bought him a business, she had two children in her own house and a few pieces of real-estate besides. She might still be in the millinery factory where she started out, over the Loop on Wabash Avenue. That was the observation we heard after Cousin Anna had come to talk to her – as one comes to a wise woman – amassed herself into a suit, hat, shoes, and sat at the kitchen table looking at herself in the mirror as she spoke, not casually, but steadily, sternly, with wrathful comment; even at the bitterest, even when her mouth was at the widest stretch of tears, she went on watching. Mama, her head wrapped in a bandanna, was singeing a chicken at the gas plate.

'*Daragaya*, nothing will happen to your son; he'll come back,' said the old woman while Anna sobbed. 'Other mothers have their sons there.'

'I *told* him to stop going with the undertaker's. What kind of friend was that for him? He dragged him into it.'

She had the Kinsmans down for death-breeders, and I found out that she made a detour of blocks when shopping to avoid Kinsman's parlors, though she had always boasted before that Mrs. Kinsman, a big, fresh, leery-looking woman, was a lodge sister and friend of hers – the rich Kinsmans. Coblin's uncle, a bank officer, was buried out of Kinsman's, and Friedl Coblin and Kinsman's daughter went to the same elocution teacher. She had the impediment of Moses whose hand the watching angel guided to the coal, Friedl, and she carried her stuttering into fluency later. Years after, at a football game where I was selling hot dogs, I heard her; she didn't recognize me in the white hat of the day, but I remembered coaching her in 'When the Frost Is on the Punkin'.'And recalled also Cousin Anna's oath that I should marry Friedl when I was grown. It was in her tears of welcome when she pressed me, on the porch of the house that day. 'Hear, Owgie, you'll be my son, my daughter's husband, *mein kind!*' At this moment she had once more given Howard up for dead.

From The Adventures of Augie March (1953)

SAUL BELLOW (1915–), American novelist, dramatist and academic, was born in Lachine, Canada. *The Adventures of Augie March* was his third novel, and won the National Book Award. He was awarded the Nobel Prize for Literature in 1977.

Arthur Miller

SECOND SIGHT

Most of the time anguish was absorbed into the games that came around with each changing season, but something happened now and then that could burn your insides. Because Kermit had a library card, I too had to have one. When I was enrolled in school and entitled to join the library near Fifth Avenue on 110th, I finally walked into the place one hot spring afternoon. It was so dark and cool in there, like no other place I had ever been, and the pink-cheeked lady leaning over her polished mahogany counter spoke in such a funereal whisper that something supernatural seemed to be present, something sacred that must not be disturbed by ordinary tones of voice, and so I stood on tiptoe as close to her ear as possible and whispered back the answers to her questions. My name, my address, my age, school, my mother's name – Augusta. At this something began knotting up inside my belly; no one had ever called her anything but Gus or Gussie, so I was already telling a kind of untruth, donning a disguise. Now the lady asked my father's name. I had not expected any of this, thinking I was simply going into this place to happily claim my rightful card, the same as my brother had done. It was going to be my turn not to be a baby anymore. Looking up into her blue eyes, I could not bring to voice my father's so Jewish name, Isidore. I was paralyzed, could only shake my head. 'What does your mother call him?' I was trapped. The smile went from her face, as though she suspected me of something. My cheeks were burning. 'Izzie' being impossible, I finally managed 'Iz.' She looked puzzled. 'Is?' she asked. I nodded. 'Is what?' I rushed out into the street, and I am sure that within minutes I was back with the gang playing ring-a-levio or banging a ball against a building in a game of stoopball.

I was six the year I entered school, and I could not, myself, ever have heard an anti-Semitic remark. Indeed, had I thought about it at all, I would have imagined that the whole world was Jewish except maybe for Lefty the cop and Mikush. Through those short years on the floor studying peoples' shoes, the lint under the couch, the brass casters under the piano legs, my skin had been absorbing some two thousand years of European history, of which, unbeknown to me, I had become part, a character in an epic I did not know existed, an undissolved lump floating on the surface of the mythic American melting pot. To use the latter-day jargon, I had already been programmed to choose something other than pride in my origins, and this despite my father's seemingly confident authority and his easy way with police and yelling cab drivers and even Mr. Mikush, who could put the fear of God into a brown bear. From my father some undefinable authority emanated, perhaps because his great height, fair skin, blue eyes, square head, and reddish hair cast him as an important Irish detective. Holding his hand, I often saw him simply pause at an alleyway and with his blank look disperse a crap game. He assumed without thought that he would be well served in restaurants, where he need hardly lift a finger to attract a waiter, and he never hesitated, but without fuss, to send back a dish that wasn't right. Knowing his past, I could never understand where this baronial attitude came from. He even had a way of listening that without any show of skepticism would cause the speaker to stop exaggerating. His open, relaxed stare, blue-eyed and innocent, brought blushes to the faces of people unsure of themselves. It would have astonished him to be credited as some kind of moral force – if indeed he could have understood such an idea. Life was just too hard to allow most people most of the time to act unselfishly, least of all himself. Nevertheless, his minority anxiety had moved into me, I am sure, though among his very few words of advice only one sentence explicitly conveyed it. We were passing an automobile accident on 110th Street, my hand in his and my brother on his other side. When we both pressed forward to see what had happened, he drew us back and steered us gently on, saying, 'Stay away from crowds.' That was all. It may have been enough.

Yet I doubt that such fright as I showed the librarian had come from him, at least not mainly. Throughout his life he declined instinctively to sentimentalize Jews, unlike my mother, who tended to expect a higher sensitivity and even morality from them, thus being endlessly and angrily disappointed. He sometimes was impatient with these idealizing waves that would repeatedly rise and break over her, and even laughed and shook his head at her naiveté. But there was no discernible apprehension disturbing his air of quiet confidence. My mother's father, Louis Barnett, once instructed me never to walk under a large lighted cross overhanging the sidewalk outside a Lenox Avenue church; if by accident I did, I must spit when I realized what I had done, in order to cleanse myself. There was a certain mild fear of that particular cross after this, but mainly that it might break loose and fall down on me. Nothing of the theology or history behind such admonitions was ever mentioned, leaving them in the realm of superstition or in a kind of immanent symbolism of menace.

There was, in fact, a certain disinclination to explain rationally anything at all that might impinge on the sacred, even in the Hebrew teacher who came to the house a few days a week to tutor Kermit and me in preparation for our bar mitzvahs, still years off. This bearded ancient taught us purely by rote, pronouncing the Hebrew words and leading us to repeat after him. In the book, the English translations of the passages from Genesis faced the Hebrew, but there were no English translations of the English: what did *firmament* mean? The worst of it was that when I spoke a passage correctly, the old man would kiss me, which was like being embraced by a rosebush. Once he leaned over and, laughing, gave my cheek a painful pinch and called me *tsadik*, wise man, a compliment whose cause I understood neither then nor later. I would have to pump up all my self-control to appear to welcome his furry arrival. The lessons were boring and meaningless, but my rebellion may simply have been caused by an undisciplined spirit: I hated piano lessons, too, or any set of rules that interfered with fantasies of magically quick accomplishment. When the violin suddenly became 'my' instrument, as mysteriously and irrevocably as second base had become my position, my mother found a teacher who, poor man, loaned me a small violin to begin on. I found that a rubber ball would take a lively bounce off the back of it as well as causing all the strings to hum, and I went downstairs to use it as a tennis racket until the neck broke in my hand. My mother carefully laid the pieces in the case and returned the instrument, and I went back to walking in my sleep, which was far more interesting than studying. So the root of that choking fear that suddenly gripped me as I looked into the face of the kindly librarian is so deeply buried that I can only imagine I had been denying, quietly and persistently, what I surely must have been hearing from my position on the floor – stories, remarks, fear-laden vocal tones that had been moving me by inches into a beleaguered zone surrounded by strangers with violent hearts.

Mikush was doubtless one of those, the sole mythic enemy who had a face and a name, as far as I knew. But the fears of Mikush sprang far less from mythic antagonisms than from the cat-and-mouse game all the boys in the building played with him on the roof. A favorite sport, of which my brother was a master, was to stand up on a parapet and leap across a shaftway to the other side over a drop of six stories. Terrified as I already was of such a drop from my sleepwalking experiences, I could not bear to watch Kermit standing tall on the parapet. Mikush was endlessly popping up out of the hatchway to chase us, not that he cared if one of us went into the abyss, but our heels made holes in the tar roofing material. 'No touch-a roof!' he would roar as we dodged him and clattered down the iron stairway into the building. As we flew down into the lower stories, his Polish war yells echoed along the ceramic-tiled floors of the hallways.

Because he was a Pole, the Jews in the building had to believe he hated them just as his countrymen for the most part had in Radomizl, where pogroms and tales of pogroms were woven into the very sky overhead, and where only the Austrian emperor Franz Josef and his army kept the Poles, egged on by their insatiable priests, from murdering every last Jew in the land. But I nevertheless had an ambiguous relation of sorts with Mikush; I brought my badly bent almost-new bike to him after an experiment of no-hands riding banged the front fork into a lamppost in the park. He straightened it with his bare hands, a memorable feat of strength that I imagined no one else in the whole world was capable of. I must have had some faith in his goodwill toward me, Pole or no Pole; my fear of him was less than total. Such a relationship made it understandable, a decade or so later, that German Jews – even those who could afford to – did not immediately leave when Hitler came to power. Had we lived in Germany, Mikush would likely have been the Nazi representative in the building, but it would have been hard to imagine even Mikush, anti-Semitic as he undoubtedly was, going from apartment to apartment with a list of names and ordering us out into trucks bound for a concentration camp and death. After all, he had straightened out the fork of my bike.

Perhaps I was so unprepared, so surprised by my own terror in the library, because of what was to be a lifelong inability to believe that all reality was of the visible kind. We all are taught how to receive our experiences, and my mother, my prime teacher, saw secret signs of other worlds wherever she looked; she was talked to by people without benefit of telephone, and even by the dead. As with others so inclined, this gave her, I suppose, an enhanced sense of her importance in the scheme of things and helped make life more interesting. Whatever the cause, I had clearly put out of mind a certain childish recognition of infinite human brutality until suddenly the librarian seemed to challenge me to identify myself as a candidate for victimization, and I fled. I had been taught to recognize danger – even where it did not exist – but not how to defend against it. The dilemma would last a long time. The same quandary, and the effort to locate in the human species a counterforce to the randomness of victimization, underlie the political aspect of my play *Incident at Vichy*. But as history has taught, that force can only be moral. Unfortunately.

For me, my mother's mysticism set death lurking everywhere. It has prejudiced me against teaching children religion; too often God is death and it is death that is being worshiped and 'loved.' If I learned early on how to disregard her dark and pessimistic surges, the fact was that they too often turned out to be prophetic. Her brother Moe, who had been a mule driver carrying ammunition up to the front in France, returned from a funeral with her one rainy afternoon, and as he sat on the pinkish satin Louis Something straight chair in the living room, she screamed and her hands flew up to her hair: he must immediately go out the apartment door and wipe a smear of gray cemetery mud off one of his heels lest it bring death to this house. They were beautiful brown calf shoes with a white bead around the seam between soles and uppers. He quickly left the living room, limping to keep the heel off the carpet.

In appearance, I would grow up to resemble Moe, a tall, thin man of great gentleness whose spirit the Great War seemed to have broken. It was as though in more than the physical sense he could never quite catch his breath. Even then I noted that joy never seemed to collect around him, even for his wedding there was no great party, no welcoming of his tiny wife, Celia, who was barely five feet tall. He was constantly bending to her as they walked, with one gentle hand against her back as though she were a child. Trying to get with the spirit of the twenties, he made it down to Florida to speculate in real estate, but his nerve soon waterlogged, his investment melting into the sea during a great land boom in which immense fortunes were made and innocents like himself fleeced. All Moe returned with was a nice tan that encouraged my mother to believe that his health was permanently restored, but he was soon back in the Veterans Hospital at Saranac Lake, where he died. The cemetery mud on his shoe could not help but cross my mind, and with it the lurking suspicion of some validity in the superstition. That only my mother knew the rules and regulations tended to leave me with all of the attendant apprehensions and none of the satisfactions of prediction – 'I knew, *I knew!*' she wailed when we heard the news of his death.

It was the same when, out of a deep sleep in an Atlantic City hotel where we were spending the High Holidays, she suddenly sat up and said, 'My mother died' – which she had, it turned out, and at approximately that hour of the night. Of course, her secret powers were not all negative and would as often send her into prescient highs of optimism, especially about me. I need only draw a straight line to hear myself praised as a coming da Vinci; my failures she simply swept aside as the fault of my teachers or a momentary fogging of my mind. This worked pretty well until Miss Fisher, the principal of P.S. 24, summoned her to a conference about my unruliness.

Miss Fisher had been the principal when my mother was a pupil in the same school. Holding me by the hand in the office, my mother seemed to blush in girlish shame as her onetime goddess said, 'I do not understand, Augusta, how a fine student like you can have brought him up so badly.' Miss Fisher wore a lace net collar with little ivory stays that pushed into the flesh under her jaw hinges and kept her from bending her neck. It was hard to look up at her without grimacing with pain. She was white-haired and wore ankle-length skirts and white long-sleeved blouses with starched pleated fronts. Tears formed in my mother's eyes. 'Kermit is such a well-behaved boy,' the great lady went on, 'and so quick in his studies . . . ' I began crying too, already feeling the sting of my mother's hand on the side of my head and imagining the stars I was about to see, but worst of all was her face wracked with disappointment. What was the matter with me? Why was I like this? Dear God, please let me be good like my mother and father and brother! At times like this all life seemed like rowing forever through a sea of remorse.

Between my terror in the library and Miss Fisher's condemnation, I seemed to have joined some underworld of disapproved people. My father and brother lived well beyond the sparkling blue line of demarcation – they were wholly good – but placing my mother was not so simple. We had hardly gotten out onto 111th Street when she violently shook me, holding my wrist, gave me a clout on top of the head with her pocketbook, and then bent over me and screamed into my face, 'What are you doing to me!' A double condemnation, since even at that moment I knew she wasn't condemning for her own sake – she adored everything I did – but as an agent for Miss Fisher and implicitly my father and Kermit and the whole United States of America. Thus it was even more painful for her to have to be cursing me when deep within her she thought I hadn't done anything very wrong. And so we were closer than ever as we reentered the apartment and I pretended deep remorse and she pretended black despair, and in a little while we both had some hot chocolate. Only then did a conspiratorial practicality enter her voice as she said, 'Listen' – I looked up from my cup – 'I want you to behave.' I said, 'I'm going to,' and I meant it. And I did for a while.

From Timebends (1987)

ARTHUR MILLER (1915–), American dramatist and author of *Death of a Salesman* and *The Crucible*, was born in Manhattan.

Norman Mailer

THE TRAINS

The trains used to go by, used to go by very fast in the field past the road on the other side of my house. I used to go down there and walk and walk through the fields whenever Mom and Pop were fighting, fighting about money like they always were, and after I'd listen awhile, I'd blow air into my ears so I couldn't hear them, then I'd go out in the field, across the road from my house and slide down the steep part of the grass where it was slippery like dogs had been dirty there, and then I used to climb up the other side, up the big hill on the other side, and walk and walk through the fat high grass until I would come to the railroad tracks where I'd just keep going and going and going.

Why don't we have any money, we never have any money, what kind of man did I marry, what good is he, what good is he, look at him, look at his boy there, look at your boy there, look at him, he takes after you, look at him walk away like he never hears us, look at him, no good like you, why don't you ever get any money?

The grass sticks would be rough and sharp sort of, like sharp pages in a book, and I had to walk with my hands in my pockets so I wouldn't cut my fingers. They were tall, the grasses, and sometimes they would hit me in the face, but I would hit them back, only that used to cut my fingers, and I'd start crying, but I stopped soon, because there was nobody around, and I knew that when there was nobody to hear me, I always stopped soon, although I never could figure it out, because I always could cry for a long time, and say I was going to run away and die if people were around.

I can't help it if I'm not making money, my God there's limits to what a man can do, nag, nag, nag, all the time. My God I can't help it, there's limits, there's depression, everybody's losing money, just worry about keeping the house, and don't compare the child to me, the God-damn child is splitting us up the middle, I can't help it if he's a stupid kid, he's only nine, maybe he'll get smarter yet, I can't help it if he's dumb, there's a depression going on I tell you, everybody's losing money, there just isn't any money around.

The railroad tracks made a funny kind of a mirror. I could see myself in them, one of me on each side, I was so tall in them, but I was awfully short, as short as my arm, but I was awful tall, I looked as tall as Pop, except as tall as if I was to see Pop all the way in the distance coming up the hill to our house, when he looked as tall as my arm, but I knew anyway that he was oh ten times bigger then me.

Why is the boy always disappearing, why don't you find him, you haven't a job, you just sit around, you might keep him near you, you might teach him to be like you, and sit around all day, and make it easier for me so at least I wouldn't have to look for him, but you can't even teach him that, I never saw such a man like you, they didn't make my father out of men like you.

If I walked and walked along the tracks, there was a spot where I could get to a place where all the big slow trains came into town. If I was careful I could sneak up in the grass near to where the men who jumped off the big trains camped in the fields.

They were dirty old men, they just sat around, and smoked pipes and washed their dirty old shirts in the yellow water spot where I used to go swimming before Mom started yell yell yell about the dirty old men and wouldn't let me swim there.

They're filthy old things, you'll get sick and die, they're diseased, they're diseased, why did the town let them camp and flop in a meadow like that, right on the town limits, what's the good of living out of town when our only neighbours are bums, what's the good, what's the town mean, why aren't they put in the coop where they belong, why should they be flopping so near our house in a meadow?

I didn't like the men, they used to talk and laugh to themselves all the time, sometimes they would sing songs. I knew they were dirty men 'cause Mom said they would give me diseases, but one time I came up and talked to them, when I went out Mom and Pop were shouting, and the men looked at me, one of the old ones who was sitting on his old stork bundle bag sort of, got up and looked at me, he made fun of me, he said sonny got a dime for a poor old man to have some coffee, and then all the men started laughing, haw haw haw kind of laughing. The other men came around me, one of them said he was going to take my shirt and use it for a snotrag, and they all laughed again, the big man in the middle of them making believe he was going to throw dirt at me only I didn't know he was going to fool me until I started crying, and he laughed too, and dropped the dirt.

That boy is going to get in trouble, why don't you take care of him, keep him around you, he goes off into the meadow, and God knows what those bums are going to do to him, they're all vile, they don't live like men, they're not men I heard, they're no more men than you are, both of you are, why don't you take care of him, he'll turn out weak in everything like you, those bums will get him in trouble.

Pop came over, grab-me picked me up, and carried me upstairs, and licked me, and locked the door on me, and then he went downstairs, and he and Mom yelled and yelled right through my crying. I waited and waited for them to hear me, but I must have fallen asleep because the next thing it was morning, and I didn't remember stopping and rubbing my hands on my nose to wipe off the crying. They unlocked the door before I sneaked downstairs, the front door was open and Mom and Pop were sitting around front, not saying anything, I hated them, I ran out the door between them, and hid around the side of the house. Pop and Mom came running out, they ran the wrong way calling to me, they were looking for me, and they weren't smiling, but they were talking nice the way they did when they didn't mean it, just like when they wanted to catch our dog, and that made me feel sad, and oh I felt just terrible, and then when they started coming back I didn't want to get another licking so I ran away without their seeing me, and sneaked across the road further down, into the field, and up the slippery hill, run run running way off until I got to the railroad tracks. I sneaked along them to where the dirty men with the disease were, and I hid down in the grass, and hid behind some to look at them, but they were all gone, there weren't any of them, but the old man who had made fun of me the day before, and he was lying on the ground crying and yowling like he was hurt or dead.

I walked over to him, he looked at me, he started crawling to me. I could see it was his foot that was hurt 'cause it was all bloody like, and bleeding near the knee. Help me kid, help me kid, he kept yelling.

Go ahead, hit the child, hit it, hit it, it deserves it, playing with dirty old men, hit it, it's a terrible child, it never listens to us, there's something wrong with it.

The old man looked like a snake, and I stepped back to run away from him, but he kept crawling after me, yelling don't go away kid, I won't hurt you, please don't go way kid, but he looked like a snake, only bleeding. I yelled at him, I said go away, you're a dirty old man, but he wouldn't stop, and I picked up a rock, and threw it at him, it missed him, but I threw another rock, and it hit him in the head, he stopped moving to me, he was crying something terrible, there was a lot of blood all over his face.

Why kid, why kid, why kid, why hit me?

You're a dirty old man, leave me alone, I don't like you, you're a dirty old man.

Kid for God's sakes help me, I'm going crazy kid, don't leave me here, it's hot here kid, it's hot here kid.

Then I picked up a stone, and threw it at him again, only I didn't see if it hit him because I was running away. I heard him crying, screaming, and I was scared, but I kept running and then I said I hate them, I hate them, the grass kept cutting at me, I couldn't run with my hands in my pockets, kept cutting at me and cutting at me, I fell down, and then I got up and kept running home.

I walked down the last part of the hill, and across the road, and when I got back Mom and Pop were sitting around again, and I started crying. I cried and cried, they asked me what's the matter, what's the matter with you, why are you crying, but I just kept saying the dirty old man, the dirty old man.

And Mom said I thought they all were kicked out of town, I don't know how any of them were left, you're not lying?

I'm not lying, I'm not lying.

And Pop got up, and said to Mom I told you not to do it, you get an idea in your head, and you can't stop, those men were beaten, I don't know how any were left in the dark, we had flashlights, but there might have been, it's the boy's own fault, he had no business going around there today, and anyway he wasn't hurt, he didn't start crying until he saw us, I saw him before he saw me.

And Mom said, if you were a man you'd go over there now, and finish them off, you wouldn't even go last night without any help, if I were a man I'd thrash the man that touched my boy, but you just sit there and talk talk talk that it's the boy's fault.

Pop got up, and walked around and around, and he said it isn't the boy's fault, but it isn't the man's either, and then he stood up, and said I'm not going to do anything about it, what with the boy between us, and the job ruined, and everything God-damn else, I might be one of them myself, maybe next year, and then Pop stood up and walked off down the road only farther out of town, not the way the old man was. I could see that Pop's shoulders were screwed up around his neck, and then I was happy, because all I could think of was that I'd seen two big men cry that day, and maybe that meant I was getting bigger too, and that was an awful good feeling.

From Advertisements for Myself (1959)

NORMAN MAILER (1923–), American novelist, dramatist and journalist, was born in Long Branch, New Jersey. His Pacific war novel, *The Naked and the Dead* (1948), won him considerable fame. *The Executioner's Song* (1980) won the Pulitzer Prize for Fiction.

Michael Meyer

INTO THE ARCH

Adrian told me that he remembered little of what went on inside the house, although he spent the first ten years of his life there. He remembered the blue Wedgwood plaques on the drawing-room ceiling, and the black and white marble squares in the hall, on which he used sometimes to spit surreptitiously from upstairs; the narrow stairs, brown-carpeted and flanked by slender wrought-iron banisters with lead embellishments, and the gate on the nursery landing to prevent him from running or falling downstairs, the lock being operated by pressure on a small diamond-shaped metal lozenge. The nursery had a table with legs shaped like sticks of barley-sugar, and bars to the windows to prevent him from falling out. Sometimes, when Nurse was away in the bedroom, he would lean through the bars to spit or fire his water-pistol into Portland Place.

That was all he remembered of the house, except the blue-walled night nursery, with its big bed for Nanny and its small bed for him, and a narrow unlit passage, leading from the night nursery to the day nursery, known as the Arch. The Arch, which had originally been designed as a powder-closet, now served two purposes. It contained a large cupboard recess, which was used to house Adrian's toys, and, being completely unlit, it served as a primitive dungeon for Adrian to be thrust into as a special punishment. Being sent into the Arch was Adrian's worst memory of childhood. It happened to him seldom, and usually, he had to admit, deservedly.

Once he had been given a gun which you loaded with a wooden rod. The rod was headed with a rubber suction cap, so that it stuck where it landed. The evening after receiving this, he crawled round the floor with the gun in his hand until he found himself behind the sofa, under which he could see the blue-veined calves of Nanny's legs, she having taken off her shoes and stockings to rest her feet after the day's work. He had not had any particular target in mind when he had begun to crawl, but the sight of the plump calves, one foot resting across the instep of the other, was too much for him. He fired, and the wooden rod fastened itself by the rubber suction cap to the blue-veined flesh.

'You little devil!' roared Nanny. 'I'll teach you! You get into the Arch!' All Adrian's howls and protestations of repentance availed nothing. Into the Arch he went. The door was closed on him and locked.

The darkness pressed itself horribly against him, a great, smooth-haired gorilla forcing its chest against his and its sleek thighs against his thighs. He held his breath, praying for it to spare him; but, quietly and slowly, it clutched his throat with its fat, stealthy fingers. He tried to push it away, but in vain; his fists sank into the soft, furred body without effect. The familiar smell of the piled toys a few feet away, with their odour of paint and glue and faint rust, made his terror greater; it was as if his playthings, his familiar companions of everyday, were watching the scene impassively, taking neither side. They had no power over this fat, furred blackness. The railway guard, the water-pistol, the Chinese mandarin with the nodding head, the passengers in the train, and even Rex the bulldog, who, by some cunning device, jumped out of his miniature kennel when you shouted his name, sat there and watched him being strangled. 'Help! Help!' he shouted, and kicked with his heels against the wall as he lay pressed against it. But although he knew that they were watching him, they did nothing. In the end, it was Nanny who opened the nursery door; and the plump, furred fingers fled at her approach.

Sometimes, visitors used to come to the nursery. Old Simon Raphael, his mother's father, came over by bus several times a year from Pembridge Avenue to see his only grandchild. He had been born in Düsseldorf just before the Crimean War and had come to settle in England during the late seventies, but had omitted what had seemed to him, in the days when one could visit most European countries without a passport, the formality of taking out naturalization papers. As a result, he had been interned in the Crystal Palace at the height of the Zeppelin terror. This had broken the old man's spirit, and he had never returned to the business life which he had been forced to relinquish. Simon Raphael had never learned to speak really good English, partly because his wife talked German fluently and used it to converse with him. He was a big, bald-headed old man, who still retained remnants of his earlier jollity, and, once Adrian had got over his preliminary distrust of the guttural voice, he used to look forward to his grandfather's visits. One day, in early December, Simon said to Adrian:

'If you're a good boy, Adrian, I'll give you a sovereign for Christmas.'

Adrian knew what a sovereign was, for he had often heard Nanny talk about them; but he had never seen one, and was greatly excited at the prospect of actually owning one for himself.

A few days before Christmas, Simon came up to the nursery and said:

'Nurse, has Adrian been a good boy like I said?'

'No worse than usual, sir,' replied Nanny.

Then Simon put his hand in his pocket and said: 'Come here, my boy.'

Adrian went over to him, trembling with excitement, ready to receive the gold sovereign. But when Simon took his hand out of his pocket, it contained only a dirty piece of crumpled paper.

'Put out your hand, my boy,' said Simon. 'This is for you.'

Adrian put out his hand, and took the note, saying 'Thank you'; but he was unable to conceal his disappointment.

Simon was hurt and perplexed at the boy's lack of enthusiasm, and, pointing to the writing on the note, said: 'Can you read what this says, my boy?'

Adrian read the words aloud: 'One Pound.'

'That's yours, Adrian,' said Simon.

'Thank you, Grandfather,' said Adrian, still disappointed; and old Simon never discovered why his gift had failed to arouse the delight he had hoped to see on his grandchild's face.

Despite this annual sovereign at Christmas, Nanny used to say that Simon was a mean old man at bottom. One afternoon, when Adrian was very young, Simon gave him a penny to play with, and then took it back before he left. The relation of this incident caused unprecedented merriment below stairs and, next afternoon, in the Botanical Gardens. Another time, he arrived without warning just as Nanny was frying something for high tea. After he had been sitting down for a few minutes, Nanny, without looking up from her frying-pan, said:

'You won't like what I'm frying him for tea, Mr. Raphael.'

'Why, Nurse, what's that?'

'Bacon.'

The effect on his grandfather of this, to Adrian, perfectly normal and everyday word, was startling. The jolly mouth went rigid; the eyelids snapped close together like shutters, so that hardly any white was visible through them. When he spoke, it was in a tone that Adrian had never heard him use before.

'You shouldn't give him that. It's not clean meat.'

Nanny gave him one of her contemptuous, round-the-corner smirks. 'Why not, sir? The pig's a clean animal.'

'How can it be?' growled old Mr. Raphael. And after he had sat there for another minute or two without saying anything, he got up and stumped out.

Adrian waited until his footsteps had died away, and then said to Nanny: 'Why did he look so angry?'

'Your grandfather doesn't like your eating pig,' said Nanny.

'Why on earth not?' said Adrian. 'Doesn't he think we ought to kill animals?'

'He's Jewish, that's why,' said Nanny, dishing out the bacon. 'Jews aren't allowed to eat bacon or pork.'

'Why ever not?' asked Adrian.

'It's the cloven hoof,' replied Nanny mysteriously. And this sinister phrase rather frightened Adrian, so that he said: 'Oh, I see,' although he didn't understand at all.

Sometimes when he was naughty, or raised his voice, Nanny used to say: 'You're a German Jew, you are' or 'You've got German blood in you' or just 'You take after your grandfather'; and Adrian remembered what she had said about the cloven hoof, and wondered what it meant; but he never dared to ask. Until one Sunday morning, when he was sitting downstairs with me, and, after looking at me in silence for a long time, he said:

'Uncle Paul, what's the cloven hoof?'

I said: 'Why, the devil, I suppose. What's the context?' But he said nothing in reply, so I assumed he had got the answer he wanted.

From The End of the Corridor (1951)

MICHAEL MEYER (1921–   ), British novelist, biographer, and translator of Ibsen and Strindberg, was born in London.

Martyn Goff

A MILD CASE OF SCUM

We start with a simple fact: Clifton College is Britain's only public school which has a Jewish house. The house, named Polacks, has had a number of members of that family as its housemaster from time to time. When I went there in 1935 it was Albert I. Polack, a man of warmth, erudition and firmness. At least once a year he made his standard joke:

> 'When was cricket first mentioned in the Bible?'

If you were new to the house, you waited anxiously for the answer. By year three or four it was difficult to contain your laughter, and, with half a dozen who also knew it, to stop that laughter degenerating into uncontrolled giggles.

> 'Nobody know? Well, when Rachel came out with a full pitcher, of course.'

And then the laughter could become open and full-throated, but not always controlled.

When I went there, did I know that it was a *Jewish* house, that the other seven or eight houses had no Jews in them and that Polacks alone took no part in Saturday school life? I cannot remember, but I doubt it. This in turn underlines the most amazing thing of all: there was no anti-semitism. Imagine it: a group of special boys, worse still, from God's chosen people, privileged to have Saturday *and* Sunday off, not to mention high and holy days like New Year and Yom Kippur, and neither resentment nor envy were to be seen or heard. There was the usual keen rivalry between the houses and the inevitable insults and catcalls among the rivals, but if the word 'Jew' were spoken pejoratively, I never heard it.

Polacks occupied a large house in a residential road adjoining the main school buildings. There was a 'private' side where the housemaster, his large, jolly wife and their clever children resided; and the school side, which housed some fifty boys, their studies, dormitories, a reasonable library and a dining-hall. The private side was rarely visited, though I remember one or two dinners in the Polacks' dining room, including one that was mildly catastrophic. A Middle-eastern-looking youth, whose name I still remember, gave the largest burp I have ever heard almost at the start of the meal. The boys present, myself included, collapsed into uncontrollable laughter (again!), and it took the whole of two courses for us to recover. I cannot recall ever being invited again, though that may have been due to another, less innocent story.

I became enamoured of a young boy, blond, lithe, tough. The affair, if such it could be termed, became fairly public knowledge. So much so that at a pre-Christmas lunch when prominent house footballers and cricketers were being hailed, there were also chants of 'Martyn and Mick'. We planned to stay with each other in the following year's summer holidays. We, or perhaps I, wrote letters. Mick pushed these under his clothes at the back of his wardrobe at home. In the Christmas holidays his mother was ironing, found the handle of the iron too hot, reached into the open wardrobe behind her and seized the first thing that came to hand, a small bundle of papers. Her eyes caught the words of one of my letters and the fat was in the fire.

Mr Polack was at his firmest, yet still concerned and understanding. Such things happened at our age, had no special significance and would soon pass when we reached the larger world where girls had their rightful place. At least, I thought, I am not to be expelled. He reached his peroration. Then the blows came. 'Of course you will have to see the Headmaster.' I shivered in silence. 'You understand?' 'Yes, sir.' 'And your mother will be informed.' The interview was over.

In part I had been sent to a boarding school because my parents had divorced when I was about 8 years of age, my father having met another woman and gone off with her (how easily this trips off the tongue when reality was more than two years of hideous quarrelling, of shouting matches and delayed Sunday lunches, and, finally, of *Daily Mirror* publicity for the court case). Clifton, with its Jewish house, had presumably been chosen because, with the departure of my father and the disgrace of divorce, I was in need of religious backing and instruction. Indeed, my barmitzvah took place in the charming small synagogue which Polacks house also contained. Mr Polack himself trained me for my part in the service.

This domestic crisis had left my mother to adjust to a whole new style and way of life, for my father was comparatively rich but treated her shoddily; and, as a successful businessman, had looked after much of the larger items of their domestic life: buying and altering houses; laying out new gardens; installing or repairing central heating and the like. Nor was she, an intelligent but largely uneducated woman, qualified to deal with the manners and conventions of public schools. Yet she was to be summoned and told that her darling youngest son had seduced a boy two years younger than himself and written unspeakable letters to the boy.

I do not know what Albert Polack said to her when she arrived, nor she to him. Was she shown the foul letters ('scum' was the Headmaster's word when I was finally ushered into his august and intimidating presence)? Was she told of what actually *happened*? It may make me smile to think of it now, but the horror for a woman on her own presented with a side of life probably never before even glimpsed can be imagined. There must have been gay Jews in the Twenties and Thirties, but I doubt whether they were ever mentioned or discussed. Camp music hall figures may have received slighting references, but I suspect that was the limit. And here she was, sitting in the housemaster's study and being told that her good Jewish son had written gutter letters and done unimaginable things.

The College is not far from the Downs, elegant buildings in a pleasant setting. I was summoned on the day of her visit to the 'private' side. Five minutes of excruciating conversation took place as Albert Polack tried, I imagine, to signal that all was fairly well and that I was not, in his eyes, a pariah even if I had fallen. My mother looked worried and smiling by turns. 'I hope,' said Mr Polack in conclusion, 'you enjoy your lunch together.' We were in the street.

We walked, not to our usual restaurant, at least not straightaway, but to those Downs. We hardly spoke. Once or twice I asked questions about home which were answered briefly. Then suddenly my mother stopped in the middle of a path, grass and trees on both sides of us, a wintry sun just shining. 'I suppose,' she said slowly and firmly, 'you were the unlucky one, the only one to get caught?' I nodded fervently. 'Right, then let's go and get some lunch and forget about it.' She had found a formula that let me off the hook without actually exonerating me.

MARTYN GOFF OBE (1923–), novelist, historian, musical and literary critic, and bookseller, was Director of Book Trust (formerly National Book League) 1970–88.

Dannie Abse

THE CLYTEMNESTRA BUST

In the hall, the stone bust of Clytemnestra stood on its stone 'Greek' pedestal. It had been newly whitewashed and I remembered how, when I was five or so, when visitors were about to leave the house, I pressed her one stony nipple that peeped over a fold of her stone dress. My father was in the middle of a farewell conversation and Dafydd Morgan had a fit of coughing. I turned round, still with my finger pressing the nipple of Clytemnestra, and mother, who was watching me, quickly averted her gaze. I posed in that position for quite a while as Clytemnestra stared down at the floor blankly. The visitors seemed a trifle embarrassed, talking a little too quickly, and Dafydd Morgan's loose cough exploded in the stuffy stiff air of the hall. The moment seemed to last forever – my index finger on the stony nipple, the accelerated conversation – before the door banged and mother ushered me into the living-room gently, without explanation. Though now I was fourteen, I felt a secret compulsion, as I stood there in the afternoon hall, to touch Clytemnestra again. I could hear the voices behind the door of the drawing-room so that now my mother's indignant comments distracted me from my silly intention.

'Mrs Goldblatt was there. A *baitsema*, I tell you. Such a woman! And she was wearing her straight black hair, shoulder-length, with a schoolgirl's fringe. With a schoolgirl's fringe cut across her forehead! And at *her* age! She had on long jade ear-rings, a shell necklace and a low-cut sweater with a long black taffeta skirt. Imagine! And she smoked through a cigarette-holder as long as a fountain-pen. And fingernails! Long! Plum colour like her thick lipstick. Powder – excuse me, Leo, I'm not exaggerating – an inch thick. Making sheep's eyes at all the young men, and flashing her diamond rings in their faces to dazzle 'em.'

I heard Leo saying, 'She certainly impressed you,' and mother replying, 'Why, I hardly looked at her, I couldn't be bothered.'

Before I went into the room I looked in the mirror with satisfaction. I had gummed down my hair with Wilfred's hair-cream and had a parting worth an advertisement. Not that it was really anything to do with Lydia Pike. After all, how could I be in love with her when we hadn't even exchanged pleasantries; but I thought of her a great deal. 'Hullo, Lydia,' I said to Clytemnestra, touching her cold nipple before I walked into the living-room with a casual indifference. They looked up from their chairs when I came in, then resumed their conversation as if nobody had entered. I leaned against the sideboard, raising my left eyebrow, for I had seen how effective this pose was in the mirror.

'What's the matter, are you ill?' asked Leo.

I gave him a look which I had also practised but it didn't seem to work out, so nonchalantly I hummed:

> I'm the man, the very fat man
> that waters the workers' beer.
> What do I care if it makes them ill
> if it make them terribly queer.
> I've a yacht, a car and an aeroplane
> and I waters the workers' beer.

'Shut up,' said Leo.

'I'm the man, the very fat man,' I sang.

'What do you want to pour so much of that poison on your hair for?' asked Dad.

'I'm not keen on curly hair,' I explained.

'You'd better give up eating crusts,' Mama said. 'Besides I'm tired of finding the loaves with all their outsides cut off.'

'You'll get bald when you're older,' Wilfred said. 'Leave *my* hair-cream alone.'

'You need a haircut,' Leo said.

'What did I give birth to,' asked Mam, 'a tailor's dummy?'

'It's unnatural to be so clean at fourteen,' remarked Leo.

'Leave me alone.'

'You dirty the pillows with such a greasy head,' scolded Mam.

'Oh stop going on about it.'

'Now don't be impudent,' said Dad.

'Leave off,' I said.

'Don't speak to your father that way,' said Leo.

'It's your father too,' I said.

'Enough,' said Dad, 'or I'll put your head under the tap.'

'Anyway, what are you smothering your head with hair-cream for? *My* hair-cream,' asked Wilfred.

'Yes, why?' asked Leo.

I looked at their inquiring faces: Leo with his dark smouldering brown eyes, Wilfred wiping his spectacles with the end of his tie, Dad with his greying hair, and Mother with her corrugated brow.

'Haven't you a tongue in your head?' demanded father.

I wanted to rise from my chair and break something.

'What have we given birth to, a mute?' mother asked.

I looked down at my feet, hurt.

'Leave the poor boy alone,' said father.

'Go on now, wash your hair,' Leo said.

'Leave him be,' said Mam, 'You're always teasing the boy.'

'Who, me?' asked Leo. 'I like your cheek.'

'Do you realise you're speaking to your mother?' shouted father.

'I realise it,' said Leo.

'You're not too old to prevent me giving you a hiding,' threatened Dad.

'Oh stop arguing with your boys,' said mother.

'They're your boys too,' said father.

Through the November streets we roamed: Bob, Basil, Ken, Alun (who had just moved into the district) and myself, the youngest. We hung round Lydia Pike's house just to receive a glimpse of her. Alun hadn't seen her yet. We waited expectantly.

'She goes to The Parade,' volunteered Bob.

'The Parade's the girls' high school,' I informed Alun.

'I'm not interested in women,' said Alun.

'Nor am I,' said Bob with alacrity.

'Nor am I,' said Basil.

'Nor am I,' said Ken.

They looked at me anxiously.

'Nor am I,' I said.

We stood there at the corner, half-way up Cyncoed Hill, the other side of the disused quarry. The new row of grey shaded houses overlooked the chimney-pots of Cardiff as they slanted down to the Bristol Channel. Soon they would erase the view by building houses on the south side of the street, and so destroy the feeling one had of almost being in the country; for further down the road, to the east, the tarmac came abruptly to an end and a stony skeleton of a path continued onwards through a gate, into a field, following a lovers' walk past a famous spot where a middle-aged woman, a few years before, had been casually murdered.

Lydia Pike's house, with its garage and front lawn, stood unfriendly behind us. And its blind windows gazed out, over the smoky beer-coloured weather of autumn, at the distant sea on which some child artist had drawn with a lead pencil the silhouette of a static cardboard ship.

'Let's go then,' said Alun.

'No point waiting here,' said Basil.

'Absolutely no point,' I said.

'Stupid, isn't it?' said Ken.

'Besides,' said Bob, 'what would we do if she came?'

'Ask her for a date,' said Basil.

'Bet you you wouldn't,' screamed Bob.

'Bet you a shilling,' I said.

'I'm not interested in women,' said Alun.

'If I was interested I'd make a date,' Basil pronounced.

'Bet you wouldn't,' I said.

'Lets go,' said Alun. 'None of us are interested.'

'Where'll we go?' Ken asked.

'Nowhere to go,' Bob said sadly.

'May as well stay here,' I said.

'You're a bunch of ladies' men,' jeered Alun. 'Women,' he added knowingly. 'Women . . . *Ach y fu*.'

'Well, where'll we go?' asked Basil.

'Anywhere, but let's go. It's cold standing about,' said Alun.

The noises of the evening gathered on a web of silence: the sound of a faraway train, a lone dog barking, shouts of a 'rag and bone' man coming down Cyncoed Hill, a queer chirping cry of some unseen bird. And beneath all these, the whine of silence that oozed from the gouged-out eye of the disused quarry.

Lydia Pike came round the corner on her own. We politely moved out of the way, clearing the pavement. She minced past us in her black sweater, nose tilted in the air, her blown golden hair falling like water over the back of her shoulders. She ran up the steps, gave us a dazzling look, and in a moment she had disappeared inside the house and not one of us had spoken a word.

'Let's go,' said Basil.

'Yes,' said Bob.

'Silly waiting here,' I said.

Suddenly, some anonymous futuristic man, a long way away in the power house, touched some gigantic switch and the lamp-posts jerked to life; and, though it was not dark, the electricity demarcated the country from the town more absolutely than any fumbling sunshine of a windy summer afternoon. . . . We began to walk away silently.

'Where'll we go, Alun?' asked Bob.

'Boy,' said Alun. 'She's certainly got a pair of tits on her!'

We looked at him surprised, aghast, mouths open; then with a certain reverence.

From: Ash on a Young Man's Sleeve (1951)

DANNIE ABSE MRCS, LRCP (1923–), Welsh poet and doctor, was born in Cardiff. His *Collected Poems* was published in 1977, and a further autobiography, *Poet in the Family*, in 1974.

Wolf Mankowitz

THE HAMMER V THE PYTHON

In the Whitechapel Road it was all bright lights and crowds of people, smart as paint, taking a Saturday night stroll after working the week as machinists and under-pressers and cabinet-makers.

They queued at the Roxy for the second house, two big pictures, while an acrobat turned somersaults in the road for pennies, and sang *Any old iron*, jangling a string of real medals. They crowded into restaurants for lemon tea, and swelled out of the public houses waving bottles, their arms about each other's necks, their children waiting at the door with glasses of lemonade clasped to their narrow chests. They walked slowly along, bright ties and high-heeled patent leather shoes, eating chips out of newspaper, careful not to let the vinegar spill onto their new clothes. Arm in arm they walked, trilby hats, brims down, girl-friends with bright lips and dark eyes and loud laughter, mothers and fathers arguing together, calling to children licking toffee apples and taking no notice, old men talking quietly raising their eyebrows, knowing the truth of things.

Joe strode ahead of his mother, who chatted with Mr Kandinsky, while Sonia dawdled talking to a girl with heavy pencilled eyebrows and glossy silk stockings, out with her new fiancé, a bookie's runner and flash with wide padded shoulders to his double-breasted suit. Joe took giant strides past Russian Peter with his crooked beard and Russian peaked cap. Russian Peter usually had wreaths of garlic cloves and pyramids of home-picked cucumbers on his barrow, a large box with handles mounted on two wheels, but now he had a tray with packets of sweets and chewing gum and toffee apples. Instead of calling out 'Cumber, knobbel, cumber, knobbel,' as he usually did, he said, 'Taffee eppls, taffee eppls,' in the same high voice. Russian Peter's cucumbers were pickled by a special recipe he brought with him from Russia, with his peaked cap. Joe went back to ask his mother for a toffee apple. Sure enough, it had a special taste, strange, black glistening treacle.

They allowed plenty of time for the walk to the baths, which was just as well, because what with Sonia saying hello to all her friends and their new fiancés, and Mr Kandinsky talking to this one and that, and different people asking Joe's mother how was his father, they would be lucky to get there at all. As it was, when they arrived at the baths, Joe heard a great roar from inside, and thought, that's it, that's the end of the fight, we've missed it. But they hadn't. It was still the last round of the fight before.

For the wrestling season, the swimming baths were boarded over, a relief to Joe who had been wondering how they could wrestle in baths. There were big lights over a ring in the middle, and you could make out the diving boards at one end, dim in the darkness, with canvas sheets hanging over them. There was no water beneath the boards though, because Joe dropped a small stone through them and there was no splash. It was like the railings over the pavements in the streets. If you made up your mind they were fixed, it was all right. People sat in rows, on seats in front and benches behind while further back still they stood on wide steps, sitting on the floor in the intervals.

Men went round with trays selling hokey-pokey ice creams, roasted peanuts, and cold drinks, and there was a great hum of noise, which, during the fights, quietened down so that only one or two voices would be heard over the grunting of the wrestlers. Two wrestlers were tied up together on the floor of the ring, one of them grunting as he pressed down harder and harder, the other shouting out 'Oh, oh, oh, oh!' every time he was pressed. He wore a red mask but he was losing all the same.

Someone called out 'Wheel 'em out,' and someone else shouted 'Carve-up,' and a red-headed woman screamed 'Tear his arms off, Mask.' All around people munched peanuts and drank ice-cold drinks out of bottles. As Joe sat down a man in a big coat started to eat a sandwich and a pickled yellow cucumber at once. At the end of the row where they were sitting, Joe saw Madame Rita and Lady R. Madame Rita had his arm round Lady R. He shouted 'Chuck 'em out, they're empty,' waving a cigar in his other hand. Lady R watched the wrestlers closely. Her eyes stared and her lips moved in a small tight smile, and when one threw the other, she clasped her hands together, breathing out hard between her teeth. Then, when they finished, she sank back in her seat and looked round with shining eyes at Madame Rita, who squeezed her shoulder in case she was frightened.

The end of the fight came while Mr Kandinsky was buying them roasted peanuts. The bell rang, and one of the wrestlers, puffing and blowing, had his arm held up by the referee, while the other one still writhed on the floor. Half the people cheered, and the other half booed. The two wrestlers left the ring, sweating hard, their dressing gowns draped over their shoulders. One of them tripped on the ropes.

There was a good echo in the baths, although with all the shouting and laughing it was difficult to hear it, but sometimes there was a gap in the noise, people were suddenly quiet, as if getting their wind, and then one voice would ring out and the echo pick the words up and throw them back into the smoke and the smell of ozone. Joe would have liked to shout for the echo, but while it was all right under the arches, you didn't like to in front of so many people, and anyhow as soon as you decided to try it, the noise started again.

'Wheel 'em in,' they shouted. 'Money back, get on with it.' But nothing happened because it was the interval.

At the ends of the aisles St John's men in uniforms with polished peaks and white bands sat looking out for people to faint, but no one did. Programme sellers went up and down, shouting out that the lucky programme number got two ringsides for next week. Madame Rita had two but bought two more, just to show off. The hokey-pokey men in white jackets did very well, and almost everyone was sucking oranges and pink ice creams or drinking from bottles or eating peanuts, crunching the shells under their feet.

Then, just as the crowd was getting bored with lucky programmes and hokey-pokey, and restless for the big fight to start, the M.C. climbed into the ring. There was a great roar, and though he held up his arms, it went on. He shook his arms, turning from one side to the other, and the dickie front of his evening suit opened a little. 'Ladees and gentlemen!' he shouted, 'your attention if you please, ladees, your attention gentlemen, please.'

The crowd quietened and the M.C. smiled. 'For your entertainment, at great expense, Sam Spindler the well-known harmonist, will entertain you.' There was a groan as Sam Spindler, a thin bald-headed man in a Russian silk blouse with red ruching, and black trousers cut wide at the bottom but tight in the waist, climbed through the ropes with a piano accordion, all ivory and silver and red enamel, on his back. He bowed twice and played *Tiger Rag*, getting the tiger so well that lots of people threw pennies into the ring when he finished. Then he played a medley of songs like *My Old Dutch* and *Tipperary* and everyone sang, but when he stopped and got out a piece of wood, took his accordion off and started to tap-dance, the crowd started to boo. He had to play the accordion again, which was a shame, because Joe was interested in tap-dancing and liked to watch the arms and the legs bent at the knees and the little head jerks

A lot more pennies were thrown, then someone shouted, 'We want Python,' and a whole crowd took it up. Another crowd answered 'We want Hammer,' and soon you couldn't hear Sam playing at all. He stopped and looked down at the M.C.'s seat with a worried expression on his face. The M.C. came up and thanked Sam, who was picking up his pennies. He spread out a big poster on the floor and started to read out the programme for next week, but the noise was so great he gave up. He beckoned towards the dark door through which the other wrestlers had passed after their fight. A little wiry man in shirt sleeves and blue braces came bounding up the aisle, and leaped into the ring. After him marched the wrestlers.

First Shmule, in a crimson dressing gown gleaming in the light, with Blackie and Oliver bustling round him. A man leaned over to pat his back as he passed, and when he sprang into the ring there was quite a big cheer. Shmule bowed towards the cheers and looked proudly at the small group who booed. He waved to Joe, and Joe waved back. Sonia blew kisses and Mr Kandinsky said, 'A fine boy, good luck to him.' Then Shmule started stretching himself, so as not lose a moment's development.

After him came the dreaded Python with his manager, a man with a square blue jaw, like polished rock. The Python wore a black silk dressing gown and a white towel round his neck, and he towered above the seconds dancing round him. He climbed into the ring, not so full of spring as Shmule but with one powerful hitch of his arm. There was, true, a bigger cheer for Python, but Shmule's friends booed hard, Joe hissed like a goose, Sonia shouted out 'Carcase meat,' and Mr Kandinsky said 'What a bull.'

The M.C. introduced Shmule first. He called him the white hope of Aldgate, the sensational young former amateur championship contender, a clean-fighting local boy, and so on and so forth. All the while the Python was baring his teeth and growling and shaking his fist at Shmule's supporters. Shmule slipped out of his crimson dressing-gown and now his muscles rippled in the ring lights, his spotless white hammer shining like a star against the crimson briefs. Oliver and Blackie clustered round his corner with towels and pails and a chair for him to sit on between rounds. They looked worried, although after all that saying he was a gonner, Shmule looked as if nothing could ever frighten him. There was a fresh feeling about him, as if he felt there were so many tailors expecting him to make a good fight, especially with the trade being so up and down, and so much unemployment, they lent him the strength they had been saving for work.

The dreaded Python Macklin was very angry. He strained like a fierce bulldog at the rope, just waiting for the bell to sound to throw himself on Shmule, tearing him limb from limb like the Christian martyrs, just as Mavis said. The black hair on the Python stood up in fury and he ground his teeth together. When the M.C. pointed in his direction and called out his name, famous contender for the championship of the world, and veteran of the ring all over Europe, the Python drew himself up and the muscles on his chest and back were swollen with pride and power. He grinned, his teeth clamped tight together, and when the red-haired woman screamed out, 'Murder him, Py,' he stared at her as if he was hungry and she was a juicy steak.

'A forty-minute contest,' the M.C. shouted through his megaphone, 'of eight five-minute rounds, for a purse of not ten, not twenty, but twenty-five pounds.'

He drew the two men together and whispered to them, the Python sneering, Shmule looking serious. Mr Kandinsky said again, 'Good luck,' and then the bell rang. In the sudden silence it echoed well.

Joe sat with his seat tipped up to see over the head of the man in front. This man had a head like a smooth water melon with a bit of hair round the edges, pasted down with oil as if painted. As soon as the bell rang he started to talk slowly in a gruff voice like a gate swinging on rusty hinges in the wind. The woman next to him had grey hair permanently waved and never spoke, except to say, 'Have a nut.' The man was very helpful to Joe because he was an expert and explained the whole fight, hold by hold.

At first the wrestlers circled watchfully round one another looking for an opening. The man with the painted head said, 'You watch, Em, he'll be on to him, just give him that opening, watch, it's coming – no, hold it, now – no, he missed it, he's waiting to put the scissors on him.'

The Python prepared to spring on Shmule, who stood quite still waiting. Then, as the Python bent his legs to jump, Shmule stepped aside and Python fell on his face with a heavy slap.

'He missed him,' said the man with painted hair, and even as he spoke Shmule leapt on to the Python, catching both legs below knee level in the crook of his arm, and pulling sharply.

'Ouch!' shouted Python.

'Ouff!' said the man with painted hair. 'He got the old calf-lock on him.'

The Python shook himself like a alligator, and one of his knees slipped free and bowled Shmule over. The Python caught hold of Shmule by the foot and thigh and prepared to throw him but Shmule pressed into the canvas with both hands, and heaved his body into the Python's ribs like a battering ram. The Python reeled into the ropes, and the bell rang.

Shmule turned to his corner, but the Python came after him. The crowd roared with one voice, 'Look behind you!' Shmule turned sharply, and the referee jumped in front of Python, and forced him to his corner. The Python was furious and pushing his seconds off the ring, he picked up his chair and punched his fist through the seat.

'Phoo,' said the man with painted hair, 'what a round, the dirty bastard turning on him like that after the bell, the dirty great bleeder.'

'Have some nuts, Fred,' the permanently waved woman said.

'The swine,' said Sonia with tears in her eyes, 'did you see that?'

The seconds rubbed them down and waved towels while the wrestlers spat into pails, and breathed deep and even, glaring at one another across the ring, listening to their manager's advice. The crowd wasn't shouting, 'Carve up,' any more. They could see it was serious. The bell rang for the second round.

The Python at once shot from his corner, his fingers crooked to seize Shmule, his face rigid, calling the muscles of his body to attention. Shmule crouched like a panther, waiting.

'He's giving him half a stone,' the man with the painted head said. 'He's got to play a waiting game, let the Python use hisself up, then come in quick. Ahh!'

The Python had his arms about Shmule and was hugging him like a bear. Shmule's arms were pinned to his sides, and he couldn't move. He twisted to one side then to the other, but the Python shortened the hug, working the grip of one hand upon the other wrist slowly up his arm. Shmule's face twisted with pain.

'Let him get out of that one,' the man said. Sonia clenched and unclenched her hands, and Joe's mother looked away. Mr Kandinsky was breathing hard, but Joe just stared, wondering what Shmule would do now. The crowd was shouting, 'Finish him, Python!'

Then Shmule moved his hand up and down in fast little movements against his thigh and the referee jumping about watching saw the sign, and told Python to let go, the Hammer gave in. But Python wouldn't let go, and Shmule bit his lips in agony. Now the crowd shouted against the Python but that didn't help Shmule. The referee and all the seconds jumped on to him to tear him away, and the bell rang.

Blackie and Oliver helped Shmule to his corner and gently rubbed him, putting wet towels on his face. The crowd was furious with the Python, but he didn't care. He shouted back at them, showing off his muscles and asking if any one would like to try them. 'Filth!' Mr Kandinsky shouted, but poor Shmule looked pale and his eyes were closed.

'He's a dirty fighter,' the man with painted hair said, 'but give credit, he's got a grip like iron, the bleeder.'

'Get us some more nuts, Fred,' the woman replied.

Blackie and Oliver were working hard on Shmule, who breathed deeply, the colour coming back into his face. By the time the bell rang for the third round, he seemed as good as new.

'But you can't tell,' the man with the painted head said, 'he could have a couple ribs broke clean and he wouldn't know till after.'

'Has he got a couple ribs broke?' Joe asked.

'God forbid,' Mr Kandinsky answered, 'God forbid.'

Blackie and Oliver must have told Shmule not to waste time, because he came out fast and made straight for the Python who, being pleased with himself, was a bit careless. Shmule clasped his hands together and raised them for a rabbit punch, but he was too late. The Python crouched away, out of distance, not careless any more. Then a look of pain suddenly crossed Shmule's face, and the Python grinned and came in to attack, his hands low.

'He's hurt,' Sonia whispered.

'He's hurt all right,' the man in front of Joe said.

But what a surprise. Shmule suddenly leaped forward and caught the Python a great crack on the jaw with his left fist. The Python looked surprised and fell down.

'No boxing,' the crowd yelled.

The Python started to get up at once, but Shmule was on top of him, his knees to either side of his stomach, his hands firmly planted on his shoulders, pressing them to the canvas. As he pressed he strengthened the grip of his knees. The Python groaned, shouted. He jerked and jumped and twisted, but he couldn't throw Shmule off.

'He can give it,' the man said, 'but he can't take it. Go on boy, do him!'

The Python beat the floor with both hands and Shmule let go at once.

'Good boy,' the man said.

'He should give him the same as he got,' Sonia said, 'Why should he fight him clean?'

The crowd cheered Shmule, but the Python wasn't hurt as much as they thought, because as soon as Shmule broke away, he leaped to his feet. Not fast enough though. Shmule wasn't so green now. He didn't stop watching the Python for a second, and he saw him tensed to leap. Ready for him, he caught the Python another crack on the chin as he came up. The Python went down with Shmule on top of him, but he was saved by the bell.

'That's more like it,' the man said, 'he's got the old Python on the squirm, proper.'

'Get us some nuts, Fred,' the woman said.

'Fancy an ice?' the man asked.

'Some nuts, Fred,' the woman said again.

'How's the boy doing now, Sonia?' Mr Kandinsky asked.

'He's all right,' Sonia said, 'another round like that and he'll win.'

'We're winning,' Joe told his mother.

'That's good,' she replied. 'It's awful to see their faces.'

In the fourth round the Python set out to finish Shmule off. He tried all the fancy holds, the Indian death lock, the flying mare, the cobra, but Shmule was like an eel, he didn't stay still long enough for the grips to take.

'He's using his speed now,' the man said, 'Let's see the Python catch up with that.'

But the Python couldn't catch up with that. After a couple of minutes the crowd started to laugh, because the Python lumbered like a great ox, while Shmule danced circles round him, cracking him on the back and chest every so often. Now the Python was on his guard against face blows, and being careful made him even more clumsy. He was furious with the crowd for laughing. He looked at Shmule through slit eyes wanting to murder him.

'Let me get my hands on you, laughing boy, that's all,' he growled.

Then suddenly Shmule nipped in close, his foot jabbed out, and the Python fell heavily on to the canvas, his arms round Shmule's legs. But as he fell Shmule struck the Python a heavy blow to the stomach, and pulled his leg free.

The Python held on to his stomach with both hands. His head came forward. His neck bent towards Shmule like a beast to the slaughterer.

Shmule folded his hands together as if to pray. He lifted them and carefully aiming, brought a rabbit punch with all his force clean on to the Python's neck. The Python slumped forward over his hands. Shmule stood back, watching. The Python didn't move.

'Cold meat!' someone shouted.

'Hammer!' all the tailors yelled.

'Hammer!' shouted Joe.

The Python was out cold.

From A Kid for Two Farthings (1953)

WOLF MANKOWITZ (1924–), British novelist, dramatist and authority on antiques, was born in Bethnal Green, London.

David Marcus

ONLY THE BEST

Shifting sands, that summed it up – shifting sands under which he had buried memories of events, situations, comments that were now pushing up into his thoughts like poisonous weeds. 'Pig's ear, wah, wah,' rang again in his ears, and with its sound he saw once more the gaping nine-year-old, aghast at the band of ragged street urchins bundling up the corners of their threadbare coats into their fists and wagging the simulated pigs' ears at him as they shouted their crazy, almost comical taunt.

Was that his first experience of anti-Semitism, the beginning of it all? If so, he had been neither frightened nor angered, only surprised. Its lack of hostility, its mindlessness, gave him no understanding of the daily deprivation and discrimination he had heard his parents and *zeide* recount of their lives in Lithuania. But he had not long to wait for such insights. Soon afterwards, when the time came for him to commence his secondary education, he had to face the ordeal that followed his mother's refusal to enrol him in the local St Dominic's which the other Jewish boys attended. Was it the best school in Cork? Bertha Cohen asked, in a tone that clearly dared any of her family to say it was. Of course they couldn't. St Dominic's was average, at best adequate. They agreed that there were far better schools in the city. But she knew, didn't she, that they refused to take Jewish students?

'I shall go to Max Klein,' she declared. 'He's the President. Let *him* do something about it. Let him go to the Lord Mayor. Let him go to the Government. That's his duty. What does he think he's President for? Just for the *yichas*? Just for the honour?'

Jacob had recognised the familiar signs of battle in his mother's gestures – the way she flicked a wisp of black hair from her eyes as if to see the enemy more clearly, the way she rubbed her hands up and down her apron like a wrestler positioning for an opening. He wished she wouldn't get such ideas into her head. St Dominic's would have suited him. It was used to Jewish students; he would have companions there, boys he already knew. Joshua, too, was upset, and had thrown his eyes up to heaven in despair at his wife's obstinacy. He was heartsore in advance for the defeat she was going to suffer, for the bitterness of soul that would be visited on her. She was not one to lose easily. When did she ever give best before? But this time. . . . If Max Klein couldn't get his own sons into a better school – and everyone knew that Dora had insisted he try – then what chance had he of getting someone else's son in?

'You're wasting your time,' Joshua told his wife.

'We'll see,' was all Bertha Cohen replied.

'You're wasting your time, Mrs Cohen,' the President echoed after all his arguments had failed to move her.

His words only roused her to anger. Why were men such sheep?

'What do you mean? Why should my son not have the best? Isn't our money as good as the Christians'?'

In his impatience Max Klein almost made to grasp the lapel of Bertha Cohen's coat the better to persuade her of her wrong-headedness. But remembering that she was a woman, and a *baaleboosta* into the bargain, he continued to plead.

'Mrs Cohen, I can't help you. *Hub a bissl sechel* – have some sense. Send Jacob to St Dominic's. That's where all the *Yiddisheh* boys go. Why shouldn't he go there like all the others?' Like his own sons, he would have added, if he had thought his visitor wouldn't know of his own unsuccessful efforts to place them elsewhere.

Bertha Cohen gave him a cold look that said *her* son wasn't like all the others. The others' parents might be content with St Dominic's – she refrained from adding that in her opinion the President was a weakling to settle for it – but she had made her mind up. All she wanted was the best for her son, and St Dominic's was not the best.

'Of course it's not,' Max Klein agreed. 'But it's not the worst, either. Take my word for it.'

'The best. Only the best.' Her voice was firm. 'You tell me: *vos iz* the best?'

Max Klein sighed. What could he do with such a blockhead of a woman?

'I don't know which is the best, Mrs Cohen. There are two or three supposed to be very good. They're all run by *galuchim* – religious Orders. But I told you: you're wasting your time. They just don't take Jews.'

'Two or three! And none of them takes Jews. A *skandale*! What are their names, Mr. Klein?'

'Well, there's Presentation Brothers College on the Western Road –'

'Thank you. That will do. Jacob shall go there.'

And there Jacob went.

Seven years had passed since the interview with the Superior, and now as Jacob sat in the bandstand waiting for Deirdre and gazing vacantly on the lonely-looking Mardyke cricket ground he experienced the same trapped feeling. Once again his religion was an issue – not his abilities, his ambitions, his opinions, or even his defects, but something as unasked for and as irreversible as his maleness, and as inexorably deciding so much of his life. He closed his eyes but found that blotting out the leafless elm-trees lining the Mardyke Walk and the backdrop of Sunday's Well's corniched gardens only sharpened the images that had been dormant for so long. He saw again the book-lined study, the mahogany desk impersonally bare of anything but a calendar and an empty letter-tray, the walls with a monster portrait of some imperious clergyman as the centrepiece flanked by rows of scholarship-class photographs and the shelves and glass cases of silver trophies, shields and medals won on the playing-field. Everything he had encountered on that first visit made him conscious to a greater degree than ever before of his foreignness – from the black-cassocked Brothers he had passed in the college grounds to the Superior himself, a chunky man, at home in a massive carved chair, his face angrily criss-crossed by tiny red veins, eyes peering out from behind gold-rimmed spectacles, and his head crowned with a biretta, a piece of headgear Jacob had never seen before and which reminded him uncomfortably of the hats worn by pirates and highwaymen in his childhood tales.

Mrs Cohen, however, seemed in no way put out by the surroundings or by Brother Connolly's appearance. She matched colour for colour and argument for argument. Almost equally forbidding-looking in a boxy dark hat with a veil, her black fur-trimmed coat buttoned up to the neck, and a muff she wore only on chilly winter burials, she contrived to give the impression that her presence was in the nature of a formality, as if she was there merely to make the acquaintance of the Superior and to provide the usual information he would require when enrolling a new pupil.

Brother Connolly had pointed out that as all the students in the school were Christian a Jewish boy would be bound to feel lonely and unhappy – to which Mrs Cohen replied that Jacob had had plenty of Jewish company in his primary school and what he wanted now was to mix with non-Jewish boys if he was to learn tolerance, as the Jewish religion taught. She was sure the Catholic religion preached tolerance, too?

'Tolerance, Mrs, is not something young boys think about much,' said the Superior. 'They can be quite cruel to anyone who is different from themselves.'

'My son understands that' – and she turned to Jacob as if expecting his endorsement. 'But he will make friends quickly. As long as the teachers . . .' Bertha Cohen left the rest unsaid.

Brother Connolly had raised an eyebrow and mused for a moment before saying, half to himself: 'Of course, Presentation College hasn't had any Jewish students before. . . . '

Jacob feared this was just the Superior's polite way of telling them that the school's doors were closed to Jews, but his mother seemed to miss the point.

'My son will have a great honour on his head, then. It will be a great distinction for him. He will repay it. I am certain of that. He is a very good scholar.'

To Jacob it seemed that there was a slight tremor in his mother's voice – whether of tension or of determination he was not sure. He glanced quickly at her hands, hidden from the Superior's sight under the desk. They were still tucked inside their muff, but now the muff was alive with movement as if there were some small animal nervously turning this way and that within it.

'Of course he's a good scholar, Mrs Cohen,' Brother Connolly accepted, 'of course he is. I'm sure he's a bright boy.'

In the silence that followed Jacob held his breath almost in an effort to deny his very presence in the room. He felt he himself did not matter. His religion was all that concerned Brother Connolly, and his mother's ambition for him was all that worried her.

'Have you applied to any other school, Mrs Cohen?'

'No. Only here.'

'Why here? There are other very good secondary schools in Cork.'

Bertha Cohen measured her reply. '*You* may call them good schools, but they do not take Jews. How can an Irish school be good if it refuses an Irish pupil? These schools, they are run by men of God. Did God tell them to refuse Jews?' She paused and then added: 'Did God tell anyone to refuse Jews?'

Jacob looked at Brother Connolly, but the Superior showed no inclination to answer for God. Instead he turned to Jacob. 'And why do you want to come to Pres., young man?'

Jacob started. He had not been prepared for such a question, and the use of the shortened name by which the school was known everywhere lulled him into thinking he might be on the brink of admission. He could spoil it all with the wrong answer. In his confusion he glanced at his mother. Her look reminded him.

'Because my mother wants me to,' he said.

'Good boy. Sound man. Honour thy father and thy mother – isn't that right? Do you know what number that Commandment is?'

'It's the fifth Commandment.'

'The fifth?' the Superior repeated questioningly. Then he immediately added: 'Of course, of course. The Jews' Commandments and the Christians' are the same but in a different order. "Honour thy father and thy mother" is our fourth. Sound man, sound man. I think you'll do well here.'

For the first time Bertha Cohen took her hands out of her muff and agitatedly raised one towards the Superior.

'Religion, Father. He wouldn't be made to attend any religious classes?'

'Certainly not, Mrs Cohen. A half an hour every day is devoted to religious instruction, but Jacob will be able to put the time to equally good use. And by the way, Mrs Cohen, I'm not a Father, I'm a Brother. Just Brother Connolly. We're all brothers here – in both senses of the word, I think I can say. Never you fear now, I'll take a special interest in this little man. I'll look after him like a father.'

Brother Connolly had been true to his word. Jacob remembered the day the Superior had quietly slipped into their English class. The Shakespeare play for study that year was *The Merchant of Venice* and the teacher, Brother Terence, had assigned the part of Shylock to Jacob. That had appealed to his classmates as a great joke and a few of them had addressed him as 'Shylock' at the lunch-break. But the day after the Superior's visit Brother Terence switched the role to someone else and Jacob was made to read the part of Portia. He had not relished the change; he had felt that reading Portia was sissyish.

Had that been his only reaction? he wondered now. He certainly couldn't remember being upset by that incident – or by any other. The one Jew among hundreds of Catholics, and his Jewishness, instead of making him vulnerable, had in fact been his armour. It was as if he didn't exist outside of Jewtown, as if the Jacob attending Presentation College was some *doppelgänger* sent to suffer the pinpricks of its alien world while the real Jacob remained cocooned in his *Yiddisheh veldt*. But now he was seeing that Jewish world for what it was – an anachronism not only of time but of place, too. As long as one didn't have to move outside it, its defences might hold. But if one had to have any traffic with the outside world, then its age was a a fragile protection. Growing up – that's what did it. Growing up meant growing out, and in the religious straitjacket of Celtic Crescent growing out was impossible.

From A Land Not Theirs (1986)

DAVID MARCUS (1924–), Irish novelist, critic and publisher, was born in Cork.

Sammy Davis

SHOW BUSINESS

The judge glanced around the courtroom. 'Where's the mother?'

Mama stood up. 'No telling' where she is, y'honor. She's chorus girling somewhere.'

'Who are you, Madam?'

'I'm the child's grandmother, Mrs. Rosa B. Davis, sir.'

'Oh yes. I received a telephone call from your employer. I'm told you're a fine woman and you have a nice little boy. She said you've cared for her children for years and she feels you're capable of raising this boy, too.'

'Yes, Judge, I love him and I can do it. I want to give him a home like a child should have and keep him out of show business where he doesn't eat every day and sometimes has no place to sleep, but I can't do that 'less he's mine.'

Back at the apartment Mama laid down the law to Will and my father. 'You heard with your own ears. The judge said his own father and mother ain't capable of raising him and he gave Sammy to me. Legal! So, from now on, you can't just pack up Sammy and go to this place and that place and just leave me a note.'

My father didn't say anything. He just looked miserable. Will cleared his throat. 'Uh – Mrs. Davis, I just got us a fine booking up in Boston next week. Naturally it's your say if we can take Sammy along with us.'

Mamma looked at me and stroked my head. I wanted desperately to go with them. After a while she said. 'All right, Sammy. I know you want to sing and dance and be in show business more than anything, so you can go. Mastin, you and Sam sit there and listen to me tell you how you'll take care of this child. You won't let him eat no hot dogs, and no hamburgers neither. Give him chicken and be sure and give the leg, not the breast, it's too dry. And don't let him eat close to the bone. And when he says he's had enough don't you tell him "There's food on the plate." Let him leave it. He'll eat as much as he wants and that's enough. And don't give him no pork chops. You and Sam can all eat the pork you want and all the pigtails but don't you give none to Sammy. If you can't get him chicken legs, then give him a piece of beef. Don't you upset his stomach. If he gets sick on the road, you won't have the money to call a doctor and you'll kill my child.'

'All right, Mama, we'll do just like you say.'

She handed him a bottle of Scott's Emulsion. 'Always keep a bottle of this and give it to him three times a day 'til he's sixteen. There'll be times you don't have heat in the room and this'll keep him from catching cold. . . . '

After dinner Mama gathered up the dishes and washed them. I helped her dry them. She seemed tired. 'You work hard, don't you, Mama?'

'Yes, I do.'

'I work hard, too.'

'But you make more money than me. Let me ask you something, Sammy. Does your father take your money to a table where he puts it down and sometimes he can't pick it up?'

'Sure, Mama, he gambles.'

'That's what I thought.'

'But he gives me what I want.'

'While you're on the road – you ever been hungry?'

'No. Daddy and Massey been hungry, but never me.'

She nodded, satisfied. 'But the first day you come home and tell me you been hungry then that's the end of show business. And don't let nobody sew up nothing for you or put patches on you. You understand what I'm talkin' about? If there's a little hole in your stocking, then you tear it and make it such a big hole that nobody can sew it up for you. You don't need to wear nothing mended. I'll always buy you whatever clothes you need. You're my little boy now, Sammy, and I love you like I always loved you and I'll always be here 'til you don't need me no more.'

I tugged at my father's arm as he, Massey, and I approached Grand Central Station. 'Where we goin', Daddy?'

'We're goin' to the railroad station.'

'But where else we goin'?'

He winked at Will, 'Well, let's see . . . from there we're catchin' the smokey to Boston.'

'I *know* that, but where else?'

He hoisted me onto his shoulders, laughing, 'We're goin' back into show business, Poppa. Back into show business.'

From Yes I Can (1965)

SAMMY DAVIS JR (1924–), singer, dancer, impressionist, was born in New York City.

Allen Ginsberg

GREGORY CORSO'S STORY

The first time I went
    to the country to New Hampshire
When I was about eight
    there was a girl
I always used to paddle with a plywood stick.

We were in love,
    so the last night there
We undressed in the moonlight
    and showed each other our bodies
then we ran singing back to the house.

ALLEN GINSBERG (1926–), American poet and dramatist, is regarded as a founder of the 'beat' school. His *Collected Poems* was published in 1985.

Bernard Malamud

BLACK WRITING

Bill insisted on showing the writer the first chapter of the novel he had recently begun. Lesser asked him not to just yet, but Bill said it would help him know if he had started off right. He said this was a brand-new book although there were some scenes from the other novel, brought from Mississippi to Harlem, where most of the action would take place. Bill asked Lesser to read the chapter in his presence. He sat in Harry's armchair, wiping his glasses and looking at a newspaper on his knees as the writer, chain-smoking, read on the sofa. Once Harry glanced up and saw Bill sweating profusely. He read quickly, thinking he would lie if he didn't like the chapter.

But he didn't have to. The novel, tentatively called *Book of a Black*, began in Herbert Smith's childhood. He was about five in the opening scene, and nine at the end of the chapter; but in truth he was an old man.

In the opening scene, one day the boy drifted out of his neighbourhood into a white neighbourhood and couldn't find his way home. Nobody spoke to him except an old white woman who saw him through her ground-floor window, sitting on the kerb.

'Who are you, little boy? What's your name?'

The boy wouldn't say.

In the afternoon this old-smelling white woman came out of the house and took the boy by the hand to the police station.

'Here's a boy that's lost,' she said.

He wouldn't answer the white pigs when they asked him questions. Finally they sent in a black cop to find out where he belonged.

'Can't you talk, boy?'

The boy nodded.

'Then talk and tell me where do you live at.'

The boy wouldn't answer.

The black cop got him a glass of milk to drink, then lifted the boy into his car and drove into Harlem. They walked from street to street, the policeman asking people sitting on the stoops if they knew this kid. No one did. Finally a fat black woman, fanning herself though the day was cool, said she did. She led them two blocks up the street to the tenement where she said the boy lived.

'Do you live in this here house?' asked the cop.

'He sure do,' said the fat woman.

The boy said nothing.

'You sure are a terror,' said the cop. 'If you was mine I would blast your ass.'

In a flat on the top of the house they found the mother drunk in bed. She was naked but did not pull up the blanket.

'Is this you boy?'

She turned her head and wept.

'I asked you to tell me is this you boy?'

She nodded and wept.

The cop left the boy there and went downstairs.

The woman wept.

The boy smeared a slice of stale bread with some rancid lard and went down to the street to eat it.

In the last scene of the chapter the mother has a visitor who drops in every other night.

. . . He was an ofay who liked to pretend to talk nigger talk. It made him feel good to do it though it was fake black talk. He did not come from the South, he came from Scranton, Pa. He came to my mama because she charged one dollar and it wasn't before long that he used to get it for free. And also my mama did all the things he wanted her to do. Sometimes he left us a loaf of sandwich bread on the table or a can of pears, or string beans, or mushy canned fruit. I remember he left a can of tomato paste that my mama smeared on the bread and gave it to me to eat. Sometimes he also gave her two packs of Lucky Strikes. My mama was about twenty-seven years then and I was nine years old. On the street they called this guy 'Rubber Dick.' He was a tall stringy Charlie with long legs and a big prick. He liked to take it out and show it to me and scare me off. I hated him and had thoughts to kill him off with my zip gun but was afraid to. I told my mother to warn him to stay out of the house but she said she didn't mind having him for company.

'Is he comin here tonight?' I asked her.

'Well, he jus might.'

'I hope he dies before he gets here. I hope I kill him if he comes in this here room.'

'I gon wash your mouth with soap if you say that word again.'

'I got nothin to be shame of.'

'He treats me real fine. Las week he buy me a pair of pretty shoes.'

I know he didn't buy her no shoes.

I left the house but when I came back to eat some supper, he was there, smoking a Lucky Strike cigarette.

'Wheah at is Elsie?' he asked me in nigger talk and I said I didn't know.

He looked at me in a way that was supposed to witch me and he sat on the bed with a shit smile on his mouth.

'I gon wait for her.'

He told me to come over to him on the bed, he wouldn't hurt me.

I was scared so nauseous I thought if I moved one teensy bit I would crap in my pants. I wanted my mother to come back fast. If she came back I would not mind what they did to each other.

'Come heah, boy, and unzip mah pants.'

I told him I didn't want to.

'Heah's a nice tin cints piece you kin have.'

I didn't move at all.

'Heah's a quotah mo. Now unzip mah pants and the money yo's. Bof the dime and the quotah.'

'Don't take it out, please,' I asked him.

'Not till you show me kin you open yo mouf wide an covah yo teef wif yo lips like this.'

He showed me how to cover my teeth.

'I will do it if you stop talking nigger talk to me.'

He said honey he would, and also I was a smart boy and he loved me very much.

He was talking like a whitey again.

Lesser said it was a strong chapter and praised the writing.

'How is the form of it?'

'It's well formed and written.' He said no more than that, as they had agreed.

'Damn right, man. It's strong black writing.'

'It's well written and touches the heart. That's as much as I'll say now.'

Bill said that in the next chapter he wanted to get deep into the boy's black consciousness, already a fire of desire and destruction.

He lived that day in a potless triumphant high.

That night both writers, over water glasses filled with red wine, talked about being writers and what a good and great thing it was.

Lesser read aloud a passage he had written in a notebook: 'I am convinced more and more day by day that fine writing is next to fine doing the top thing in the world.'

'Who said that?'

'John Keats, the poet.'

'Fine dude.'

'And here's something from Coleridge: "Nothing can permanently please which does not contain in itself the reason why it is so and not otherwise." '

'Copy that down for me, man.'

From The Tenants (1981)

BERNARD MALAMUD (1914–86), American novelist and short story writer, was born in Brooklyn. *The Assistant* (1957) and *The Fixer* (1966) between them won several awards, and he was accorded the Premio Mondello in 1985.

Marghanita Laski

THE ORPHAN

It had grown cold while Hilary had been inside the orphanage, cold and dark. The colours were fading from the trees and the walls, and a thin damp mist was rising from the ground. What the devil shall we do, he thought in dismay, and he turned to the child waiting beside him and said, 'You'll have to tell me where to go because I don't know your town at all.'

Jean said breathlessly, 'Do you like trains, monsieur?'

'I like trains very much,' said Hilary, hopefully.

'There is a level-crossing.' said Jean, 'I think – do you think, monsieur – it would be nice to go that way?'

'Nothing could be nicer,' said Hilary. 'Come on, you show me where it is,' and they walked down the steps together.

Outside the gate Jean stopped and looked up at Hilary doubtfully. 'Yes,' said Hilary, as he might have reassured a dog. 'I do really want to see the trains,' and suddenly the boy seemed sure of him and for the first time gave him a natural happy little boy's grin. 'Robert said it was this way.' he said, and they started off down the hill.

At first Jean walked sedately by Hilary's side, every now and then glancing sideways up into his face. Each time he did so, Hilary found he must inevitably smile at him, telling him without words that all was and would be well, and at last the boy seemed reassured. He started to run about, a few steps this way, a few steps that, sometimes running just a little way ahead, but always quickly coming back to look into Hilary's face and, at last, to smile at Hilary before Hilary smiled at him.

'Look!' said Hilary after they had gone a hundred yards or so, 'There's your level-crossing right at the bottom of the hill,' and he pointed down a side turning to the tall posts reared erect beside the road.

Jean stood still and put his head on one side and looked at them. Then, one last glance at Hilary, and he started to run down the hill.

Hilary lengthened his stride to keep close behind. He didn't have to lengthen it very much. The thin legs in the clumsy boots were incapable of going very fast and Hilary and Jean reached the bottom of the hill together.

Just as they arrived, the heavy posts fell slowly and majestically over the road, their dangling iron curtains hitting the ground with a splendid clang. Jean clutched Hilary's coat and said with a kind of ecstatic tremor, 'Robert said that after the gates go down the train comes,' and at that moment they both heard the chuff of the engine coming towards them.

It was a slow old goods-engine dragging what seemed to Hilary a really surprising number of coal-filled wagons and it took a long time to pass. He watched it with the absorption a passing train can always command and momentarily forgot the little boy at his side. Then the last wagon went by and the rumble and clatter slowly died away and Hilary heard a small incredulous voice saying, 'I've seen a train.'

Hilary demanded, 'Haven't you ever seen a train before?'

The boy was frightened at Hilary's tone. He said, 'No, monsieur,' and his eyes opened widely in apprehension.

'But don't you ever come this way on your walks?' asked Hilary.

'No, monsieur,' whispered Jean, 'we always go the other way.' His eyes pleaded for forgiveness.

It's unbelievable, thought Hilary savagely, it's intolerable and I can't stand it. Then he looked at Jean and saw that he, completely uncomprehending, was finding this moment intolerable too, and with an effort of deliberate physical relaxation he made himself say warmly, 'Look, Jean, the gates are still down. I think another train's going to come.'

They waited and watched a rusty tank engine puff strenuously by. 'Look, monsieur,' shouted Jean, 'Look, it's going backwards!' and he burst into wild laughter, and Hilary laughed with him.

Then the gates went up again and Hilary discovered that he was feeling cold. He suggested, 'Let's go to that café over the road and sit in the warm. We can still see the trains out of the window.'

Jean nodded quickly, grinning to show how much he liked the idea, and followed Hilary into the café.

Inside it was warm and comfortable. A big stove was burning in one corner and rexine-covered benches backed with high boards made convenient private alcoves. Hilary set the child near the window at an empty table and sat down facing him.

'Now,' he said 'what would you like to drink?'

Jean looked puzzled, and Hilary, realising that a café was as novel an experience as a train, ordered a beer and a raspberry syrup.

'It's a pretty colour,' Jean said timorously when this was set before him.

'Taste it,' urged Hilary, and Jean tasted and then drank the whole lot down with loud sucking gulps. 'Well, what do you think of it?' Hilary asked, and Jean said boldly, 'I even think I could drink another,' and Hilary laughed and ordered it for him.

Jean seemed to have forgotten about the trains. His eyes were roving the room now with eager interest. 'Look, monsieur,' he cried suddenly, pointing to a dusty green plant in a pot, 'look, there's a little palm tree!'

'How do you know it's a palm tree?' asked Hilary, interested.

'I saw it in a book,' Jean said casually.

'Do you like reading?' Hilary pursued.

Jean said, 'I like reading about Africa.'

'And what else?' asked Hilary.

Jean said, 'I haven't got a book about anything else.'

From Little Boy Lost (1949)

MARGHANITA LASKI (1915–88), British novelist, biographer, critic, lexicographer and broadcaster, was born in Manchester.

Lionel Blue

PICKLES AND PIETY

I never wanted to be a fireman or an engine driver, and when I was given fire engines or Meccano sets I stacked them away in a cupboard until I learned to recycle them. I must have been a precocious child because I wanted to be a high-powered lawyer and make love to Shirley Temple. As regards both ambitions I have been an under-achiever, or perhaps non-starter would be more accurate.

Instead I became a rabbi, which puzzled both my family and myself. My mother said I did it to spite her and my father, and there certainly was an aggressive twist to it, because for some years my poor father had to eat forbidden food in the bedroom, not to offend my piety. With the years my mother's puzzlement has increased. 'Why,' she says, 'if you have to be a rabbi, must you be the only one who writes a cookery column for a Christian paper?'

'Why, indeed, do I mix pickles and piety?' I brooded. And I knew the answer straightaway. It was my grandmother, God rest her soul, who mixed food and faith so well in my belly and my being, that I have never been able to separate them since.

Her parents were killed in a Russian pogrom. So her village clubbed together and bought her a steerage ticket to England, where it was rumoured she had a rich uncle who ate chicken and sat in a parlour wearing a gold watch. She was an orphan of about nine, so they put a label round her neck giving her name, and the possible name of her possible uncle. On the boat she met my future grandfather, who was not much older, making his way to America from the Tsar's army. When they arrived, the two children were given soup at the London docks, and they clung to each other for some years, and eventually set up home together.

For some years my grandfather thought this was America. My grandmother couldn't work it out, and returned to her kitchen where she cooked enormous pots of soup, ladling it out to penniless Yiddish poets, Irish immigrants and miracle rabbis, who couldn't perform the miracle of a decent meal for themselves.

All the while I, as a child, sat on the boiler by the steaming pots and listened to my grandmother's commentary on the human condition. Every Thursday night she woke me, and together we dropped little parcels of food or money through the letter-boxes in our block, to homes where there was illness or no job, so they could celebrate the Jewish Sabbath which was the birthday of creation. We went out at night to spare them the shame of charity. She never had a proper holiday. But once a year she looked up rooms to let in high-class areas like Golders Green or Hampstead and together we visited them, not because she could ever dream of taking them but because she wanted a glimpse into the life of rich people who ate smoked salmon, unafraid of bailiffs or pawnshops.

A Catholic friend of mine took me to a mass, and when I heard the words of invitation to the Lord's supper I thought of her, and said the memorial prayers for her under my breath. Because of her I understand why Christians experience God's presence on their tongues, and Jewish rabbis in the Middle Ages asked for their coffins to be made out of the holy planks of their kitchen tables, presumably leaving their widows bereft of holy husbands and cooking space.

'Blessed are You, Lord our God, king of the Universe, who feeds the whole world.' Just like Granny, in fact!

RABBI LIONEL BLUE (1930–) has been Convenor of the Beth Din of the Reform Synagogues of Great Britain since 1971. He is also an author, broadcaster and cook.

Bernard Levin

The Taste of Food

I cannot get out of my head the belief that when I peel a banana, if I do not, before eating it, remove also the fine stringy threads that run along the divisions between the segments of the fruit, I shall contract leprosy. I am quite unable to remember when and how this extraordinary idea got into me; usually, such beliefs stem from a superstition current in the holder's childhood, but I have never met anyone, whether my contemporary or older than I, who has ever heard of it, much less held it. Possibly it was based on a misunderstood remark of my mother's, though it is so specific I cannot well see how that could be. Certainly she did hold a wide variety of superstitious beliefs, as most women of her time and background did: I remember being taken to see a family friend, a woman always spoken of at home in a somewhat reserved tone, and before we set out my mother took a tiny fragment of coal, wrapped it in a scrap of paper and thrust it into my pocket, bidding me leave it there until we returned and to say nothing about it. I had not the slightest idea of the purpose of this action, nor did she explain it, but in the trusting way of childhood I assumed that it must mean *something*, and since the burden of the coal and the simultaneously enjoined secrecy was not great, I made no objection.

It was many years later, and not from my mother, that I learned the meaning of the strange ceremony; apparently, the woman whom we were to visit was reputed to have the Evil Eye, and the coal, it seemed, was a charm against it. In the instant of my discovery, I remembered another inexplicable moment from that afternoon – one so puzzling that memory had until then suppressed it altogether. On leaving the home of the *malocchio*, my mother turned first to her left, then to her right, spitting each time on the pavement as she did so; this action, familiar in some form in many primitive cultures, is likewise reputed to keep evil spirits at bay. I also believe, as firmly as I hold the leprosy-inducing banana-strings theory, that a cut between the thumb and forefinger will lead inevitably to lockjaw.

The belief about the banana, even though its origins are undiscoverable, is my earliest memory of anything to do with food; it even antedates my first recollections of the food I ate as a child. But next to it in time is the memory of an episode so painful that, as I embarked on this sentence, I had to break off and occupy myself in something altogether different for an hour, before I could feel calm enough to tell the story, and as I put these words on paper I live again the hour of that day, more than forty years ago, as though it had only just happened.

The unleavened bread called *matzo*, which Jews eat instead of ordinary bread at Passover, was to be found in my home, on and off, throughout the year: I loved it, and still do. But it has – or had in my childhood home –

culinary uses wider than as a substitute for bread. A dish which my mother used to cook quite frequently was based upon it; I have remembered the recipe well, despite the trauma it led to, and often cook it myself when I am eating at home alone.

The dish was called *matzobrei*, the 'brei' being from the Yiddish (and before that from the German) and meaning something like a mash or puree. At my elementary school, the day began, before my lessons were embarked upon, with an assembly of all the pupils. It is possible that there was a hymn or other collective activity, but this I have forgotten: I do remember, though, that the assembly concluded with any special or general announcements, before we dispersed to the classrooms.

On the fateful day, the announcements were not the end of assembly. Whether some sociologist was conducting an experiment, whether there were fears (as well there might have been in those days and in that neighbourhood) that many children were not getting enough to eat at home, whether somebody had had a bright idea in the staff common-room, I do not know, and nobody explained. Nor did it matter. What happened was that each child was invited to stand up, in turn, and say before all the others what he or she had had, that day, for breakfast. This did not, when it was announced, strike me as alarming or strange, and I patiently awaited my turn, halfway through the alphabetical order. When it came, I said that my breakfast had been a *matzobrei*.

It had not occurred to me that a word with which I was perfectly familiar, which described a simple and customary dish, would be utterly unknown to three hundred other children and the entire staff of the school. I was asked to repeat what I had said, the teacher in charge assuming that he had not heard correctly. I repeated it. I was asked to repeat it again, and did so. By now murmurs were breaking out throughout the hall; everybody had heard clearly what I said, but it conveyed no meaning to any mind there. I was asked to come from my place, to the front of the hall, *on to the platform*, and say it again. I did so; there was a pause, during which I stood where I was, alone and in full and prominent view, while the staff held a whispered conference, trying to make out what I was talking about. One of them then advanced to the centre of the stage – the questioning had been conducted throughout with the greatest mildness and tact – and bent his head gently to my face, asking me to say it once more, close to his ear. I did so. He straightened up, shook his head, patted my shoulder, and motioned me to go back to my place. The next child was asked to say what he had had for breakfast.

The episode took perhaps six or seven minutes; in that time, any meaning the world might have held for me had vanished. I could think of no explanation whatever that would make sense at all of the experience I had just been through. Had I misheard the word at home? Of course not. Had they misheard the word from me at school? Not after three repetitions. Was everybody mad? Was I mad? Was the Devil in charge of the universe after all?

I went back to my place in the hall; my schoolfellows instinctively moved away from me as I passed among them, lest the contagion should come upon them: they were as baffled as I was but safe, and I don't think any of them had even laughed. When I got back to my row the children on either side of me stared straight ahead as though I was not there at all; the breakfast call-over finished, assembly ended, the school day began. I went through the day's lessons in a trance; I said nothing when I got home, and from that day until this hour, I have never said a single word about it to any human being.

It was a long time ago, and nothing much to get excited about. The explanation is, and was when it occurred to me only a year of two later, obvious: no one not familiar with Yiddish could have known the word or even guessed at its meaning. Children have had far worse experiences and survived them smiling. And yet I, a middle-aged man not at all given to dwelling in the past or keening over my inability to rewrite it, can bring back, instantly and completely, the experience I have described, and in doing so can feel all the pain I felt that day, and all the terror of its inexplicability.

It is a wonder I ever ate breakfast again, or anything else. But there were goods things to eat in my childhood home, though, as I learned only later, and then gradually, it was sometimes touch and go whether there would be anything at all; I cannot remember noticing, or if I did being puzzled by the fact, that the silver candlesticks, and sometimes my mother's rings, would vanish from their accustomed place for a few weeks, returning as mysteriously as they had gone. My mother was not a natural cook, much less a trained one; but she had learned a small repertoire, mainly from her own mother, of standard Jewish dishes, and those she did well and with complete consistency. I don't think she ever thought of what she was doing as cooking at all, much less as 'cuisine'; she was simply making dinner for the family. I cannot recall ever seeing a cookery book, for instance, or any wine except once a year with the Passover dinner, when it was invariably something called Palwin.

This may well still exist, though I hope not, for a more powerful force for instilling the idea that wine is disgusting I cannot imagine; the first time I drank real wine, many years later, I could not believe my taste buds, and I have no doubt that many children exposed to Palwin grew up as lifelong teetotallers in consequence. It was made in Palestine, as its name suggests, and tasted like very heavily over-sweetened prune juice; I have no recollection of any alcohol content in it at all, though there must have been some, I suppose, for my mother, who had the lightest head of anyone I have ever known, would never take a second glass for fear of the consequences, or more than a sip or two of my grandmother's cherry brandy, though that I recall as being very powerful. The only other drink I can recall clearly, apart from endless cups of tea (coffee was unknown, though I seem to remember a bottled concentrate called Camp, which bore much the same relation to coffee as Palwin did to wine, and must have had much the same effect on those exposed to it early), was a patent juice called Lucozade, most devoutly believed in my home to have almost miraculous medicinal properties, and another called Tizer, similar to Lucozade but not believed capable of restoring the dead to life.

If there was nothing interesting to drink, there was a short but interesting menu, and the taste it gave me for Jewish cooking has lasted the rest of my life. Grilling was unknown; practically everything was fried, and most of what wasn't was roasted. The heart of the repertoire was fried fish, more often plaice than anything else, but with cod a good second and occasionally halibut. Fresh salmon was, of course, unknown, being far too expensive (so was carp, though important to classic Jewish cuisine, if there is such a thing); it came only in the tinned form, which was certainly not salmon but a variety of inferior fish, and out of this my mother would make fried rissoles, of which I was particularly fond. The fried fish was always done in batter, and always accompanied by *chren*, in the making of which my grandmother was the acknowledged family expert (as she was with the cherry brandy I have mentioned, which I suppose – I did not understand the process – she must have made in an illicit still). *Chren* was home-made horseradish sauce; it was mixed with beetroot, partly to make it milder and partly to make it taste and look more interesting. I loved to watch as my grandmother grated the horseradish, cooked and prepared the beetroot, added the sugar and combined the ingredients in the correct proportions; no witches' cauldron was ever more carefully tended.

The result, however, was, and was meant to be, enormously strong, even toned down by the beetroot. Sniffing the *chren* jar had exactly the same effect as the most powerful smelling-salts, and I remember one of my uncles daring the other to put his nose right into the jar and breathe in sharply; the dare was accepted, and a moment later the experimenter was flat on his back on the floor, semi-conscious and gasping for breath. I have not tasted the real thing for years; even good Jewish restaurants serve a feeble diluted version, and the bottled kind is beneath the contempt of anyone who ever tasted any Jewish grandmother's. There was also *gefillte* fish, a kind of *quenelle*, served cold.

The fish was always accompanied by chips, fine-cut and done to crisp perfection; olive oil was too expensive to be the sole cooking-medium, and was therefore eked out by kosher lard. Sometimes, when money was even shorter than usual, and both the candlesticks and the rings were on holiday, the fried fish became a tin of sardines ('a makeshift' was my mother's term for such a meal), but the chips were never cancelled.

As fried fish was the left hand, so the right was boiled chicken, or more rarely, roast. When it was boiled, there would, naturally, be chicken soup, which – if any single dish may claim the title – must be regarded as the staple of Jewish cookery. The broth was rarely served clear; it contained *lokshen*, a kind of very fine vermicelli, or *kreplach*, a similarly superior cousin to *tortelloni*, or *kneidlach*, which were dumplings. The roast chicken was invariably accompanied by oven-roast potatoes. Meat of any kind was unusual; I do not think there was ever roast beef *à l'anglaise*, let alone lamb, or even veal, and strangely enough I do not think I can remember salt beef. Occasionally there was a steak, though since nothing was grilled (I think it possible that my mother had never encountered the technique at all), this was always done in a frying pan and, bizarre though it may sound, doused and recooked in boiling water, in the same pan, before being served. It thus became – not that I knew it at the time – a kind of *Tafelspitz*. I enjoyed it greatly, and never met a real steak until years later.

Chopped liver; a mixture of chopped egg and fried onions; a kind of pancake, made from a mixture of potato flour and *matzo* meal (the fine-ground kind was the equivalent of flour and the coarser was used for the batter in which the fried fish was coated), which was called a *luttke*, and was my mother's speciality, much in demand at family gatherings (my sister and I gave her a surprise party for her eightieth birthday, and arranged with the Dorchester, where it was held, for a stove and the utensils to be provided, while we got the ingredients, and at a given signal drew back the curtain behind when all was in readiness, whereupon, after we had draped a monster apron round her finery, she turned to and cooked 'Rosie's *luttkes*' for all); baked apples; these are among the other dishes I recollect from my childhood with pleasure. There was virtually nothing cooked in my childhood home that I did not enjoy, except *lokshen* pudding; this was a dessert, made from the same vermicelli that went into the soup, but in this form compacted, sweetened and baked. My favourite dish, though, was a sweetmeat that went by the name of *taygelach*, and its making was the highlight of the year: it did not appear more often than annually, because it was very expensive to make, using prodigious quanties of Tate and Lyle's Golden Syrup. I dare say that that delectable, viscous substance still exists, and if it doesn't I would be perfectly happy, should Tate and Lyle wish to revive it, to shut my eyes and draw the old tin from memory; it had a lion on it, for reasons which will be known to those familiar with the zoologically improbable story of Samson and the lion in *Judges*, chapter 14, a story which incidentally includes the first nagging wife in recorded history.

The *taygelach* were made of a kind of dough, rolled out into cylinders somewhat thicker than a pencil; these were then lightly baked and dropped into a huge saucepan in which the syrup was boiling. Removed from the liquid, the strips were laid side by side on greaseproof paper, and cut diagonally into rhomboids about the size of a domino. They were then sprinkled with ginger, and left to set hard. The result was an incomparable form of toffee; as the teeth crunched into it they went through the coating of hardened syrup and encountered the dough, which crumbled at once; the ginger was the perfect spice, hot but sweet. When she was making it, my mother would use just enough dough to absorb the syrup, but inevitably there were bits of dough left over, and the saucepan was still coated, so my sister and I were allowed to mop the scraps in the still warm liquid.

Vegetables, apart from potatoes, were rare; there were carrots with the boiled chicken and the cold *gefillte* fish, peas (I can remember helping my mother to shell them) and buckwheat, called *kasha*, which I loved, though I have not seen it these many years. There was cabbage, though only in the form of the wrapping for forcemeat, and I have a very faint memory of runner beans also, but I am sure there was never any spinach, broccoli, haricots or mushrooms, and as for the now common courgettes, aubergines, artichokes and the like, they would have been considered as exotic as ortolans' tongues or first-growth claret. There were no shellfish, and no crustaceans; the former were banned under the faint vestiges of obedience to the Jewish dietary laws that reigned at home, and the latter in addition were too expensive and viewed with intense suspicion as likely to cause food-poisoning. I have grown up unable to eat oysters, mussels or clams, but devoted to every kind of crustacean from the tiniest shrimp, as served in the *crevettes Alfonso* at L'Epicure, in Soho, to the vastest lobster, as served in the Hostellerie du Moulin du Maine Brun at Angoulême.

Over the simple pleasures of my infant dinner table a cloud was forming, though I did not know it and could not possibly have guessed what lay ahead, nor done anything about it if I had. Only those who attended an English public school as boarders doing the Second World War can truly say that they have experienced the very lowest level that food can reach and still be classified as food. If the memory of the *matzobrei* is too painful to think about, that of the food served at my school is too nauseating; there were the usual schoolboy rumours that the meat, invariably in the form of a glutinous and quite extraordinarily disgusting stew, came from the rotted carcasses of beasts gathered from the hedgerows in which they had perished of disease, or from zoos which were culling their less edible specimens, and none of us would have been in the least surprised if the rumours had turned out to be true.

I was clearly in danger of starving to death from the effect of the food served and the culture shock it would have given me even if it had been the finest *haute cuisine*, for I had never eaten anything except the cooking of my home; of most of what faced me I was quite literally unable to swallow a mouthful (the school had a most sensible rule that, although we had to finish anything we took, were not obliged to take anything we did not want), and I lived almost entirely off potatoes and bread, and later off peanut butter, which I think I got from a shop in the nearby town.

The horrors of school food might have been thought likely to lead to a complete lack of interest in the subject (I have just remembered some filth described as liver, though what animal it came from I dare not guess, and I know that I would not touch liver thereafter until I was in my late twenties); I think, however, that instead it encouraged a taste for food.

It meant that I could not, as I might otherwise have, come to believe that the narrow range of Jewish cooking I was used to was the only kind that existed; in addition, from the fact that the muck at school could not possibly be the only other kind of food there was I derived an interest in discovering what else there might be in a world elsewhere. This was an almost fully conscious feeling, which seems odd now, because it meant that I was interested in seeking out something of which I had had no experience at all, and I cannot remember reading about food, or even coming across descriptions of banquets or meals in fiction.

From Enthusiasms (1983)

BERNARD LEVIN (1928–   ), British journalist, was born in London. His articles and reviews of politics, the theatre, books, television and contemporary life have appeared in many journals.

Evelyn Cowan

BETTY THE HEN

The morning after our arrival, my sisters went about their business. Lily had already made some contacts. Parcels were ready for delivery. The other girls set out for Largs, Gourock, and Dunoon. Stripped to the waist, Jacky, Wally, and I went fishing from the rocks, or swimming from the open bathing station. We appointed ourselves unpaid seamen, helping to dispatch the *May Queen* on its hourly trips round the bay.

One day in that summer of 1929 my mother made an important discovery. We were not the only Jewish family on the Island of Bute. In the course of one of her shopping expeditions into Rothesay, she made the acquaintance of Mrs Nubilsky, whose husband ran a bicycle and pram-renting shop just opposite the putting green.

An equally important part of the conversation proved to be the fact that Mr Nubilsky was an accredited shochet, a man qualified to kill animals according to the laws of the Jewish religion. Ma was delighted to hear this. Because of the distance from our kosher butchers in Glasgow, the purchase of fresh meat created a major problem. Non-kosher food never entered our home. She permitted herself to buy newly-caught fish from the boats that tied up in the harbour. Milk and eggs were delivered from a farm nearby.

One of my married sisters occasionally loaded a parcel of egg loaves from the bakers in the Gorbals on to the old *Kyle-more*. With this we made do. But Ma had an irresistible urge to make real Shabbos dinner with chicken soup and all the trimmings. Off we went to see Mr. Cross the poultry-farmer. I trotted along beside Ma. My small schoolgirl figure and her tall bulky shape threw contrasting shadows on the sunlit hedges.

It was a shimmering hot June day. And in all the years that have passed since then, memory makes it more brilliant each time I remember it.

Rolling heavily in her almost bandy walk, Ma trudged up the hot dusty farm road. 'This heat is firing my bunions,' she winced. Towards the end she limped badly. She adjusted her worn black leather shopper on her arm and shouted to a big rugged red-haired man 'Goot morning. Are you Mr. Cross?'

He touched his cap. 'Morning, missus. Yes, I am.'

'I'm the woman from Libya on the Ardbeg Road. I get all my eggs here.' Hens were clucking all round us. 'Oh, yes.' His freckled hand wiped the perspiration from his brow. 'I mind now. You're the lady with all those nice-looking daughters.'

Ma threw him a suspicious look. 'Never mind that. Have you got a good fat hen for sale?'

'Sure we have. But I don't usually sell 'em this way.' Mr. Cross laughed. 'Going to start a farm in opposition to me?'

'No, tanks. I got plenty to do. I just want someting for the week-end dinner.' I scarcely listened to all this, enveloped as I was in my mother's long skirt. At first I peeped out in fear and then courageously put my hand out to touch the strutting parade. Ma ran her eyes over the noisy farmyard. 'Hey! There's a nice fat one.' She pointed to a lovely white regal-looking bird. 'How about that one?'

Mr. Cross ran over and grabbed it. 'It looks all right to me. I don't see why you shouldnie have it.' Ma poked around in her purse. 'Well, just tell me how much it is, and I'll take it.'

'O.K.' said the farmer. 'I'll go up the road to the house and gauge its weight, and then I'll wring its neck for you.'

'Don't do that, please,' Ma pleaded hurriedly. 'Say how much. And I'll take it in my shopping bag.'

'You mean, you want it alive, missis?'

'Yes, please, Mr Cross. Just tie some string round its legs. And I'll pop it in the bag.'

As we rolled along the road home, I tried to help with the heavy bag. I put my hand up to lift an end. The hen's innocent blue eyes gazed down into mine. It was love at first sight. I called her Betty.

As I have said, I was the youngest of a poor widow's family. And it may sound incredible, but it is quite true when I say that I never possessed a doll, or for that matter, a toy of any description. There was no lack of love in our home. I felt safe and secure always. I loved my mother deeply. But she was just there, like the sun and the moon and the clouds in the sky, taken for granted.

Everyone fondled and cuddled me, the baby. I was bathed, romped and loved by all the older sisters and brothers. I longed for something of my very own. Betty the Hen was my first true love. She fulfilled my need. Within a few hours my two brothers, Wally and Jacky, made a little wooden hut surrounded by a wire pen for my pet. I painted the name 'Betty' in dark blue on white wood.

After meals, I brought out scraps of food for her. I even tried to clean and brush Betty's feathers. The bird seemed to thrive on all this attention. Her feathers looked whiter, her stature more regal than before. She clucked happily (I thought) whenever she saw me approaching. We gazed into each other's eyes. I said little. Young love does not need much conversation.

Betty had been bought from the farm on a Monday. On Thursday, Ma sent a message to Mr Nubilsky's house above the bicycle shop, to say his services were required that evening.

My two brothers and myself were out picking brambles for jam in the Skeoch woods all day Thursday. It had been a happy, carefree day. We were exhausted from the heat. I knew that Betty was well stocked with food and water. So I did not go round the back yard. We flopped into our threesome bed, and I lapsed into a heavy childish sleep.

The next morning, Friday, before breakfast, I discovered the little hut was empty. Not a sound from the yard. All was silence. I ran into the kitchen. 'Ma, for goodness, Ma. The hen's gone.'

Feathers flew in all directions. My mother was busy plucking. 'Ach, here it is. Surely you knew I wanted it for Shabbos dinner. As soon as it is cleaned, I will kosher it and start it in the big pot. For tomorrow is Sabbath . . . Saturday.'

I could not raise my eyes further to the bleeding mass on her lap. Surely that was not Betty! Feeling sick, I raced across the promenade to the shore. I threw pebbles aimlessly in the water. Small waves rippled back at me. I thought of my make-believe puppy and the old stray cat I'd wanted for my own. Yet I never dreamed of begging for Betty's life. We were a large, hungry family. Although I had deluded myself for a short time, I knew in my young-old heart that Betty was for eating. I kicked my thinly-clad foot against a rock until my toes almost bled.

On Saturday morning I awakened on a pillow of grief. It was Shabbos, a quiet day, when no rough games were allowed. You had to keep your clothes in Sunday-best condition. Time dragged by. At last I heard my mother's voice echoing across the promenade. 'Children, keender, come on, now! Wash your hands and get ready for Shabbos dinner.'

We filed into the seldom-used dining room. Each child went to his or her place. After Kiddush wine and a little prayer murmured by all, we were served steaming plates of chicken soup with little knaidle doughballs dancing about on the surface. I turned away from this, the fragrant essence of my love. Then came the main course. This was stuffed roast chicken carried in on a large platter surrounded by 'cholent' brown potatoes and green vegetables.

Eagerly plates were pushed at Ma from both sides of the long table.

'I like the leg,' shrilled Wally.

'Give me the wing,' cried Jacky.

Cannibals! I raged into myself. My own brother, too! Uninvited, a piece of white meat appeared in front of me. I blinked down at it. My tears made a gravy on the plate.

From Spring Remembered (1974)

EVELYN COWAN (1926–), Scottish novelist and journalist, was born and lives in Glasgow.

John D. Rayner

KRISTALLNACHT

There were – there must have been – sunny, happy, carefree days when I played with my sister in the garden, dominated by a huge pear tree, of the little terrace house in the housing estate on the southern outskirts of Berlin where I grew up; but they have mainly faded from my memory. When I try to conjure up visual images of that far-off world, the sky is always overcast in subconscious symbolism of the atmosphere of fear that grew darker as the swastikas multiplied.

The fear first gripped me one day in 1934 when I was not yet ten years old. The headmaster of the local primary school walked into our classroom and ordered the Jewish children – I was the only one – to stand up. He then read out some proclamation the gist of which was that decent, self-respecting Germans should have nothing to do with Jews. Thereafter I was ostracised, and even the class mistress, who was a kind, gentle, motherly woman, only permitted herself an occasional, surreptitious, reassuring smile.

Next term I found myself at a Jewish school, of Zionist orientation, subsequently named Theodor Herzl Schule, in West Berlin, near the sports stadium where, two years later, the Olympic Games were held. My parents were not religious; they called themselves 'freethinkers', and I am not sure whether, before Hitler, I even knew that I was Jewish. Still less were my parents Zionists. But the school had a good reputation and was conveniently near the home of my favourite uncle and aunt. Nevertheless, it was a long train journey, and my parents were always relieved when I got safely home.

Soon I knew the map of Palestine better than the streets of Berlin and began to think that one day I might live there; the sandy school yard with its fir trees seemed to prefigure that possibility. I joined a Zionist youth club but felt ill-at-ease with the propaganda and regimentation that went with it. I also joined a clique of friends who shared a common passion for athletics and table-tennis. One of them, known as Abu, came from a religiously observant home, where I experienced my first Seder.

Nearly every Friday night and Saturday morning Abu and I went together to a little synagogue in an old people's home in a remote suburb called Lichterfelde, served by a Student-Rabbi with piercing eyes and a Cantor with a miraculously lyrical tenor voice. There, within a fortnight of each other, we cantillated our Bar-Mitzvah portions.

Academically, my best subject was English, which came to me so easily that sometimes I seemed to be drawing on forgotten memories of a previous, English-speaking incarnations. I also had a brilliant teacher with a flair for phonetics, Fräulein Dr Jarislowsky, who, moreover, would frequently lose her voice and then call on me to conduct the class for her, which gave me an added incentive.

After four years at Theodor Herzl I was transferred to another, more academic school, recently opened by the Jewish Community in Wilsnacker Strasse. There another woman teacher, whose name I can no longer recall, opened my eyes to German literature and prompted me to try my hand at writing poetry in the style of Rainer Maria Rilke.

At home, life became less easy. My father was dismissed from his post at the Deutsche Bank, where he had been French correspondent, and our petit-bourgeois income was reduced to subsistence level. From now on the only permitted luxury was a piece of cake on Saturday afternoon, while we listened to a radio programme called Laterna Magica. Conversation became increasingly hushed – for walls had ears and our neighbours on both sides were Nazis and quite capable of denouncing us – and turned almost exclusively on one subject: emigration. My own contribution to these discussions was to suggest Iceland, since surely nobody else would have thought of going there.

On the evening of 9 November 1938, the Berlin sky had a curiously reddish tinge – I remember my parents remarking on that. Next morning I went to school as usual and only then learnt what had happened, including the burning of the synagogues: it had been Kristallnacht. The German literature teacher assembled the class and, with a tremulous but decisive voice which I can still hear, said: 'Hitherto the Foreign Powers have kept silent; now they are sure to act.' Then she dismissed us and sent us home.

That afternoon two plain-clothes Gestapo men came for my father. My mother screamed: 'They have denounced us!' But my father quietened her and said: 'You must not make such accusations.' He was allowed to pack a bag, to use the toilet, leaving the door open, and to pay for the privilege of riding in a taxicab rather than a police-car to wherever they were taking him. About a week later we received a postcard from the concentration camp and knew that he was alive. After seven weeks, by which time we had been expelled from Lindenhof and taken a shared flat in Marburger Strasse, my father returned, a skeleton from which hung clothes thick with mud. It took me some seconds to recognise him, and my mother many weeks to nurse him back to physical heath.

He hardly ever spoke of his experiences, though he once let slip about a torture which still gives me nightmares. He also mentioned Rabbi Rautenberg, who had been incarcerated with him and had amazed my father by his tranquillity.

From now on efforts at emigration became frantic. My favourite uncle had settled in Uruguay: my mother had sent him an SOS telegram; he had wired back 'visa obtained'; and on the strength of that my mother had obtained my father's release. But my uncle had been swindled by a middleman, and it all fell through. Now my parents concentrated on getting their children out and submitted our names for every scheme that was going.

On my fifteenth birthday a Quaker lady, Frau Landmann, telephoned to say that I had been offered a place at Durham School. I wanted to decline it because my heart was set on going to Palestine, but my parents insisted, and on 10 August 1939, I left for England with a children's transport. At Harwich the sun shone and the grass looked greener than I had ever seen. At Liverpool Street Station we were dumped in a huge hall. One by one, the children were collected by relatives or friends. Finally a strange lady took me to King's Cross and put me on the Flying Scotsman. I chatted with my neighbour, in adequately fluent English, all the way to Newcastle, where I was met by a saintly Christian clergyman, R. W. Stannard, then Rector of Bishopwearmouth, Sunderland. He and his wife, 'Uncle Will' and 'Aunt Muriel', became my guardians, and I spent my school holidays in their home. They also brought my sister over, to train as a nurse. She arrived a fortnight after me, terrified because she was convinced that the man who had sat opposite her on the train was a Nazi agent. A week later the war broke out.

After that our only means of communication with our parents was by 25-word Red Cross message. The last message from them, which took months to reach us, was dated 13 December 1942. It was evidently written just before they were deported; it asked us to pray for them. As a boarder, I threw myself with zest into school life, but my parents were never far from my mind, and often, as I looked into the distance from the top of the hill on which the school chapel stood, I wished I had an aeroplane so that I could fly over and rescue them.

Years later, when the war was over and I was a lieutenant in the Durham Light Infantry, I heard from Abu. He had narrowly survived the concentration camps and was in Brussels. I flew over to see him. Later he settled in Brazil, where I attended his son's Bar-Mitzvah in 1964 and co-officiated at his daughter's wedding in 1977.

I also obtained compassionate leave to search for any traces of my parents in Berlin. But there had been no survivors among the 800 with whom they were sent to Auschwitz. In Lindenhof, the little terrace house of my childhood was a ruin, but a portion of the front wall still stood, and the pear tree still dominated the garden, but there were no children playing in its shade.

RABBI JOHN D. RAYNER (1924–) has been senior minister at the Liberal Jewish Synagogue, St John's Wood, since 1961. He is a vice-president of Leo Baeck College, and the co-author of *The Jewish People* (1987).

Anne Frank

HIDING

Thursday, 25th May, 1944

Dear Kitty,
There's something fresh every day. This morning our vegetable man was picked up for having two Jews in his house. It's a great blow to us, not only that those poor Jews are balancing on the edge of an abyss, but it's terrible for the man himself.

The world has turned topsy-turvy, respectable people are being sent off to concentration camps, prison, and lonely cells, and the dregs that remain govern young and old, rich and poor. One person walks into the trap through the black market, a second through helping the Jews or other people who've had to go 'underground'; anyone who isn't a member of the N.S.B. doesn't know what may happen to him from one day to another.

This man is a great loss to us too. The girls can't and aren't allowed to haul along our share of potatoes, so the only thing to do is to eat less. I will tell you how we shall do that; it's certainly not going to make things any pleasanter. Mummy says we shall cut out breakfast altogether, have porridge and bread for lunch, and for supper fried potatoes and possibly once or twice per week vegetables or lettuce, nothing more. We're going be hungry, but anything is better than being discovered.
Yours, ANNE.

Friday, 26th May, 1944

Dear Kitty,
At last, at last I can sit quietly at my table in front of a crack of window and write you everything.

I feel so miserable, I haven't felt like this for months; even after the burglary I didn't feel so utterly broken. On the one hand, the vegetable man, the Jewish question, which is being discussed minutely over the whole house, the invasion delay, the bad food, the strain, the miserable atmosphere, my disappointment in Peter; and on the other hand, Elli's engagement, Whitsun reception, flowers, Kraler's birthday, fancy cakes and stories about cabarets, films and concerts. That difference, the huge difference, it's always there; one day we laugh and see the funny side of the situation, but the next we are afraid, fear, suspense and despair staring from our faces. Miep and Kraler carry the heaviest burden of the eight in hiding, Miep in all she does, and Kraler through the enormous responsibility, which is sometimes so much for him that he can hardly talk from pent-up nerves and strain. Koophuis and Elli look after us well too, but they can forget us at times, even if it's only for a few hours, or a day, or even two days. They have their own worries, Koophuis over his health, Elli over her engagement, which is not altogether rosy, but they also have their little outings, visits to friends, and the whole life of ordinary people. For them the suspense is sometimes lifted, even if it is only for a short time, but for us it never lifts for a moment. We've been here for two years now; how long have we still to put up with this almost unbearable, ever-increasing pressure?

The sewer is blocked, so we mustn't run water, or rather only a trickle; when we go to the W.C. we have to take a lavatory brush with us, and we keep dirty water in a large Cologne pot. We can manage for today, but what do we do if the plumber can't do the job alone? The municipal scavenging service doesn't come until Tuesday.

Miep sent us a currant cake, made up in the shape of a doll, with the words 'Happy Whitsun' on the note attached to it. It's almost as if she's ridiculing us; our present frame of mind and our uneasiness could hardly be called 'happy.' The affair of the vegetable man has made us more nervous, you hear 'shh, shh' from all sides again, and we're being quieter over everything. The police forced the door there, so they could do it to us too! If one day we too should . . . no, I mustn't write it, but I can't put the question out of my mind today. On the contrary, all the fear I've already been through seems to face me again in all its frightfulness.

This evening at eight o'clock I had to go to the downstairs lavatory all alone; there was no one down there, as everyone was listening to the radio; I wanted to be brave, but it was difficult. I always feel much safer here upstairs than alone downstairs in that large, silent house; alone with the mysterious muffled noises from upstairs and the tooting of motor horns in the street. I have to hurry for I start to quiver if I begin thinking about the situation.

Again and again I ask myself, would it not have been better for us all if we had not gone into hiding, and if we were dead now and not going through all this misery, especially as we should no longer be dragging our protectors into danger. But we recoil from these thoughts too, for we still love life; we haven't yet forgotten the voice of nature, we still hope, hope about everything. I hope something will happen soon now, shooting if need be – nothing can crush us *more* than this restlessness. Let the end come, even if it is hard; then at least we shall know whether we are finally going to win through or go under.
Yours, ANNE.

From The Diary of Anne Frank, *tr.* B. M. Mooyart-Doubleday (1953)

ANNE FRANK (1929–45), was born in Germany, but emigrated with her parents to Amsterdam in 1933. They went into hiding in 1942, where they remained until betrayed in 1944. Anne and her elder sister died in Belsen. 'Kitty' is her imaginary correspondent.

Elie Wiesel

The Violin Player

On the way it snowed, snowed, snowed endlessly. We were marching more slowly. The guards themselves seemed tired. My wounded foot no longer hurt me. It must have been completely frozen. The foot was lost to me. It had detached itself from my body like the wheel of a car. Too bad. I should have to resign myself: I could live with only one leg. The main thing was not to think about it. Above all, not at this moment. Leave thoughts for later.

Our march had lost all semblance of discipline. We went as we wanted, as we could. We heard no more shots. Our guards must have been tired.

But death scarcely needed any help from them. The cold was conscientiously doing its work. At every step, someone fell, and suffered no more.

From time to time, SS officers on motor-cycles would go down the length of the column to try and shake us out of our growing apathy:

'Keep going! We are getting there!'

'Courage! Only a few more hours!'

'We're reaching Gleiwitz.'

These words of encouragement, even though they came from the mouths of our assassins, did us a great deal of good. No one wanted to give up now, just before the end, so near to the goal. Our eyes searched the horizon, for the barbed wire of Gleiwitz. Our only desire was to reach it as quickly as possible.

The night had now set in. The snow had ceased to fall. We walked for several more hours before arriving.

We did not notice the camp until we were just in front of the gate.

Some Kapos rapidly installed us in the barracks. We pushed and jostled one another as if this were the supreme refuge, the gateway to life. We walked over pain-racked bodies. We trod on wounded faces. No cries; a few groans. My father and I were ourselves thrown to the ground by this rolling tide. Beneath our feet someone let out a rattling cry:

'You're crushing me . . . mercy!'

A voice that was not unknown to me.

'You're crushing me . . . mercy! mercy!'

The same faint voice, the same rattle, heard somewhere before. That voice had spoken to me one day. Where? When? Years ago? No, it could only have been at the camp.

'Mercy!'

I felt that I was crushing him. I was stopping his breath. I wanted to get up. I struggled to disengage myself, so that he could breathe. But I was crushed myself beneath the weight of other bodies. I could hardly breathe. I dug my nails into unknown faces, I was biting all round me, in order to gain access to the air. No one cried out.

Suddenly I remembered. Juliek! The boy from Warsaw who played the violin in the band at Buna . . .

'Juliek, is it you?'

'Eliezer . . . the twenty-five strokes of the whip. Yes . . . I remember.'

He was silent. A long moment elapsed.

'Juliek! Can you hear me, Juliek?'

'Yes . . . ' he said, in a feeble voice. 'What do you want?'

He was not dead.

'How do you feel, Juliek?' I asked, less to know the answer than to hear that he could speak, was alive.

'All right, Eliezer . . . I'm getting on all right . . . hardly any air . . . worn out. My feet are swollen. It's good to rest, but my violin . . . '

I thought he had gone out of his mind. What use was the violin here?

'What, your violin?'

He gasped.

'I'm afraid . . . I'm afraid . . . that they'll break my violin . . . I've brought it with me.'

I could not answer him. Someone was lying full length on top of me, covering my face. I was unable to breathe, through either mouth or nose. Sweat beaded my brow, ran down my spine. This was the end; the end of the road. A silent death, suffocation. No way of crying out; of calling for help.

I tried to get rid of my invisible assassin. My whole will to live was centred in my nails. I scratched, I battled for a mouthful of air. I tore at decaying flesh which did not respond. I could not free myself from this mass weighing down my chest. Who knows? Was it a dead man I was struggling against?

I shall never know. All I can say is that I was justified. I succeeded in digging a hole through this wall of dying people, a little hole through which I could drink in a small quantity of air.

'Father, how are you?' I asked, as soon as I could utter a word.

I knew he could not be far from me.

'Well!' answered a distant voice, which seemed to come from another world. I tried to sleep.

He tried to sleep. Was he right or wrong? Could one sleep here? Was it not dangerous to allow your vigilance to fail, even for a moment, when at any minute death could pounce upon you?

I was thinking of this when I heard the sound of a violin. The sound of a violin, in this dark shed, where the dead were heaped on the living. What madman could be playing the violin here, at the brink of his own grave? Or was it really an hallucination?

It must have been Juliek.

He played a fragment from a Beethoven concerto. I had never heard sounds so pure. In such a silence.

How had he managed to free himself? To draw his body from under mine without my being aware of it?

It was pitch dark. I could hear only the violin, and it was as though Juliek's soul were the bow. He was playing his life. The whole of his life was gliding on the strings. His lost hopes. His charred past, his extinguished future. He played what he would never play again.

I shall never forget Juliek. How could I forget that concert, given to an audience of dying and dead men! To this day, whenever I hear Beethoven played my eyes close and out of the dark rises the sad, pale face of my Polish friend, as he said farewell on his violin to an audience of dying men.

I do not know for how long he played. I was overcome by sleep. When I awoke, in the daylight, I could see Juliek, opposite me, slumped over, dead. Near him lay his violin, smashed, trampled, a strange overwhelming little corpse.

From Night, *tr.* Stella Rodway (1960)

ELIE WIESEL (1928–), writer and historian, was born in Sighet, Transylvania, and has been Andrew Mellon Professor of Humanities, Boston University, since 1976. He was awarded the Nobel Prize in 1986.

Bernard Kops

JEWISH CHRISTMAS

Nearly thirteen years old, when I should have been studying and practising for my Bar Mitzvah, I found myself in Buckinghamshire in a church hall at that. A picture of Christ on the wall, and my young sister sitting beside me hiding her eyes.

I thought that we had travelled to the other end of the earth, yet when I asked one white-haired old lady where we were, she replied, 'Denham dearie, where the film studios are.' But my mind wasn't on film stars. 'Where's that?' I asked. I was told that it was only twenty miles from London, and as a matter of fact two miles away at Uxbridge you could get a tube train on the Central Line to Liverpool Street Station. I kept that in mind.

My sister perked up when I told her how close we were to home. So there we were, September the First 1939, Friday night, when we should have been having lockshen soup, waiting to be billeted on a family who wanted us about as much as we wanted them.

But later we really did want them because, owing to the fact that my sister and I wouldn't be separated, the billeting officer had a very hard time trying to get us off his hands. We were the last ones left in that church hall.

'But won't you be separated – you'll be awfully near each other, Denham's such a small place.'

Rose shook her head about twenty times and clutched me tighter. 'No,' she replied, 'I promised my mum.'

Near to midnight the billeting officer was getting quite desperate. Then he drove us around in a car from house to house trying to sell us. His desperation must have eventually made him a better salesman, because a young woman and an old woman, standing at the door, nodded their heads up and down. We were in. And no sooner in than whisked straight upstairs to the bedroom, Rose practically walking in her sleep.

'Poor mites,' I heard the woman say. And no sooner did I sit on the bed when morning came.

Rose whispered. She whispered for days. Everything was so clean in the room. We were even given flannels and toothbrushes. We'd never cleaned our teeth up till then. And hot water came from the tap. And there was a lavatory upstairs. And carpets. And something called an eiderdown. And clean sheets. This was all very odd. And rather scaring.

Now I had become the mother. Rose wouldn't let go of me. I thought for one dreadful moment that I would have to go to the lavatory with her.

Mr and Mrs Thompson were very kind and her mother, Mrs Patmore, had white clicking teeth. Mrs Thompson had a sister called Aunt Mabel who had two dogs and a perpetual smile. I don't think I heard her utter more than a few words all the months I was there.

I felt it my duty, on the very first morning, to tell Mrs Thompson we were Jewish. She told us she knew, for it was already all around the village that Stepney Jewish schoolchildren had been inflicted upon them.

'Mind you, they're terribly well-behaved,' I heard her telling the woman next door. Then we sat down to eat our breakfast. We never had breakfast in Stepney Green, just a cup of tea and a slice of bread. There we were, in a shining little room that smelled of polish, and a table all set out with knives and forks and marmalade. And we were eating soft-boiled eggs. Well, if this was evacuation I was all for it.

Next day our teachers called us together, told us that we were the representatives of the Jewish people and they expected us to be well behaved. There were two masters, a young one, Mr Lipschitz, and an old one, Mr De Haan. I was drawn towards the older one.

The people I was staying with were quite kind, but I very much envied some of the other boys who were billeted on the actor Conrad Veidt, 'Cor we have servants waiting on us and the same food as him.'

My sister started crying, 'I want to go home'. One day away and already she wanted to go home. I decided to be short with her. 'Shut up,' I said, thinking that ought to do the trick. She wept more bitterly, so I had to be kind. But I must say she got much happier after a few days and colour came to her cheeks.

I couldn't understand the Thompson family for no-one had yet mentioned the coming war. During that day I kept on asking, 'What's the news? What's the news?' They looked at me incredulously and said to each other things like 'Don't forget to pick up the seeds', or 'The hens are a bit off today.' They were living in a different world. I suppose most of the people in England were rather like that. Why don't they curse the Germans? Why can't they see the enemy? I boiled inside.

Over tea I tried to tell them about my family in Amsterdam. Told them that to be Jewish meant to be persecuted. Mrs Thompson sliced up a tomato, put some salt on it and said, 'Don't you worry your head about that.'

The next day was memorable enough. September the Third. A beautiful day. We went blackberry picking. Memorable because we had our first sight of open fields. Memorable because of our delight in rolling over in the grass and seeing the baby rabbits scampering for the hedges.

All at once I saw life in a different way. For now I realised that the world was an open place of light, air and clouds. A tree was a miracle. How strange! It poked through the earth and stood there waving. Trees were alive and so was grass and earth and everything. Here I could see the sky but London was a maze of stones. Here things were growing and there, beyond Uxbridge, was an artificially created world of brick. A world that was about to blow itself to smithereens, as if we hated our trap and wanted to destroy it to start again. The trouble was we might kill ourselves in the process.

Doubt entered my mind that sunny day. Doubt and conflict. For though I lay in the sunshine chewing grass and watching the birds swoop, I loved that trap. I was part of that world and I knew that I would soon tire of this one. I was not cut out for country.

We ran across the fields laughing and shouting our heads off, and we both got stung by nettles which we plucked, thinking they were ordinary leaves.

Mrs Thompson had warned us not to be late for lunch, but when we came across a whole hedge of blackberries we just went mad. Soon our mouths, our legs and our hands were completely stained purple.

I was stooping towards the ground when I heard sirens. 'What's that?' Rose said.

'Sirens, they're practising.'

She said she was scared and I told her there was nothing to worry about but, nevertheless, we walked across the fields towards our foster home. The sirens went right through me, touched something deep within me. But the day was too lovely to worry about war or death. The grown-ups knew what they were doing, didn't they?

Walking across those fields I heard more than sirens. Or rather, deeper sirens pulling me towards the rocks, tugging me inland, into myself, where doubt and fear were the only certain signposts in that city of my confused thoughts.

Sirens that called to me from within the maze of myself.

That day was memorable because of the war that had come to the world, but on that day my war also started. A war that had nothing to do with the crossing of frontiers and the destruction of cities, at least not directly.

When we reached the main road a policeman shouted at us. 'What are you kids doing out, don't you know there's a war on?' His words left me cold and I noticed he had a tin helmet on. We started running towards the house, but by the time we reached the gate the all-clear was sounding. We rushed into the house. 'There's a war on! It's war isn't it? It's war!' My sister's words got jumbled up with mine then quietly I said, 'Is it war?' Mrs Thompson's mother nodded. She was laying up for lunch and she was polishing up the plates. We all sat down quietly to eat lunch. This was the first real, square, ordinary meal I had ever sat down to at a laid-up table.

'Horse-radish sauce?'

Now the Stukas were diving on Polish towns and the Nazis were goose-stepping through frightened villages and we were eating roast beef and Yorkshire Pudding.

But I certainly enjoyed the food.

They wouldn't talk about the war. 'What do you think will happen?' I kept asking. 'What about my mum and dad?' 'Will they bomb the cities?'

Events, and not the Thompsons, gave me the answer. For nothing happened at first and we settled down in Denham and became more familiar with the ways of ordinary English people. And we realised how different we were from them. We spoke the same language but meant different things.

There were a few books in the house. Books of quotations, a Home Doctor and Gems of English Poetry.

The leaves fell and as the nights drew in and I sat poking the fire and stroking the cat and reading the poems of Robert Burns and the sonnets of Shakespeare. There was one poem in particular, 'My mother bore me in the southern wild and I am black but O my soul is white. . . . '

And another one by that same poet called William Blake, 'Piping down the valleys wild'. I used to wander in the garden reading the first four lines over and over again until I learnt them by heart. I heard the sirens of poetry that autumn. Vera Lynn sang on the radio, 'Yours till the stars lose their glory –' and everyone said that the war would be over very shortly.

When Christmas came they bought us toys. They didn't seem to understand that Christmas wasn't our festival.

'Don't tell 'em,' I said to my sister.

But we became more intensely Jewish that December and I tried to tell them about our Chanucah. 'Do you know why there wasn't room at the inn?' I said. 'Why Christ was born in a manger?' They all shook their heads. 'Because everywhere was full up for Chanucah,' I said. I don't know if this was a fact, but it certainly impressed them. I realised then you could invent stories and people would believe you.

Christmas morning and our room was full of toys, sweets and fruit. Later, laughing, they told us they had fitted a microphone under the bed to hear our reaction to the presents. At first I worried. What had I said about them? Then I was furious. 'Bloody nerve, spying on us.'

We had a wonderful time that Christmas, even Auntie Mabel spoke, but I searched that bedroom thoroughly ever after.

From The World Is a Wedding (1963)

BERNARD KOPS (1926–) is the author of novels, poetry and plays.

Jack Rosenthal

Evacuees

21. Int. Mrs Graham's hallway.

[DANNY *and* NEVILLE *stand in the hall, their caps on their heads, their luggage at their feet. They stand for a moment or two, looking at each other, nonplussed.*]

DANNY: She's scrammed!
NEVILLE: She went up the dancers.
DANNY: What for?
NEVILLE: *I* don't know!
DANNY*: Has she gone to bed?*
   [They stand there. Small. Lonely.
   The bathroom door at the top of the stairs opens, we hear the sound of running water. MRS GRAHAM *appears at the bathroom door.]*
MRS GRAHAM: Come along, children. A nice hot bath.
NEVILLE. We had a bath on Sunday.
MRS GRAHAM: Upstairs please, like big boys.
   [She goes back inside.
   They start upstairs.]

22. Int. Mrs Graham's lounge/dining room. Evening.

[*The house and furniture are comfortably middle-class.*
MRS GRAHAM *is preparing the table for tea.*
MRS GRAHAM *is in an armchair listening to Hitler giving a speech – punctuated by a chorus of thousands shouting 'Sieg Heil' on the wireless. From time to time* MR GRAHAM *shakes his head sadly and sighs.*
DANNY *and* NEVILLE *enter from upstairs, scrubbed clean after their exhausting day, wearing identical fair-isle pullovers, and their school caps.*
DANNY *stops dead on hearing Hitler's voice – and on seeing* MR GRAHAM *listening to it. He at once suspects him of being a German spy. He glances at* NEVILLE, *who understands but dismisses the theory with an impatient shake of the head.*
MRS GRAHAM *looks at them.*]

MRS GRAHAM: Oh! No caps, children! Not indoors.
NEVILLE: We've always worn them.
MRS GRAHAM: I don't think so. [*She takes their caps off.*]
MRS GRAHAM: To the table, children. [*To* MR GRAHAM] Tea, dear?
MR GRAHAM: Atta girl!
   [*He switches the wireless off, makes his way to the table and sits down.*
   MRS GRAHAM *also sits down – in the only remaining chair. The two boys look*

blankly at the table, wondering where they're supposed to sit. Two plates have been laid for them – each bearing one cold sausage – but no chairs.
Mr Graham *bows his head in prayer.* Mrs Graham *likewise.*
The two boys stand at the table facing their plate of cold sausage.

MR GRAHAM: For what we're about to receive, may the Lord make us truly thankful. Amen. [*He digs into his meal.*]
MRS GRAHAM: Amen. [*To the boys*] 'Amen'.
NEVILLE: Amen.
MRS GRAHAM: Danny?
DANNY: Amen – what is it?
MRS GRAHAM: 'What is it, Mrs Graham?'
DANNY: [*confused*]: What? [*Looks down at the sausage.*]
MRS GRAHAM: Silly lad. It's a sausage.
NEVILLE [*to* MRS GRAHAM]: Shall we stand here?
MRS GRAHAM: You boys like football?
DANNY: Yes.
MRS GRAHAM: 'Yes, Mrs Graham.'
NEVILLE: [*to* DANNY]: You've to say 'Mrs Graham' at the end of the sentence. [*To* MR GRAHAM] Sometimes, Mr Graham.
MR GRAHAM: I watch Blackpool now and then. Top of the first division. Saw them wallop the Wolves on Saturday. [*Which doesn't please* DANNY.] Two-one. Jock Dodds got both.
DANNY: I don't like cold sausage, Mrs Graham.
MRS GRAHAM: Of course you do! It's real pork.
   [DANNY *and* NEVILLE *exchange an immediate frantic glance of panic. Real pork is the biggest crisis they've ever had to face.*]
NEVILLE: Is there anything else instead, Mrs Graham?
MRS GRAHAM: [*putting down her knife and fork*] Neville. One thing I shall not entertain. And that's impertinence. Mr Graham and I like boys who are grateful for being taken off the streets and given a home. [*She continues eating.*]
NEVILLE: Could we have the corned beef we brought – do you think – Mrs Graham?
MRS GRAHAM: No. That stays in the larder for when there's a shortage.
DANNY: We've never had pork sausage, Mrs Graham. We're not allowed it.
MR GRAHAM: [*with consummate wisdom*]: How do you know you don't like it, then, eh? Mmmmm? Can't answer that one, can you? Eh, boys? Blinded by science, eh?
MRS GRAHAM: [*to the boys, annoyed*]: Just don't know there's a war *on*, do you.
   [MR *and* MRS GRAHAM *continue eating their meal.*
   DANNY *and* NEVILLE *look at each other.*
   NEVILLE *realizes he has to take the lead and make a decision. He struggles through a little crisis of conscience, then cuts a small piece of his sausage – whispers a short Hebrew prayer to himself – hand on head – and eats.*
   DANNY *watches. Accepts the decision and puts his hand on his head to whisper the Hebrew prayer.*

MRS GRAHAM *glances at him. He pretends he's scratching his head, then drops his hand and eats.*]

24. Int. The boys' bedroom. Night.

[DANNY *and* NEVILLE *are lying back to back in bed – both tired but awake. Faintly, from downstairs, we hear on the wireless 'Monday night at 8.00 o'clock'. The boys are silent for a few moments. Looking into space, mulling over the events of the day.*]

DANNY: If he isn't a spy, why was he listening to Her Hitler?
NEVILLE: *Herr* Hitler. He isn't. Go to sleep.
DANNY: Your big fat elbow's only sticking in my ribs.
[NEVILLE *shifts position slightly. Tears imminent.*]
Neville . . .
NEVILLE: Go to sleep.
DANNY: It'll be over by Christmas, won't it? Any money?
NEVILLE: 'Course.
DANNY: We'll write to Mam tomorrow. [*Pause.*] Railings can't do much against *tanks*. You can only make spears out of railings.
[*A long pause. They seem to be settling down to sleep. We hear* DANNY *quietly sobbing to himself.*
NEVILLE *listens to him – fighting back his own tears.*]
NEVILLE: We'll be all right.
[DANNY *continues sobbing.*]
Sssshhh.
[DANNY *continues sobbing.*]
NEVILLE *gets up on one elbow and belts his brother across the head.*]
Now, shurrup!!
[DANNY *quietens down. A pause.*]
DANNY: I forgot to say my prayers.
NEVILLE: Do you want another good hiding?
[DANNY *whispers his prayers to himself.*]
DANNY: Boruch atto adonai Elohanu melech ho'oulom. Hamapeel chevlai . . . er . . . [*He's lost. He tries again.*] Hamapeel chevlai . . . er . . . [*Lost again. Tries again.*] Hamapeel chevlai shano, al anai . . . er . . . al anai . . . [*He gives up and continues in English.*] Blessed are Thou O Lord Our God, King of the Universe. Please look after Mam and Dad and everyone, and let Hitler get a railing up his tochass. Amen.

From The Evacuees (1975)

JACK ROSENTHAL (1931–), British dramatist and award-winning television writer, was born in Manchester.

Norman Podhoretz

IMPROPERLY DRESSED

Given the fact that I had literary ambitions even as a small boy, it was inevitable that the issue of class would sooner or later arise for me with a sharpness it would never acquire for most of my friends. But given the fact also that I was on the whole very happy to be growing up where I was, that I was fiercely patriotic about Brownsville (the spawning-ground of so many famous athletes and gangsters), and that I felt genuinely patronizing toward other neighborhoods, especially the 'better' ones like Crown Heights and East Flatbush which seemed by comparison colorless and unexciting – given the fact, in other words, that I was not, for all that I wrote poetry and read books, an 'alienated' boy dreaming of escape – my confrontation with the issue of class would probably have come later rather than sooner if not for an English teacher in high school who decided that I was a gem in the rough and who took it upon herself to polish me to as high a sheen as she could manage and I would permit.

I resisted – far less effectively, I can see now, than I then thought, though even then I knew that she was wearing me down far more than I would ever give her the satisfaction of admitting. Famous throughout the school for her altogether outspoken snobbery, which stopped short by only a hair, and sometimes did not stop short at all, of an old-fashioned kind of patrician anti-Semitism, Mrs. K. was also famous for being an extremely good teacher; indeed, I am sure that she saw no distinction between the hopeless task of teaching the proper use of English to the young Jewish barbarians whom fate had so unkindly deposited into her charge and the equally hopeless task of teaching them the proper 'manners.' (There were as many young Negro barbarians in her charge as Jewish ones, but I doubt that she could ever bring herself to pay very much attention to them. As she never hesitated to make clear, it was punishment enough for a woman of her background – her family was old-Brooklyn and, she would have us understand, extremely distinguished – to have fallen among the sons of East European immigrant Jews.)

For three years, from the age of thirteen to the age of sixteen, I was her special pet, though that word is scarcely adequate to suggest the intensity of the relationship which developed between us. It was a relationship right out of *The Corn Is Green*, which may, for all I know, have served as her model; at any rate, her objective was much the same as the Welsh teacher's in that play: she was determined that I should win a scholarship to Harvard. But whereas (an irony much to the point here) the problem the teacher had in *The Corn Is Green* with her coal-miner pupil in the traditional class society of Edwardian England was strictly academic, Mrs. K's problem with me in the putatively egalitarian society of New Deal America was strictly social. My grades were very high and would obviously remain so, but what would they avail me if I continued to go about looking and sounding like a 'filthy little slum child' (the epithet she would invariably hurl at me whenever we had an argument about 'manners')?

Childless herself, she worked on me like a dementedly ambitious mother with a somewhat recalcitrant son; married to a solemn and elderly man (she was then in her early forties or thereabouts), she treated me like a callous, ungrateful adolescent lover on whom she had humiliatingly bestowed her favours. She flirted with me and flattered me, she scolded me and insulted me. Slum child, filthy little slum child, so beautiful a mind and so vulgar a personality, so exquisite in sensibility and so coarse in manner. What would she do with me, what would become of me if I persisted out of stubbornness and perversity in the disgusting ways they had taught me at home and on the streets?

To her the most offensive of these ways was the style in which I dressed: a tee shirt, tightly pegged pants, and a red satin jacket with the legend 'Cherokees, S.A.C.' (social-athletic club) stitched in large white letters across the back. This was bad enough, but when on certain days I would appear in school wearing, as a particular ceremonial occasion required, a suit and tie, the sight of those immense padded shoulders and my white-on-white shirt would drive her to even greater heights of contempt and even lower depths of loving despair than usual. *Slum child, filthy little slum child.* I was beyond saving; I deserved no better than to wind up with all the other horrible little Jewboys in the gutter (by which she meant Brooklyn College). If only I would listen to her, the whole world could be mine: I could win a scholarship to Harvard, I could get to know the best people, I could grow up into a life of elegance and refinement and taste. Why was I so stupid as not to understand?

In those days it was very unusual, and possibly even against the rules, for teachers in public high schools to associate with their students after hours. Nevertheless, Mrs K. sometimes invited me to her home, a beautiful old brownstone located in what was perhaps the only section in the whole of Brooklyn fashionable enough to be intimidating. I would read her my poems and she would tell me about her family, about the schools she had gone to, about Vassar, about writers she had met, while her husband, of whom I was frightened to death and who to my utter astonishment turned out to be Jewish (but not, as Mrs. K. quite unnecessarily hastened to inform me, *my* kind of Jewish), sat stiffly and silently in an armchair across the room, squinting at his newspaper through the first *pince-nez* I had ever seen outside the movies. He spoke to me but once, and that was after I had read Mrs. K. my tearful editorial for the school newspaper on the death of Roosevelt – an effusion which provoked him into a full five-minute harangue whose blasphemous contents would certainly have shocked me into insensibility if I had not been even more shocked to discover that he actually had a voice.

But Mrs. K. not only had me to her house; she also – what was even more unusual – took me out a few times, to the Frick Gallery and the Metropolitan Museum, and once to the theater, where we saw a dramatization of *The Late*

George Apley, a play I imagine she deliberately chose with the not wholly mistaken idea that it would impress upon me the glories of aristocratic Boston.

One of our excursions into Manhattan I remember with particular vividness because she used it to bring the struggle between us to rather a dramatic head. The familiar argument began this time on the subway. Why, knowing that we would be spending the afternoon together 'in public,' had I come to school that morning improperly dressed? (I was, as usual, wearing my red satin club jacket over a white tee shirt.) She realized, of course, that I owned only one suit (this said not in compassion but in derision) and that my poor parents had, God only knew where, picked up the idea that it was too precious to be worn except at one of those bar mitzvahs I was always going to. Though why, if my parents were so worried about clothes, they had permitted me to buy a suit which made me look like a young hoodlum she found it very difficult to imagine. Still, much as she would have been embarrassed to be seen in public with a boy whose parents allowed him to wear a zoot suit, she would have been somewhat less embarrassed than she was now by the ridiculous costume I had on. Had I no consideration for her? Had I no consideration for myself? Did I want everyone who laid eyes on me to think that I was nothing but an ill-bred little slum child?

My standard ploy in these arguments was to take the position that such things were of no concern to me: I was a poet and I had more important matters to think about than clothes. Besides, I would feel silly coming to school on an ordinary day dressed in a suit. Did Mrs. K. want me to look like one of those 'creeps' from Crown Heights who were all going to become doctors? This was usually an effective counter, since Mrs. K. despised her middle-class Jewish students even more than she did the 'slum children,' but probably because she was growing desperate at the thought of how I would strike a Harvard interviewer (it was my senior year), she did not respond according to form on that particular occasion. 'At least,' she snapped, 'they reflect well on their parents.'

I was accustomed to her bantering gibes at my parents, and sensing, probably, that they arose out of jealousy, I was rarely troubled by them. But this one bothered me; it went beyond banter and I did not know how to deal with it. I remember flushing, but I cannot remember what if anything I said in protest. It was the beginning of a very bad afternoon for both of us.

We had been heading for the Museum of Modern Art, but as we got off the subway, Mrs. K. announced that she had changed her mind about the museum. She was going to show me something else instead, just down the street on Fifth Avenue. This mysterious 'something else' to which we proceeded in silence turned out to be the college department of an expensive clothing store, de Pinna. I do not exaggerate when I say that an actual physical dread seized me as I followed her into the store. I had never been inside such a store; it was not a store, it was enemy territory, every inch of it mined with humiliations. 'I am,' Mrs. K. declared in the coldest human voice I hope I shall ever hear, 'going to buy you a suit that you will be able to wear at your

Harvard interview.' I had guessed, of course, that this was what she had in mind, and even at fifteen I understood what a fantastic act of aggression she was planning to commit against my parents and asking me to participate in. Oh no, I said in a panic (suddenly realizing that I *wanted* her to buy me that suit), I can't, my mother wouldn't like it. 'You can tell her it's a birthday present. Or else I will tell her. If I tell her, I'm sure she won't object.' The idea of Mrs. K. meeting my mother was more than I could bear: my mother, who spoke with a Yiddish accent and of whom, until that sickening moment, I had never known I was ashamed and so ready to betray.

To my immense relief and my equally immense disappointment, we left the store, finally, without buying a suit, but it was not to be the end of clothing or 'manners' for me that day – not yet. There was still the ordeal of a restaurant to go through. Where I came from, people rarely ate in restaurants, not so much because most of them were too poor to afford such a luxury – although most of them certainly were – as because eating in restaurants was not regarded as a luxury at all; it was, rather, a necessity to which bachelors were pitiably condemned. A home-cooked meal was assumed to be better than anything one could possibly get in a restaurant, and considering the class of restaurants in question (they were really diners or luncheonettes), the assumption was probably correct. In the case of my own family, myself included until my late teens, the business of going to restaurants was complicated by the fact that we observed the Jewish dietary laws, and except in certain neighborhoods, few places could be found which served kosher food; in midtown Manhattan in the 1940s, I believe there were only two and both were relatively expensive. All this is by way of explaining why I had had so little experience of restaurants up to the age of fifteen and why I grew apprehensive once more when Mrs. K. decided after we left de Pinna that we should have something to eat.

The restaurant she chose was not at all an elegant one – I have, like a criminal, revisited it since – but it seemed very elegant indeed to me; enemy territory again, and this time a mine exploded in my face the minute I set foot through the door. The hostess was very sorry, but she could not seat the young gentleman without a coat and tie. If the lady wished, however, something could be arranged. The lady (visibly pleased by this unexpected – or was it expected? – object lesson) did wish, and the so recently defiant but by now utterly docile young gentleman was forthwith divested of his so recently beloved but by now thoroughly loathsome red satin jacket and provided with a much oversized white waiter's coat and a tie – which, there being no collar to a tee shirt, had to be worn around his bare neck. Thus attired, and with his face supplying the touch of red which had moments earlier been supplied by his jacket, he was led into the dining room, there to be taught the importance of proper table manners through the same pedagogic instrumentality that had worked so well in impressing him with the importance of proper dress.

Like any other pedagogic technique, however, humiliation has its limits, and Mrs. K. was to make no further progress with it that day. For I had had enough, and I was not about to risk stepping on another mine. Knowing she would subject me to still more ridicule if I made a point of my revulsion at the prospect of eating non-kosher food, I resolved to let her order for me and then to feign lack of appetite or possibly even illness when the meal was served. She did order – duck for both of us, undoubtedly because it would be a hard dish for me to manage without using my fingers.

The two portions came in deep oval-shaped dishes, swimming in a brown sauce and each with a sprig of parsley on top. I had not the faintest idea of what to do – should the food be eaten directly from the oval dish or not? – nor which of the many implements on the table to do it with. But remembering that Mrs. K. herself had once advised me to watch my hostess in such a situation and then do exactly as she did, I sat perfectly still and waited for her to make the first move. Unfortunately, Mrs. K. also remembered having taught me that trick, and determined as she was that I should be given a lesson that would force me to mend my ways, she waited too. And so we both waited, chatting amiably, pretending not to notice the food while it sat there getting colder and colder by the minute. Thanks partly to the fact that I would probably have gagged on the duck if I had tried to eat it – dietary taboos are very powerful if one has been conditioned to them – I was prepared to wait forever. And in fact it was Mrs. K. who broke first.

'Why aren't you eating?' she suddenly said after something like fifteen minutes had passed. 'Aren't you hungry?' Not very, I answered. 'Well,' she said, 'I think we'd better eat. The food is getting cold.' Whereupon, as I watched with great fascination, she deftly captured the sprig of parsley between the prongs of her serving fork, set it aside, took up her serving spoon and delicately used those two esoteric implements to transfer a piece of duck from the oval dish to her plate. I imitated the whole operation as best I could, but not well enough to avoid splattering some partly congealed sauce onto my borrowed coat in the process. Still, things could have been worse, and having more or less successfully negotiated my way around that particular mine, I now had to cope with the problem of how to get out of eating the duck. I need not have worried. Mrs. K. took one bite, pronounced it inedible (it must have been frozen by then), and called in quiet fury for the check.

From Making It (1957)

NORMAN PODHORETZ (1930–), American editor and writer on current affairs, was born in Brooklyn.

Chaim Bermant

BAR-MITZVAH BOY

I was the first person in synagogue. Father had a last-minute panic about his top hat. He had worn it only once before, seven years ago, and it was now too small. Mother advised him to wear a homburg, but he wouldn't have it. 'A homburg on a Bar-Mitzvah? Never!' They were still arguing about it when I left, but father for once had his way and he arrived breathless and triumphant, with the topper balanced on his head like a jug. It fell off about twenty times in the course of the morning. Once while he was standing by the ark with the scrolls of the law in his hand, it toppled over, rolled down the short flight of stairs and settled in the aisle. But the real calamity had nothing to do with father or his hat. It came during the service when I was being addressed by the Rabbi. I stood in the front pew between the synagogue wardens like a prisoner in the dock, directly facing the pulpit, while the Rabbi's words flowed over me. He had a long face, made longer by a pointed beard, and long arms which, in his turbulent, black canonicals, looked like vultures' wings.

'My dear Bar-Mitzvah boy,' he began, but I was not listening. I gazed at him for a while, then my eyes wandered round the congregation. My father, with one hand to his hat and the other to his ear; Uncle Motie, with his thin moustache coming down the sides of his mouth as if it was melting; Uncle Boruch, with his face raised to heaven, fast asleep; Uncle Yehudah looking into his prayer book with a pained look on his face; Uncle Peter picking his nose; Uncle Freddy, eyeing the women; Uncle Reuben, facing the Rabbi, with his shoulders drooping in sleep. I looked up to the gallery: a few old ladies scattered loosely about the place, and a glossy cluster grouped round my mother, all silver foxes and straw hats. When the sermon was over I would have to go upstairs and kiss them; I steeled myself for the task. An occasional sentence from the pulpit reached me: '. . . remember therefore that you are standing in the congregation of Abraham, Isaac and Jacob. . . . Children can err, but only man can do wrong, and henceforth you are a man. . . .'

I sank into a reverie and began to tally up my Bar-Mitzvah presents: thirty-two pounds in notes; forty-seven pounds in cheques; the Five Books of Moses, five times over; a child's version of the Talmud; the life of Lord Nelson; two histories of Mary Queen of Scots; *The Decline and Fall of the Roman Empire*; seven books on Jewish ethics; five sets of prayer books; three wallets; a trouser press; eleven ties; four watches; a pair of gold cuff links; five pairs of non-gold cuff links; a bottle of Palestinian wine made in Manchester; a manicure set; and eleven fountain pens. And I continued to comfort myself with my riches, when the raised voice of the Rabbi burst in upon me:

'. . . and therefore I say to you, there are two roads in life, the road of iniquity and the road of virtue. Which road shall be yours?'

'The road of iniquity,' I shouted before I could recover my bearings. And at once the whole synagogue rose in commotion.

Father did not think this a happy omen, and when I went upstairs to kiss mother and my aunts, mother boxed my ears before the full congregation.

The reception which was to have taken place for the next day was cancelled because mother became violently ill and for the next fortnight the house was busy with the passage of comforting aunts. That same Saturday, Kadisch won some piffling prize scholarship. I can't remember what it was, but his picture appeared in the *Evening Times* and it didn't help mother's recovery a bit. By then I was beginning to give up the race with him, but mother did not. 'I wouldn't bother if I thought you were an idiot,' she said, 'but you're not. There's nothing wrong with you which good tuition can't cure.' Uncle Boruch was the only one who took my side on this issue: 'Are you sure,' he asked, 'that there's nothing right with him which bad tuition might spoil?' But Uncle's philosophy was never highly rated in our household and for several years there was hardly an evening to the week which was not darkened by some bleak-faced tutor. I was a form of outdoor relief for superannuated schoolmasters. Happily, there was always the Sabbath.

From Jericho Sleep Alone (1963)

CHAIM BERMANT (1929–), British novelist and journalist, was born in Poland, and brought up and educated in Glasgow. His non-fiction works include *The Jews* (1978) and *What's the Joke* (1986), a study of Jewish humour through the ages.

T.G. Rosenthal

NOT KOSHER

My childhood was spent in a part of Manchester called Withington, in a modest, rented house off Palatine Road. The next district was Didsbury. Didsbury was known as Yidsbury and Palatine Road as Palestine.

My father, then an impoverished Lecturer in Hebrew at Manchester University, was the only Jew in the area, apart from the doctor (also a German refugee), who was not in the cotton trade. All my Jewish friends were Iraqis and the local synagogue was dramatically orthodox (with the women segregated upstairs), and even more dramatically Sephardic in its practice and its liturgy. The Sephardic rite is infinitely exciting and I'm sure it's responsible for my later passion for opera, particularly Verdi. The Sephardim had – and have – all the best tunes and I found, on our move to London after the war, the local Ashkenazi form curiously anaemic. My best friend, with whom I often shared the main North Country meal of the day, High Tea, eaten at 6 o'clock, was not Jewish. One evening being, at least as far as my elders were concerned, a polite little boy, having just eaten a plateful of superb cold white meat, thinly sliced, I thanked his mother for 'the best cold chicken I've ever eaten'. She roared with laughter and asked, with total incredulity, if I'd never eaten pork before. . . .

This was clearly a major catastrophe and, as they say, I made my excuses and left at once for my own home, some three hundred yards away. I don't know which of the two facial colours that afflicted me on that seemingly eternal journey was the more extreme, the pork-like whiteness of terror (read James Joyce on the fear of Hellfire) or the scarlet of gastronomic shame. My father opened the door, saw my evident distress and asked why I was home so early.

I blurted out my agonised confession – no Joycean Catholic teenager could possibly have felt worse – and my father, then as now, a wise and humorous man, proceeded with the following interrogation:

Him: 'Did she tell you she was serving pork?'
Me: 'No.'
Him: 'Did you have any reason to think it was pork?'
Me: 'No. I thought it looked like chicken.'
Him: 'Well, in that case you've committed no sin. But you'll always in future, if in doubt, ask what the meat is.'
Me: 'Yes.'
Him: 'So you'll never do it again?'
Me: 'No.'
Him: 'Well, that's alright then. Now, tell me honestly, did you enjoy it?'
Me: 'Yes. It was marvellous!'
Him: 'Hmmm. Well, at least that's something in favour of this whole episode. Now let's both forget it and watch what you eat when you're with Goyim in future. . . . '

Many years later, aged about twenty-five, I deliberately ate my first piece of bacon, simply as an experiment in both taste and sin. By the time I was thirty, I had reached some kind of maturity and was eating bacon, pork, ham and shellfish, not to sin but because I enjoyed them. I challenged my father about the validity of these prohibitions, which were very proper health safeguards in the Judean desert five thousand years ago, but made little sense in the age of refrigeration. Once again he delivered the ultimate in devastating answers. He was as free not to eat certain foods as I was to choose to eat them but, since my ancestors had suffered and indeed, died for the right not to, he saw no reason to change his ways. . . .

I once asked my father, when I was clearly under the influence of several Goulds, Cowans, Greens and other previously foreign named Jews, why he did not change our name. (My mother's maiden name, by the way, was Marx and she claims collateral descent, alas, from boring old Karl rather than glorious Groucho.) He replied that he would not, for three very convincing reasons – at least to the ten year old me. It was an attractive name, meaning valley of roses; it had been the recorded name of the family for about five hundred years and it would, in any case, be professionally awkward for him to change it, even if he wanted to – which he did not – because he had already used it to publish various learned books and articles. I had no choice but to agree with him and, over forty years later, my two grown up sons feel the same way.

My childhood, while one of shabby genteel poverty, was not unhappy and I even, with some reservations, enjoyed the three schools I attended in Manchester.

The first, from about the age of four to six, was of all things a Church of England school, which, out of respect for my father's academic distinction, took me in as its only non-Christian pupil. The male teacher, the husband, was a contemporary of my father and progressed from being a mere Rev. and Rector of Fallowfield (next door to Withington) to being the Rt. Rev. John Moorman, Bishop of Ripon; the female teacher, his wife Mary, a daughter of the great G.M. Trevelyan, taught me to read before going on to higher things and becoming this country's leading Wordsworth scholar. I was indubitably well taught very early in life, and when my parents asked me how I was enjoying the school, I replied that it was all very good except for too many spells of enforced kneeling. With the clarity and the benefit of hindsight I remember that neither of those splendid Moormans ever tried to entice me away from Judaism, and that their forcing me to kneel with the rest was simply an enlightened way of making sure that their only Jew was not – the ultimate childhood sin – made to appear conspicuous. Conspicuous, at my next school, Beaver Road Primary School, I most certainly was.

My conspicuousness consisted in the revelation, in those specially tiny and smelly urinals to be found in old primary schools, of a penis whose knob was entirely unconcealed and unfettered by a foreskin. For the first year or so I possessed one of only two such in the school. For the last year or so I had the only one after my Jewish friend Eddie left for better things.

I have no doubt that I was a fairly obnoxious child anyway, since I was the only pupil who could fulfil the Headmistress's criterion for being a first class reader, namely, mastery of the intricacies of the Leader columns in the Manchester Guardian. This would cause her to draw – much dreaded – particular attention to me and frequently aver that I was a future prime minister in the making. (She was, I think, unaware that Disraeli had been, at the behest of his prescient father, baptised; who knows what might have happened if the gentle Moormans had been of a proselytising persuasion . . .)

Since it was not worth prosecuting a future politician and, amazingly, no one seemed to know what was happening in Germany – the full body count of dead Rosenthals only emerged, even for us, years later, I was persecuted as a filthy little Yid and chased home with an unappealing mixture of foul language, thrown stones and blows. My father, not yet in the army, and even then definitely a scholarly type who would probably not have been a success in Irgun or the Hagannah, shrewdly consulted our local Rabbi, a magisterial, splendidly bearded man and a very tough cookie indeed. Definitely the synagogue militant. . . .

He summoned my father and me to tea one Saturday afternoon and, despite being an orthodox, Sephardic, spiritual leader, tolerated no nonsense about the sanctity of the Sabbath. His son was home on leave, a large man wearing the uniform of a sergeant in the Royal Air Force. 'Now, young man,' the Rabbi said, 'my son here is a Physical Training Instructor and an excellent boxer. He's going to take you into the next room and teach you how to teach those bullying swine the only lesson they'll understand.' And he did.

The next school day, as usual, I was taunted and prodded by the school's chief bully who was, as is often the case with bullies, no mere blusterer but was known as the school's 'champion fighter'. I had been pushed beyond endurance and I had been well taught. I was also lucky, in that my first, unexpected, punch landed on his nose and drew instant and copious blood. I decided that I rather liked that and, taking advantage of the surprise, proceeded to beat hell out of him, till he ended up limp, not unconscious, but certainly motionless on the ground. He never touched me again and I was never again called a filthy Yid, at least not at Beaver Road Primary School. I also, to this day, have never again resorted to violence.

Sometime after that, as a result of untold sacrifice by my parents, involving my father sending home virtually all his army pay and my mother storing up for herself terrible arthritis in her hands later on, by crocheting myriad tablemats for a sweatshop owner (inevitably himself a Jewish refugee), I was sent to an eccentric, run down, fee-paying day preparatory school. As one might expect of such an establishment in wartime, it was staffed by those unfit even for munitions work, let alone military service. Yet the Headmaster, an intimidating, one-armed, World War One veteran, and Cambridge graduate, was a superb teacher and propelled me to a Foundation Scholarship to Manchester Grammar School.

He was, however, not a great theologian. As the only Jew in my class, and because my parents had made their views very clear, I was excused Religious Instruction. The lesson was always the last before the mid-morning break, and, if the weather was good, I was allowed out early into the school playground. One fine, bright summer day I was outside, on my own, practising leg breaks with a battered, composition, cricket ball against a plane tree, when I heard the usual exodus from the classroom. In a matter of seconds I was surrounded by my ten or so classmates who began, at first raggedly, and then in terrifying unison, to shout at me 'Christkiller! Christkiller! Christkiller! . . . ' for what seemed like forever but was, I now suppose, perhaps a mere two minutes.

Because my religious knowledge was exclusively that of the synagogue and the Old Testament, I was totally at a loss. I was silent. I was confused. Above all, I did not understand. I could make no connection with the image those nice Moormans had made me kneel to.

I never took up my hard-won scholarship to Manchester Grammar School because my father, released from the army, had, to the shame of Academe, no job left for him at Manchester University, so we moved to London, where he worked at the British end of the German Control Commission. I went to a North London grammar school where, intellectually, thanks to the redoubtable Mr Oliver, I vegetated for two years, even, for half a term, avoiding school. I did a milk round in the mornings, actually driving an Express Dairy horse and cart and filled in, on the phone, in the afternoons, for a friendly estate agent who wanted his office manned when business was slack so that he could go to his (alas, Jewish) golf club.

When not thus employed, however, I quite liked that school. It was co-educational and the girls sat on one side and the boys on the other. The desks were in pairs bolted together. You therefore could not escape the attentions of your neighbour. Mine, a cheerful and friendly soul, who told me authoritatively that the royal family did not actually perform the sexual act but produced their offspring by artificial insemination, leaned over one day in between lessons, in a thoroughly conspiratorial way.

''Ere', he said, 'you one of them Scottish Jews then?'

This being North London, there were about twenty per cent Jewish pupils, but it took me some time to understand his question.

Not only was I a Christkiller. I also had a Manchester accent.

TOM ROSENTHAL (1935–), British publisher and critic, was born in London. He is Joint Chairman and sole Managing Director of Andre Deutsch Ltd.

Frederic Raphael

A SECOND CHILDHOOD

I had two childhoods. Like my parents, one was American and the other British. For my first seven years, I had an American accent and American expectations. Somewhere in a trunk I still have a copy of the *New York Herald Tribune* (with a mock-up headline) announcing 'FREDDIE RAPHAEL VISITS WORLD'S FAIR'. I still pay the occasional pilgrimage to 30 W 70th street, N.Y.C., just off Central Park West, where we lived until 1938. There were candle-style lamp-brackets in the living room (no American ever used the term 'drawing room', let alone 'lounge'). I had a black nanny called Fleggy and then an Irish one, whose name I forget but of whose flaming hair I later thought when I heard that red-heads were passionate.

My mother was born in St Louis and I was born in Chicago. My father was born in London. His family, I have always been told, was among those first invited to return to England by Cromwell. My mother's father was German; his name was Max Mauser and he travelled from Bad Kreuznach to St Louis, by himself, at the age of fourteen, in order to work for a supposedly rich uncle. He became the most patriotic possible American. It was from his lips that I learnt my first words of a foreign language, although my knowledge of

German never progressed beyond the simplest nursery terms. During the war, when I was in England, I typed a letter to Max on a W.V.S. Royal Sovereign, while my mother was busy organising a Car Pool in central London. When I failed to use the shift key when writing 'germany', I covered my error by affecting deliberately to have docked that country of its capital: 'It doesn't deserve one, does it?' I never considered how far my grandfather shared my assumption that the land of his birth was beyond the community of proper names. Probably he was not offended. He was a man of rare geniality and the keenest of Uncle Sam's adopted nephews. I still have an album of childhood snaps, captioned by him, in white ink on the black pages, with such phrases as 'Attaboy!' and 'Punch him right in the nose!' and 'Home run!' I used to get into his bed on Sunday mornings (he lived with us when he and my grandmother, Fanny, fell out for a while) and we would read the Funnies together. I hated 'Little Orphan Annie', but I liked (never loved) Dick Tracy and Dagwood Bumpstead. Comedy was the essence of American culture in my first childhood: my father read Greats at Oxford, but he loved Jack Benny. We would always hurry home from Jones's Beach, on summer afternoons, in time to hear Rochester say 'Yes, Mr Benny'. You could park the Dodge right in front of the house in those days. I liked to listen to Eddie Cantor, but my parents thought him vulgar. 'Jeepers Creepers' was, of course, a cryptic recension of Jesus Christ; Cantor's catch-tune was, in a way, blasphemous and they probably thought it unwise of a Jew to make such play with Christianity.

My parents loved to dance (my father had been Tango Champion of the World), but here again there were limits: Guy Lombardo was never missed on the radio, but I was not allowed to listen to Hillbilly music. It came from the American South where prejudices were rampant; it was just as well that the Rebels had been defeated, but Jews were still liable to meet hatred down there. When I was a little boy, they still held parades of the veterans from the Civil War. For some reason, perhaps wholly sartorial, I had a secret preference for the gentlemen of the South, for all their disreputable opinions. The Union hats were rather absurd, I still think. When I was a small English schoolboy drawing pictures of war in the desert and of street-fighting at Stalingrad, I continued to have a certain penchant for the head-gear of the wrong side: the caps of the German officers fascinated me with their haughty crowns.

My American grandmother was of Lithuanian origin, though I think she was born in St Jo, Missouri. She was a woman of forthright style and prejudices, who always said what she thought. When she dressed up for a function, or to play Canasta with the girls, she would say, 'I look like a lady tonight.' My father would always say, 'But you *are* a lady, Fanny.' She was not flattered: she was a worker. Even in her nineties, when she came to live in England, with her daughter, she would jump up to make me a cup of coffee whenever I came to visit. She and Max, in the years when they managed to stay together, ran a delicatessen in Kansas City. Her brother had been murdered by the mob, when he left a poker game with more money than he had been supposed to win. My grandfather knew several of the Prendergast mob, who ran K.C. just as Capone ran Chicago. Max was straight, but well-liked. They offered him the job of City Health Inspector. He thanked them but said that he had his hands full with the delly, without doing anything else. They told him that he wouldn't have to do anything else, just collect the salary, but he declined. He was, I suppose, the nicest kind of loser. He always dreamed of becoming a millionaire, but the only means which appealed to him was through inventing a typically American gadget. He designed shoes which could be repaired at home by sliding off the heel and replacing it with a new one. His partner swindled him out of the idea but I doubt if it ever made him rich. Max was the kind of American who thought that the world would be paradise if there were a good five-cent cigar. He was a Jew who, on High Days and Holydays, would take my mother for a ham sandwich while Fanny sat in the synagogue gallery.

When, in 1938, my father was offered a promotion in Shell, which involved moving to London, he did not long hesitate, even though he loved the American way of life. There were, of course, no negroes among his personal friends, but he adored black music and black dancers. He and my mother would go, with their friends, to the Cotton Club in Harlem and I can remember him 'trucking' in the hallway of our apartment house. He wore seersucker suits in the summer and admired Jack Dempsey, with whose children I played in Central Park (there were still red squirrels there then). But there was a side of America which did not appeal to him. His boss in Rockefeller Centre was a man called Kittinger, who did not like Jews. In the thirties, the German-American Bund held rallies of intimidating strength; support for Nazism was ominously fervent. Father Coughlin broadcast anti-Semitic sermons to huge audiences. I overheard the old story about a hotel in New England where there was a sign 'No dogs or Jews admitted'. It was certainly true that the New York Athletic Club did not welcome Jewish members; nor did Country Clubs all over the country. My grandfather might believe that I could be President of the United States one of these days, but the President of the United States is unlikely to have shared his hopes. The Jews were numerous, and articulate, in New York, but they were also, in many cases, marginalised and wary. If they were confident, it was often in the name of more universal ideals than Judaism: the intelligent preferred Ethical Culture to ethnical cults. They supported Socialism and Music, Business and Tolerance, Democracy and (though I saw small evidence of the fact) Literature. I had never heard of Zionism; I never did until after the war. My father was both sorry and not sorry to be transferred. He told me, in one of those formal talks to which he would invite me, while he was shaving (in boxer shorts and sock-suspenders), that I should now have the opportunity to grow up 'as an English gentleman and not an American Jew'. I do not recall my heart leaping up at the prospect.

I had made two or three earlier visits to the U.K. Since my father was British, he had the right to 'home leave' every three years. We would go Cabin Class on a Cunarder. It was a voyage of rare luxury. One could play ping-pong at any hour of the day or night. Nothing on the lavish menu was denied me. There was 'Bingo' and there was 'horse-racing'. My parents always had friends in First Class (those higher in Shell usually) and we would be invited to share their panelled pleasures. Often I was left in the nursery, but sometimes I saw the dinner jackets and the evening dresses. Sentimental memories of those white-starred days, and nights, impelled me to take my wife on the Q.E.II, first class, to America recently. What a fall was there! Ghastly food, plastic décor, insolent crew: never again. I prefer to remember 1938, on the Britannic, when my 'a's' were still short and I thought Macy's better than Harrod's and the Empire State Building finer than St Paul's.

As for being a Jew, the nearest I ever came to a synagogue in N.Y.C. was when we went to play in the park. We crossed by the Spanish and Portuguese Synagogue, with its Palladian façade and its black railings. One winter I was frostbitten, under the jaw, as my mother and I fought our way home, against the wind, by hauling ourselves along those gleaming iron bars. Being an only child, I overheard many adult conversations; anti-Semitism was often mentioned, but I never met any manifestation of it until I came to England. I can still see the great airship, the Hindenberg, as it sailed high over Central Park in 1936 on its way to disaster somewhere on Long Island. The crash horrified America and, such was the humane naiveté of the time, not a single murmur was heard even hinting at a certain pleasure at the misfortune of the Nazi's proudest symbol. The days of the licensed malice were, despite the cruelties of the time, to come later; partisanship was not yet without shame. Nowadays, commentators do not weep at the sight of horrors; professionalism involves articulate callousness. The indifference with which governments treated the Final Solution has entered the heart of mankind. When I was a little American boy, a few dozen people burning to death in the flames of what had been a beautiful machine seemed like an unthinkable outrage. By the time I had become an English adolescent, his Majesty's diplomats, educated men like Sir Frank Roberts and the Duke of Portland, had winced with officious distaste at the wailing of Europe's Jews and had done their fastidious best to stifle their pleas and their protests but nothing to impede their massacre. I am less than convinced that the English gentleman, which I was intended to become as the result of the education I finally received, is necessarily an article in every respect superior to the American Jew. My childhood in England was Jewish only in the sense that I was too guileless to deny my Jewishness and too alone to experience it as anything but a source of apprehension. Sometimes I am asked, in a challenging tone, whether I am proud of being a Jew. I am not sure that pride in what cannot be changed is particularly noble, but I cannot, in all honesty, claim to vaunt myself on my Jewishness. I do not believe either in God or, generally speaking, in men. If one can no more deny being a Jew than deny one's shadow, that scarcely entails that one should affect superiority on that account. I accept George Steiner's dictum – part defiance, part confession – that 'in the 20th century, Jewishness is a club from which there can be no resignations' – but I cannot pretend that I never wished that that particular cup should pass from me. I discovered the English and their values in what were, I daresay, soft circumstances, but if I was a Jew (and they made it clear that I was, and what it meant to them), I was never part of a Jewish community; I had none of the consolations of fellowship. Both at my prep school and at Charterhouse, I believed myself to be utterly alone. When other Jewish pupils approached me, I did not, I admit, welcome the news of our supposed affinity. When my father decided that I should receive instruction from the Liberal Jewish synagogue in the rudiments of a faith which he rarely practised (candles were not lit in S.W.15), I dreaded the drab envelopes which brought me the story of Nehemiah and his associates. These envelopes bore the word 'synagogue' on the front and they were stamped 'Student's Exercise'. In 1947, in Godalming, the word 'student' was almost as off as the word 'Jew' which, in Carthusian slang, meant a swindler or a miser. I suppose that my rather long childhood could be said to have ended soon after a certain Provost of Guildford preached a sermon in Charterhouse chapel in which, to amuse the boys, he pictured the young Jesus as the carpenter's apprentice taking his week's work to the local shopkeeper. 'And the shopkeeper, being a Jew, would give him as little as possible for it.' This sermon was preached only three or four years after the revelation of the camps. I was a timid, even a cowardly child, but I was more afraid of my peers than of my elders. I wrote a letter to the Provost in which I sought, in quite vivid terms, to alert him to the impropriety of his remarks. A bigot might have retorted with shamelessness; a gentleman might have apologised. The Provost merely reported me to the headmaster, a certain George Turner, who ordered me to apologise to 'a guest of the school'. I was almost eighteen and I wept. I wept, but I did not write. I was therefore barred from sitting for a closed scholarship to Christ Church (whose limited number of entrants was decided by Charterhouse) and thus I did not, as I had hoped, follow my father to Oxford. I could, of course, have taken an open scholarship, later in the academic year, but by that time I had sat for an open scholarship to Cambridge, which I obtained. I was advised by Ivor Gibson, the only master at Charterhouse whom I liked, to take it, and I did. My childhood ended with the letter I wrote to George Turner informing him, with a measure of pride, that I was beyond his orbit. I disposed of my school uniform and went to America that summer and bought a pair of fawn trousers with a zip instead of fly-buttons. I was a man, if not a gentleman.

FREDERIC RAPHAEL (1931–), novelist, screenplay and television writer, and critic, was born in Chicago. He won the Royal Television Society's 'Writer of the Year' award for *The Glittering Prizes* (1976). His latest novel on a Jewish theme is *After the War* (1988).

Leonard Cohen

FOR WILF AND HIS HOUSE

When young the Christians told me
how we pinned Jesus
like a lovely butterfly against the wood,
and I wept beside paintings of Calvary
at velvet wounds
and delicate twisted feet.

But he could not hang softly long,
your fighters so proud with bugles,
bending flowers with their silver stain,
and when I faced the Ark for counting,
trembling underneath the burning oil,
the meadow of running flesh turned sour
and I kissed away my gentle teachers,
warned my younger brothers.

Among the young and turning-great
of the large nations, innocent
of the spiked wish and the bright crusade,
there I could sing my heathen tears
between the summersaults and chestnut battles,
love the distant saint
who fed his arm to flies,
mourn the crushed ant
and despise the reason of the heel.

Raging and weeping are left on the early road.
Now each in his holy hill
the glittering and hurting days are almost done.
    Then let us compare mythologies.
I have learned my elaborate lie
of soaring crosses and poisoned thorns
and how my fathers nailed him
like a bat against a barn
to greet the autumn and late hungry ravens
as a hollow yellow sign.

LEONARD COHEN (1936–), Canadian poet, novelist, composer and singer, was born in Montreal. His *Selected Poems* was published in 1969.

Mordecai Richler

PRE-MED?

'Why do you want to go to university?' the student counsellor asked me.

Without thinking, I replied, 'I'm going to be a doctor, I suppose.'

A doctor.

One St. Urbain Street day cribs and diapers were cruelly withdrawn and the next we were scrubbed and carted off to kindergarten. Though we didn't know it, we were already in pre-med school. School starting age was six, but fiercely competitive mothers would drag protesting four-year-olds to the registration desk and say, 'He's short for his age.'

'Birth certificate, please?'

'Lost in a fire.'

On St. Urbain Street, a head start was all. Our mothers read us stories from *Life* about pimply astigmatic fourteen-year-olds who had already graduated from Harvard or who were confounding the professors at M.I.T. Reading *Tip-Top Comics* or listening to *The Green Hornet* on the radio was as good as asking for a whack on the head, sometimes administered with a rolled-up copy of *The Canadian Jewish Eagle*, as if that in itself would be nourishing. We were not supposed to memorise baseball batting averages or dirty limericks. We were expected to improve our Word Power with the *Reader's Digest* and find inspiration in Paul de Kruif's medical biographies. If we didn't make doctors, we were supposed to at least squeeze into dentistry. School marks didn't count as much as rank. One wintry day I came home, nostrils clinging together and ears burning cold, proud of my report. 'I came rank two, Maw.'

'And who came rank one, may I ask?'

Mrs. Klinger's boy, alas. Already the phone was ringing. 'Yes, yes,' my mother said to Mrs. Klinger, 'congratulations, and what does the eye doctor say about your Riva, poor kid, to have a complex at her age, will they be able to straighten them . . . '

Parochial school was a mixed pleasure. The old, underpaid men who taught us Hebrew tended to be surly, impatient. Ear-twisters and knuckle-rappers. They didn't like children. But the girls who handled the English-language part of our studies were charming, bracingly modern and concerned about our future. They told us about *El Campesino*, how John Steinbeck wrote the truth, and read Sacco's speech to the court aloud to us. If one of the younger, unmarried teachers started out the morning looking weary we assured each other that she had done it the night before. Maybe with a soldier. Bareback.

From parochial school, I went on to a place I call Fletcher's Field High in the stories and memoirs that follow. Fletcher's Field High was under the jurisdiction of the Montreal Protestant School Board, but had a student body that was nevertheless almost a hundred per cent Jewish. The school became something of a legend in our area. Everybody, it seemed, had passed through FFHS. Canada's most famous gambler. An atom bomb spy. Boys who went off to fight in the Spanish Civil War. Miracle-making doctors and silver-tongued lawyers. Boxers. Fighters for Israel. All of whom were instructed, as I was, to be staunch and bold, to play the man, and, above all, to

> Strive hard and work
> With your heart in the doing.
> Up play the game,
> As you learnt it at Fletcher's.

Again and again we led Quebec province in the junior matriculation results. This was galling to the communists amongst us who held we were the same as everyone else, but to the many more who knew that for all seasons there was nothing like a Yiddish boy, it was an annual cause for celebration. Our class at FFHS, Room 41, was one of the few to boast a true Gentile, an authentic white Protestant. Yugoslavs and Bulgarians, who were as foxy as we were, their potato-filled mothers sitting just as rigid in their corsets at school concerts, fathers equally prone to natty straw hats and cursing in the mother-tongue, did not count. Our very own WASP's name was Whelan, and he was no less than perfect. Actually blond, with real blue eyes, and a tendency to sit with his mouth hanging open. A natural hockey player, a born first-baseman. Envious students came from other classrooms to look him over and put questions to him. Whelan, as was to be expected, was not excessively bright, but he gave Room 41 a certain tone, some badly needed glamour, and in order to keep him with us as we progressed from grade to grade, we wrote essays for him and slipped him answers at examination time. We were enormously proud of Whelan.

Among our young school masters, most of them returned war veterans, there were a number of truly dedicated men as well as some sour and brutish ones, like Shaw, who strapped twelve of us one afternoon, ten on each hand, because we wouldn't say who had farted while his back was turned. The foibles of older teachers were well-known to us, because so many aunts, uncles, cousins and elder brothers had preceded us at FFHS. There was, for instance, one master who initiated first year students with a standing joke. 'Do you know how the Jews make an "s"?'

'No, Sir.'

Then he would make an 's' on the blackboard and draw two strokes through it. The dollar sign.

Among us, at FFHS, were future leaders of the community. Progressive parents. Reform-minded aldermen. Anti-fallout enthusiasts. Collectors of early French Canadian furniture. Boys who would actually grow up to be doctors and lecture on early cancer warnings to ladies' clubs. Girls who would appear in the social pages of the Montreal *Star*, sponsoring concerts in aid of retarded children (regardless of race, colour, or creed) and luncheon hour fashion shows, proceeds to the Hebrew University. Lawyers. Notaries.

Professors. And marvelously with-it rabbis, who could not only quote Rabbi Akiba but could also get a kick out of a hockey game. But at the time who would have known that such slouchy, aggressive girls, their very brassieres filled with bluff, would grow up to look so serene, such honeys, seeking apotheosis at the Saidye Bronfman Cultural Centre, posing on curving marble stairwells in their bouffant hair styles and strapless gowns? Or that such nervy boys, each one a hustler, would mature into men who were so damn pleased with what this world has to offer, epiphanous, radiating self-confidence at the curling or country club, at ease even with pot-bellies spilling over their Bermuda shorts? Who would have guessed?

Not me.

From The Street (1969)

MORDECAI RICHLER (1931–), Canadian novelist and dramatist, was born in Montreal. His novel *The Apprenticeship of Duddy Kravitz* (1959) also draws on memories of his youth.

Philip Roth

MY BASEBALL YEARS

In one of his essays George Orwell writes that, though he was not very good at the game, he had a long, hopeless love affair with cricket until he was sixteen. My relations with baseball were similar. Between the ages of nine and thirteen, I must have put in a forty-hour week during the snowless months over at the neighborhood playfield – softball, hardball, and stickball pick-up games – while simultaneously holding down a full-time job as a pupil at the local grammar school. As I remember it, news of two of the most cataclysmic public events of my childhood – the death of President Roosevelt and the bombing of Hiroshima – reached me while I was out playing ball. My performance was uniformly erratic; generally okay for those easygoing pick-up games, but invariably lacking the calm and the expertise that the naturals displayed in stiff competition. My taste, and my talent, such as it was, was for the flashy, whiz-bang catch rather than the towering fly; running and leaping I loved, all the do-or-die stuff – somehow I lost confidence waiting and waiting for the ball lofted right at me to descend. I could never make the high school team, yet I remember that, in one of the two years I vainly (in both senses of the word) tried out, I did a good enough imitation of a baseball player's *style* to be able to fool (or amuse) the coach right down to the day he cut the last of the dreamers from the squad and gave out the uniforms.

Though my disappointment was keen, my misfortune did not necessitate a change in plans for the future. Playing baseball was not what the Jewish boys of our lower-middle-class neighborhood were expected to do in later life for a living. Had I been cut from the high school itself, *then* there would have been hell to play in my house, and much confusion and shame in me. As it was, my family took my chagrin in stride and lost no more faith in me than I actually did in myself. They probably would have been shocked if I had made the team.

Maybe I would have been too. Surely it would have put me on a somewhat different footing with this game that I loved with all my heart, not simply for the fun of playing it (fun was secondary, really), but for the mythic and aesthetic dimension that it gave to an American boy's life – particularly to one whose grandparents could hardly speak English. For someone whose roots in America were strong but only inches deep, and who had no experience, such as a Catholic child might, of an awesome hierarchy that was real and felt, baseball was a kind of secular church that reached into every class and region of the nation and bound millions upon millions of us together in common concerns, loyalties, rituals, enthusiasms, and antagonisms. Baseball made me understand what patriotism was about, at its best.

Not that Hitler, the Bataan Death March, the battle for the Solomons, and the Normandy invasion didn't make of me and my contemporaries what may well have been the most patriotic generation of schoolchildren in American history (and the most willingly and successfully propagandized). But the war we entered when I was eight had thrust the country into what seemed to a child – and not only to a child – a struggle to the death between Good and Evil. Fraught with perilous, unthinkable possibilities, it inevitably nourished a patriotism grounded in moral virtue and bloody-minded hate, the patriotism that fixes a bayonet to a Bible. It seems to me that through baseball I was put in touch with a more humane and tender brand of patriotism, lyrical rather than martial or righteous in spirit, and without the reek of saintly zeal, a patriotism that could not so easily be sloganized, or contained in a high-sounding formula to which you had to pledge something vague but all-encompassing called your 'allegiance.'

To sing the National Anthem in the school auditorium every week, even during the worst of the war years, generally left me cold. The enthusiastic lady teacher waved her arms in the air and we obliged with the words: 'See! Light! Proof! Night! There!' But nothing stirred within, strident as we might be – in the end, just another school exercise. It was different, however, on Sundays out at Ruppert Stadium, a green wedge of pasture miraculously walled in among the factories, warehouses, and truck depots of industrial Newark. It would, in fact, have seemed to me an emotional thrill forsaken if, before the Newark Bears took on the hated enemy from across the marshes, the Jersey City Giants, we hadn't first to rise to our feet (my father, my brother, and I – along with our inimical countrymen, the city's Germans, Italians, Irish, Poles, and, out in the Africa of the bleachers, Newark's Negroes) to celebrate the America that had given to this inharmonious mob a game so grand and beautiful.

Just as I first learned the names of the great institutions of higher learning by trafficking in football pools for a neighborhood bookmaker rather than from our high school's college adviser, so my feel for the American landscape came less from what I learned in the classroom about Lewis and Clark than from following the major-league clubs on their road trips and reading about the minor leagues in the back pages of *The Sporting News*. The size of the continent got through to you finally when you had to stay up to 10:30 p.m. in New Jersey to hear via radio 'ticker-tape' Cardinal pitcher Mort Cooper throw the first strike of the night to Brooklyn shortstop Pee Wee Reese out in 'steamy' Sportsmen's Park in St. Louis, Missouri. And however much we might be told by teacher about the stockyards and the Haymarket riot, Chicago only began to exist for me as a real place, and to matter in American history, when I became fearful (as a Dodger fan) of the bat of Phil Cavarretta, first baseman for the Chicago Cubs.

Not until I got to college and was introduced to literature did I find anything with a comparable emotional atmosphere and aesthetic appeal. I don't mean to suggest that it was a simple exchange, one passion for another. Between first discovering the Newark Bears and the Brooklyn Dodgers at seven or eight and first looking into Conrad's *Lord Jim* at age eighteen, I had done some growing up. I am only saying that my discovery of literature, and fiction particularly, and the 'love affair' – to some degree hopeless, but still earnest – that has ensued, derives in part from this childhood infatuation with baseball. Or, more accurately perhaps, baseball – with its lore and legends, its cultural power, its seasonal associations, its native authenticity, its simple rules and transparent strategies, its longueurs and thrills, its spaciousness, its suspensefulness, its heroics, its nuances, its lingo, its 'characters,' its peculiarly hypnotic tedium, its mystic transformation of the immediate – was the literature of my boyhood.

Baseball, as played in the big leagues, was something completely outside my own life that could nonetheless move me to ecstasy and to tears; like fiction it could excite the imagination and hold the attention as much with minutiae as with high drama. Mel Ott's cocked leg striding into the ball, Jackie Robinson's pigeon-toed shuffle as he moved out to second base, each was to be as deeply affecting over the years as that night – 'inconceivable,' 'inscrutable,' as any night Conrad's Marlow might struggle to comprehend – the night that Dodger wild man, Rex Barney (who never lived up to 'our' expectations, who should have been 'our' Koufax), not only went the distance without walking in half a dozen runs, but, of all things, threw a no-hitter. A thrilling mystery, marvelously enriched by the fact that a light rain had fallen during the early evening, and Barney, figuring the game was going to be postponed, had eaten a hot dog just before being told to take the mound.

This detail was passed on to us by Red Barber, the Dodger radio sportscaster of the forties, a respectful, mild Southerner with a subtle rural tanginess to his vocabulary and a soft country-parson tone to his voice. For the adventures of 'dem bums' of Brooklyn – a region then the very symbol of urban wackiness and tumult – to be narrated from Red Barber's highly alien but loving perspective constituted a genuine triumph of what my English professors would later teach me to call 'point of view.' James himself might have admired the implicit cultural ironies and the splendid possibilities for oblique moral and social commentary. And as for the detail about Rex Barney eating his hot dog, it was irresistible, joining it as it did the spectacular to the mundane, and furnishing an adolescent boy with a glimpse of an unexpectedly ordinary, even humdrum, side to male heroism.

Of course, in time, neither the flavor and suggestiveness of Red Barber's narration nor 'epiphanies' as resonant with meaning as Rex Barney's pre-game hot dog could continue to satisfy a developing literary appetite; nonetheless, it was just this that helped to sustain me until I was ready to begin to respond to the great inventors of narrative detail and masters of narrative voice and perspective like James, Conrad, Dostoevsky, and Bellow.

PHILIP ROTH (1933–), American novelist, was born in Newark, New Jersey. His novella *Goodbye Columbus* (1959) won the National Book Award for Fiction and the Daroff Award, Jewish Book Council of America. This article was written for the *New York Times* in 1973.

Yaël Dayan

A CASE OF SECURITY

In the meantime, a series of articles appeared, published by the editor who had befriended me. The authorities were very upset, and when Father was in New York, all hell broke loose. Some clues concerning a security leak had led the Intelligence Service to me. They searched my room, read my diary, and went through my school copybooks. They cross-examined my mother, and she was dumbfounded. There was no way she could face me, and hectic cables were sent to my father to return home. He was reluctant to do so, and as the whole affair was highly classified, he wasn't even sure what it was all about. He wrote letters twice a day, to my mother and to me, and I claimed partial innocence. Yes, we were friends. Yes, I occasionally told him about a party or a social gathering, and no, nothing more. What's more, I didn't care or know details about any of the subjects I was asked about. 'Asked about' in a roundabout manner. A friend of my parents was given the unhappy mission of questioning me, an assignment later undertaken by my Uncle Ezer. The questioning was pathetically naïve and obvious, an attempt to drive me to tell things that didn't happen. I was rebellious, I was different, I was treading on dangerous ground without knowing it, perhaps I was taken advantage of by smarter people, but I did not say or write or give away anything that was damaging or secret.

My father was wild with frustration and anger. He wrote Mother: 'I couldn't understand anything from our phone conversation, though it was long and cost fifty dollars. I can't understand why I should cut my trip short because of our 14½-year-old daughter, and how to explain it to others. Can't you, your parents, Ezer or my parents put some sense into her? If you think I should return immediately, I will, but this will create an even greater scandal, for me and for her, which may mark her for life. It makes me blush to think I will have to go to Eban and tell him I have to cut my trip short because something happened with my daughter. I cabled Yaël asking her to listen to you and enable me to finish what I have to do here. I asked her to terminate her friendship with you know who, and put it to her as if she was doing me a great favour . . .' etc., etc.

A letter a day, telephone calls and cables, and yet he didn't cut his trip short by one day. I was terrified of his arrival and was forever grateful that he didn't cancel any of his 'national obligations.' Though I wasn't worried about the actual 'scandal' or any of the public aspects, I was not looking forward to a confrontation with him. My mother was sick. Unable to cope with, or face, or even understand the circumstances, she became physically ill, which was probably a combination of shattered nerves and too much crying, and moved for a few days to her sister's house. Now another guilt was loaded on me, by my uncle, who pointed her out to me through a curtain, lying in bed, swollen-eyed and red-faced. 'Look what you did to your mother.' He explained that her entire world was shattered, and that my behaviour was a blow to the strong foundations she had so carefully built for our family, that she was in a state of shock and felt hopeless about the future, too. At that point, rather than melting with shame and misery, I felt that I was forming a shield. I hated sacrificial attitudes, I couldn't stand the missionary approach, I didn't feel guilty and wasn't even falling into the trap of self-pity. I promised not to see the man in question. I said I was beginning to feel like a scapegoat, maybe someone was guilty of leaking something to somebody, but, as it wasn't me, they were wasting their time, and interfering with my studies and playing spy in the wrong arena. I derived from my absent father the strength to answer back, and from the fact that he was far away and less alarmed now, and from a night-long decision-taking analysis of the situation.

When Father returned, the scene was brief, painful, and enlightening in many ways. I found him in my room. My diary, which he had obviously just read, was open on the desk. He kissed me warmly, as we hadn't seen each other for a long while, and then he slapped my face, so hard I was almost thrown across the room. He threw the diary on the floor. I cried from the pain, and all I could mutter was 'Why?' 'What did I do?' He wasn't very clear when he tried to answer, and I managed to compose myself and even assume a certain detachment. 'I am not talking about Kibya, or Lavon or the Intelligence Service report. You are fourteen and a schoolgirl, and you are not yet smart, or wise, or experienced enough to know when you are taken advantage of. So don't take risks until you are fit for them.' He was furious about the incident in the Scout summer camp as read in my diary – shocked and somehow hurt.

'It is partly fiction,' I said, 'and I learned my lesson.'

'Oh, did you? And went on to sleep with a man who could be your father?'

The use of the term 'who could be your father' from my own father made me smile. At my smile, he slapped me again, and this time I could detect regret in his eye as he did it.

'I didn't sleep with him. I am a virgin, for what it matters, and I'm not even interested. I can't say the same about many of my girlfriends, and that isn't important either.' I was afraid to smile, but I felt a devilish grin inside when I added: 'One of the intelligence officers who talked to me, in a very fatherly way, and made me cry, also tried to kiss me in a way which was not fatherly at all. So I'm on guard now, Father, and I am in control, but so many people around me are not, and maybe you should handle them first.'

'And so I will. But you'd better watch yourself.' It was obvious that the conversation was over. He was uncomfortable. We both let out steam and were aware of the dangers of melodramatizing, and he was looking for a way out. 'Come up and see the dresses I bought you. I hope the sizes are right.'

'Don't you want to talk some more?' I tested him.

'The subject is closed as far as I am concerned.'

It sounded like 'Roger and over and out,' and I was grateful. We walked up the stairs, and before we entered the apartment, he kissed me again, and said, 'I love you very much, but don't take advantage of it.'

The dresses were beautiful, and so were the other gifts. My mother managed to relax and pretend it was all over for her too, and no apologies were exchanged at any time. Though we had all handled the given situation badly, the nearness between my father and myself was not impaired, and the distance between Mother and me didn't diminish. I had a notion of the price I had to pay for fame, notoriety, and independence, and the 'straight talk' with my father was satisfactory only to him. There were things he couldn't ignore but wanted shelved, and he absolved himself rather than support me. He, too, wanted to be free of guilt and anxieties as a father, and I offered him an easy way. No blames, no psychology, no question marks as to how we ever reached this gap or rift, and, above all, no moralizing. Two slaps, five sentences, a diary which was to be burned and forever discontinued and a renewed façade of happiness and unity which supplied a good alibi for both of us. We both wanted, with different degrees of legitimacy, not to be slaves to the confining dictates of family routine.

A month later, my father reached the top of the military pyramid and was appointed Chief of Staff of the Israeli Armed Forces, and we moved to our own new house in the suburb of Zahala.

From My Father, His Daughter (1985)

YAËL DAYAN (1939–), Israeli novelist and journalist, was born in Nahalal, the daughter of Moshe Dayan, statesman and soldier, and granddaughter of Schmuel Dayan.

Julia Pascal

BALLERINA!

Blackpool in the 1950s – pleasure beach for northern workers, a place of seaside showbiz and tat. I go to the Grand Theatre and see Hilda Baker – she knows-you-know; I impersonate her and everyone laughs. Ken Dodd is at the end of the pier and the local paper has a Girl Of The Year contest. 'You should be Girl Of The Year,' my father tells me, 'when you're sixteen.' So I think I have a chance to enter a whole magic world of showbiz. A cousin of mine, Valerie Carton, comes to the Grand in a touring show. I sit in the audience and watch this blonde girl sing a song while hanging mid-air on a moon. It is strange and wonderful. At six I am dancing to the music on the radio, the lines on the carpet become lines of people applauding my performance.

Memory: I am in Victoria Hospital and a doctor is looking at my feet. I am given physiotherapy for flat feet and they teach me to pick up pens and marbles with my toes. 'But if you really want the arches to improve,' says the doctor, 'you should send her to ballet classes.' Paradise begins here. Laura Webb's Ballet School at the top of Whitegate Drive is freedom once a week, and soon I progress to tap and musical comedy. 'Casey would waltz with the strawberry blonde and the band plays on, he'd waltz cross the floor with the girl he adored and the band played on.' Pastiche-of-the-thirties waltzes and soft-shoe shuffles are taught to Blackpool's daughters as they compete for medals and fight to come first in the Blackpool Summer Dance Festival. I compete in ballet and wear a pink tutu and a band of pink rose-buds in my hair.

I came across a photo of a plump little Jewish girl in pink tulle recently and saw in her face that she wanted to be Margot Fonteyn. The little fattie was me. And as I came second in ballet I looked out in the hall for my mother – for what use success if nobody sees it? – but she wasn't there. She arrived late and I was mortified.

'Why weren't you there?' I asked. 'I was too busy, darling,' she told me. I felt miserable that she hadn't seen me step forward for my medal. She was my beloved mother but too often she was busy or else David or my father 'needed' her so she forgot me. It was the beginning of a pattern which I could not understand as a child. But it goes back much further.

'A lovely baby, just like a doll,' she used to tell me, but the doll was too demanding and the doll was given away. Soon after my birth she sent me to her parents in Manchester. 'You learned to walk and talk with us,' said my grandmother with pride, and the early years are Manchester years in a large, damp house in Prestwich with two old people. I never understood why I was sent to them at 32 Hereford Drive; I must have done something terrible that my mother sent me away, but I never knew what this was. I remember lying in bed as a young child and my grandmother putting a chair at the side of the bed, 'so you won't fall out'. I remember being ill with scarlet fever and being taken to Bury Hospital in an ambulance and then being put in strict isolation. I felt panic. Not only was I sent away from my parents but now I was sent away from my grandparents.

Finally they came to see me and brought me a jigsaw and some books, but there was nothing I could say to them. I had got stuck in a shell of solitude where only the nurses talked to me and then it was to tell me off because I refused to eat the hospital greens and hid them under my plate. One nurse slapped me and I felt how unjust the world was. But there were moments of pleasure. Radios were installed in the isolation cubicles and I remember listening to 'Stranger In Paradise' on the earphones and now, whenever I hear that record, I am taken back to those weeks in isolation.

My parents were in Israel during this period. I must have been about six. When they heard I was ill they sent me a parcel of clothes: jumpers and dungarees. I was angry; not only had they not taken me with them, but they'd sent me dungarees and only boys or very young children wore those – I wanted a dress. . . .

Memory: my grandparents are sitting in their living room in Manchester listening to the news and the Billy Cotton Band Show. My grandfather takes us out to town and I watch my first film with them on a rainy Saturday afternoon. It is *The Blue Angel* with Sammy Davis Junior and Mae Britt. 'He's a Jew,' they tell me and I wonder how a black man can be a Jew. But the film is very sad and the black Jew is alone while the blonde woman goes off with someone else. The sophistication of the film escapes me but the tone of it does not. My grandfather drives us home in his Ford Popular and as we go down Corporation Street I look out of the window and see daubed on the wall 'SAVE THE ROSENBERGS'. I wonder who they are and hope they will be saved.

They go to Hallé Orchestra concerts in the Free Trade Hall and sometimes to weddings. I go to synagogue with them on Saturday mornings and am shown off as being the first grand-daughter. But their pride means little to me and I wonder how my mother is and when I am going to see her next. On Saturday afternoons my grandmother takes me to Lewis's in Market Street to 'try and find a bargain' and then we go to Kendal's. She takes me to the Ladies Powder Room. It is a vast space with lots of toilet cubicles and a large carpeted room with wide porcelain bowls and padded stools where Manchester ladies sit down to powder their noses in front of a curtained mirror. I stare in fascination at the powder and lipstick ritual and have to be dragged away.

At night I lie in bed counting the weeks until I can go home. It's dark and rainy and I'm in a single bed; my grandparents are next door. I can't sleep so I sit up and take an imaginary dagger and stick it in my chest, and in my head my mother's voice: 'I wish I was dead, I wish I was dead.' Childish morbidity or a playing out of my mother's fantasies? Whatever it was it was a displacement which was part of a longer chain of events.

My mother's parents came from Romania at the beginning of the century. Grandmother Esther had been married off to my grandfather against her wishes but he was the third suggestion so she had little choice. He, however, was passionately in love with his blonde, tall wife, and the pain of the marriage was his warmth and her coolness. They left a traditional Jewish middle-European culture for strange exile in Manchester. My grandmother, who loved Wagner and Strauss, wanted to settle in Germany, but my grandfather had family in Manchester and wanted to join them. So, she settled in foggy, rainy Manchester and pined for Bucharest – the sunny Paris of the Balkans. She retained memories of Europe which outshone the reality of the damp Manchester streets, and, although she was happy being a mother to her four children, she did not enforce any religious orthodoxy or strong sense of cultural bonding. My grandparents were the last of the Yiddish speakers and with the loss of the language there was the loss of a cultural heritage. They did not teach their children Romanian because they wanted them to assimilate.

But their children knew that although they were English they were also continentals. Either they sank into conservative provincial Jewish attitudes, worrying that their children might 'marry out', or they floated free, divorced from traditional values but caught in a no-man's land between the Yiddish past and the English post-war present. The fifties gave my parents an economic stability which their parents had never known and the jump from immigrant to middle-class English respectability was effected.

My mother's family were never radicals: her father came to Manchester and built up a textile business in Faulkner Street which today is Manchester's Chinatown. But my father's Lithuanian background was steeped in talmud study and a disdain for materialism. My father was something of a Fabian Jew, caring little for his good income which he occasionally gave to needy patients, much to my mother's rage. If they were mismatched it was because my mother had chosen my father for his status: she was attracted to the idea of being a doctor's wife. She expected the man to be 'a pillar of strength' to the woman, and when she discovered he was as weak as any other human being, she was bitterly disappointed.

Memory: sitting in the front row at the Palace Theatre, Manchester, watching The Royal Ballet. New stars, Lynn Seymour and Merle Park, dance in 'The Sleeping Beauty'. I am going to be a ballerina. I announce I am going to study seriously, am going to audition for The Royal Ballet School at White Lodge. This will mean going to London and, if I pass, boarding there. I tell my parents of my decision. The next morning my mother hardly speaks to me, my father takes me to one side. 'Your mother was up all night worrying about you. She doesn't want you to go away. What sort of a daughter thinks of leaving her mother, especially as she's always so ill? Put the idea out of your mind immediately.' My mother keeps silence for days. I stop talking about the audition but resolve to lose weight.

Memory: David calls me 'fattie' which isn't fair as he's fat too. I call him 'fattie' back but he doesn't seem to care. Mother's cooking is erratic. When she's happy meals are good but when she's upset – which is most of the time – they are extraordinary. One teatime she makes stewed apple for herself and mashed potato and poached eggs for us. But she is flustered and gets it wrong so we are presented with a plateful of stewed apple and egg. I complain and she bursts into tears. 'I hope your children treat you the way you treat me,' she cries.

We devise ways of getting rid of food. David saves brown paper bags and we bring them down to meals in our pockets. When Mother isn't looking we hide most of the food in the bags and then sneak them down the toilet. But one day David hurls his bag out of the window and into the neighbour's garden: we are discovered.

Breakfast is less painful, though the amounts are always huge. Father makes breakfast and then brings Mother hers up on a tray. It's three courses of porridge, eggs, beans or spaghetti on toast, followed by more toast and several cups of tea. We go to school with lead in our stomachs. Victor Sylvester is on the radio and my father tells us that the bandleader has gone to the studio at six o'clock with his band to play especially for us. We don't realise he's having us on.

One morning he's cooking breakfast in shorts – he's just been for an early-morning run around Stanley Park opposite where we live. 'Did you know that you have a fifty million to one chance of being you?' he asks. 'Millions of sperms fight to get to the egg and only one survives – all the others die.' I imagine fish swimming but I don't really know what he's talking about or why this is so fantastic. What does he mean a fifty million to one chance of being me? I am me – what more is there to say?

Memory: I am looking at myself in the mirror and in my ballet dress I look fat. I ask my mother, 'Can I please go on a diet. I'd like to lose weight.' She goes white with rage. 'On no account. You'll make yourself ill. You're lucky you've got food. Thousands haven't. If you go on a diet your nose will get even longer.' Quite a threat to a pubescent Jewish girl who longs to be blonde, thin and snub-nosed.

There was a secret garden in Stanley Park, a covered way with a shed in it. I imagine running away and hiding there but I never do. Instead I take a tram down to the sea and walk along the prom. It's blustery, even in spring and early summer, but I let the wind almost pull me over while I hang on to my skirt. Everywhere there are pigeons and seagulls. I like the gulls and want to put my hand up in the air and stroke their chests, but they are too far away. The sea is soothing and magic. Blackpool, out of season, is best without tourists and kiss-me-quick hats. One day the school takes us to Fleetwood. The town smells of fish because of Fleetwood kippers. We go into a trawler and have to bend our heads low to go into a cabin where there are pictures of bare women on the cabin wall.

Memory: King's Road School, Manchester. It's my first day in a new primary school during one of the long stays with my grandparents. Children play two-ball on the wall and I learn too. Others do hand stands but I'm afraid of falling so just watch. The teacher gives me a book to read all about an elephant; I read it before breaktime and the teacher is astonished. 'It's supposed to be read all week. Go back and read it again.' I'm pleased because my father taught me to read before going to school. He sat with me and showed me David's comics and the first line I read was 'Little Plum Your Redskin Chum' in the *Beezer*. Now, at school, I'm quicker at reading than anyone else but then it's boring because I've got to go back and read the same book all over again.

Lunchtime at King's Road School and a bus is hired to take the Jewish children to a kosher canteen. I go too. It's quite different from my Blackpool school – everyone seems more adult. On the coach they all sing 'Love and Marriage, Love and Marriage, they go together like a horse and carriage, you can't have one, you can't have one, you can't have one without the other.' I want to join in but don't because I don't really know anybody, though I'm not shy at singing.

My parents and grandparents are in Blackpool's Savoy Hotel one Sunday for tea. There is a small band playing Victor Sylvester style. I go up and ask if I can sing. The family all watch as I sing 'Che sera' without inhibition. Everybody loves me and pinches my cheeks hard, especially my grandparents who praise me in Yiddish and kiss me. Then David and I go and play in the lift until suddenly it stops between floors and I get frightened and cry. David isn't frightened. He teases me. 'It'll be stuck for ever and we'll run out of air and die.' I'm hysterical and when it starts up again I rush out as soon as we reach the ground floor and run to my parents.

It's cold, always cold. Even though the Aga cooker is supposed to heat the house, it never does. One of my jobs is cleaning the flues. I don't mind this. It entails dipping a long square-bowled spoon down a long chimney and lifting out the soot. I then wrap the soot in a newspaper and throw it away. But even after cleaning the Aga every room is cold. And it's the same in Manchester. My grandmother's toilet is coldest of all. I rush out of it as quickly as possible and then suffer constipation pains. She gives me syrup of figs or Ex-Lax chocolate, and then the cramps start and it's back to the freezing toilet with knives in the stomach.

From 'Prima Ballerina Assoluta' in Truth, Dare or Promise, *ed.* Liz Heron (1985)

JULIA PASCAL (1949–), British writer and stage director, was born in Manchester.

Joseph Heller

My Daughter Is Unhappy

'You never like to talk to me, do you?' my daughter says to me softly and earnestly, speaking this time not merely for effect.

'Yes, I do,' I reply, avoiding her eyes guiltily. (She is vulnerable in her candor. I do not want to hurt her.)

'You don't even like to look at me.'

'I'm looking at you now.'

'Only because I just said so. You were looking over my shoulder, like you always do, until I just said so.'

'I was watching a fly. I thought I saw one. When I do look at you, you want to know why I'm staring at you. You do the same thing with Mommy. *You* yell.'

'If I come in here to talk to you, you always look annoyed because I'm interrupting you, even when you're not doing anything but reading a magazine or writing on a pad.'

'Sometimes you keep saying good night to me for an hour or two and keep coming back in with something else you want to take up with me. Five or six times. I keep thinking you've gone to bed and I can concentrate and you keep coming back in and interrupting me. Sometimes I think you do it for spite, just to keep interrupting me.'

'I keep thinking of other things to say.'

'I'm not always that way.'

'I'm the only one who ever comes in here.'

'Am I always that way?'

'Everybody else is afraid to.'

'Except the maid,' I say, trying a mild joke.

'I'm not counting her.'

'I do come in here to work, or to get away from all of you for a little while and relax. I don't know why everyone around here is so afraid of me when I never do anything to anybody or even threaten to. Just because I like to be alone every now and then. I know *I* certainly don't get the impression that people around here are afraid to come in here and interrupt me when they want to, or do or say anything else to me, for that matter. Everybody always is.'

'You spend nearly all your time at home in here. We have to come in here when we want to talk to you.'

'I have a lot of work to do. I make a lot of money. Even though it may not seem like much to you. My work is hard.'

'You keep saying it's easy.'

'Sometimes it's hard. You know I do a lot of work in here. Sometimes when I just seem to be scribbling things on a pad or reading I'm actually thinking or doing work that I'll need in the morning the next day. It isn't always easy to do it at the office.'

'If you ever do say you want to speak to me, it's only to criticize me or warn me or yell at me for something you think I did.'

'That's not true.'

'It is.'

'Is it?'

'You never come into my room.'

'Is *that* true?'

'When do you?'

'You told us not to come in. You don't want me to. You keep the door closed all the time and you ask me to please get out if I do knock and come in.'

'That's because you never come in.'

'That doesn't make sense, does it?'

'Yes, it does. Mommy would know what I mean. You never want to come in.'

'I thought you didn't like Mommy.'

'Sometimes I do. She knows what I mean. All you ever do when you come into my room is to tell me to open a window and pick my clothes up off the floor.'

'Somebody has to.'

'Mommy does.'

'But they're always on the floor.'

'Sooner or later they get picked up. Don't they? I don't think that's so important. I don't think that's the most important thing you have to talk to me about. Is it?'

'I'll try never to say that to you again. What is important?'

'I've got posters on my wall and some funny lampshades that I painted myself and some funny collages that I made out of magazine advertisements. And I'm reading a book by D.H. Lawrence that I'm really enjoying very much. I think it's the best book I ever read.'

'I'm interested in all that,' I tell her. 'I'd like to see your posters and your funny lampshades and collages. What's the book by D.H. Lawrence?'

'You don't like D.H. Lawrence.'

'My own taste isn't too good. I'd like to see what you've done with your room.'

'Now?'

'If you'd let me.'

She shakes her head. 'You don't want to. You'd only pretend to look around for a second and then tell me to pick my clothes up off the floor.'

'Are they on the floor?'

'You see? You're only interested in joking. You're not really interested in anything I do. You're only interested in yourself. You're not interested in me.'

'You're not interested in me,' I retaliate gently. 'When I do start to ask you questions about yourself, you think I'm snooping into your affairs or trying to trap you in a lie or something.'

'You usually are.'

'Not always. You do tell lies. You do have things you try to hide.'

'You won't let me hide them. You want to know everything. Mommy too.'
'Sometimes they're things we should know.'
'Sometimes they've got nothing to do with you.'
'How can I tell until I find out what they are?'
'You could take my word.'
'I can't. You know that.'
'That's very flattering.'
'You do lie a lot.'
'You don't enjoy talking with me. You never want to discuss things with me or tell me anything. Unless it's to make me do my homework. Mommy spends more time talking to me than you do.'
'Then why don't you like her more?'
'I don't like what she says.'
'You aren't being fair. If I do try to tell you something about the company or my work, you usually sneer and make snotty wisecracks. You don't think the work I do is important.'
'You don't think it's important, either. You just do it to make money.'
'I think making money for you and the rest of the family is important. And doing my work well enough to maintain my self-respect is important, even though the work itself isn't. You know, it's not always so pleasant for me to have the work I do at the company ridiculed by you and your brother. Even though you're joking, and I'm not always sure you are. I spend so much of my life at it.'

(*Why* must I win this argument? And why must I use this whining plea for pity to do it? Why must I show off for her and myself and exult in my fine logic and more expert command of language and details – in a battle of wits with a fifteen-year-old child, my own? I could just as easily say, 'You're right. I'm sorry. Please forgive me.' Even though *I'm* right and not really sorry. I could say so anyway. But I can't. And I *am* winning, for her look of resolution is failing, her hesitations are growing, and now it is her gaze that is shiftily avoiding mine. I relax complacently, with a momentary tingle of scorn for my inferior adversary, my teenage daughter. I am a shit. But at least I am a successful one.)

My daughter replies apologetically. 'I'm interested in your work,' she tries to defend herself. 'Sometimes I ask you questions.'
'I always answer them.'
'With a wisecrack.'
'I know you're going to sneer.'
'If you didn't wisecrack, maybe I wouldn't sneer.'
'I promise never to wisecrack again,' I wisecrack.
'*That's* a wisecrack,' she says. (She is bright, and I am pleased with her alertness.)
'So is that,' I retort (before I can restrain myself, for I suppose I have to show her that I am at least as good).
My daughter doesn't return my smile. 'See? You're grinning already,' she charges in a low, accusing tone. 'You're turning it into a joke. Even now, when

we're supposed to be serious.'

I turn my eyes from her face and look past her shoulder uneasily at the bookcase on the wall. 'I'm sorry. I was only trying to make you feel better. I was trying to make you laugh.'

'I don't think there's anything funny.'

'No, I'm not. I'm sorry if you thought so.'

'You like to turn everything into a joke.'

'I don't. Now don't get rude. Or I'll have to.'

'You start making fun of me. You never want to talk seriously to any of us.'

'That isn't true. That's the third time you've made me deny it.'

'You always try to laugh and joke your way out whenever something serious comes up.'

'That's the fourth.'

'Or you get angry and bossy and begin yelling, like you're starting to do now.'

'I'm sorry,' I say, and pause to lower my voice. 'It's my personality, I guess. And my nerves. I'm not really proud of it. What you have to try to remember, honey, and nobody seems to, is that I've got feelings too, that I get headaches, that I can't always control my own moods even though I seem to be the one in charge. I'm not always happy either. Please go on talking to me.'

'Why should I?'

'Don't you want to?'

'You don't enjoy talking to me.'

'Yes, I do.'

'Now?'

'Yes. Tell me what you want to. That's how I'll know. Please. Otherwise I always have to guess.'

'Was Derek born the way he is?'

'Yes. of course. We think so.'

'Or was it caused by something one of us did?'

'He was born that way.'

'Why?'

'Nobody knows. We all think he was. That's part of the problem. Nobody knows what happened to him.'

'Maybe that's what I'll be when I go to college. An anthropologist.'

'Geneticist.'

'Did you have to say that now?'

'You want to learn, don't you?'

'Not always.'

'I thought you'd like to know the difference when you make a mistake.'

'Not now. You knew what I meant. You didn't have to stop me just to show you're smarter. Did you?'

'You're very smart. You're very bright and very clever. Maybe you should be a lawyer. That's a compliment. I don't pay you compliments often.'

'I'll say.'

'You like to force people into a corner. I'm the same way.'

'I think I try to be like you.'

'I was happier.'

'Was your family disappointed in you?'

'I can't remember. Is yours?'

'I don't know.'

'I think my mother was. But later on, not when I was a child. When I was older and moved away.'

'You never kiss me,' my daughter says. 'Or hug me. Or kid with me. Like other fathers.'

She has black, large shadows under her eyes, which are swollen, gummy, and red suddenly, and she looks more wretched than any other human being I have ever stared at before. (I want to wrench my gaze away.)

'You stopped wanting me to kiss you,' I explained softly with tenderness, feeling enormous pity for her (and for myself. Whenever I feel sorry for someone, I find that I also feel sorry for myself). 'I used to. I used to want to hug you and kiss you. Then you began to pull away from me or draw your face back with a funny expression and make a disgusted sound. And laugh. As a joke at first, I thought. But then it became a habit, and you pulled away from me every time and made that same face and disgusted sound every time I tried to kiss you.'

'So now you've stopped trying.'

'It wasn't pleasant for me to be insulted that way.'

'Were you hurt?' There is that glitter of too much eagerness in her expression. 'Did it make you unhappy?'

'Yes.' We are talking in monotones. (I don't remember when it really did begin to hurt me deeply each time she pulled away from my demonstrations of affection with signs of mock revulsion; and I also don't remember when it stopped bothering me at all.) 'I was very unhappy. My feelings were hurt.'

'You never said so.'

'I wouldn't give you the satisfaction.'

'I was little then.'

'It was still very painful.'

'I was just a little girl then. Wouldn't you give up just a little bit of your pride to satisfy me, if that's what I wanted?'

'No. I didn't.'

'Would you do it now?'

'I'm not.'

'You won't?'

'No. I don't think so. I don't think I'll ever let you get any satisfaction out of me that way.'

'You must be very disappointed in me?'

'Why?'

'I'll bet you are. You and Mommy both.'

'Why should we be?'

'I know *she* is. I'm not good at anything.'

'Like what? Neither am I.'

'I've got a greasy scalp and skin. And pimples. I'm not pretty.'
'Yes, you are.'
'I'm too tall and fat.'
'For what?'
'I'm not even sure I want to be. I don't know what I'd do even if I was good at anything.'
'Like what?'
'Like art. I can't paint or sculpt. I'm not very smart. I'm not good at music. I don't study ballet.'
'I don't study ballet either.'
'It's not funny!'
'I'm not trying to be.' (I *was* trying to be.) 'We're not good at those things either.'
'I'm not even rich.'
'That's my fault, not yours.'
'At least that would be something. I could be proud of that. Are we ever going to be? I mean really rich, like Jean's father, or Grace.'
'No. Unless you do it.'
'I can't do anything. Should I be ashamed?'
'Of what?'
'Because we're poor.'
'We aren't poor.'
'Of you.'
'At least you're frank.'
'Should I be?'
'What would you expect me to say?'
'The truth.'
'Of me? I hope not. Being ashamed is something you either are or aren't, not something you do because you should or shouldn't. I do well enough. Jean is ashamed of her father because he's mean and stupid, and thinks I'm better. Isn't she? So is Grace. I think Grace likes me a lot more than she does her father.'
'I'm never going to be anything.'
'Everybody is something.'
'You know what I mean.'
'Like what?'
'Famous.'
'Few of us are.'
'I don't blame you. I don't blame you for being disappointed in me.'
'We're not. Do you think we'd be disappointed in you just because you aren't good at anything?'
'Then you never expected anything of me, did you?' she accuses, with a sudden surge of emotion that catches me by surprise.
'Now you're not being fair!' I insist.
'It's not funny.'
'Honey, I – '

302

But she is gone, disappearing intransigently with a look of mournful loathing as I put my arms out to comfort her (and I am left again by myself in my study with my empty hands outstretched in the air, reaching out toward nothing that is there).

From Something Happened (1974)

JOSEPH HELLER (1921–), American novelist and dramatist, achieved instant fame with his first novel, *Catch-22* (1961).

Julia Neuberger

BELIEF AND PRACTICE

It was – it always seemed to be – the second day of a Jewish festival. I do not remember which one. It might have been Sukkot, or even the preceding Shavuot. It was 1962, and I know it was not Passover because there was no smell of food. We were talking, my cousins and I, in the upstairs drawing room of my grandmother's house in Hampstead. I can still feel the prickling, uncomfortable sensation of the green rep on the sofa against the backs of my knees. My father still believes that all proper furniture ought to be upholstered in green rep. To set the scene completely, my cousins and grandmother were orthodox, whilst my parents and I were Reform Jews.

I was sitting there with a bag of sewing on my knees. I wanted to do some patchwork. This was particularly odd, and might even have been perverse, since neither then nor now am I at all skilled at such handiwork. Nevertheless, the determination was strong. It was therefore particularly irritating to be told by my younger cousin, always the more forthright, that I could not use my scissors because it was a festival.

'But *you* don't need to use them,' I pointed out, 'And it's not our festival any longer anyway. Besides, I'm allowed to cut things on festivals even if you're not.'

'But you ought not to be cutting out,' continued my younger cousin, 'It's a festival. . . . '

'For you but not for me. I'm not asking you to use the scissors, just not to stop me doing so. . . . '

My grandmother was downstairs. My elder cousin, always the gentle peace-maker, was contemplating descent to seek guidance. My grandmother was by then far too ill to be able to climb the stairs, and she slept in what had always been the dining room, and sat in the downstairs drawing room, on a rubber ring to stop her getting sore. Poor thing – she was reduced from a big, strong woman to someone almost pitifully thin, with a curiously waif-like expression. Her will was still formidable, however, and her strength of personality and her mental powers still indomitable. Nevertheless, we did not bother her unless we needed to, as she was probably using all her energy in talking to one of the adults, possibly even lambasting them with her tongue, a spectacle all the cousins enjoyed if we got the chance to witness it.

She was holding forth on this occasion to one of the very few refugee women whom she had helped before and during the war, when she had chaired the Refugee Committee, who still came to see her. Her subject was, as it so often was, the decline in the sense of duty amongst the Jewish middle classes of London. Where were the young women who ran, as she had, as a young matron in the twenties, clubs for the less well off, or youth clubs for the disaffected and depressed? Where was that social conscience she had always possessed in excess herself? And why were her children and grandchildren not interested in those things which had so motivated her? A disappointment to her, the lot of them. All these assertions were made in a German accent, which her family could not hear but everyone else was all too conscious of. She had come to England as a young woman when she had married my grandfather and they had left Frankfurt together. All her adult life had been lived in England – by this time nearly fifty years. She loved the country and its people, and never ceased to be grateful for the number of Jewish refugees Britain had accepted, partly as a result of her nagging and insistence, in the late 1930s.

This was the formidable woman my cousin wanted to consult. And yet something held her back. Was it the fear of this being thought a trivial matter, far too slight to bother her grandmother about? Was it the sense that our grandmother, orthodox as she was, would not feel that I had to abide by their rules if what I was doing did not harm them? Was it a sense that somehow, as the oldest of us, she ought to be able to sort it out without a fight? Or was it the sense, which certainly grew over the years, that the division between orthodox and non-orthodox was going to divide us more completely than living half-way across the world from each other ever could?

It was a strange day, certainly. My cousin continued to hesitate. She began to ask me questions about what I, we Reform Jews, believed and thought. How did we justify our position of only observing one day of festivals? How did we decide what to observe and what not to observe? Wasn't it just a convenient way of doing exactly what we wanted, without, as in the case of many orthodox people who did not observe all the rules either, the sense that that was really what we ought to be doing? And instead of getting angry with each other, as we were to do in later life when it became clear that we were miles apart on these issues, we began to discuss the whole matter quite seriously. I was all of twelve at the time, and my cousins were eleven and thirteen. It seemed strange just a couple of years later to look back at that discussion. It had been so intense, and yet we were hardly yet at the age for such concentration, such devotion to the minutiae of argument. It would be another ten years before I realised that there was intense religious feeling in girls in their early teenage years. At the time, it was a complete surprise. The serious conversations I had with my school friends were much more likely to be about politics than religion, about the Cuba crisis, the headmistress's clear worry about Reds under the beds, despite the fact it was a day school, about the Holocaust, about which we were learning. But questions of belief had passed me by. We discussed them neither at school nor at religion school on Sunday mornings. We discussed them very rarely at home. I was aware – if I was aware of anything at all – that Christians seemed to be more worried about what they believed in than we did, and it seemed that we were much more worried about what we did, or did not do, as far as observance was concerned. Yet for all three of us that afternoon with my scissors poised was an eye-opener. I had eventually put the scissors down because I had got too interested in the discussion to want to sew anyway. Susan, who had, I suspect, started it all off in order to keep the peace, was flushed with excitement as she put her case. Aviva, the younger cousin, was saying with her customary authority: 'But you can't believe that. . . !' And we all realised that nobody had ever given us a serious chance to discuss what it was we really believed in.

The discussion about the nature of revelation, though we did not call it that and I am not at all sure that we knew the word, continued all afternoon. We were, finally, summoned for tea. There was a sticky cake, a Sachertorte, I think. All three of us were greedy. My aunt and my mother turned to us and asked why we had been so quiet. We tried to explain, but it was like talking to two brick walls. My aunt could not understand why we should be talking about belief rather than practice and my mother thought religion in general the most boring subject in the world and one she had heard far too much of since marrying into the family. And so we left the subject, because there was nothing else to do.

I picked it up with my father, who was genuinely interested in questions of belief, that evening. But the three cousins never really took it any further, which was a great shame. For we might have understood each other better if we had. But it did teach me one thing, that children and young adolescents are not to be underrated in their religious quest, and the discussions about truth and authority, revelation and the sense of the numinous are discussions which can take place quite early if the interest is there, and if the vocabulary is carefully chosen. I wish that Susan, Aviva and I had finished our debate. I doubt now that we ever will, from our entrenched positions on either side of the orthodox-progressive divide. We see each other rarely, though affection remains. But understanding is another matter, and what we could have achieved at eleven, twelve and thirteen we are unlikely to manage in our late thirties.

RABBI JULIA NEUBERGER (1950–   ) has been minister of the South London Liberal Synagogue since 1977. She is also a broadcaster, critic and writer.

Gary Kasparov

CHECKMATE

My memory of my father is shadowy, since I was such a small boy when he died. I still carry a photograph of him everywhere in my wallet. Inevitably, I regard him as a hero or a saint. His face is like mine except for the nose. It is a strong, handsome face. Everyone says he was a man of firm principles, so maybe I have inherited my stubbornness from him. My mother says his character was a mixture of me and my Uncle Leonid, who is a more jolly, open, outgoing character, around whom there are always plenty of laughs and high spirits. People say I am just like my father when I talk on the telephone or when I make gestures. Like me, he tended to explode about things, then quickly get over them. As they say in Azerbaijan, he never kept a stone hidden inside his clothes. Like me, too, he could bring himself to say things he did not mean, just for the effect they would create.

He was away for medical treatment in Moscow for many months before he finally died from lung cancer at the age of thirty-nine. I stayed with my grandfather and grandmother Kasparov during this time and after his death. My father did not want me to see him during his last illness because he didn't want me to remember him like that, and he thought it might also frighten me.

I knew something unusual was happening, but I didn't know what. I thought maybe he was on a business trip, though I could see that my mother was deeply unhappy and preoccupied. My mother had been to see my teacher, Rosa Azatorovna, to explain that she had to be in Moscow with my father and please to look after me. Shortly before he died my father himself went to my school to see Rosa and asked her to take good care of me. She told him he should be happy to have such a good son, and he thanked her. I wasn't taken to his funeral because the family thought I would find this too upsetting, like the boy in the opening scene of Pasternak's *Dr Zhivago*.

People didn't like to talk directly to me about my father's death, and I think I wanted to hide the full knowledge from myself. So it became a forbidden subject. I was afraid to ask. I kept talking about my father as if he was still alive, almost daring people to tell me the truth which I knew in my heart. My teacher never referred to it, because she thought it might be painful for me. But one day I took her a photograph of myself and compared it with one of my father at the same age, so that she would know that I was ready for my father to be mentioned. On International Women's Day, in the March just before my eighth birthday, I sent my mother a greetings card because I knew my father always did that every year and that he couldn't do so any more. I didn't want her to be the only woman in the Soviet Union who was not congratulated by her menfolk on that day. In my excitement I mixed up the wording on the postcard. Clara – known to close friends in Baku as 'Aida' – devoted herself to me and imbued me with her great zest for life. . . .

At an early age my parents had to decide whether I should make a special study of music, as my father's family expected. He saw no point in this unless I had an aptitude for it. They knew I had a gift for analysis. They were still discussing what hobby I should be encouraged to pursue when my talent for chess suddenly emerged out of a clear blue sky. Nobody expected it. My mother says it was as if God had spoken at exactly the right moment. My father was not a serious chess player, but my mother had shown a precocious ability for the game at the age of six. She was considered a 'wunderkind' and played with boys, even men. But it was the beginning of the war and nobody paid much attention to chess. Everybody thought only about how to get food in those terrible days.

One spring evening, just before my sixth birthday, my parents were trying to solve a chess problem in the newspaper set by the old master Abramian. I had never played chess, but I watched them closely as they struggled to solve the problem and then gave up in despair. Next morning I showed them the move that solved the problem. They were astonished. After breakfast my father got out a chess set and took me through the moves and notations. Even though no one had ever shown me before, I knew the chessboard off by heart. 'If he knows the end of the game, I'd better show him the beginning,' my father said, teaching me the opening rules. Half a year later, I could beat him. By the age of six I was playing all the time. I challenged every friend who came when I was six. . . .

When I was seven, I was taken to the Young Pioneers' Palace in Baku for special chess instruction and at ten I went to the Botvinnik School, run by the great Soviet grandmaster and former world champion. But chess lessons were only twice a week. The rest of the time I was going to ordinary school in Baku, School 151, and learning a full curriculum. The school was named after a famous Soviet girl partisan, Zoja Kosmodemjanskya, who became a national hero when she was killed by the German invaders close to Moscow. I remember when I was in the second form, at the age of eight, we had a class competition and I was captain of our team. My task was to list all the fairy stories I knew. I remembered twenty-one of them, which shows that my memory was in good working order from an early age. I was the first of the forty-six pupils in the class; a boy called Igor was my chief rival.

Apart from Rosa, the other teacher who was very important to me was Alexandra Pavlovna, who is now director of the school. I try to go and see my teachers before and after every tournament. They recently found some of the essays I wrote as a child, which make interesting (and sometimes embarrassing) reading now. At seven I said I wanted to be a military surgeon to save soldiers' lives. Whether, unconsciously, I was influenced by my father's illness and his time in hospital, I don't know. Maybe, in my childish way, I was thinking that if I was a doctor I might have saved his life.

I started to go abroad to play in chess tournaments from the age of thirteen. Every time I would discuss the country I was going to visit with the teacher, and on my return I would tell the other pupils what I had seen with my own eyes. Alexandra remembers me saying about my first visit to France that I couldn't decide what I looked forward to most – seeing beautiful Paris, the so-called Capital of Europe, or fighting for the honour of my country. I used to return so full of impressions that I couldn't sleep. My childish mind was very impressed, for example, by the fact that everybody could sit on the green grass in Paris. There were no regulations there. . . .

Girls did not impinge on my mind very forcefully until I was about sixteen. In fact, being an only child, I was rather disdainful and perhaps a little afraid of them. My mother remembers standing at a bus stop with me one day, on our way to visit Uncle Leonid, when I said: 'Why do girls spend so much time studying at their lessons? Why are they such limited people? I hate them.' She adds with a gale of laughter when telling this story: 'Only six months later he had fallen in love – for the first, but not the last time!'

When I was in the third class, aged eight or nine, a girl had a note to me passed around the class. When it reached me, I opened it and read. 'I love you. I want you to marry me!' I'm afraid my response was less than gallant, saying I wasn't interested in her stupid wedding. Unfortunately – or maybe fortunately in the circumstances – this note was intercepted by Rosa, the teacher, before it could break my admirer's heart. Rosa then told my mother about this infant passion.

When I did finally fall in love, it was typical that I should do so head over heels, one hundred per cent, not in some faint-hearted fashion. The girl was younger and in another class, so I needed to draw myself to her attention in a way that would show me in a flattering light. I arranged for my friends to stage-manage the situation. They pretended to threaten her in the playground – it was early summer – and I appeared on the scene like a heroic fighter to save the damsel from distress. It worked like a charm. To declare my passion I sent up a display of fireworks, including rockets, which everybody still remembers. I was ever the maximalist, all or nothing, not one to hide my light under a bushel.

When I was nine I had my appendix out. My Uncle Leonid took me to the hospital and came back early the next day to see how I was recovering from the operation. When my bed was empty he became alarmed. The nurse led him to the doctors' room and said: 'Don't worry, he's fine. Look in there.' Leonid looked in and saw that I was playing a chess 'simul' with all ten doctors at once.

Poor Uncle Leonid was the only person around in an earlier medical crisis, when I was five and swallowed a twenty-kopek piece. My grandmother rang him because both my parents were at work and he, being a composer, worked at home. He took me to the hospital, where an X-ray showed that the coin was in my stomach. What could be done? The doctor's prognosis was simple: 'Take him to the toilet and wait.' Three hours later, the penny dropped! . . .

When I was ten the doctors began to worry about my heart. They told my mother it was important that I should not catch any colds because that might strain the heart, so she always carried a syringe to keep me injected every twenty-eight days with an antibiotic vaccine. She had to take this into my training camps, sometimes up in the hills, where there was no doctor. So she was mother, father and doctor in one. On occasions she even injected my trainers. The doctor told my mother I should give up competitive chess because of the strain, but she knew it was vital to me to have this interest after my father's death. This regime went on until I was fourteen, then I resumed a normal life, taking up swimming, football, badminton and cycling. I have had no ill-effects since. . . .

People are puzzled that I changed my name from Weinstein to Kasparov around the age of eleven and assume this was to disguise my Jewish background. This is quite wrong. In any event, taking an Armenian name was simply exchanging one minority for another. It made no difference politically. The reason was that I had gone to live with my mother's family, the Kasparovs, from the time my father first became ill and it seemed more natural to use their name. My parents had a small flat in the same courtyard in Yerevan Prospect. The Kasparovs had had three girls, so there was no boy to carry on the family name. When my Uncle Leonid had his fine son, Timur, there was another Weinstein to continue that line of the family into the next generation. It is wonderful to hear the two of them playing a duet, with Leonid at the piano and Timur playing a harmonica. Last time I was at their flat they were playing a tune by Stevie Wonder, but it could equally well be a classical melody or a song Leonid had written himself or something by Dave Brubeck or Charlie Parker.

It is not clear why I was called Garik. My father took a great interest in names, but on this occasion he could not decide, so I had no name at all for two months. When his brother was born, fourteen years my father's junior, he had happened to be reading *Spartacus* and suggested Leonidas. What book he was reading when I was born we never discovered. At home in Baku most people pronounce my name 'Harry' because of the soft Russian 'G' sound.

My grandfather Weinstein, the musician, died a few months after I was born, so I never knew him. But my grandfather Kasparov, the oil engineer, I came to know very well. He had reached pensionable age when I was a boy, so I used to come home at two o'clock and have my lunch with him every day, because my mother didn't return from her work until six o'clock. He taught me politics and philosophy. He was an old Communist so he introduced me at an early age to political literature. We read many documents together about questions affecting our country. We had a map of the world, so our discussions ranged very widely. Our arguments were not always resolved in his favour. After my father died it was natural that I should become very important to him, like another son.

From Child of Change (1987)

GARY KASPAROV (1963–   ), world chess champion since 1985, was born in Baku, Azerbaijan.

Acknowledgements

The editors are particularly grateful to Martyn Goff, Josephine Kamm, Julia Neuberger, Frederic Raphael (copyright © Byronic Investments 1988), John D. Rayner, T.G. Rosenthal and Sir Roy Welensky for responding to their requests for contributions to this book. Thanks are also due to the following for permission to reproduce copyright material: extract from *Ash on a Young Man's Sleeve* by Dannie Abse reproduced by permission of Vallentine Mitchell & Co. Ltd; Collins Publishers for the extract from *It Ain't Necessarily So* by Larry Adler; Phaidon Press Ltd for the extract from *Essays: Letters: Memoirs* by Ahad Ha-Am; Vision Press Ltd for the extract from *The Great Fair* by Shalom Aleichem; extract from *The Promised Land* by Mary Antin © 1912 Houghton Mifflin Company; Methuen, London for *Karl-Yankel* from *Collected Stories of Isaak Babel*; Odhams Press for the extract from *My Own Story* by Bernard Baruch; S.N. Behrman and A.M. Heath Ltd for the extract from *The Worcester Account;* Harriet Wasserman Literary Agency on behalf of Saul Bellow for the extract from *The Adventures of Augie March;* extract from *Jericho Sleep Alone* © Chaim Bermant; *Pickles and Piety* from *Bright Blue* by Rabbi Lionel Blue by permission of BBC Enterprises Ltd; George Weidenfeld and Nicholson Ltd for the extract from *Memoirs* by Sely Brodetsky; extract from *My Life* by Marc Chagall reprinted by permission of Peter Owen, London; extract from *A Bundle of Time* by Harriet Cohen by permission of Faber & Faber; Leonard Cohen and Jonathan Cape Ltd for *For Wilf and His House;* Evelyn Cowan and Canongate Publishing Ltd for the extract from *Spring Remembered;* David Daiches and David Higham Associates Ltd for the extract from *Two Worlds;* Farrar Straus & Giroux Inc. for the extract from *Yes I Can* by Sammy Davis Jr; Routledge & Kegan Paul for the extract from *The Promised Land* by Schmuel Dayan; Yaël Dayan and George Weidenfeld Ltd and Nicholson for the extract from *My Father His Daughter;* Peter Owen, London for the extract from *Immoral Memoirs* by Sergei Eisenstein; William Heinemann for the extract from *Let There Be Sculpture* by Jacob Epstein; *My Father* from *The Last Supper* by Howard Fast reprinted by permission of Sterling Lord Literistic, Inc.; *A Peculiar Treasure* by Edna Ferber © 1939 by Edna Ferber © Renewed 1966 by Edna Ferber, reprinted by permission of Harriet F. Pilpel, as trustee and attorney for the Ferber Proprietors; Century Hutchinson Group Ltd for the extract from *My Crazy Life* by Bud Flanagan; extract from *Anne Frank's Diary* reprinted by permission of Vallentine Mitchell & Co. Ltd; A.P. Watt Ltd on behalf of Timothy D'Arch Smith for permission to reprint the extract from *Self-Portrait* by Gilbert Frankau; extract from *The Interpretation of Dreams Volume IV* by Sigmund Freud, reprinted by permission of Unwin Hyman; *Gregory Corso's Story* from *Collected Poems 1947–1980* by Allen Ginsberg (Viking Books 1985), © Allen Ginsberg 1984; Ralph Glasser and Chatto & Windus Ltd for permission to reprint the extract from *Growing Up in the Gorbals;* and Victor Gollancz Ltd for permission to reprint the extract from *My Dear Timothy* by Victor Gollancz; Joseph Heller and Jonathan Cape Ltd for permission to reprint the extract from *Something Happened;* extract from *An Unfinished Woman* by Lilian Hellman by permission of Macmillan, London and Basingstoke; extract from *Wedding Preparations in the Country* by Franz Kafka reprinted by permission of Martin Secker & Warburg Ltd; extract from *Child of Change* by Gary Kasparov reprinted by permission of Century Hutchinson Publishing Group Ltd; extract from *Arrow in the Blue* by Arthur Koestler reprinted by permission of A.D. Peters & Co. Ltd; extract from *The World is a Wedding* by Bernard Kops reprinted by permission of Vallentine Mitchell & Co. Ltd; extract from *Little Boy Lost* by Marghanita Laski reprinted by permission of Bookward Ltd; Jonathan Cape Ltd for extract from *Enthusiasms* by Bernard Levin; Isaac Löwy extract from *Wedding Preparations in the Country* by Franz Kafka reprinted by permission of Martin Secker & Warburg Ltd; extract from *Advertisements for Myself* by Norman Mailer reprinted by permission of André Deutsch; the estate of Bernard Malamud and Chatto & Windus for permission to reprint the extract from *The Tenants;* extract from *A Kid for Two Farthings* by Wolf Mankowitz by permission of André Deutsch; extract from *A Land Not Theirs* © David Marcus 1986 published by Bantam Press; extract from *Groucho and Me* by Groucho Marx by permission of Bernard Geis Associates Inc, Publishers; extract from *Collected Works 1* by Karl Marx reprinted by permission of Lawrence and Wishart Ltd; Curtis Brown Group Ltd on behalf of the estate of André Maurois for the extract from *Memoirs* © 1970 André Maurois; George Weidenfeld and Nicholson Ltd for the extract from *My Life* by Golda Meir; Grafton Books, a division of the Collins Publishing Group, for the extract from *Letters of Felix Mendelssohn;* David Higham Associates for the extract from *The End of the Corridor* by Michael Meyer; Cannongate Publishing Ltd for the extract from *The Heritage of the Kaiser's Children* by Ruth Michaelis-Jena; extract from *Timebends* by Arthur Miller by permission of Methuen, London; Gerald Duckworth & Co. Ltd for a poem from *Sunset Gun* by Dorothy Parker; Julia Pascal for the extract from *Prima Ballerina Assoluta;* Richard Scott Simon Ltd and A.M. Heath for the extract from *Making It* by Norman Podhoretz; George Weidenfeld and Nicholson Ltd for the extract from *The Evacuees* by Jack Rosenthal (all rights whatsoever in this play are strictly reserved and application for performances etc should be made before rehearsal to Margaret Ramsay Ltd, 14a Goodwin's Court, St Martin's Lane WC2. No performance may be given unless a licence has been obtained); Leo Rosten for permission to reprint *A Book was a Book* from *The Leo Rosten Bedside Book;* Jonathan Cape Ltd for *My Baseball Years* by Philip Roth; Sir John Rothenstein and Michael Rothenstein for permission to reprint the extract from *Men and Memories* by William Rothenstein; The Helena Rubinstein Foundation Inc. for permission to reprint an extract from *My Life for Beauty;* extract from *What Makes Sammy Run* by Bud Schulberg reprinted by permission of the Dorese Agency Ltd, copyright by Bud Schulberg © 1941, renewed 1969, all rights reserved; George Weidenfeld and Nicholson Ltd for the extract from *A Private View* by Irene Mayer Selznick; Isaac Bashevis Singer for permission to reprint the extract from *Love and Exile;* Bethel Solomons Jnr for permission to reprint the extract from *One Doctor In His Time;* extract from *Wars I Have Seen* by permission of Random House Inc. and the estate of Gertrude Stein; extract from *My Life* by Leon Trotsky (Penguin Books 1975), © Pathfinder Press Inc. 1970; extract from *Some of These Days* by Sophie Tucker (Hammond Hammond 1945) by permission of Laurence Pollinger Ltd; *A Man* is reprinted from *Job's Daughter, New Poems and Old Favourites* by Jean Starr Untermeyer, by permission of W.W. Norton and Co, Inc. copyright © 1967 by W.W. Norton and Co. Inc.; extract from *Trial and Error* by Chaim Weizmann copyright 1949 by Weizmann Foundation reprinted by permission of Harper & Row Publishers Inc.; extract from *Night* by Elie Wiesel by permission of Richard Scott Simon Ltd; extract from *Sowing* reprinted by permission of the estate of Leonard Woolf and The Hogarth Press; extract from *Inside Outside* by Herman Wouk reprinted by permission of Collins Publishers Ltd; extract from *How I Found America* by Anzia Yezierska copyright © Louise Levitas Mennksen 1985 first published by Virago Press 1987; extract from *From Apes to Warlords* by Solly Zuckerman by permission of Collins Publishers Ltd; extract from *The World of Yesterday* by Stefan Zweig by permission of Cassell Publishers Ltd. Every effort has been made to identify, trace and obtain a response from owners of copyright material. The publishers would be only too pleased to complete the normal formalities where for any reason they have so far been unable to do so.

Index

Abse, Dannie 221
Adler, Larry 199
Ahad Ha-Am 18
Aleichem, Shalom 20
Antin, Mary 69
Asch, Sholem 59

Babel, Isaak 112
Baruch, Bernard 49
Behrman, S.N. 143
Bellow, Saul 204
Bermant, Chaim 273
Bernhardt, Sarah 8
Blue, Lionel 243
Brodetsky, Sely 106

Chagall, Marc 109
Cohen, Harriet 150
Cohen, Leonard 283
Cowan, Evelyn 251

Daiches, David 187
Davis, Sammy 236
Dayan, Schmuel 118
Dayan, Yaël 289
Disraeli, Benjamin 1

Eisenstein, Sergei 123
Epstein, Jacob 52

Farjeon, Benjamin 12
Fast, Howard 194
Ferber, Edna 102
Flanagan, Bud 138
Frank, Anne 257
Frankau, Gilbert 91
Freud, Sigmund 16

Ginsberg, Allen 238
Glasser, Ralph 191
Goff, Martyn 219
Golding, Louis 134
Gollancz, Victor 128

Hart, Kenneth 171
Heine, Heinrich 1
Heller, Joseph 297
Hellman, Lilian 160

Kafka, Franz 86
Kamm, Josephine 176
Kasparov, Gary 306
Koestler, Arthur 159
Kops, Bernard 261

Laski, Marghanita 241
Levin, Bernard 245
Levin, Meyer 168

Löwy, Isaak 66

Mailer, Norman 212
Malamud, Bernard 238
Mankowitz, Wolf 225
Marcus, David 232
Marx, Groucho 147
Marx, Karl 7
Maurois, André 98
Meir, Golda 125
Mendelssohn-Bartholdy, Felix 4
Meyer, Michael 215
Michaelis-Jena, Ruth 164
Miller, Arthur 207

Neuberger, Julia 303

Parker, Dorothy 149
Pascal, Julia 292
Pasternak, Boris 122
Podhoretz, Norman 268
Proust, Marcel 26

Raphael, Frederic 278
Rayner, John D. 254
Richler, Mordecai 284
Rosenthal, Jack 265
Rosenthal, T.G. 274
Rosten, Leo 181
Roth, Philip 286
Rothenstein, William 31
Rubinstein, Helena 33

Schulberg, Bud 193
Selznick, Irene Mayer 184
Shinwell, Emanuel 89
Singer, Isaac Bashevis 155
Solomons, Bethel 96
Stein, Gertrude 45
Stern, G.B. 132

Trotsky, Leon 40
Tucker, Sophie 81

Untermeyer, Jean Starr 101

Weizmann, Chaim 35
Welensky, Roy 179
Wiesel, Elie 259
Wolfe, Humbert 92
Woolf, Leonard 56
Wouk, Herman 201

Yezierska, Anzia 74

Zangwill, Israel 23
Zuckerman, Solly 152
Zweig, Stefan 64